WHAT IS THE EMERGING CHURCH?

By David Cloud

What Is the Emerging Church?
Copyright 2008 by David Cloud
Second edition November 2008
Third edition January 2009
Fourth edition November 2009
ISBN 978-1-58318-112-6

Published by
Way of Life Literature
P.O. Box 610368, Port Huron, MI 48061
866-295-4143 (toll free) • fbns@wayoflife.org (e-mail)
http://www.wayoflife.org (web site)

Canada
Bethel Baptist Church,
4212 Campbell St. N., London, Ont. N6P 1A6
• 519-652-2619 (voice) • 519-652-0056 (fax)
• info@bethelbaptist.ca (e-mail)

Printed in Canada by
Bethel Baptist Print Ministry

OUTLINE

I. What Is the Emerging Church? 5
II. A Great Blending and Merging 17
III. The Liberal Emerging Church 26
   Leading Voices   28
   A Magnet for Rebels   41
   Errors of the Liberal Emerging Church
   Rejecting Infallible Inspiration & Sole Authority of Scripture   60
   No Clear Testimony of Salvation   75
   A Non-Dogmatic Approach to Doctrine   87
   Glorifying Doubt over Faith   108
   Contemplative Mysticism   115
   A Social-Justice, Kingdom Building Gospel   244
   Rejection of Dispensationalism   278
   Low Key about Evangelism   290
   Worldliness   295
   Loving to Drink   324
   Ecumenism   330
   Tending toward Universalism   340
   Downplaying Hell   362
   Weak on the Issue of Homosexuality   366
   Weak on the Substitutionary Atonement   373
   Female Church Leaders   381
IV. The Conservative Emerging Church 386
   Some Influential Voices   388
   New Evangelicalism Sets the Stage   390
   Errors of the Conservative Emerging Church
   Worldliness   396
   Contemplative Mysticism   408
   The Incarnational Doctrine   408
   A Positive, Non-Judgmental Approach   417
   Ecumenicalism   423
   Traditional Evangelism/Church Planting No Longer Works   425
   Anti-Fundamentalist   429
   Social-Justice, Kingdom-Building Emphasis   436
   Rejecting "Agenda" of Winning Lost to Christ   438
   Only Major Doctrines Should Be Points of Division   441
   Music Is a Matter of Preference   446
   Rejection of Dispensationalism   454

V. Brian McLaren: Emerging Church's Biggest Mouth....457
VI. Cain the First Emergent Worshiper..........................471
VII. Charles Spurgeon Exposed the Emergent Church...473
VIII. Bibliography 476
IX. Index 486

WHAT IS THE EMERGING CHURCH?

"We're all trying to stumble along and take some steps in the right direction" --Brian McLaren

Nothing has made me more conscious of the vicious battle that is raging for the very life and soul of Bible-believing churches than my research into the emergent church. It is frightful, because so many are falling into the devil's trap and so many more will doubtless fall in the coming days.

Emerging church leaders have the objective of proselytizing our children and grandchildren. In his 2008 book *Finding Our Way Again: The Return of the Ancient Practices,* Brian McLaren describes his plan to infiltrate churches and Christian institutions that are currently rejecting the emerging church. He says:

> "But over time, what they reject will find or create safe space outside their borders and become a resource so that many if not most of the grandchildren of today's fundamentalists will learn and grow and move on from the misguided battles of their forebears [Biblicist Christians]" (p. 133).

McLaren is saying that emerging church teachers will infiltrate Biblicist churches from without through "resources" such as books, videos, and web sites. That is exactly how New Evangelicalism has so deeply infiltrated fundamental Baptist churches over the past two decades and it is doubtless how the more radical emerging church doctrines will infiltrate over the coming decades. It is more imperative than ever that pastors train their people to discern the error of these heresies and that they exhort them to avoid the writings of false teachers. It is imperative that fundamentalist Bible Colleges and Institutes prepare their students to resist this tide of error. Too often it can be said of Bible-believing churches today what was said of Israel of old, *"My people are destroyed for lack of knowledge"* (Hosea 4:6).

The average member of a fundamentalist Bible-believing church is not equipped to deal effectively with the spiritual dangers that lurk on the shelves of the typical Christian bookstore and on the airwaves of the typical Christian radio station. The average church member receives little practical warning from his pastors and teachers and has no interest in building a library of material that can help protect him from spiritual dangers. If this situation is not rectified, the Brian McLarens of this world will doubtless devour many of our children and grandchildren.

At the same time, it is exciting to study the emerging church, because it reminds us that the hour is very, very late and we need to be busy in the Lord's service and always "looking up."

At the Soularize gathering in 2002 in Minneapolis, Minnesota, Brian McLaren said, "This is a small part of something very big and in its very early stages."

We could not agree more, but when it reaches terminal velocity, the Antichrist himself will be at the helm!

I have made a great effort to understand the emerging church. In the past several months I have read more than 80 books and a great many articles by emerging church leaders and their teachers.

In a movement as complicated and diverse as this, there will be exceptions to the rules, but I am confident that the following review is an accurate representation of the emerging church movement as a whole.

THE EMERGING CHURCH'S INFLUENCE

The *emerging church* is the name that has been coined for a new approach to missions and church life among some "evangelicals" for these present times.

In reality, the emerging church is simply the latest heresy within the broad tent of evangelicalism. It is the twenty-first century face of New Evangelicalism. When the "neo-evangelicalism" swept onto the scene in the late 1940s with its bold repudiation of "separatism" and its emphasis on dialogue with heretics, the door was left open for every sort of heresy to infiltrate the "evangelical" fold, and that is precisely what has happened. The Bible does not warn in vain, *"Be not deceived: evil communications corrupt good manners"* (1 Corinthians 15:33).

Emerging church teaching tends to be complicated, convoluted, contradictory, and confusing.

Coming to grips with it is like trying to pin a glass marble to a table with an ice pick. It is movable and if forced to stand still and be consistent, it shatters!

In addition, it is evolving as I write, and there is a "conservative" side to the emerging church issue that further complicates things.

Regardless, we must deal with the emerging church because its influence is growing.

Dwight Friesen of the Emergent Village says, "... we have a few thousand churches in the United States and more around the world" ("Emergent Village and Full Communion," a paper presented to the National Council of Churches Faith & Order Commission, March 17, 2007, http://dwightfriesen.blog.com/1616648/).

Emerging church books are published by evangelical publishers such as Zondervan, InterVarsity, and Baker.

Brian McLaren, a prominent and very liberal emerging church voice, was included in *Time* magazine's list of the 25 most influential evangelicals in America in 2005

The exceedingly influential Rick Warren has promoted McLaren on his *Ministry Toolbox* web site. Warren also recommends emergent Leonard Sweet's book *Soul Tsunami* (his recommendation is printed on the cover), which says, "It is time for a Postmodern Reformation ... Reinvent yourself for the 21st century or die" (p. 75). Warren and Sweet collaborated on an audio set entitled *Tides of Change*, and Sweet was scheduled to speak at Saddleback Church in January 2008 for a small groups training conference.

In October 2001, Sweet spoke for the Southern Baptist Convention's Lifeway Christian Resources in Nashville.

The emerging church is also supported by Bill Hybels and Willow Creek Community Church. Emergents Brian McLaren, Scot McKnight, and Shane Claiborne spoke at Willow Creek's Shift conference in April 2008.

In the section on Blending and Merging we will give more documentation on the emerging church's influence within evangelicalism.

EVERYTHING IS CHANGING

The emerging church emphasizes the fact that great changes are occurring throughout the world, and particularly in North American and British society. They use the terms "postmodern" or "post-Christian" to describe this, and they contend that since the world is changing, the churches must change.

In addition to "post-modern" they use terms such as "new paradigm" and "paradigm shift" (a change in one's worldview), "tipping point," "changing times," and "transformation."

Eddie Gibbs and Ryan Bolger write, "The church must recognize that we are in the midst of a cultural revolution and that nineteenth-century (or older) forms of church do not communicate clearly to twenty-first-century cultures" (*Emerging Church*, p. 17).

Long-time Wheaton College professor Robert Webber wrote in 1999:

> "Currently, Western society is in a transition from the modern world to a postmodern world. The new revolutions ... are shifting us toward the affirmation of new values. ... These shifts are resulting in a whole new culture and raise new questions about the way a biblical Christianity is to be understood and communicated" (*Ancient-Future Faith: Rethinking Evangelicalism for a Postmodern World*, p. 15).

Dan Kimball describes this change in his book *The Emerging Church*:

> In the post-Christian era ... the values and beliefs of a person raised in America are shaped by a global, pluralistic atmosphere. This person has instant exposure to global news, global fashion, global music, and global religions. There are many gods, many faiths, many forms of spiritual expression from which to choose. In a postmodern atmosphere, a person grows up learning that all faiths are equal but that Christianity is primarily a negative religion, known for finger-pointing and condemning the behavior of others. In this atmosphere, the Ten Commandments aren't taught and the Bible is simply one of many religious writings. Ethics and morals are based on personal choice, as families encourage their children to make their own decisions about religion and to be tolerant of all beliefs. A major influence on a postmodern person's ethics and morals is what they learn from the media and what is accepted by their peers. ... relativism is more of a norm. ...
>
> In a post-Christian world, pluralism is the norm. Buddhism, Wicca, Christianity, Islam, Hinduism, or an eclectic blend—it's all part of the soil. The basis of learning has shifted from logic and rational, systematic thought to the realm of experience. People increasingly long for the mystical and the spiritual rather than the evidential and facts-based faith of the modern soil [referring to the 20th century]. The

way people respond and think is more fluid than systematic, more global than local, more communal than individualistic. And in postmodern soil a high value is placed on personal preference and choice, as opposed to predetermined truth. ...

At the University of California at Santa Cruz ... the non-Christian student religious groups on campus conspicuously outnumber the Christian groups. They have a Muslim group, a Buddhist group, a Baha'i group, even a Wiccan group. Religious diversity such as once was found only in metropolitan areas now flourishes in suburbs and rural areas. ... The times are definitely changing as we see all types of religious faiths in mainstream America. ... Diana Eck ... has written a book called *A New Religious America: How a 'Christian Country' Has Become the World's Most Religiously Diverse Nation.* ...

In order to think like missionaries we need to recognize that America is a nation that offers an ever more accessible mix of spiritual choices, all perceived as equal. So we shouldn't be surprised to hear statements like the one Madonna said in a 1990 interview on *60 Minutes*: 'I go to synagogue, I study Hinduism ... all paths lead to God.' This is the religious anthem of those growing up in a post-Christian world. ... What is interesting is that most people in the emerging culture have no problem believing in a 'God.' But this 'God' is pieced together from a mix of world religions and various personal beliefs. Since having contradictory beliefs is not a problem in postmodern culture, this is acceptable. Though she embraced aspects of Hinduism and practices the Jewish mysticism of kabbalah, Madonna has no problem having her son baptized in an Anglican church. ...

Something we cannot underestimate is the way that communications media affect our worldview. Just as the printing press transformed Europe in past centuries, we are in the midst of another communications revolution with the internet, which almost every household in America has access to. Unlike any other time in history, emerging generations have instant access to world news. ... We have global access to endless volumes of information, including about religion and world faiths of all kinds. This information changes how we see the world. Because we are in a global community, even trends in fashion, entertainment, and music are no longer merely regional. ...

"A new group of prophets, philosophers, and theologians are teaching the emerging culture about spirituality and even Christian theology. ... Movie theaters all across America (and the world) show a steady stream of movies that deal with spiritual themes ... Spirituality is taught quite often in popular music. ... To add to the confusion, famous celebrities claim they are Christian and talk about God or Jesus yet promote a lifestyle contrary to Scripture (*The Emerging Church*, pp. 59, 60, 67, 70, 71, 73, 75, 85, 86).

We agree that the world is changing dramatically and we believe that there are adjustments that churches should make in regard to this. I am nearly 60 years old and have seen the great changes with my own eyes. And as a preacher with 35 years experience, including nearly two decades in cross-cultural church planting in one of the darkest parts of the world, I understand the need to try to understand the culture in which one ministers and to do everything possible within the biblical framework to preach the gospel in a meaningful way, but the emerging church is going far beyond biblical boundaries in its adaptation to culture.

HOW AND WHEN DID THE EMERGING CHURCH BEGIN?

On his website, Brian McLaren says, "Emergent grew out of the Young Leader Networks, which was launched in the mid-90's by Leadership Network, a Dallas-based foundation."

The Leadership Network was formed in the mid-1980s to stimulate discussion of new ideas, to disseminate those ideas, and to network innovative leaders within evangelicalism. It was a network of leaders led by megachurch pastors. Founded by Bob Buford, a business guru with the objective of building the kingdom of God in the world in this present time, the Leadership Network was designed from its inception as a radical change agent. Buford "introduced Leadership Network as a 'resource broker' to churches, hoping to help leaders of 'innovative churches' connect together" (Roger Oakland, *Faith Undone*, p. 23). (I am thankful for Roger Oakland's ground breaking research into the history of the Leadership Network.) "Buford's goal was to be a resource to the megachurch, because he saw it as a highly influential instrument for societal changes. ... Buford described Warren and Bill Hybels (Willow Creek) as 'change makers'" (*Faith Undone*).

Buford, in turn, was mentored by Peter Drucker (1909-2005, a business management guru who was deeply influenced by Soren Kierkegaard's mystical existentialism and Martin Buber's pantheistic universalism. Drucker believed that we have moved into a new era in which we need to rethink everything. He said that we need a great imaginer "of a new synthesis, of a new philosophy" (*Landmarks of Tomorrow*, 1957, p. x). He used terms such as "age of transition," "post-modern," "shift to innovation," "new frontiers," "changing times." Drucker wrote, "Mankind ... needs the deep experience that the Thou and the I are one, which all higher religions share" (*Landmarks of Tomorrow*, p. 265). Drucker promoted interfaith dialogue and established the Leader to Leader Institute, "an interspiritual thought forum, which to this day includes Buddhist sympathizers, globalists, evangelicals, and New Age sympathizers" (*Faith Undone*, p. 27). Drucker believed that doctrine is less important than "people's needs." Thus, some of the chief earmarks of the emerging church were evident in Drucker's philosophy: believing that we need a new Christianity for a new times, promoting mysticism, downplaying doctrine, learning from heretics, interfaith dialogue, and kinship with New Agers. (Speaking at the Pew Forum on Religion in 2005 Rick Warren called Drucker "my mentor" and said he had "spent 20 years under his tutelage.")

In the mid-1990s the Leadership Network formed the Young Leaders Network. It targeted innovative youth workers who represented the Leadership Network's philosophy. The Young Leaders Network spread its influence through books, conferences, and Internet blogs. Its chief personalities included Doug Pagitt, Brian McLaren, Chris Seay, Tony Jones, Dan Kimball, Andrew Jones, and Brad Smith. When he was brought into the Young Leaders Network, Pagitt was a youth pastor at Wooddale Church in Minneapolis. His pastor, Leith Anderson, in his 1992 book *A Church for the 21st Century*, had already called for a new roadmap for the future. He wrote, "[W]e need a paradigm shift for the future." This refers to a dramatic change in one's worldview.

The Young Leaders Network morphed into the Terra Nova (new earth) Project. It involved seminars and conferences to teach evangelicals how to be change agents in churches, denominations, and Christian organizations and kingdom builders in the world. For example, the one at University Baptist Church in Waco, Texas, February 22, 2001, was described as a "working lab." It combined social-justice theology with the arts to prepare the participants to "act as a transforming presence."

The Young Leaders Network eventually morphed into the Emergent Village.

Roger Oakland documents the close association between the Leadership Network and two large publishing houses, Zondervan and Jossey-Bass. Zondervan, which was purchased by Rupert Murdoch's News Corporation in 1988, is the publisher of Rick Warren's mega bestseller *The Purpose Driven Life*. Warren has stated that he is Murdoch's pastor ("Murdoch Pastor Gets Heat for Mogul's Porn Channels," W*orldNetDaily*, May 10, 2007). As for Jossey-Bass, Peter Drucker was one of the board members. "Through this strong-arm publishing alliance of Jossey-Bass and Leadership Network, the handful of carefully selected young men began writing books, and with the Drucker/Buford marketing energies, these young emerging leaders became known world-wide in just a few years, so much so, that in 2005, *Time* magazine named Brian McLaren one of the country's top 25 'Most Influential Evangelicals' (*Faith Undone*, p. 37).

TWO STREAMS OF THE EMERGING CHURCH

The emerging church is not a unified system; it is multi-faceted, and for the purposes of this book we will describe two distinct streams that feed the broad river of the movement.

One is the more radical side that is represented by Brian McLaren and the Emergent Village. We will call it **THE LIBERAL EMERGING CHURCH**. *In doctrine*, it is flexible, tolerant, non-dogmatic, rethinking, evolving. It is dismissive of the Bible as verbal-plenarily inspired, infallible, and the sole authority for faith and practice. It is hesitant about holding a doctrinal statement of faith and if it does hold one it is usually very limited (such as the so-called Apostles' Creed). *In worship*, it is experimental and borrows heavily from "ancient spirituality," incorporating candles, incense, dim lighting, ambient music, labyrinths, icons, prayer stations, art, dance, meditation, silence. *In mission*, the emphasis is on kingdom building in the world today and developing relationships with the unsaved, with no strict line between the church and the world. It is heavily involved with a social-justice-environmentalist gospel and often accepts people as part of God's family even when they do not have personal faith in Jesus Christ.

The other stream is less radical. For lack of a better term we will call it **THE CONSERVATIVE EMERGING CHURCH**. It is represented by men such as Mark Driscoll of Seattle and the Acts 29 church planting network. They have a higher view of the Bible and want to maintain a solid doctrinal foundation (particularly Calvinistic Reformed theology), but they are open to worldly, "cultural affirming" techniques of church growth because "the old methods aren't working." One report says that they are "not necessarily trying to rewrite theology, but offer innovative methods of ministry" ("Conference examines the emerging church," Baptist Press, Sept. 25, 2007). Driscoll claims to be "theologically conservative and culturally liberal."

Many men have made an effort to distinguish between the various streams of the emergent church.

Mark Driscoll uses the terms "emergent liberals" and "emerging evangelicals," putting himself into the latter group (*Confessions of a Reformission Rev.*, pp. 21-23).

We believe, though, that an attempt to make a sharp distinction between the terms *emergent* and *emerging* is confusing to the average person and won't hold up in the long term. The two terms are often used as synonyms. Further, even those of the liberal stream of the emerging church fall within the broad category of "evangelicals," so the distinction between "emerging liberals" and "emerging evangelicals" cannot be maintained. The emerging church in all of its facets fits under the broad umbrella of modern evangelicalism, so it is "evangelical" even when it is liberal. (If you find that confusing, I am not surprised, but it is only because of the confusion that reigns within contemporary evangelicalism.)

Ed Stetzer of the Southern Baptist Convention coined the term "relevant" to describe the more conservative stream, because they want to be "relevant" to modern culture. Yet the term "relevant" could as easily be applied to both streams of the emerging church, since the desire to be relevant to modern culture is a distinguishing feature of the entire field. They differ only in how far they will go in this venture.

Some use the term "missional" to describe the conservative side of the emerging church, but the liberal emerging churches also like that term, so it is of little help in distinguishing between various aspects of the movement.

I considered using the terms *doctrinal* and *non-doctrinal* to distinguish the two major streams of the emerging church, since one stream is much more oriented toward doctrinal truth and less relativistic than the other. But in the end I decided that those terms are too cumbersome.

We have decided to use the terms "liberal" and "conservative" to describe the two branches, though these are not ideal. While "liberal" is a perfectly good term for the most radical side of the emerging church, it is with great difficulty that we use the term "conservative" to describe the less liberal type of emerging churches. They are "conservative" only when compared to the liberal stream!

We will begin our study by examining the liberal stream and then we will look at the more conservative side.

A GREAT BLENDING AND MERGING

It is important to understand that it is difficult to draw a strict line between the two streams of the emerging church.

There is a blending and merging going on that will cause all lines to be blurred eventually. This is the devil's grand plan that is leading toward the formation of the end-time one-world church, and the New Evangelicals are unwittingly a part of that program.

Phyllis Tickle says the emerging church is blending the four major streams of American Christianity: Evangelicalism, Charismaticism, mainline liberal Protestantism, and liturgicalism (Catholicism, Orthodoxy). She says, "WHERE THE QUADRANTS MEET IN THE CENTER THERE'S A VORTEX LIKE A WHIRLPOOL AND THEY ARE BLENDING" ("The Future of the Emerging Church," March 19, 2007, *Leadership Magazine*).

Brian McLaren has said, "A lot of mixing is taking place-- Lutherans using Catholic liturgy, Catholic churches using Pentecostal stuff, evangelicals borrowing the Episcopal Book of Common Prayer" ("Young Pastors Explore New Forms of Worship," *Christian Science Monitor*, Oct. 31, 2002).

Indeed, everywhere you look there is a whole lot of mixing going on!

TAKE ED STETZER, FOR INSTANCE. He is an influential Southern Baptist and rejects the more radical elements of the emerging church, but he does not believe in separating from the liberal emergents and often recommends their writings. After admitting that the liberals deny "the substitutionary atonement, the reality of Hell, the nature of gender, and the nature of the gospel itself," a very serious accusation, Stetzer makes the following amazing and very dangerous statement: "The revisionist emerging church leaders should be treated, appreciated, and read as we read mainline theologians" (*Breaking the Missional Code*, 2006, p. 190). This type of bold rejection of biblical separation (e.g., Romans 16:17; 2 Corinthians 6:14-18; 2 Timothy 3:5; 2 John 7-11) on the part of the conservative emerging church leaders is why the blending and merging will continue.

At a Convergent Conference at Southeastern Baptist Theological Seminary in September 2007, Stetzer gave another very weak and mixed signal about the liberal emerging church. He said that instead of being upset about emerging churches, Southern Baptists should affirm their faith statement and share their witness for Christ ("Conference examines the emerging church," Baptist Press, Sept. 25, 2007). In fact, Bible-believing people should stand fast in sound doctrine, should be zealous in evangelism, AND should earnestly contend for the faith against every heresy such as the emerging church. God's people should definitely be upset about false doctrine. The Psalmist testified, "I esteem all thy precepts concerning all things to be right, and I HATE EVERY FALSE WAY" (Psalm 119:128). That is the proper biblicist attitude.

Stetzer is a participant in Shapevine, the emerging church blog that features liberal emergents such as Brian McLaren, Tony Jones, Sally Morganthaler, Alan Hirsch, and Leonard Sweet. Shapevine is called "a global community of COLLABORATORS," and Southern Baptist "conservatives" are collaborating in this forum with the most radical of emergent heretics. Collaboration is the very opposite of separation.

Stetzer is on the board of the Acts 29 church planting network, and he is not the only member of Acts 29 that is participating on Shapevine. Darrin Patrick, pastor of The Journey in St. Louis, has participated non-critically in

Shapevine. Instead of rebuking the emergents who congregate on this blog, the "evangelical relevant" Patrick is buddy-buddy with them, dialoguing with them instead of rebuking them plainly and separating from them as a plain witness against their heresies.

CONSIDER DAN KIMBALL. He says that he has "a fundamental belief in the inspired Scriptures being my guide and my authority" and that he "cannot read the New Testament and consider it all inspired and then downplay or ignore the repeated teaching about the blood of Jesus being shed on the cross for the payment of our sin" (*Listening to the Beliefs of Emerging Churches*, pp. 97, 100). That sounds good, but he undermines this by his principle of allowing people to question traditional doctrines and his idea that "we are supposed to approach theology more with a sense of wonder, awe, and mystery than like trying to solve a mathematical puzzle" (p. 91). This position reduces the plain teaching of divine revelation to something mysterious and uncertain. Kimball recommends books by Emergent Village people such as Tony Jones. Kimball's book *The Emerging Church* was forwarded by Brian McLaren and Kimball quotes McLaren several times with no warning about his heresies. Kimball joined McLaren and other emerging church leaders as a contributor to *An Emergent Manifesto of Hope* and did not have one word of warning about their agenda to tear down the Bible and find saving faith in non-Christian religions. As a contributor to the book *Listening to the Beliefs of Emerging Churches*, Kimball joined hands with liberals Doug Pagitt and Karen Ward, a female preacher, and said that he has tremendous respect for them (p. 86). Kimball praised Ward and her church and said her contribution to this book "was the one that moved me most emotionally" (pp. 190-191). He had little substantial criticism of her views, even though she plainly denied that the Bible is the sole authority for faith and practice, rejected the infallibility of Scripture, dismissed the doctrine of substitutionary atonement as a "theory," refused to reject the doctrine of universalism, claimed that the Bible's stories are not always literal, said that a church's theology should be like a "potluck" with everyone contributing his own ideas, and claimed that baptism is the beginning of the Christian life.

CONSIDER RICK MCKINLEY OF IMAGO DEI OF PORTLAND. The church has a doctrinal statement that, though brief, does cover some important things such as the infallible inspiration of Scripture (though how exactly they define this and to what extent they actually believe and defend it in practice, we do not know). Yet when McKinley published a blog entitled "My Thoughts on the Emerging Church" on October 18, 2007, and distanced himself a bit from it, he did not reprove its heresies but merely said he has some "concerns." He used the blog to take a cheap shot at the fundamentalist's "need to divide Christians into categories," because "it's just not that cut and dry." This is exactly the type of vagueness and non-dogmatism that we find in the liberal emerging church. McKinley says that it is wrong and dangerous to "simply want to know what category they fit in so we can pronounce our judgment if we disagree with them." He says we shouldn't force the emerging church leader to define himself, and if we do we are "putting a yoke upon him that will crush all the life and creativity." He says that the emerging church is a "young and fragile thing" and we must be careful that we don't harm it. He says it is "a new thing that God is doing and we should respect it as such." He says he feels responsible "to create space for what is coming up behind us," that though he has built his faith "on the foundation of orthodoxy and the gospel of the reformers," yet he says, "I think there is a lot of room for theological progress. Not denying the foundation but building on it." He concludes, "I hope that those of us that have gone before them will not be so full of fear that we kill their vision and quench the Spirit, for I fear that we will have to answer for that one day."

It is obvious that this type of approach is unscriptural and dangerous. Resisting heresy is not quenching the Spirit! We are exhorted in Scripture to prove all things (1 Thess. 5:21). The Bereans were commended because they *"searched the scriptures daily, whether those things were so"* (Acts 17:11). We must understand that there are false christs, false gospels, false spirits and we are thus to be exceedingly careful in theological matters (2 Cor. 11:1-4). We are not instructed to give the heretic space to develop but *"after the first and second admonition reject"* (Titus 3:10). When some "false brethren" tried to teach a different gospel, Paul dealt with them quickly. He said, *"To whom we gave place by subjection, no, not for an hour; that the truth of the gospel might continue with you"* (Galatians 2:5). The Bible warns that *"a little leaven leaveneth the whole lump"* (Gal. 5:9); thus, error must be dealt with quickly.

McKinley's foundational error is his heresy pertaining to the kingdom of God and the church's mission in this present world. He says, "I hope that we can leave the next generation great theology on the Kingdom of God that seems to have gotten confused in the enlightenment. I hope that we can expand our theology of the Trinity from a static doctrine to a dynamic and living theology of community and transformation." He is exceedingly sympathetic with even the most radical elements of the emerging church because he holds the same heresy pertaining to the kingdom of God. This is true of all of the conservative emerging church leaders.

CONSIDER DONALD MILLER. His popular book *Blue Like Jazz* is a harsh rant against traditional evangelical Christianity and he frequently takes shots at doctrinal dogmatism, speaking so much like a liberal emergent that it is difficult to know where to place the man. For example, in discussing his involvement in church in his youth he writes, "I wished I could have subscribed to aspects of Christianity but not the whole thing" (*Blue Like Jazz*, p. 30). He said, "In order to believe Christianity, you either had to reduce enormous theological absurdities [i.e., Garden of Eden, universal flood] into children's stories or ignore them" (p.

31). He wanted to believe the gospel "free from the clasp of fairy tale" (p. 35). Thus he wanted to pick and choose what parts of the Bible he would believe. At a book signing event, one enthusiastic reader of *Blue Like Jazz* said: "I love *Blue Like Jazz* because it's, like, a Christian book, but it doesn't make you feel bad about yourself" ("A Better Storyteller," *Christianity Today*, June 2007). Miller even claims that terms such as "inerrancy" are relatively new to church history and that "much of biblical truth must go out the window when you approach it through the scientific [literal] method" (*Searching for God Knows What*, p. 160).

Yet Miller is a member of Imago Dei, which has a doctrinal statement that includes an affirmation of the infallibility of Scripture and knows personally and speaks highly of Mark Driscoll, who returns the compliment in *Confessions of a Reformission Rev*. Driscoll writes, "The church [Imago Dei] is doing great, and so is Donald" (p. 97).

CONSIDER DALLAS THEOLOGICAL SEMINARY. This institution is also looking at the emerging church far too sympathetically. In 2004 they invited Brian McLaren for a one-day conference. He was critiqued by the faculty, but the fact remains that he was there by invitation and he had an opportunity to spread his harmful influence among the students. Dallas Seminary sells Dan Kimball's CD set *The Emerging Church* at the Resources section of their web site, and there are no warnings. Emergent blogger Andrew Jones praised Dallas' three-set podcasts on the emerging church, concluding, "I wish all seminaries would take THIS LEARNING POSTURE towards the emerging church" (http://tallskinnykiwi.typepad.com/tallskinnykiwi/2006/06/3_seminary_podc.html). He would not have said this if Dallas Seminary were treating the liberal emerging church as the gross heresy it is and separating from it as the Bible commands.

CONSIDER MARK DRISCOLL. Though he has distanced himself somewhat from some emerging church radicals and has warned of some of their errors, he has not separated from them after a biblical fashion. He calls them friends rather than the dangerous heretics that they are, continues to recommend some of their writings, and joins hands with them in contributing to the same books.

Two of the titles on Driscoll's "Short List of Books of Missional Church Planters" are by Lesslie Newbigin, an author greatly beloved by the liberal emergents (*The Gospel in a Pluralist Society* and *The Open Secret*) (http://mrclm.blogspot.com/2007/10/mark-driscoll-short-list-of-books-for.html). In *The Radical Reformission*, Driscoll gives "thanks to Lesslie Newbigin for his prophetic voice" (p. 9). Newbigin was a bishop in the very liberal Church of South India and was Associate General Secretary in the radically heretical World Council of Churches. In *The Gospel in a Pluralist Society,* Newbigin denied that the Bible is the verbally inspired Word of God and said the 18th century defenders of the faith were in error when they taught that the Bible is "a set of timeless truths." Newbigin falsely claimed that Jesus did not leave behind "a book, nor a creed, nor a system of thought, nor a rule of life" (*The Gospel in a Pluralist Society*, p. 20). Though the Lord Jesus did not write anything with His own hand, He promised to send the Holy Spirit to guide the apostles into all truth and the New Testament Scripture is the product (John 16). Paul testified that he spoke in Christ (2 Cor. 2:17) and called the New Testament Scriptures "the word of Christ" (Col. 3:16). Further, Newbigin said, "All so-called facts are interpreted facts. ... What we see as facts depends on the theory we bring to the observation" (p. 21). This is a liberal emerging church principle, that all facts are merely human interpretations and all interpretations of the Bible are therefore imperfect. Newbigin called the split between liberals and fundamentalists "tragic" (p. 24) and taught that there is the possibility of salvation apart from personal faith in Christ.

These are all liberal emerging church heresies, and the man who held them is highly recommended by conservative emerging church pastors. You can see the confusion, the blurring of lines.

Driscoll also recommends five books by Dan Allender, the president of Mars Hill Graduate School, which has a very radical liberal emerging church philosophy. Brian McLaren is an adjunct professor there, and the school sponsored McLaren's "Everything Must Change" tour.

On a visit to the Ballard campus of Driscoll's Mars Hill Church on January 27, 2008, I saw the following books by heretics for sale in the small bookstore in the main lobby: *The Essential Kierkegaard*, *The Cost of Discipleship* by Dietrich Bonhoeffer, *The Gospel in a Pluralistic Society* by Lesslie Newbigin, and *Mere Christianity* by C.S. Lewis.

CONSIDER BIOLA UNIVERSITY. In May 2005, they hosted an emerging church conference. Though some of the professors have rejected elements of the liberal emerging church, it is obvious that they are dialoguing with it and not separating from it in a biblical fashion. For example, J.P. Moreland, a Biola professor, critiques the emerging church in his book *Kingdom Triangle*. While he criticizes the emerging church for rejecting objective truth, he hastens to add: "I do not wish to be harsh or inappropriately critical of my brothers and sisters who are part of the emerging church. There is much good in the problems they are bringing to the surface and in some of the solutions they are offering. For now, I simply register my concern about what I believe is their unnecessary association with postmodern language."

This approach won't get the job done.

The liberal emerging church philosophy will continue to have an influence among evangelical "relevant" churches like Driscoll's and Kimball's and Warren's and Hybels' and schools like Biola and Multnomah and Dallas because their approach toward heresy is too soft and the line of demarcation is not clear enough and separation, in fact, is despised and because of their folly of recommending books by and quoting men that are unsound.

As we have seen, the Achilles heel of New Evangelicalism from its inception has been the renunciation of separatism. When Harold Ockenga coined the term "Neo-evangelical" in 1948 and proclaimed its standard in a speech that year, he twice stated, "We repudiate separatism" (Ockenga's foreword to Harold Lindsell's *The Battle for the Bible*).

New Evangelicals want to dialogue rather than separate. They want to take a more positive stance. They don't like naming the names of false teachers and labeling them heretics. Compared to the biblical pattern, they are soft and tolerant toward error.

The fact is that New Evangelicals despise biblical separatists more than they hate theological modernism!

The New Evangelical philosophy, which has permeated the evangelical world over the past 50 years, set the stage for the emerging church heresy and facilitates its progress.

THE LIBERAL EMERGING CHURCH

The emerging church says that since the world is changing we need a new type of Christianity. Modern people don't respond to the old type; in fact, they are offended by it, so we need to devise a new one. We need to rethink everything. Leonard Sweet says:

> "A sea change of transitions and transformations is birthing a whole new world and a whole new set of ways of making our way in the world.... It is time for a Postmodern Reformation ... Reinvent yourself for the 21st century or die" (*Soul Tsunami*, pp. 17, 75).

The liberal emerging church is infatuated with novelty and change. One of the articles in *An Emergent Manifesto* begins with this quote from the elf queen Galadriel in the mythical movie *The Fellowship of the Ring*: "The world is changed. I feel it in the water. I feel it in the earth. I smell it in the air" (*An Emergent Manifesto*, p. 226).

The same quote appears in the foreword to Brian McLaren's book *A Generous Orthodoxy,* and I have seen it referenced in at least two other emerging books.

Emergent Tim Keel says that since the world has changed, facts alone are not adequate; we must follow "the artists, poets, prophets, contemplatives, and mystics among us" because "they are leading us somewhere" (*An Emergent Manifesto*, pp. 228, 229).

The liberal emerging church is an open-ended pursuit of mysticism into an unknown future.

It reminds us of the Athenians who "*spent their time in nothing else, but either to tell, or to hear some new thing*" (Acts 17:21). It is "*ever learning, and never able to come to the knowledge of the truth*" (2 Tim. 3:7).

It downplays the preaching of the gospel and the winning of souls while aiming to create "meaningful relationships" and transform the world by building the kingdom of God through socio-political-environmental-artsy endeavors (they call this "missional" work).

It calls for positive dialogue among professing Christians rather than doctrinal evaluation and separation.

It downplays the importance of doctrine and the infallibility and sole authority of Scripture ("we committed ourselves to lives of reconciliation and friendship, no matter our theological or historical differences," Emergent Village).

It looks upon doctrine as something that is always evolving.

It says we should develop intimate relationships with the unsaved without an "agenda" of trying to win them to Christ.

It is intimately involved with Roman Catholic contemplative forms of "spirituality," such as silent meditation, mantras, centering prayer, and monasticism.

It looks upon life as a party to be enjoyed and participates freely in the world's music, art, fashion, movies, etc. It "communicates with" the world's culture rather than condemning it.

A *Christianity Today* article about emerging church, which analyzes the liberal side, says that emergents "are looking for a faith that is colorful enough for their culturally savvy friends, deep enough for mystery, big enough for their own doubts," and, "To get there, they are willing to abandon some long-defended battle lines" (Andy Crouch, "The Emergent Mystique," *Christianity Today*, Nov. 2004).

Thus, emergents want a Christianity that is worldly enough to attract those who love the world and non-dogmatic enough to allow for doubts and heresies.

LEADING VOICES

The following are some of the leading voices for the liberal emerging church. We have included some individuals who, though deceased, have a major influence on the emerging church through their writings.

MARK BATTERSON is senior pastor of National Community Church in Washington D.C. ("one church in multiple locations"). Seventy percent of the church membership is composed of young people in their twenties. Batterson is author of *In a Pit with a Lion on a Snowy Day: How to Survive and Thrive When Opportunity Roars* (2006).

ROB BELL (b. 1970) is pastor of Mars Hill Bible Church in Grandville, Michigan, and author of *Velvet Elvis* (2005) and *Sex God: Exploring the Endless Connections between Sexuality and Spirituality* (2007). In the January 2007 issue of *The Church Report*, Bell was named #10 in their list of "The 50 Most Influential Christians in America" as chosen by readers and online visitors. He also produces the popular series of short films called *NOOMA*.

RYAN BOLGER is Assistant Professor of Church in Contemporary Culture in the School of Intercultural Studies at Fuller Theological Seminary and coauthor with Eddie Gibbs of *Emerging Churches: Creating Christian Community in Postmodern Cultures* (Baker, 2005).

SPENCER BURKE is the founder of an emergent church in Los Angeles and the host of SOULARIZE, an annual emergent conference; his web site, TheOOze.com, which is described as "a safe place to ask questions and work through issues," is said to have 250,000 unique visitors every month. Burke is author of *Making Sense of Church* (2003), *Stories of Emergence* (2003), and co-author of *An Heretic's Guide to Eternity* (2006). Matt Palmer, a member of Burke's church, says, "Our goal is to be there for each other and try to find activities [through which] we can service our community" ("These Christians Radically Rethink What a Church Is," http://www.fuller.edu/news/html/emerging_church.asp).

TONY CAMPOLO (b. 1935) is professor emeritus of sociology at Eastern University and an ordained minister in the American Baptist Church. He co-authored *Adventures in Missing the Point* with Brian McLaren, and McLaren endorsed Campolo's book *Speaking My Mind: The Radical Evangelical Prophet Tackles the Tough Issues Christians Are Afraid to Face* (2004). Campolo is also the author of *How to Rescue the Earth without Worshiping Nature* (1992), *Red Letter Christians* (2008) and the co-author with Mary Darling of *The God of Intimacy and Action* (2007), which promotes Roman Catholic-style contemporary spirituality. Some of the testimonies in the book *Emerging Churches* by Eddie Gibbs and Ryan Bolger mention Campolo as an influence.

G.K. CHESTERTON (1874-1936) was a Roman Catholic whose writings have a large influence within the emerging church. He is often quoted, and his book *Orthodoxy* is recommended by many emergents. He believed that the so-called Apostles' Creed, which briefly states a few very basic doctrines, is a sufficient summary of the Christian faith; he used humor to break down walls of differing doctrinal opinions; he was philosophical and complicated rather than straightforward and plainspoken; he accepted theistic evolution (*Orthodoxy*, p. 30); he loved to drink liquor. A 2001 edition of *Orthodoxy* has an introduction by Philip Yancy that explains Chesterton's attraction. Yancy says, "Chesterton seemed to sense instinctively that a stern prophet will rarely break through to a society full of religion's 'cultured despisers'; he preferred the role of jester. ... In a time when culture and faith have drifted even further apart, we could use his brilliance, his entertaining style, and above all his generous and joyful spirit. When society becomes polarized, as ours has, it is as if the two sides stand across a great divide and shout at each other. Chesterton had another approach: He walked to the center of a swinging bridge, roared a challenge to any single combat warrior, and then made both sides laugh aloud" (*Orthodoxy*, Image Books, 2001, p. xix). The fact that this is not the type of "prophet" that we see in Scripture doesn't bother the emerging church one iota.

CHRISTIANITY TODAY magazine is a strong promoter of the emerging church. A page of their web site, called "The Emergence of Emergent," is dedicated to it, and they have published many positive articles dealing with it, including several by Brian McLaren. Marshall Shelley, vice president of *Christianity Today*, said of Spencer Burke's *An Heretic's Guide to Eternity*, which is forwarded by Brian McLaren: "Spencer is a winsome walking companion for those who find traditional dogma too narrow. It's a thoughtful conversation" (http://www.spencerburke.com/pdf/presskit.pdf).

TIM CONDOR is a member of the coordinating team for Emergent Village, pastor of Emmaus Way, an emergent community in Durham, North Carolina, and a member of the board of directors of the Mars Hill Graduate School. He authored *The Church in Transition: The Journey of Existing Church into Emerging Culture* (2006).

EMERGENT VILLAGE, headquartered in Minneapolis, Minnesota, is not a village in a traditional sense, nor is it a church or denomination. It is described by Dwight Friesen as "a type of ecumenical movement of Christian churches from various ecclesial non/traditions, parachurch organizations, and Christian social-advocates linked together in a generative conversational network around mission" ("Emergent Village and Full Communion," a paper presented to the National Council of Churches Faith & Order Commission, March 17, 2007, http://dwightfriesen.blog.com/1616648/). The Emergent Village claims "to have everything from a Texas Baptist pastor to a New England lesbian Episcopal priest" (Roger Moran, "The Emerging Church movement Calls for Biblical Scrutiny by

Missourians," http://www.mbcpathway.com/article97073c482768.htm). Thus the Emergent Village is an ecumenical linking of professing Christians or various stripes who accept the basic premises of the liberal emerging church. Its objective is to facilitate "mission," which refers to social justice projects and artistic living geared toward the building of the alleged kingdom of God.

CHRIS ERDMAN is senior pastor of University Presbyterian Church, Fresno, California, professor at the Mennonite Brethren Biblical Seminary, and contributor to *An Emergent Manifesto of Hope*.

DAVID FOSTER (b. c. 1969) is founding pastor of Bellevue Community Church, Nashville, and author of *A Renegade's Guide to God: Finding Life outside Conventional Christianity* (2006). This book is recommended by Brian McLaren, Tim Stevens, pastor of Granger Community Church, Bill Cornelius, pastor of Bay Area Fellowship in Corpus Christi, Texas, Ron Phillips, pastor of Abba's House, Jim Henderson of Off the Map, and Tony Morgan of WiredChurches.com.

DWIGHT J. FRIESEN is a teacher at Mars Hill Graduate School, founder of an emerging church in Seattle, and member of the Faith & Order Commission of the National Council of Churches.

FULLER THEOLOGICAL SEMINARY is a hotbed of emerging church theology and sympathies. Fuller professors Ryan Bolger and Barry Taylor contributed highly supportive articles to the book *An Emergent Manifesto*. In March 2007, Doug Pagitt joined Bolger in co-teaching a 40-hour Doctor of Ministry class. Spencer Burke has also lectured at Fuller.

STANLEY GRENZ (1950-2005) was a Baptist pastor and professor at several schools (including North American Baptist Seminary, Regent College, and Baylor University) and author of books that are promoted in the emerging church. These include *A Primer on Postmodernism* (1996) and *Beyond Foundationalism: Shaping Theology in a Postmodern Context* (2000), which he coauthored with John Franke. Grenz was influential in the formation of the "theological roots" of Mars Hill Graduate School in Seattle.

ALAN HIRSH is founder of Forge, author of *The Forgotten Ways: Reactivating the Missional Church*, and co-author of *The Shaping of Things to Come* (2006). The foreword to the latter was written by Leonard Sweet, who said: "Hirsch has discovered the formula that unlocks the secrets of the ecclesial universe like Einstein's simple formula (e=mc2) unlocked the secrets of the physical universe. There are some books good enough to read to the end. There are only a few books good enough to read to the end of time. *The Forgotten Ways* is one of them." The book is also recommended by Tony Jones and Brian McLaren.

TONY JONES is National Coordinator of Emergent Village and ministers to youth and young adults at Colonial Church of Edina in Minnesota. He is the author of *Postmodern Youth Ministry: Exploring Cultural Shift, Creating Holistic Connections, Cultivating Authentic Community* (2001), *The Sacred Way: Spiritual Practices for Everyday Life* (2005), *Soul Shaper: Exploring Spirituality and Contemplative Practices in Youth Ministry* (2003), and *The Sacred Way: Spiritual Practices for Everyday Life* (2005).

TIM KEEL is the founder of Jacob's Well Church in Kansas City, Missouri. He is a member of the board of directors for Emergent Village and his interests "include monastic life and culture, reading, writing, and all things Middle Earth" (*The Relevant Church*, p. 161).

LEADERSHIP NETWORK

We described the Leadership Network's history and workings in the first chapter.

C.S. LEWIS (1898-1963) is very popular with both streams of the emerging church. This is not surprising, of course. A *Christianity Today* reader's poll in 1998 rated Lewis the most influential evangelical writer. In an article commemorating the 100th anniversary of Lewis's birth, J.I. Packer called him "our patron saint" and said that Lewis "has come to be the Aquinas, the Augustine, and the Aesop of contemporary evangelicalism" ("Still Surprised by Lewis," *Christianity Today*, Sept. 7, 1998). The cover story of the December 2005 edition of CT was "C.S. Lewis Superstar." Doubtless the emerging church loves Lewis so much because he denied the inerrancy of Scripture and the substitutionary atonement, and because of his ecumenical philosophy, and because he preferred the Romanizing branch of the Anglican Church. Or maybe it is because his testimony of salvation was as vague and unscriptural as theirs typically is or because of his three decades long relationship with a woman to whom he was not married. Or maybe they love him for his life-long fascination with paganism and his strong universalistic tendencies and because he loved to drink beer and whiskey.

KEN AND DEBORAH LOYD are the founding pastors of The Bridge Church in Portland, Oregon, and contributors to *An Emerging Manifesto of Hope.*

DONALD MCCULLOUGH is an ordained minister in the Presbyterian Church USA, president of Salt Lake Theological Seminary, and former president and professor of theology and preaching at San Francisco Theological Seminary. He is the author of *If Grace Is So Amazing Why Don't We Like It?* (2005).

SCOT MCKNIGHT is Professor of Religious Studies at the very liberal North Park University in Chicago. Prior to that, he taught at Trinity Evangelical Divinity School. His web page and blog is called "Jesus Creed." He is the author of several books, including *The Real Mary: Why Evangelical Christians Can Embrace the Mother of Jesus* (2006). In this book McKnight claims that evangelicals and Catholics can find common ground in Mary. His latest book is *Turning to Jesus: The Sociology of Conversion in the Gospels* (2007), in which he claims that "conversion" can be through liturgy (which refers to sacraments such as baptism) or through socialization (growing up in a Christian home) or through personal decisional faith in Christ. Thus, he is deeply confused about salvation itself. McKnight is an advocate of the "New Perspective on Paul" that makes the strange and unscriptural claim that Judaism taught salvation by grace. According to the New Perspective, Paul did not write against Judaism's legalism but against its claim to be the only people of God. James Dunn, one of the fathers of the New Perspective, says that "Paul was reacting primarily against the exclusivism that he himself had previously fought to maintain" ("Paul's Theology," *The Face of New Testament Studies*, p. 336). McKnight got his Ph.D. under Dunn's tutelage at the University of Nottingham in England. Thus, it is obvious that McKnight has been on the road of "rethinking" doctrines of the faith for a long time, and was deeply influenced by heretics before he jumped on the emerging church bandwagon.

BRIAN MCLAREN (b. 1956) is a board member for Sojourners and a member of the international steering team for Emergent Village. He has authored many books promoting emerging theology, including *A New Kind of Christian* (2001), *A Generous Orthodoxy* (2004), and *Everything Must Change: Jesus, Global Crises, and a Revolution of Hope* (2007). *Christianity Today* (November 2004) identified McLaren as "the de facto spiritual leader for the emerging church." McLaren rejects the infallible inspiration of the Bible, the substitutionary atonement of Christ, and the doctrine of eternal punishment in hell fire. He says the Bible is "not a look-it-up encyclopedia of timeless moral truths, but the unfolding narrative of God at work" (*A Generous Orthodoxy*, p. 190). He says that it is wrong and Pharisaical to look upon the Bible as "God's encyclopedia, God's rule book, God's answer book" (*A New Kind of Christian*, p. 52). McLaren has "a strong conviction that THE EXCLUSIVE, HELL-ORIENTED GOSPEL IS NOT THE WAY FORWARD" (*A Generous Orthodoxy*, p. 120, f. 48). McLaren mocks the "fundamentalist expectations" of an imminent return of Christ with its attendant judgments (p. 305), calling this "pop-Evangelical eschatology" (p. 267). McLaren epitomizes the emerging church's radical ecumenism by calling himself "evangelical, post-protestant, liberal/conservative, mystical/poetic, biblical, charismatic/contemplative, fundamentalist/Calvinist, anabaptist/anglican, Methodist, catholic, green, incarnational, emergent" (*A Generous Orthodoxy*, subtitle to the book). The fact that these various doctrinal positions are contradictory and non-reconcilable does not bother this new emergent thinker one iota.

MARS HILL GRADUATE SCHOOL is an interdenominational institution located in Seattle, Washington, that has the objective of preparing "those who desire to obey Christ's commission to serve in the fields of ministry, counseling, spiritual direction and the arts." Thus, according to Mars Hill, the Great Commission is fulfilled through artistic endeavors but nothing is said about soul winning evangelism. Mars Hill's statement on Scripture says, "We believe interpretation or hermeneutics is neither primarily a science, nor a skill, but a living art that molds us into maturity by the Word itself, the convicting work of the Spirit, and in dialogue with the community of faith both past and present" (http://www.mhgs.edu/common/about.asp#scpriture). Thus, according to Mars Hill, the interpretation of the Bible is never absolute and dogmatic and the Bible is not the sole authority of faith and practice; it is only one source together with the tradition and teaching of churches past and present. Mars Hill's statement on Scripture also says: "We believe a person or community can never receive a hearing, nor offer the gospel, unless it incarnates the gospel through joyful participation in a culture's glory and honest engagement in its darkness. We wish to develop lovers of language, story, drama, film, music, dance, architecture, and art in order to deepen our love of life and the God of all creativity." Thus instead of preaching the Word of God to sinners and calling for repentance, as the apostles and prophets in the early churches did in the book of Acts, Mars Hill has the goal of participating in and infiltrating culture through all sorts of artistic endeavors. There is not a hint of such a thing in the New Testament Scripture. Whereas the Bible says, "Love not the world," the emerging church says, "Love it." Mars Hill's statement of faith also says, "We acknowledge one baptism for the forgiveness of sins." Thus, they teach the heresy of baptismal salvation. There is a heavy emphasis on psychology at Mars Hill. The *Wikipedia* article on Mars Hill says, "From a psychological perspective, Mars Hill Graduate School teaches its counseling courses from largely a psychodynamic modality that utilizes an existential approach along with attachment theory and object relations stressed in its curriculum." What does that mean, you say? Who knows, but it certainly sounds impressive! The teachers at Mars Hill include female pastors such as Patricia Brown of the United Methodist Church and Cheryl Goodwin, an elder in a Presbyterian church.

DONALD MILLER (b. 1971) is the author of the very popular book *Blue Like Jazz* (2003). Because he is a member of Imago Dei in Portland, which has a doctrinal statement that includes a reference to the infallibility of Scripture, it is a bit difficult to place Miller within our framework of liberal or conservative. Since he often criticizes doctrinal dogmatism, though, and wants to look at some of the Bible's teaching as "fairy tales" (*Blue Like Jazz*, pp. 31, 35) we have included him in the liberal stream.

SALLY MORGENTHALER is author of *Worship Evangelism* (1998) and "an innovator" and "trusted interpreter of postmodern culture" who seeks to involve women in leadership in every area of church and denominational life.

IAN MOBSBY is an emerging church leader in England. He is an ordained Anglican priest and a founding member of Moot, an emergent community within the Anglican archdiocese of London, England. On its website it is described as follows: "Moot is a developing community of spiritual travellers who are seeking to find a means of living a life that is honest to God and honest to now. Moot seeks to make connections and find inspirations in the meeting of faith, life and culture. Moot looks to the Christian call for justice, equity and balance as a means of living politically and ethically. We recognise the inspiration of saints, mystics, philosophers and artists throughout the centuries." Mobsby's 2007 U.S. book tour was announced by the Emergent Village. He is a proponent of the "new monasticism." He is a worship planner for the very liberal and ecumenical Greenbelt Festival.

LESSLIE NEWBIGIN (1909-1998) has had a powerful influence on the emerging church through his writings. He was a bishop in the very liberal Church of South India and was Associate General Secretary in the radically heretical World Council of Churches. In *The Gospel in a Pluralist Society* Newbigin denied that the Bible is the verbally inspired Word of God and said the 18th century defenders of the faith were in error when they taught that the Bible is a set of timeless truths. Newbigin falsely claimed that Jesus did not leave behind "a book, nor a creed, nor a system of thought, nor a rule of life" (p. 20). Newbigin wrote, "All so-called facts are interpreted facts ... What we see as facts depends on the theory we bring to the observation" (*The Gospel in a Pluralist Society*, p. 21). Newbigin called the split between liberals and fundamentalists "tragic" (p. 24). He taught that there is the possibility of salvation apart from faith in Christ.

HENRI J.M. NOUWEN (1932-1996) was a Roman Catholic priest who taught at Harvard, Yale, and the University of Notre Dame and his writings have had a powerful influence within the emerging church. A *Christian Century* magazine survey conducted in 2003 indicated that Nouwen's writings were a first choice for Catholic and mainline Protestant clergy.

DOUG PAGITT (b. 1964) is a Senior Fellow with Emergent Village and the pastor of Solomon's Porch in Minneapolis, Minnesota. He is coeditor with Tony Jones of *An Emergent Manifesto of Hope* (2007).

PETER ROLLINS is an emergent author in Ireland. In his book *How (Not) to Speak of God* (Paraclete, 2006) he says, "Thus orthodoxy is no longer (mis)understood as the opposite of heresy but rather is understood as a term that signals a way of being in the world rather than a means of believing things about the world." Thus that nasty little problem of orthodoxy vs. heresy is removed by the neat trick of redefining orthodoxy.

MARK SCANDRETTE is an Emergent Village Coordinating Group participant, director of ReIMAGINE, "a center for spiritual formation in San Francisco," and a founding member of SEVEN, a monastic community promoting "holistic and integrative Christian spirituality."

ROBERT SCHULLER (b. 1926), founder of the Crystal Cathedral, taught emerging theology before it became popular, with his *Self-Esteem: A New Reformation* (1982). He reinterprets the doctrines of the Word of God to conform to his self-esteem philosophy. To Schuller, sin is the lack of self-esteem. His christ is a psycho-savior who is "self-esteem incarnate." His gospel is to replace negative self-concepts with positive ones. Schuller wants to create a new kind of Christianity: one that believes in the Fatherhood of God and the divinity of man, one that is positive and non-judgmental, one that worships a New Age self-esteem Christ, one that denies the necessity of Christ's blood atonement, one in which salvation is to be reconciled with one's one essential goodness, one that believes in the essential truth in all religions. Schuller remains on the cutting edge of emerging philosophy with a January 2008 Rethinking Conference that brought together emerging leaders (Dan Kimball and Erwin McManus), evangelicals (i.e., Kay Warren, Henry Cloud, Chuck Colson, Gary Smalley, Jay Sekulow), and agnostics (Larry King).

CHRIS SEAY (b. 1972) is founding pastor of Ecclesia of Houston, Texas. He is the author of *The Gospel according to Tony Soprano* (2002), which finds spiritual lessons in the filthy R-rated television series. He co-authored with Greg Garrett *The Gospel Reloaded* (2003), which analyzes the R-rated *Matrix* movies "for their hidden and transparent meaning." Seay was the founding pastor of University Baptist Church in Waco. Ecclesia is very artsy, hosting poetic readings, art shows, conducting "liturgy," etc. Its mission statement says: "Culture is met, embraced, and transformed. ... Beauty, art, and creativity are valued. ... Other churches are valued and supported."

SHAPEVINE is an emerging church blog that features individuals such as Brian McLaren, Tony Jones, Sally Morganthaler, Alan Hirsch, Reggie McNeal, and Leonard Sweet. It is called "a global community of collaborators." The Shapevine goal is "to give missional leaders the opportunity to engage in live learning environments with a wide variety of authors and thought leaders" (http://movementseverywhererant.blogspot.com/2007/04/shapevine.html).

WILBERT R. SHENK was a professor of mission history and contemporary culture at Fuller Theological Seminary from 1995 until his retirement in 2005. Ryan Bolger says that Shenk had a powerful influence on his thinking, and that Shenk, in turn, was a disciple of Lesslie Newbigin (http://thebolgblog.typepad.com/thebolgblog/2005/08/you_changed_my_.html).

KAREN SLOAN is a minister in the Presbyterian Church USA who "can often be found praying in Catholic churches and hanging "around the Dominican order and monastic life." She is the author of *Flirting with Monasticism: Finding God on Ancient Paths* (InterVarsity, 2006).

SOJOURNERS was emerging church before there was an emerging church. It has been involved in leftist social-justice-environmental activities since its inception in the 1970s. It was founded by a group of "evangelical" students associated with Trinity Evangelical Divinity School. They established a pacifistic social-justice commune in Washington D.C. and began publishing *Sojourners* magazine in 1975. They describe themselves today as "a committed group of Christians who believe in the biblical call to integrate spiritual renewal and social justice." Sojourners membership includes "evangelicals, Catholics, Pentecostals and Protestants; liberals and conservatives" who "sojourn with others in different faith traditions and all those who are on a spiritual journey." JIM WALLIS and RON SIDER are leaders in this movement. SOJOURNERS FAITH & JUSTICE CONNECTION is a network of churches that are committed to Sojourners' social-justice-environmental gospel.

LEONARD SWEET (b. 1961) is a United Methodist clergyman, E. Stanley Jones Professor of Evangelism at Drew University, and founder and president of SpiritVenture Ministries. He is the author of *Quantum Spirituality: A Postmodern Apologetic* (1991), *Soul Tsunami* (1999), *Postmodern Pilgrims* (2000), *Carpe Manana: Is Your Church Ready to Seize Tomorrow?* (2001), *Jesus Drives Me Crazy* (2003), and *The Gospel according to Starbucks* (2007). He was a contributor to *The Church in Emerging Culture: Five Perspectives* (2003). Sweet promotes a New Age universalist spirituality that he calls New Light and "the Christ consciousness." He describes it in terms of "the union of the human with the divine" which is the "center feature of all the world's religions" (*Quantum Spirituality*, p. 235). He says it was experienced by Mohammed, Moses, and Krishna. He says that some of the "New Light leaders" that have led him into this new thinking are New Agers Matthew Fox, M. Scott Peck, Willis Harman, and Ken Wilber, all of whom believe in the divinity of man, plus the Catholic-Buddhist monk Thomas Merton. In *Quantum Spirituality* Sweet defines the New Light as "a structure of human becoming, a channeling of Christ energies through mindbody experience" (*Quantum Spirituality*, p. 70). He says humanity needs to learn the truth of the words of Thomas Merton, "We are already one" (*Quantum Spirituality*, p. 13).

KAREN WARD is the founding pastor of the Church of the Apostles in Seattle, Washington, which is affiliated with the Episcopal Church USA and the Evangelical Lutheran Church in America. She contributed a chapter to *The Relevant Church: A New Vision for Communities of Faith* (2004) and to *Listening to the Beliefs of Emerging Churches* edited by Robert Webber (2007).

A MAGNET FOR REBELS

The emerging church is a magnet for those who have rejected the "old-fashioned" New Testament faith and who despise traditional Bible-believing churches, dogmatic biblical preaching, and biblical "judgmentalism" in regard to lifestyle choices.

Many of the books I have read by emerging leaders make this admission.

For example, in *Blue Like Jazz* Donald Miller tells how that he refused to be restricted by the teaching of traditional-type churches. He wanted to drink beer and watch raunchy movies and talk trashy and run around with atheists and other rebels. In discussing his involvement in church in his youth he says, "I wished I could have subscribed to aspects of Christianity but not the whole thing" (p. 30). He complains, "In order to believe Christianity, you either had to reduce enormous theological absurdities [i.e., Garden of Eden, universal flood] into children's stories or ignore them" (p. 31). He wanted to believe the gospel "free from the clasp of fairy tale" (p. 35). In other words, he wanted to pick and choose what parts of the Bible he would believe. He despised dogmatic Bible preaching and hated it when preachers "said we had to follow Jesus" because "sometimes they would make Him sound angry" (p. 34).

In fact, Jesus *was* angry sometimes even in His incarnation ("*he looked round about on them with anger, being grieved for the hardness of their hearts*," Mark 3:5), and He will be *very* angry in the future when the wrath of the Lamb is poured out upon mankind as described in the book of Revelation and many other places in Scripture!

When Miller decided to attend a raunchy secular college in Portland, Oregon, where most of the students are atheists and agnostics and they use drugs and openly fornicate and sometimes run around naked, a Christian friend sat him down and warned him that God did not want him to attend there. That was good biblical advice (e.g., 2 Corinthians 6:14 -17; Ephesians 5:11; 2 Timothy 3:5; James 4:4; 1 John 2:15-17), but Miller ignored the warning and felt that the wicked atmosphere was a liberating experience. He writes: "The first day of school was exhilarating. It was better than high school. Reed had ashtrays, and everybody said cusswords" (p. 38). After spending time with drug-using, atheistic hippies who lived in the woods he said, "I had discovered life outside the church, and I liked it. As I said, I preferred it" (p. 210).

At a book signing event, one enthusiastic reader of Miller's *Blue Like Jazz* said: "I love *Blue Like Jazz* because it's, like, a Christian book, but it doesn't make you feel bad about yourself" ("A Better Storyteller," *Christianity Today*, June 2007). Another said: "I've already bought *Blue Like Jazz* 13 times. But I gotta have all these to give to people. I'm a Jesus girl, but I also like to go out and do tequila shots with my friends. This is a book I can give to those friends."

Some members of Spirit Garage meet in an Irish bar in downtown Minneapolis on Wednesday for a weekly Theology Pub, a mix of biblical discussion and beer. Lindsey Gice, a member of Spirit Garage, says that when the subject of Christianity comes up, "I always feel like I have to qualify it, like, 'I'm not that kind of Christian, I go to a cool church'" ("Hip New Churches Pray to a Different Drummer," *New York Times*, Feb. 18, 2004). Gice said that she left church after high school because her former churches were "way too judgmental."

Brian McLaren's book *A New Kind of Christian* is the story of a pastor who rejects the Bible in a "crisis of faith" and follows the guidance of a modernist. The book recounts the man's journey from a fairly solid faith in the Bible as the absolute standard for truth, in which doctrine is either right or wrong, scriptural or unscriptural, to a pliable, philosophical position in which "faith is more about a way of life than a system of belief, where being authentically good is more important than being doctrinally right" (from the back cover of *A New Kind of Christian*).

In *A Renegade's Guide to God*, David Foster mocks "Bible thumpers" and calls for a "renegade" type of Christianity that "resists being named, revolts at being shamed, and rebels against being tamed" (p. 8). He says, "We won't be 'told' what to do or 'commanded' how to behave'" (p. 10).

Nanette Sawyer, in her chapter in *An Emergent Manifesto of Hope*, begins by describing her "explicit rejection of Christianity" (p. 43). She rejected the division of people into categories of saved and unsaved. She rejected the restriction on women church leaders. She renounced the doctrine that man is "inherently bad" and the necessity of judging oneself a sinner. She complains, "This didn't leave any room for questions, doubts, or growth in faith."

The testimony of Anna Dodridge of Bournemouth, England, is featured in the book *Emerging Churches* by Eddie Gibbs and Ryan Bolger. She describes how that she grew up in a Christian home but fell in love with the world and got deeply involved in the club culture, which involves all night dance and drug parties. Her interests were "in drinking and kissing boys" (p. 262). She got fed up with the churches because they "refused to support me" and "couldn't see how I could possibly want to go into nightclubs, and they thought it was disgraceful that we were encouraging the culture." She and others that support the emerging church philosophy are "fed up with traditional church, heavy-handed guidance" (p. 264).

The membership of the emerging church congregation called Revive in Leeds, England, is "mainly made up of people who didn't fit into 'regular' church. They were too cynical, too rebellious, too radical" (*Emerging Church*, p. 273).

Jonny Baker of Grace in London, England, says: "We once did a service called 'we're right, follow us' that explored the discomfort we all feel with that old-school, arrogant approach to evangelism" (*Emerging Church*, p. 123).

Donald McCullough complains about those who make "cocksure pronouncements about God" and engage in "doctrinal warfare" and are "eager to condemn others to hell" (*If Grace Is So Amazing, Why Don't We Like It*, p. 25). He is opposed to preachers who "crack the whip of the imperative ('Do this!') [rather] than announce the news of the indicative ('God has done this!')" (p. 78). He doesn't like the type of preaching that says, "... don't do that, curb your appetites, reign in desire, discipline and sacrifice yourself" (p. 104). He claims that grace means "we may relax in our humanity" (p. 141).

These people are rebels against the plain teaching of the Bible, and as a magnet for rebellion the emerging church holds a wide attraction in these last days as prophesied in Scripture:

> "For the time will come when they will not endure sound doctrine; but after their own lusts shall they heap to themselves teachers, having

itching ears; and they shall turn away their ears from the truth, and shall be turned unto fables" (2 Timothy 4:3-4).

This prophecy describes a great turning away from the truth among professing Christians. It says they will reject the sound teaching of the Bible and desire a new type of Christianity that allows them to live after their own lusts. That is a strange type of Christianity, but we are seeing its fulfillment before our very eyes. The prophecy says there will be heaps of teachers who will give the people this new type of Christianity, and this is exactly what we see. Christian bookstores are filled with books and the Internet is filled with Christian articles and blogs, but the majority of this material does not contain the straightforward preaching of God's Word that reproves, rebukes, and exhorts (2 Timothy 4:2). Rather, they are filled with doctrine that scratches the itching ears of those who have rejected the Bible. They are filled with pop novelties, psychology, self-esteemism, pampering of the ego, friendship with the world, heresies, questionings, boastings, doubtings, illicit fellowship with error (e.g., evangelicals and contemplative spirituality), railings against "legalism" falsely so called, fairy tales, fictional romance, reconstructed history, fascination with ancient heretics wrongly called "church fathers," and many other such things.

The New Evangelicalism of the 1950s was a rebellion against strict biblical Christianity, and the emerging church is simply a step further in that fearful direction.

Rebellion is a natural product of our fallen nature. The Old Man, as it is called in Scripture, which we inherited from Adam's fall, is at enmity against God and His Word. True Christianity requires a new birth. There are no "second generation" Christians in the true biblical sense. Thus each person that grows up in a Christian home and church must come to grips with the gospel for himself and herself, and because the devil and the indwelling fallen nature are real, there is a spiritual battle that must be waged. I faced this battle in my youth. I grew up in a Bible-believing church and went through the motions of receiving Christ and joining the church, but I wanted my own way more than Christ's. I rejected the Bible, left the church, and went very far into the world before being converted at age 23. Emerging church philosophy would doubtless have been appealing to me in my unsaved, rebellious condition.

Because of this ongoing battle that rages with each new generation, the rebellion that is part and parcel of the emerging church philosophy is very enticing to a wide range of people.

COMPLICATED

The liberal emerging church is very complicated. Consider some of the terms that are used in the book *An Emergent Manifesto of Hope* edited by Doug Pagitt and Tony Jones: *generative concepts, orthopraxis, global narrative, integrative theology, hermeneutical circle, reciprocal relationship axis, radical discontinuity regarding the gospel, paradigm shifts, cosmic fulness of God's influence, generative conversational network, exegetical trajectory, missional imagination, self-theologizing church*, and my personal favorite -- *orthoparadoxy*.

Brian McLaren's speech at Wake Forest University on October 24, 2006, was entitled: "On ramp to the Postmodern Conversation: historical, philosophical, and theological background to the concepts of a paradigm shift and postmodern transition in a fast-paced, understandable and highly visual way."

If the title of a speech is difficult understand, imagine how dense the speech itself must be!

Ryan Bolger, Fuller Theological Seminary professor who promotes emerging church thinking, wrote a paper about the late church growth professor Donald McGavran entitled "Looking Back at McGavran and Finding a Way Forward." Note the following description of this paper from Bolger's blog:

> "Adding deterritorialization to people movement theory enables the formulation of a theory that maintains the dynamics of mission within spaces where people are no longer associated with particular places or cultures. If mission stations represent mission engagement in modernity, and people movements in postmodernity, the author proposes practice movements as a viable way forward for mission in global information culture."

Did you get that the first time, or should I repeat it!

The emerging church is so complicated that it would be impossible for anyone except the most highly educated to grasp its teaching, and this complexity is contrary to the gospel of Jesus Christ, which has a basic simplicity that allows even children and the illiterate to understand its major points. The complexity that is characteristic of the emerging church has been the hallmark of false teachers since the days of the apostles. The apostle Paul wrote to the church at Corinth about the false teachers that were tempting them and said:

> "But I fear, lest by any means, as the serpent beguiled Eve through his subtilty, so your minds should be corrupted from the simplicity that is in Christ. For if he that cometh preacheth another Jesus, whom we have not preached, or if ye receive another spirit, which ye have not received, or another gospel, which ye have not accepted, ye might well bear with him" (2 Corinthians 11:3-4).

The apostle stated that there is a simplicity to the doctrine of Christ. It is the devil that complicates it. It is God's will that the gospel be preached to all men (Mark 16:15), and the fact is that the vast majority of people are not highly educated. My wife and I have spent 17 years preaching the Word of God in a part of South Asia where the literacy rate is not more than 30%. The percentage of people who would be capable of understanding emerging church theology is extremely small. Though emerging church leaders claim to be following in the footsteps of Jesus, they obviously are not teaching the doctrine of the One who spent most of his time with fishermen and others who were not the elite of society.

The Lord Jesus Christ said, "*I thank thee, O Father, Lord of heaven and earth, because thou hast hid these things from the wise and prudent, and hast revealed them unto babes*" (Matthew 11:25).

There is a simplicity to sound doctrine because God has chosen the humble of this world to confound the proud, the low to confound the high. The members of the early churches were not, for the most part, from the highly educated strata of society. Paul said to the church at Corinth:

> "For the preaching of the cross is to them that perish foolishness; but unto us which are saved it is the power of God. For it is written, I will destroy the wisdom of the wise, and will bring to nothing the understanding of the prudent. Where is the wise? where is the scribe? where is the disputer of this world? hath not God made foolish the wisdom of this world? For after that in the wisdom of God the world by wisdom knew not God, it pleased God by the foolishness of preaching to save them that believe. For the Jews require a sign, and the Greeks seek after wisdom: But we preach Christ crucified, unto the Jews a stumblingblock, and unto the Greeks foolishness; But unto them which are called, both Jews and Greeks, Christ the power of God, and the wisdom of God. Because the foolishness of God is wiser than men; and the weakness of God is stronger than men. FOR YE SEE YOUR CALLING, BRETHREN, HOW THAT NOT MANY WISE MEN AFTER THE FLESH, NOT MANY MIGHTY, NOT MANY NOBLE, ARE CALLED: But God hath chosen the foolish things of the world to confound the wise; and God hath chosen the weak things of the world to confound the things which are mighty; And base things of the world, and things which are despised, hath God chosen, yea, and things which are not, to bring to nought things that are: That no flesh should glory in his presence" (1 Corinthians 1:18-29).

This passage of Scripture refutes the emerging church doctrine. Paul said that God has rejected the wise of this world and has destroyed their wisdom through the gospel. He has chosen the foolish things of the world to confound the wise. The Greeks of old pursued wisdom just like the proud emerging church leaders are doing today, but they have no true wisdom because they have rejected the beginning of wisdom, which is the humble fear of God, and the foundation of wisdom, which is submission to the gospel of Jesus Christ. (They talk much about the gospel but they commonly redefine it in terms of social justice and kingdom building.)

WHAT YOU WON'T FIND IN THE LIBERAL EMERGING CHURCH

The following are things that I have never read in a book by a liberal emerging church leader: a clear and biblical exhortation on the necessity of the new birth or a clear message on how to be born again; a description of the blood atonement of Christ as a substitutionary act necessary for the salvation of the soul; an exhortation to repentance from sin and idolatry; an exhortation to love not the world; a warning that the whole world lieth in wickedness; an exhortation that the believer's citizenship is heavenly and not of this world and to set our affection on things above not on things on this earth; a warning about false christs, false spirits and false gospels; an exhortation to separate from theological error; the mention of Hell as a real place of fiery punishment and the destiny of every person that does not put his faith in Jesus Christ; a warning against fellowshipping with idols; a warning against demonic delusion; a warning that Roman Catholicism preaches a false gospel and is filled with idolatrous and blasphemous doctrines and practices; a plain warning against theological modernism.

HYPOCRISY

There is a great hypocrisy that permeates emerging church writings. They denounce dogmatism in the most dogmatic terms! They reject judgmentalism in the most judgmental terms, having nothing to say of fundamentalist Christianity except ridicule and denunciation. They reject traditional patterns of Bible "spirituality," such as daily devotions, as dull and legalistically obligatory, but accept the most stringent forms of Catholic "spirituality," such as *lectio divina* and keeping "the hours" and monasticism as exciting and life-giving.

STRAW MAN ARGUMENTATION

Emerging church writers constantly set up straw men and knock them down with vigor.

Donald Miller, for example, describes how that he was "a fundamentalist Christian for "a summer" (*Blue Like Jazz*, pp. 79-80). During that short time he became "a Navy SEAL for Jesus." But his description of fundamentalism is a convenient straw man. He said that in those days he got upset when preachers talked too much about grace, as if biblical fundamentalists don't believe in and preach much about grace. He says he was self-righteous in those days, as if Bible fundamentalists are a bunch of self-righteous Pharisees, which simply isn't true. I have been walking in fundamentalist circles for 35 years and have met countless humble, godly, Christ-centered Christians who know that they are merely sinners saved by grace and that they have no righteousness apart from Jesus and that they are not better than anyone else. Miller says that during that summer he and some of his friends made a contract not to watch television or smoke or listen to music and to read the Bible every day and to memorize certain long passages of Scripture. Then he describes how that he gave all this up because he "got ticked at all the people who were having fun with their lives." This gives the idea that Bible-believing fundamentalists separate from the world only because they don't like to have fun and they only read the Bible every day because they are forced to. I realize that the term "fundamentalist" is very broad, but in my experience I can say that the fundamentalists I know read the Bible because they love the Lord and want to know His thoughts and walk in His ways and they separate from the world because they want to please the Lord that saved them and they don't want to be caught in the snare of the world, the flesh, and the devil.

I will give another example from Miller's writings of the straw man argumentation that permeates the emerging church. He says:

> "I do not believe a person can take two issues from Scripture, those being abortion and gay marriage, and adhere to them as sins, then neglect much of the rest and call himself a fundamentalist or even a conservative. The person who believes the sum of his morality involves gay marriage and abortion alone, and neglects health care and world trade and the environment and loving his neighbor and feeding the poor is, by definition, a theological liberal, because he takes what he wants from Scripture and ignores the rest" (*Searching for God Knows What*, p. 194).

Ignoring, for a moment, his inclusion of things such as health care and the environment as part of the Christian's obligation in this world, consider how he mischaracterizes the fundamentalist position. I don't know any Bible-believing fundamentalists who think that abortion and homosexuality are wrong while ignoring the rest of the Bible and caring nothing about loving one's neighbor and caring for the needy and a hundred and one other saintly obligations. What Miller has described is a convenient straw man.

David Foster says, "We've all heard arrogant, agitated, self-righteous know-it-alls who insist they have the absolute, one and only, true 'Christian view' on all things..." (*A Renegade's Guide to God*, p. 194). Thus he holds up a dogmatic fundamentalist approach to the Bible as arrogant and self-righteous and in doing so he sets up a convenient straw man. Who is he to think that he knows the deepest motives of the fundamentalist's heart? He doesn't, but it is much easier to dismiss the fundamentalist with a mere wave of the hand when he is labeled an arrogant, self-righteous fanatic.

The truth is that the born again fundamentalist interprets the Bible differently than the emergent and is convinced that he is not in this present world to fight against environmentalism and global injustice, but he definitely wants to obey everything in Scripture that is required of him. He believes he is obligated to *"have no fellowship with the unfruitful works of darkness, but rather reprove them"* (Eph. 5:11) and to *"love not the world"* (1 John 2:15-16), but his obligation certainly does not end there. He also believes that it is God's will for him to jealously keep his first love relationship with Christ and to walk in the Spirit not in the flesh and to put off the old man and put on the new and to obey those that have the rule over him and to love his wife as he loves himself and to train up his children in the way they should go and to be a diligent and honest worker and not to neglect the assembly and many other things, and he attempts, by God's grace and the power of the indwelling Spirit, to do these things.

Let me give another example of the emerging church's straw man argumentation. Rob Bell claims that Jesus is already with people even in their false religions, thus "the issue isn't so much taking Jesus to people who don't have him, but going to a place and pointing out to the people there the creative, life-giving God who is already present in their midst" (*Velvet Elvis*, p. 88). In his zeal to show how wrong traditional missionary work is he says that "some people actually believe that God is absent from a place until they get there" (*Velvet Elvis*, p. 88).

I don't know anyone who believes that God is absent from a certain place until a gospel missionary goes there. We know that God is everywhere present and gives to all men life and breath and every blessing that they enjoy (Acts 17:25). But we also know that God is only present *in His soul-saving power* through the gospel, and that is why Jesus commanded us to preach the gospel to every person. Those who believe are saved and those who do not believe are damned (Mark 16:15-16).

I will give one more example. Rob Bell describes a Christian who doesn't attend secular university because she had "been taught that Christianity is the only thing that's true" and "that there is no truth outside the Bible" (*Velvet Elvis*, p. 81).

Again, I don't know anyone who believes this. The world is filled with things that are true in various fields, such as mathematics, but the Bible is true in a unique way. It is the only infallible revelation from God about salvation, and it is the touchstone for truth in a dark world.

The emerging church employs straw man theology, and it works very well for the ill-informed and for rebels.

A NEW DICTIONARY

Like all false teachers, emerging church proponents put their own new definitions on words, and this can deceive the ill-informed.

They talk much about the gospel, for example, but they don't mean the gospel defined in 1 Corinthians 15:1-4. They talk about the kingdom of God, but it is not the kingdom that will be established when Christ returns but a kingdom that they are building on earth today. They talk about being led of the Spirit and listening to the Spirit's voice, but they do not mean by this that they are in subjection to the Bible in the sense that they use it as the sole authority to test everything. They speak of loving the Bible and of the Bible being an important part of the Christian life, but by this they do not mean that the Bible is infallibly inspired and the sole authority for faith and practice. The talk about "mission" (actually they prefer "missional") but by this they do not mean the mission that Jesus Christ assigned to the churches in Matthew 28, Mark 16, Luke 24, John 20, and Acts 1. They talk about redemption and reconciliation, but by these terms they don't mean the redemption of a sinner's soul through faith in the blood of Christ but rather the redemption of society and creation. They talk about Hell, but they don't mean a place of eternal fiery judgment for every unbeliever. They talk about grace, but what they mean is actually license. They talk about creation, but they really believe that Moses wrote the first few chapters of Genesis in "poetic" terms.

REFUSING TO ACKNOWLEDGE THE RELATIVISM OF ITS STANCE

Even though the liberal emerging church rejects theological dogmatism and claims that all theological interpretations are fallible, and even though it is open to new interpretations and intends to dialogue with every facet of Christianity and even with non-Christian religions from a non-dogmatic, non-judgmental stance, and even though it wants to learn from the world more than preach to it, it HAS THE AUDACITY TO CLAIM THAT IT DOES NOT BELIEVE IN RELATIVISM!

Consider the following statement by Barry Taylor:

> "'Muscular Christianity' and 'robust faith' are views that worked well in modernity's concrete world, but the viability of Christian faith in the twenty-first century is not guaranteed by claims to power and declarations of strengths and doctrinal postures. THIS IS NOT A SLIDE INTO RELATIVISM BUT A COMMITMENT TO NONDOGMATIC SPECIFICITY" (*An Emergent Manifesto of Hope*, p. 169).

Think about that last statement for a moment. It demonstrates the impossible, self-deceived stance of the emerging church. What is "a commitment to nondogmatic specificity"? If something is specific it is dogmatic, and if it is nondogmatic it cannot be specific! And what is a "nondogmatic" stance if it is not relativism?

MISUSING SCRIPTURE

Emerging church writers continually take Scripture out of context and otherwise abuse it. This comes back to the problem of unregeneration. Without the new birth, the individual does not have the indwelling Spirit of God and cannot rightly understand the Scripture. "*But the anointing which ye have received of him abideth in you, and ye need not that any man teach you: but as the same anointing teacheth you of all things, and is truth, and is no lie, and even as it hath taught you, ye shall abide in him*" (1 John 2:27).

Consider a few examples of how the emerging church misuses the Scripture.

Sherry and Geoff Maddock use Jeremiah 29:4-7 to "prove" that Christians should get involved in emerging church style "missional" work through social-justice-environmental issues (*An Emergent Manifesto of Hope*, p. 83). In fact, Jeremiah 29 speaks to a particular situation that existed in that day when Israel had been taken captive and was living in Babylon. God instructed them to settle down and live in peace and to seek the welfare of that nation. This is NOT the Christian's commission about how to live in this present world. We have been given that in Christ's Great Commission (e.g., Matthew 28:18-20; Acts 1:8) and in the New Testament epistles, and it is an entirely different thing.

Barry Taylor, a professor at Fuller Theological Seminary and a contributor to *An Emergent Manifesto of Hope*, says we should not "go out into the world to tell people what we think they ought to know" but instead we should seek "to discover what they are interested in and where they are looking for answers" (p. 170). He claims that we should listen to the world instead of preaching at it. As proof of this doctrine he cites Paul's message to the Athenians in Acts 17. He says, "Paul began with what they had and built from there." In fact, Paul preached TO the Athenians boldly and told them in no uncertain terms that they were worshipping false gods and demanded that they repent! It is true that Paul quoted from one of their philosophers and preached in a way that the Athenians could understand him, but the fact is that Acts 17 teaches exactly the opposite of the point that Taylor is trying to make.

Donald Miller also uses Paul's message on Mars Hill to support his idea that Christians should not rebuke the world's sin (such as homosexuality). He says, "In fact, in

Athens, he was so appreciated by pagans who worshiped false idols, they invited him to speak about Jesus in an open forum. ... Paul would go so far as to compliment the men of Athens, calling them 'spiritual men' and quoting their poetry, then telling them the God he knew was better for them, larger, stronger and more alive than any of the stone idols they bowed down to. And many of the people in the audience followed Him and had more and more questions. This would not have happened if Paul had labeled them as pagans and attacked them" (*Searching for God Knows What*, p. 190).

This is a make-believe view of what Paul did that day! Paul was not invited to speak because he was appreciated by the pagans, but because they constantly lusted after novel philosophy and they thought Paul was preaching "strange gods" and "new doctrine" (Acts 17:18-20). Far from appreciating Paul, the philosophers who invited him to speak on Mars Hill called him a "babbler" (Acts 17:18). And far from complimenting the men of Athens, he said they were "superstitious" (Acts 17:22). Far from being positive about their religion, Paul said their idols were nothing (Acts 17:29), called their religion "ignorance" (Acts 17:30), demanded that they repent (Acts 17:30), and warned that if they didn't repent God was going to judge them (Acts 17:30).

Dwight Friesen, a teacher at Mars Hill Graduate School, claims that "God's hope for creation is peace or shalom--wholeness." He is referring to the emerging church's social-justice-environmental gospel. To support this claim he quotes 2 Corinthians 5:18, "*And all things are of God, who hath reconciled us to himself by Jesus Christ, and hath given to us the ministry of reconciliation.*" But Paul was not saying that God has given us the ministry of reconciling the creation to God. He was saying that God has given us the ministry of reconciling MEN to God! The context makes this clear. Verse 19 says it is the forgiveness of sins that is in view here. Verse 20 says we are to beseech MEN to be reconciled to God.

Rob Bell says Christ has given believers the authority to come up with new interpretations of the Bible, and to prove this he quotes Matthew 16:19 (*Velvet Elvis*, p. 50). *"And I will give unto thee the keys of the kingdom of heaven: and whatsoever thou shalt bind on earth shall be bound in heaven: and whatsoever thou shalt loose on earth shall be loosed in heaven."* But Christ has not given Christians the authority to come up with perpetually new interpretations of the Bible, and Matthew 16:19 has nothing to do with such a thing. The statement is addressed to Peter, not to Christians in general. To Peter Christ gave the keys of the kingdom of Heaven, and Peter used those keys for the Jews when he preached the gospel on the day of Pentecost and for the Gentiles when he preached the gospel to Cornelius and his friends in Acts 10. That Christ did not give Christians the authority to come up with new interpretations of the Bible is evident from the fact that He warned His disciples to beware of false prophets (Mat. 7:15). If new interpretations of doctrine are proper, it would be impossible to identify a false prophet.

Erwin McManus contends that Christians should walk "the barbarian way," rejecting rules and boundaries, and as evidence he cites John the Baptist's statement in Matthew 3:11 that Jesus would "baptize us in both Spirit and fire." He concludes from this that "Barbarians are guided by the wind of God and ignited by the fire of God. The way of the barbarian can be found only by listening to the voice of the Spirit" (*The Barbarian Way*, p. 13). In fact, when John said that Jesus would baptize with fire, he was referring to judgment upon unbelievers! That is made clear in the context. Consider. *"I indeed baptize you with water unto repentance: but he that cometh after me is mightier than I, whose shoes I am not worthy to bear: he shall baptize you with the Holy Ghost, and with fire: Whose fan is in his hand, and he will throughly purge his floor, and gather his wheat into the garner; but he will burn up the chaff with unquenchable fire"* (Matthew 3:11-12). John plainly identified the fire as God's judgment upon rebels.

Practically every time a liberal emerging church leader tries to use Scripture, he misuses it!

TRUTH MIXED WITH THE ERROR

I don't know of one heresy that is unmitigated error. It always comes mixed with some truth, and emerging church heresy is no different. The emerging church makes some proper critiques of the weakness both of evangelicalism and fundamentalism. It says, for example, that many churches are too inward-looking and not aggressive enough about reaching the world, and this is correct. It calls on Christians to love their neighbors, and this is good and important (though we would disagree with their definition of how this is accomplished). It is opposed to self-righteousness, which is good. It is opposed to a shallow type of Christianity that is not characterized by true discipleship, and this is good.

The emerging church has a desire for real spiritual community and true fellowship, a desire to communicate effectively to the unsaved, a willingness to befriend those outside of the church and really care for people, a rejection of the program of running the church like a large business, of the "big is better" church growth policies, of glitzy services and celebrity preachers.

The problem is that any "good" that is found in emerging church teaching is corrupted by the heresies that permeate it. Further, its proposed solutions to the problems are largely unscriptural.

ERRORS OF THE LIBERAL EMERGING CHURCH

In this section we will look at some of the chief errors of the liberal emerging church.

Contents of this section

1. Rejecting the infallible inspiration and sole authority of Scripture
2. No clear testimony of salvation
3. A non-dogmatic approach to doctrine
4. Glorifying doubt
5. Contemplative Mysticism
6. A social-justice, kingdom-building gospel
7. Hating dispensationalism and rejecting the imminent return of Christ
8. Very low-key about evangelism
9. Worldliness
10. Loving to drink
11. Ecumenicalism
12. Tending toward Universalism
13. Downplaying Hell
14. Weak on the issue of homosexuality
15. Weak on the substitutionary atonement
16. Female church leaders

LIBERAL EMERGING CHURCH ERROR #1 REJECTING THE INFALLIBLE INSPIRATION AND SOLE AUTHORITY OF SCRIPTURE

According to the emerging church, the Bible is not a divinely-inspired instruction book for the Christian life and ministry, is not our sole authority, and cannot be dogmatically and authoritatively interpreted. This is the emerging church's foundational error.

Brian McLaren, in *A Generous Orthodoxy*, says the Bible is "not a look-it-up encyclopedia of timeless moral truths, but the unfolding narrative of God at work..." (p. 190). He compliments the Anglicans because to them the Bible is *A factor* in their thinking "but it is never *sola*--never the only factor. Rather Scripture is always in dialogue with tradition, reason, and experience" (p. 235). In *A New Kind of Christian*, McLaren teaches that the Bible should be only one of many authorities, such as tradition, reason, exemplary people and institutions one has come to trust, and spiritual experience (pp. 54, 55). He says that it is wrong and Pharisaical to look upon the Bible as "God's encyclopedia, God's rule book, God's answer book" (p. 52). He says that the authority of the Bible is not in the text itself but in a mystical level above and beyond the text (p. 51).

Karen Ward, founder of the Church of the Apostle in Seattle, rejects the position that the Bible is the supreme court of authority. She says: "I reference Scripture as the 'big S story,' a founding partner in a relational dance, as my friend Rachel Mee Chapman says, 'in the overlap' of text, community, and Spirit" (*Listening to the Beliefs of Emerging Churches*, p. 45). Thus, for her, the Bible is only one authority among many. Ward says, "In the Apostles' community as a whole, we do not speak of Scripture using the words 'inerrant' or 'infallible'" (p. 168).

In *Velvet Elvis*, Rob Bell makes the following statements:

> "They [the New Testament epistles] aren't first and foremost timeless truths. ... The Bible is not pieces of information about God and Jesus and whatever else we take and apply to situations as we would a cookbook or an instruction manual. And while I'm at it, let's make a group decision to drop once and for all the Bible-as-owner's-manual metaphor. It's terrible. It really is. ... We have to embrace the Bible as the wild, uncensored, passionate account it is of people experiencing the living God" (*Velvet Elvis*, pp. 62, 63).

> "The Christian faith is mysterious to the core. It is about things and beings that ultimately can't be put into words. Language fails. And if we do definitively put God into words, we have at that very moment made God something God is not" (p. 32).

To say that God can't be definitely put into words is to say that the Bible's words are fallible.

Bell claims that the apostles in their writings in the Bible didn't "claim to have the absolute word from God" (p. 57).

Chris Seay of Ecclesia in Houston, Texas, rejects the infallibility of the Scripture and believes it contains many errors (*Faith of My Fathers*, pp. 81-86). He says: "I love the Bible, and I believe it's perfect in every way IT NEEDS TO BE. But I serve a living God, not a canon" (p. 86).

Will Samson, in his contribution to *An Emergent Manifesto of Hope*, says:

> "Preachers speak of the Bible as an instruction book or as the only data necessary for spiritual living. But this diminishes some critical elements of theological knowledge. *Sola scriptura* does not account for the history of the church in shaping our theological understanding, even though, ironically, it was the church itself that shaped and determined what we know as Scripture. *Sola scriptura* also tends to downplay the role of God's Spirit in shaping the direction of the church. Of greatest importance to this discussion is the fact that often people subscribing to *sola scriptura* do not take into account the subjectivity of human interpreters" (p. 156).

Tony Jones says, "We must stop looking for some objective Truth that is available when we delve into the text of the Bible" (*Postmodern Youth Ministry*, Zondervan, 2004, p. 201).

The late Lesslie Newbigin, who is one of the gurus of the emerging church, said, "It is surely a fact of inexhaustible significance that what our Lord left behind Him was not a book, nor a creed, nor a system of thought, nor a rule of life, but a visible community" (Lesslie Newbigin, *The Household of God*, p. 20).

Tim Condor, pastor of Emmaus Way in Durham, North Carolina, and affiliated with Emergent Village and Mars Hill Graduate School, says we need to have extra-biblical sources of authority such as Judaism and Rome.

> "Particularly the Protestant church often finds its heritage solely in the Reformation and in portions of the first-century church. A sense of continuity with pre-Christian Judaism (and the scriptural narrative of God's redemptive work in Israel) and pre-Reformation Christianity [Romanism] is often absent. So many of the passions of emergent Christianity, such as mysticism, mystery, experiential faith practices, community, appreciation for the narrative of Scriptures, and monasticism, find stronger historical precedents in these 'blacked-out' eras of God's redemptive history" (*An Emergent Manifesto of Hope*, p. 105).

Donald Miller says that terms such as "inerrancy" are relatively new to church history and that "much of biblical truth must go out the window when you approach it through the scientific [literal] method" (*Searching for God Knows What*, p. 160).

Some emergents weaken the Bible's authority with a modernistic allegorical approach. Donald McCullough says the reader of the early chapters of Genesis should "remember the difference between literal facts and truths" (*If Grace Is So Amazing*, p. 35). He says, "Literal facts may be part of truth, but truth is always larger than and not dependent on literal facts." He says the Genesis account of creation might be "primeval parables, not literal history" and cites Jesus' parables as evidence. But when Jesus told parables it was clear that He was telling a parable, whereas Genesis is written as plain history. There is not a hint in Genesis 1-3 or anywhere else in Scripture to indicate that it is anything other than literal history.

McCullough also says that we can't know much about the future because Bible prophecy is couched in "highly imaginative language" (*If Grace Is So Amazing*, p. 218).

According to McCullough, the book of Jonah might be "an ancient morality play or piece of short fiction" (p. 220).

Phyllis Tickle adds her amen to the heresy that the Bible is not the sole authority for faith and practice:

> "Now, some five hundred years later, even many of the most die-hard Protestants among us have grown suspicious of 'Scripture and Scripture only.' We question what the words mean--literally? Metaphorically? Actually? We even question which words do and do not belong in Scripture and the purity of the editorial line of decent of those that do. We begin to refer to Luther's principle of 'sola scriptura, scriptura sola' as having been little more than the creation of a paper pope in place of a flesh and blood one. And even as we speak, the authority that has been in place for five hundred years withers away in our hands. ...
>
> "The new Christianity of the Great Emergence must discover some authority base or delivery system and/or governing agency of its own. It must formulate--and soon--something other than Luther's *sola scriptura* which, although used so well by the Great Reformation originally, is now seen as hopelessly outmoded or insufficient" (*The Great Emergence*, pp. 47, 151).

Doug Pagitt, in his 2008 book *A Christianity Worth Believing*, boldly denies the infallible inspiration of Scripture:

> "The inerrancy debate is based on the belief that the Bible is the word of God, that the Bible is true because God made it and gave it to us as a guide to truth. But that's not what the Bible says" (p. 65).

WHAT THE BIBLE TEACHES

A full refutation of the emerging church's grave error in regard to the Bible would require a book, but that is not necessary for those who believe the testimony of Jesus Christ and His apostles.

The claim of inspiration

Thousands of times in Scripture we are confronted with the unmistakable claim that God is the author. Phrases such as "thus saith the Lord" and "the word of God" and "the word of the Lord" permeate the Bible. By my own count, these phrases are used 2,451 times in the Old Testament. Consider the following examples:

> "And the Lord said unto Moses, Write thou these words: for after the tenor of these words I have made a covenant with thee and with Israel" (Ex. 34:27).
>
> "The spirit of the Lord spake by me and His word was in my tongue" (2 Sam. 23:2).
>
> "Whatsoever I command thee thou shalt speak ... Behold, I have put my words in thy mouth" (Jer. 1:7, 9).
>
> "Thou shalt speak my words unto them" (Ezek. 2:7).
>
> "All this was done that it might be fulfilled which was spoken by the Lord through the prophet" (Mat. 1:22; 2:15).
>
> "David himself said by the Holy Ghost" (Mk. 12:36).
>
> "He spake by the mouth of His holy prophets, which have been since the world began" (Lk. 1:70).
>
> "Whom the heaven must receive until the times of restitution of all things, which God hath spoken by the mouth of all his holy prophets since the world began" (Acts 3:21).

If the Bible is not the very Word of God, it is the greatest lie that has ever been perpetrated upon mankind.

The extent of inspiration

Consider some of the major New Testament passages on the divine inspiration of Scripture:

2 TIMOTHY 3:13-17 — *"And that from a child thou hast known the holy scriptures, which are able to make thee wise unto salvation through faith which is in Christ Jesus. All scripture is given by inspiration of God, and is profitable for* *doctrine, for reproof, for correction, for instruction in righteousness: That the man of God may be perfect, throughly furnished unto all good works."*

This is a key passage on the inspiration of the Scriptures, and it teaches many important lessons. Note that the apostle Paul wrote these verses. He was chosen by God to reveal divine truths (Eph. 3; Gal. 1). If we cannot trust this man's writings, we can trust no man's. Personally, I had much rather trust Paul's testimony than that of some critical-thinking, miracle-denying liberal or some compromising, liberally-influenced evangelical or some relativistic emergent mystic. Paul was utterly dedicated to the Lord Jesus Christ and suffered constant persecution and hardship because of his faith. He was personally called by Christ to be an apostle and he performed the signs of an apostle to authenticate his calling (2 Cor. 12:12). Let us see, then, what the apostle Paul testified concerning the nature of the Bible:

1. The Bible is set apart from all other books (2 Tim. 3:15). Here the Scriptures are called "holy." This means "set apart, different." According to Paul's teaching, the Bible cannot be compared with other books. Any theologian or textual critic that treats the Bible like other books is wrong from the outset and cannot possibly come to a right understanding of the subject.

2. The Bible is from God (2 Tim. 3:16). This verse literally says the Scriptures are God-breathed. Though written by men, the Bible is a divine product. This is the biblical doctrine of divine inspiration. When discussing its own inspiration, the Scripture does not focus on mechanics but on product. God spoke in many diverse ways (dreams, visions, angels, directly as on Mt. Sinai and the Mt. of Transfiguration, etc.) but the result in all cases was that the writings were God breathed. L. Gaussen, in *Theopneustia: The Plenary Inspiration of the Holy Scriptures* (1850), rightly says of 2 Timothy 3:16: "This statement admits of no exception and of no restriction. ... All Scripture is in such

wise a work of God, that it is represented to us as uttered by the divine breathing, just as human speech is uttered by the breathing of a man's mouth. The prophet is the mouth of the Lord."

3. The Bible is from God in its entirety (2 Tim. 3:16). All of the Scripture is said to have come from God. The word for Scripture here, *graphe*, is a word meaning "writing" or "book." This is referred to as "plenary inspiration." *Plenary* means full, complete, entire.

4. The Bible is from God in its smallest detail (2 Tim. 3:15). The word for Scripture in this verse is *gramma*, referring to a letter. This teaches that even the smallest details of the Bible are from God. This is the doctrine of "verbal inspiration." Jesus commended this doctrine when He referred to the jots and tittles of the Old Testament (Mat. 5:18).

5. The Bible is one divine book with an all-encompassing theme, and that is salvation through Jesus Christ (2 Tim. 3:15). The Bible is not just a group of disjoined religious writings. It is a unified Book planned by God to teach man the way of salvation. Compare Luke 24:44-45; John 1:45; 5:39; Ephesians 3:11.

6. The Bible can protect Christians from error (2 Tim. 3:13-15). This means that it is 100% true. If the Bible contains myths, mistakes, and untrue claims concerning authorship, miracles, and prophecies, it certainly is not a book that can give sure protection from false teaching!

7. The Bible is sufficient to make the Christian complete and mature (2 Tim. 3:17). An imperfect or incomplete book could not produce perfection. Since the Bible is able to make the man of God perfect it is obvious that nothing else is needed. The Scripture is thus the *sole* authority for faith and practice. This is not mere "Protestant" tradition; it is the Bible's own claim.

MARK 12:36; LUKE 1:70; ACTS 1:16; 3:18, 21; 4:25; 28:25 -- *"For David himself said by the Holy Ghost, The LORD said to my Lord, Sit thou on my right hand, till I make thine enemies thy footstool. ... As he spake by the mouth of his holy prophets, which have been since the world began. ... Men and brethren, this scripture must needs have been fulfilled, which the Holy Ghost by the mouth of David spake before concerning Judas, which was guide to them that took Jesus. ... But those things, which God before had showed by the mouth of all his prophets, that Christ should suffer, he hath so fulfilled. ... Whom the heaven must receive until the times of restitution of all things, which God hath spoken by the mouth of all his holy prophets since the world began. ... Who by the mouth of thy servant David hast said, Why did the heathen rage, and the people imagine vain things? ... And when they agreed not among themselves, they departed, after that Paul had spoken one word, Well spake the Holy Ghost by Esaias the prophet unto our fathers."*

The teaching of the Bible regarding its own nature is described in these verses. The Bible is God's Word given through divinely-chosen human instruments. This is the plain teaching of Scripture. Any other view is false human conjecture and heresy.

JOHN 17:8 -- *"For I have given unto them the words which thou gavest me; and they have received them, and have known surely that I came out from thee, and they have believed that thou didst send me."*

Jesus Christ received words from God the Father and delivered them to the apostles. He promised that His words would not pass away (Mat. 24:35). He further promised that the Holy Spirit would guide the apostles into all truth, would bring things to their remembrance, and would show them things to come (Jn. 14:25-26; 16:12-13). Thus, the apostles and prophets who wrote the New Testament did not have to depend upon their fallible human devices. Edward Hills wisely observed: "The New Testament contains the words that Christ brought down from heaven for the salvation of His people and now remain inscribed in holy Writ. ... *For ever, O LORD, Thy Word is settled in heaven* (Ps. 119:89). Although the Scriptures were written during a definite historical period, they are not the product of that period but of the eternal plan of God. When God designed the holy Scriptures in eternity, He had the whole sweep of human history in view. Hence the Scriptures are forever relevant. Their message can never be outgrown. *The grass withereth, the flower fadeth: but the Word of our God shall stand for ever* (Isa. 40:8)."

ROMANS 16:25-26 -- *"Now to him that is of power to stablish you according to my gospel, and the preaching of Jesus Christ, according to the revelation of the mystery, which was kept secret since the world began, but now is made manifest, and by the scriptures of the prophets, according to the commandment of the everlasting God, made known to all nations for the obedience of faith."*

Paul stated that Scripture was being written by the New Testament apostles and prophets under divine revelation. This is contrary to the idea that the New Testament authors did not know they were writing Scripture. See also Ephesians 3:4-5. *"Whereby, when ye read, ye may understand my knowledge in the mystery of Christ) which in other ages was not made known unto the sons of men, as it is now revealed unto his holy apostles and prophets by the Spirit."*

1 CORINTHIANS 2:9-13 -- *"But as it is written, Eye hath not seen, nor ear heard, neither have entered into the heart of man, the things which God hath prepared for them that love him. But God hath revealed them unto us by his Spirit: for the Spirit searcheth all things, yea, the deep things of God. For what man knoweth the things of a man, save the spirit of man which is in him? even so the things of God knoweth no man, but the Spirit of God. Now we have received, not the spirit of the world, but the spirit which is of God; that we might know* *the things that are freely given to us of God. Which things also we speak, not in the words which man's wisdom teacheth, but which the Holy Ghost teacheth; comparing spiritual things with spiritual."*

In this passage we see that Scripture is the following:

It is God's revelation (v. 10). Revelation concerns those things which man cannot know by his own investigation and intellect (v. 9). God, by His Spirit, has chosen to reveal things about Himself, salvation, and His eternal plans (vv. 10-12).

It is the deep things of God (v. 10). Emerging church writers claim that human language is not capable of making definitive statements about divinity, but Paul refutes this idea. The words of Scripture are fully capable of communicating the deep things of God. Human language is not a product of evolution; it was invented by God and given to man from the beginning for the purpose of divine Revelation. The first thing that Adam did with his new language was communicate with God.

It is the very words of God (v. 13). In verse 13 we are told that this revelation extends to the very choice of the words used to relate it. God did not merely give the Bible writers the general thoughts they were to write; He gave them the words.

It is the mind of Christ (v. 16). We cannot know Christ or His will apart from the Scriptures.

The Scripture is understood only by the spiritual man (vv. 14-15). There are three types of men described in this passage.

> *The natural man* (v. 14). This refers to the unsaved man; he cannot understand the things of God because he is spiritually blind and does not have the indwelling Holy Spirit.
>
> *The spiritual man* (v. 15). This refers to the born again man who walks in the Spirit. The spiritual man can know all things that God has revealed.

The carnal man (1 Cor. 3:1-2). This refers to the saved man who remains a spiritual baby and does not grow spiritually. The carnal man can understand only the simplest things in the Scriptures.

1 CORINTHIANS 14:17 -- *"If any man think himself to be a prophet, or spiritual, let him acknowledge that the things that I write unto you are the commandments of the Lord."*

Here we see that Paul knew that his writings were the commandments of the Lord. See also 1 Corinthians 11:2; Galatians 1:11-12; Colossians 1:25-26, 28; 1 Thessalonians 2:13; and 2 Thessalonians 3:6, 14.

1 PETER 1:10-12 -- *"Of which salvation the prophets have inquired and searched diligently, who prophesied of the grace that should come unto you: Searching what, or what manner of time the Spirit of Christ which was in them did signify, when it testified beforehand the sufferings of Christ, and the glory that should follow. Unto whom it was revealed, that not unto themselves, but unto us they did minister the things, which are now reported unto you by them that have preached the gospel unto you with the Holy Ghost sent down from heaven; which things the angels desire to look into."*

This passage deals with the mechanics of inspiration. The Spirit of God was in the prophets testifying of the things of God. The prophets themselves did not even understand all that they spoke and wrote. This shows the error of any view of inspiration that deals with the thoughts alone. The prophets were not given general thoughts and then left to record those thoughts and impressions as best they could. They were given a perfect revelation from God and were divinely-enabled in every detail of its recording.

1 PETER 1:25 -- *"But the word of the Lord endureth for ever. And this is the word which by the gospel is preached unto you."*

Peter taught that the word that was preached by the New Testament apostles and prophets is the eternal Word of God.

2 PETER 1:19-21 — *"We have also a more sure word of prophecy; whereunto ye do well that ye take heed, as unto a light that shineth in a dark place, until the day dawn, and the day star arise in your hearts: Knowing this first, that no prophecy of the scripture is of any private interpretation. For the prophecy came not in old time by the will of man: but holy men of God spake as they were moved by the Holy Ghost."*

First, we are told that the Scriptures are a light shining in a dark place (v. 19). The dark place is the world. Though it contains some truth, the world is pictured as dark because man is not able to know spiritual truth without revelation from God. The Bible is that revelation which is shining in the midst of the darkness.

Second, the Bible is not a product of man's will (v. 21). Other books are products of the will of the human author, but not the Bible. God chose certain men and moved in them to deliver His message. As the Holy Spirit moved them, the things they wrote were the words of God.

This passage explains the method whereby the Bible was given. God used men, but He used them in such a way that what they wrote was precisely God's Word. When the Bible touches on the subject of inspiration and revelation, it focuses on God and His role in the process. We are told very little about the actual mechanism. The method of inspiration is an unrevealed mystery. It was accomplished mysteriously by the Holy Spirit. We are not supposed to try to speculate on the method of inspiration; we are supposed to believe God's testimony that it happened and to have faith in the finished product, the Holy Scriptures. Modern Bible scholars usually do just the opposite of what the Scriptures do in reference to the subject of inspiration. They focus on man's part rather than upon God's. That is because most modern scholars do not operate by the principle of faith. They are operating on the level of human intellect and scholarship, yet no man can know the perfect Word of God by this means, for *"without faith it is impossible to please him"* (Heb. 11:6).

The phrase "private interpretation" refers to the writers of the Bible. In the context this refers to the giving of revelation rather than to the understanding of it. The Bible writers did not personally interpret God's revelation to mankind; they were given God's revelation by the Holy Spirit. They did not always even understand what they were writing (1 Peter 1:10-12).

2 PETER 3:2 -- *"That ye may be mindful of the words which were spoken before by the holy prophets, and of the commandment of us the apostles of the Lord and Saviour."*

Peter put the commandments of the apostles on the same level of authority as that of the Old Testament prophets. A Jew would not have dared to make such a claim if he were not convinced that the apostolic writings were Holy Scripture, because he looked upon the Old Testament prophets as the very oracles of God.

2 PETER 3:15-16 -- *"And account that the longsuffering of our Lord is salvation; even as our beloved brother Paul also according to the wisdom given unto him hath written unto you; as also in all his epistles, speaking in them of these things; in which are some things hard to be understood, which they that are unlearned and unstable wrest, as they do also the other scriptures, unto their own destruction."*

Peter called Paul's writings "scripture" and put them on the same level of authority as the Old Testament. Peter says that Paul did not write by his own understanding but by wisdom given to him of God. Peter warned about the false teachers that were attacking the Scripture even in that day. "Although some [of Paul's epistles] had been out for perhaps fifteen years, the ink was scarcely dry on others, and perhaps 2 Timothy had not yet been penned when Peter wrote. Paul's writings were recognized and declared by apostolic authority to be Scripture as soon as they appeared" (Wilbur Pickering).

1 JOHN 4:6 -- *"We are of God: he that knoweth God heareth us; he that is not of God heareth not us. Hereby know we the spirit of truth, and the spirit of error."*

John held forth the writings of the apostles and prophets as the sole and absolute standard of truth.

JUDE 17 -- *"But, beloved, remember ye the words which were spoken before of the apostles of our Lord Jesus Christ."*

In warning of false teachers, Jude refers to the *"words which were spoken before of the apostles of our Lord Jesus Christ."* He holds these words up as the sole divine standard for faith and practice.

REVELATION 1:3 -- *"Blessed is he that readeth, and they that hear the words of this prophecy, and keep those things which are written therein: for the time is at hand."*

The book of Revelation was presented as the prophetic Word of God. See also Revelation 21:5; 22:18-19.

What did Jesus Christ believe about the Scriptures?

1. Christ taught that the Old Testament is perfect to the letter. *"Think not that I am come to destroy the law, or the prophets: I am not come to destroy, but to fulfil. For verily I say unto you, Till heaven and earth pass, one jot or one tittle shall in no wise pass from the law, till all be fulfilled"* (Mat. 5:17-18).

2. Christ taught that the Old Testament cannot be broken (John 10:35). In this verse Christ was speaking of the authority of the Scriptures. He was saying that absolutely nothing written in the Scriptures can be set aside or ignored. It is authoritative to every detail--a chain with no weak link.

3. Christ taught that the Old Testament is a divinely-planned book written to prepare for His coming (Lk. 24:44).

4. Christ taught that every part of the Old Testament was cited as inspired and authoritative -- the law, the writings, and the Psalms (Lk. 24:44).

5. Christ taught that the Old Testament characters, events, and miracles are true and historical. Some of the Old Testament people and events Christ referred to are as follows:

>The creation (Mk. 13:19)
>Adam and Eve (Mt. 19:4-6; Mk. 10:6-7)
>Cain and Abel (Mt. 23:35; Lk. 11:50-51)
>Noah and the flood (Mt. 24:37-39)
>Abraham (Jn. 8:39-40)
>The destruction of Sodom and Gomorrah (Lk. 17:28-29)
>Lot's wife turning to salt (Lk. 17:32)
>Moses and the burning bush (Mk. 12:26)
>Manna from heaven (Jn. 6:31-32)
>The brazen serpent (Jn. 3:14-15)
>Jonah and the whale (Mt. 12:39-41; Lk. 11:29-32)
>Nineveh repenting at Jonah's preaching (Lk. 11:32)
>The queen of Sheba visiting Solomon (Lk. 11:31)

6. Christ taught that the writers of the Old Testament were those claimed by the Scriptures. In referring to books of the Old Testament, the Lord Jesus left no doubt that they were written by the traditional authors. According to the Son of God:

>Moses wrote the books of the Law (Lk. 24:44; Jn. 5:45-47).
>David wrote the Psalms bearing his name (Lk. 20:42).
>Daniel wrote the book bearing his name (Mt. 24:15).
>Isaiah wrote the prophecy bearing his name. Jesus quoted from Isaiah often and said the historical prophet Isaiah wrote it, not an unknown group of men. In John 12:38-41, Christ quoted from both major sections of Isaiah and said both were written by the same Isaiah.

For more about the divine inspiration of Scripture see the report entitled "Biblical Inspiration" at the Way of Life web site.

Conclusion

According to the testimony of the Bible itself, from beginning to end, it is the infallible Word of God. This is the testimony of Jesus Christ and of the apostles. The Scripture is verbally, plenarily (fully) inspired and is the sole authority for faith and practice. This doctrine refutes the emerging church heresy.

LIBERAL EMERGING CHURCH ERROR #2 NO CLEAR TESTIMONY OF SALVATION

The experience of salvation is foundational to anything pertaining to the church, because it is impossible to understand the truth properly apart from the new birth.

> "But the natural man receiveth not the things of the Spirit of God: for they are foolishness unto him: neither can he know them, because they are spiritually discerned" (1 Corinthians 2:14).

Yet in the emerging church salvation is a murky thing.

In fact, Brian McLaren says:

> "I don't think we've got the gospel right yet. What does it mean to be 'saved'? When I read the Bible, I don't see it meaning, 'I'm going to heaven after I die.' Before modern evangelicalism nobody accepted Jesus Christ as their personal Savior, or walked down an aisle, or said the sinner's prayer. I don't think the liberals have it right. But I don't think we have it right either. None of us has arrived at orthodoxy" ("The Emergent Mystique," *Christianity Today*, Nov. 2004, p. 40).

McLaren says he identifies with Anabaptists because they (allegedly) teach that "one becomes a Christian through an event, process, or both, in which one identifies with Jesus, his mission, and his followers" (*A Generous Orthodoxy*, p. 229).

McLaren's doctrine of salvation is as murky as any I have ever read.

Mars Hill Graduate School's statement of faith says, "We acknowledge one baptism for the forgiveness of sins." This is the heresy of baptismal salvation.

Scot McKnight says that "conversion" can be through liturgy (referring to sacraments such as baptism) or through socialization (growing up in a Christian home) or through personal decisional faith in Christ (*Turning to Jesus: The Sociology of Conversion in the Gospels*).

This statement reflects a deep confusion about salvation.

It is exceedingly rare to find a clear biblical testimony of salvation in the writings of emerging church leaders.

Robert Webber, who grew up in a Baptist pastor's home, argued that salvation does not have to be a dramatic conversion experience and he admitted that he didn't have such an experience. He said that repentance "can have a dramatic beginning or can come as a result of a process over time" (*The Divine Embrace*, p. 149). He saw salvation is a sacramental process that begins at baptism, and this is one reason why he left the Baptists and joined the Episcopalians and was also perfectly comfortable with Roman Catholicism.

Tony Campolo has a similar testimony. In *Letters to a Young Evangelical* Campolo described his own experience in the following words:

> When I was a boy growing up in a lower-middle-class neighborhood in West Philadelphia, MY MOTHER, a convert to Evangelical Christianity from a Catholic Italian immigrant family, HOPED I WOULD HAVE ONE OF THOSE DRAMATIC 'BORN-AGAIN' EXPERIENCES. That was the way she had come into a personal relationship with Christ. She took me to hear one evangelist after another, praying that I would go to the altar and come away 'converted.' BUT IT NEVER WORKED FOR ME. I would go down the aisle as the people around me sang 'the invitation hymn,' but I just didn't feel as if anything happened to me. For a while I despaired, wondering if I would ever get 'saved.' It took me quite some time to realize that entering into a personal relationship with Christ DOES NOT ALWAYS HAPPEN THAT WAY. ...

> In my case INTIMACY WITH CHRIST WAS DEVELOPED GRADUALLY OVER THE YEARS, primarily through what Catholic mystics call 'centering prayer.' Each morning, as soon as I wake up, I take time--sometimes as much as a half hour--to center myself on Jesus. I say his name over and over again to drive back the 101 things that begin to clutter up my mind the minute I open my eyes. Jesus is my mantra, as some would say. ...
>
> I LEARNED ABOUT THIS WAY OF HAVING A BORN-AGAIN EXPERIENCE FROM READING THE CATHOLIC MYSTICS, especially *The Spiritual Exercises* of Ignatius of Loyola (*Letters to a Young Evangelical,* 2006, pp. 25, 26, 30).

This is very frightful testimony. Campolo does not have a biblical testimony of salvation. He plainly admits that he is not "born again" in the way that his mother was, through a biblical-style conversion. Instead, he describes his "intimacy with Christ" as something that has developed gradually through the practice of Catholic mysticism.

For one thing, this is to confuse the issue of salvation with that of spiritual growth. All of the conversions that are recorded in the New Testament are of the instantaneous, dramatic variety. We think of the woman at the well (John 4), Zacchaeus (Luke 19), the Ethiopian Eunuch (Acts 8), Paul (Acts 9), Cornelius (Acts 10), Lydia (Acts 16), and the Philippian jailer (Acts 16), to name a few.

The Lord Jesus Christ said that salvation is a birth (John 3:3). That is not a gradual thing that happens throughout one's life; it is an event!

Further, Catholic mysticism itself is unscriptural. Jesus forbad repetitious prayers (Mat. 6:7). He taught us to pray in a verbal, conscious manner, talking with God as with a Father, addressing God the Father external to us, not searching for a mystical oneness with God in the center of our being through meditation (Mat. 6:9-13).

Campolo's testimony is akin to the Roman Catholicism that his mother was *saved out of*. It is repeating mantras and doing good works and progressing in spirituality.

The book *Emerging Churches* by Eddie Gibbs and Ryan Bolger contains the testimonies of about 50 emerging church leaders in Appendix A, and only a couple of them even come close to a biblical testimony. Some of them don't mention a personal salvation testimony of any sort, merely saying that they grew up in some type of church.

And remember that these are emerging church *LEADERS*.

Jonny Baker of Grace in London, England, says:

> "I loved God, or rather, knew I was loved by him, from an early age. I actually received the gift of tongues when I was just four years old" (p. 240).

She kept responding to appeals to "commit your life to Christ" until she "finally realized I must be 'in.'"

Nowhere in Scripture do we see a four-year-old child speaking in tongues. Further, committing one's life to Christ is not biblical salvation. The sinner has nothing acceptable to God that he can commit. Even his righteousnesses are as filthy rags before God (Isaiah 64:6). Salvation is not committing my life to God, it is acknowledging my sinful condition before God and putting my faith in what Jesus did on the cross so that I can be forgiven and cleansed and made acceptable in Christ.

Kester Brewin of Vaux in London, England, said:

> "I can point to a Billy Graham rally in 1984 as a conversion, but that was really more of a moment of STRENGTHENING A FAITH THAT HAD ALWAYS been there" (*Emerging Churches*, 2005, p. 248).

Jesus said we must be born again, and a birth happens at a certain time. It is not a process. Ephesians 2:1-2 says there is a time before salvation and a time after salvation. Before salvation we are dead in trespasses and sins and controlled by the devil. After salvation we have new life in Christ and belong to God. It is sometimes the case with a child who grows up in church that he does not remember the exact time that he put his faith in Christ, but true salvation is always a life-changing event and one should never say that he has always had faith.

Alan Creech of Vine and Branches in Lexington, Kentucky, says:

> "I went to catechism through the Catholic Church and was baptized at the age of fourteen" (p. 260).

The Catholic Church teaches that salvation is a process that begins with baptism and is fed by the other sacraments, confirmation being one of those, and good works. This is not biblical salvation.

Ben Edson of Sanctus1 in Manchester, England, says:

> "After a painful breakup with my girlfriend, I gave God another chance. I cried out to God at my point of need, and God met me in a profound and life-changing way" (p. 266).

Is salvation a matter of giving God a chance, of God meeting my needs and having a "profound" experience of some sort? Many people have life-changing experiences through psychology, 12-Step programs, New Age mysticism, and goddess worship.

Roger Ellis of Revelation Church in Chichester, England, says:

> "In my late teens, I had a dynamic experience of God, an encounter of the Spirit at a crazy charismatic church down the road" (p. 268).

Is salvation merely an experiential "encounter of the Spirit"? What spirit? Paul warned that there is the possibility of receiving "another spirit" (2 Corinthians 4:3-4). Ellis mentions nothing about sin, nothing about Jesus Christ's death and resurrection, nothing about repentance toward God.

Billy Kennedy of Sublime, Remix, and Cultural Shift in Southampton, England, says:

> "I was raised in church, my father being a Baptist minister. I ALWAYS had faith, but when I was eighteen years old, I left home and traveled around the U.K. with my job, seeking a faith of my own. I tried a wide variety of churches. Then I moved to Southampton, where I attended Southampton Community Church. My first week there I had a significant encounter with the Holy Spirit. I was hooked!" (p. 277).

He claims that he has always had faith, which is not possible, because when we are born into this world we are dead in trespasses and sins (Eph. 2:1). He further says that he had a "significant encounter with the Holy Spirit." What does that mean? He does not describe the new birth in a biblical manner. He doesn't mention the death, burial, and resurrection of Jesus Christ. He doesn't mention repentance toward God.

Kenny Mitchell of Tribe in New York says:

> "I began to pray at the age of five, and supernatural joy dropped on me. I began to do evangelism at supermarkets, telling people that God likes them. As a result of my reading the Bible, I wanted to be baptized. I was told I was too young, that I had to wait until I was ten. I was crushed! When I was ten, I immediately went and got baptized" (p. 288).

Is salvation an experience of supernatural joy? The devil can produce experiences like that. Is the gospel the message that God likes people? And why does he mention baptism? Does he think that baptism is a part of salvation?

Ian Mobsby of the Epicentre Network and Moot in London, England, says:

> "At seventeen, I encountered Christians of a charismatic evangelical persuasion. It felt like coming home and was very emotional, and I had a profound conversion experience" (p. 291).

There is no biblical substance to this testimony. An emotional religious experience is not biblical salvation.

Paul Roberts of Third Sunday Service in Resonance, Bristol, England, says:

> "I was ... raised in the high church tradition of the Anglican Church in Wales. I dropped out of church at the age of twelve or thirteen but returned in my later teens, partly for the girls in the church youth group, partly because of the young evangelical assistant minister who helped me make sense of Christianity as relevant and vibrant. I recommitted my life at that age, but I definitely had faith as a child" (p. 297).

So when and how was he born again? When did he repent of his sin before God? What does he mean by learning to make sense of Christianity as "relevant and vibrant"? What kind of faith did he have as a child in an Anglican church? Does he believe his infant baptism was part of salvation?

Mark Scandrette of ReIMAGINE in San Francisco says:

> "I had an early sensitivity to spiritual realities and made a primitive declaration of faith" (p. 303).

Sensitivity to what spiritual realities? A declaration of what type of faith?

Barry Taylor of Sanctuary and New Ground in Santa Monica, California, says:

> "In the end, I didn't pick Christianity. I picked Jesus instead, because Jesus seemed cool and treated people kindly. From that time I sought to follow Jesus" (p. 311).

What is a cool Jesus? Taylor mentions nothing about the Jesus who died on the cross for man's sin and rose from the dead the third day. He mentions nothing about repentance.

Andy Thornton of Late Late Service in Glasgow, Scotland, says:

> "My dad was a churchwarden in an Anglican church. ... I dated a girl who went to David Watson's church, St. Michael-le-Belfry in York, when I was seventeen. I prayed a prayer, which was not a problem, because I didn't really see myself as an unbeliever. I did feel that, strangely, something changed inside me. I felt something warm and affirming and quite energizing" (p. 314).

This man says that he became a Christian by praying a prayer even though he did not consider himself an unbeliever. Upon praying such an unscriptural prayer he had a mystical experience. This is not biblical salvation.

Sue Wallace of Visions in York, England, says:

> "I remember having what some would call a conversion experience quite early in life, at the age of four, in response to a talk about God needing laborers for the harvest. I remember praying something along the lines of, 'Okay, I'll help if you need people'" (p. 318).

Salvation is not offering oneself to assist God!

Nanette Sawyer of Wicker Park Grace in Chicago says:

> "I was born in 1961 and raised in rural Upstate New York. My family sporadically attended a small Baptist church there, but we never were really part of that community. It was a church that presented a very shame-based theology. When I asked the minister what I 'had to believe' to be a Christian, he gave me a simple 'Jesus died on the cross for your sins' answer, which made no sense to me. I made a conscious decision at that time that I was not a Christian. After many years of seeking, I took up meditation with an Indian meditation master who taught me two things that Christians never had: that God loves me, and how to be still and listen for God. In some ways, I am a Christian today because of this great Hindu woman. She inspired me to study comparative world religions, and so I went to Harvard Divinity School and received a master's in theological studies in 1997. Around that time, a friend of mine invited me to his church in south Boston. I was nervous and very hesitant. I went to a small evening prayer service and received communion with an intimate circle of people, and a transformation began in me. I felt as though Jesus himself was welcoming me at the communion table. I started showing up at that church on Sundays. This church was so different from the church of my childhood, because they welcomed me without asking for my Christian ID card, so to speak. ... They preached and lived a message of grace, emphasizing that we are all beloved children of God. Eventually, I was baptized in that church and felt my call to ministry of Word and sacrament in that church" (pp. 301, 302).

This is the most pathetic testimony of all. She's a "Christian" because of Hindu mysticism. She rejected the gospel that Jesus died on the cross for our sins and believed rather in a mystical experience of unconditional grace in a liberal church, a church that doesn't ask people when and how they were born again but just receives them and gives them communion in their unregenerate condition.

WHAT DOES THE BIBLE SAY?

It is no wonder that the emergents are as confused as they are about doctrine. Salvation is necessary for understanding spiritual matters. Paul warned that *"the natural man receiveth not the things of the Spirit of God: for they are foolishness unto him: neither can he know them, because they are spiritually discerned"* (1 Cor. 2:14).

Only by the Holy Spirit can truth be discerned and the Bible properly interpreted. The apostle John warned his readers about the false teachers that were proliferating even in his day and he taught that it is the indwelling Holy Spirit by which the believer is protected from the wiles of the devil:

> "These things have I written unto you concerning them that seduce you. But the anointing which ye have received of him abideth in you, and ye need not that any man teach you: but as the same anointing teacheth you of all things, and is truth, and is no lie, and even as it hath taught you, ye shall abide in him" (1 John 2:26-27).

Salvation involves three very important things. It involves repenting of one's sin before God. It involves believing the gospel, and it involves being born again. These are not really three different things. They are three things that come together at one time and place for salvation.

There is no salvation without **REPENTANCE.** All of the New Testament preachers demanded repentance. Jesus said, *"except ye repent, ye shall all likewise perish"* (Luke 13:3). Paul said, *"God ... now commandeth all men every where to repent"* (Acts 17:30). Paul defined salvation as *"repentance toward God, and faith toward our Lord Jesus Christ"* (Acts 20:21).

Repentance is a change of mind that results in a change of life. It is a radical change of mind about sin and about one's relationship with God. It means to surrender to God, to bow before Him as God and to repent of breaking His law and living for one's self. It means to turn around, to change directions. It is something that occurs in the heart and mind and that demonstrates itself in the life.

The Bible says there is no salvation without repentance. In fact, the Bible sometimes describes salvation in terms of repentance (Luke 24:47; Acts 3:19; 5:31; 11:18; 26:20; 2 Peter 3:9).

Further, there is no salvation without **THE GOSPEL**. The gospel is the power of God unto salvation (Romans 1:16), and the gospel is defined in the following way:

> "Moreover, brethren, I declare unto you the gospel which I preached unto you, which also ye have received, and wherein ye stand; By which also ye are saved, if ye keep in memory what I preached unto you, unless ye have believed in vain. For I delivered unto you first of all that which I also received, how that Christ died for our sins according to the scriptures; And that he was buried, and that he rose again the third day according to the scriptures" (1 Corinthians 15:1-4).

The saving gospel is the good news that Jesus died for our sins, that he was buried, and that He rose from the dead the third day. And He did all of this in fulfillment of the prophetic Scriptures. Any other gospel is a false one that brings God's curse (Galatians 1:6-8).

Therefore, biblical salvation is acknowledging that I am a sinner as the Bible says I am and requires putting my faith in the fact that Jesus died for my sin on the cross and that He rose from the dead and is alive today to save sinners. Salvation is acknowledging that I am a lost sinner and believing that Jesus Christ alone is my Saviour.

There is also no salvation without **THE NEW BIRTH**. The Lord Jesus Christ said that a man must be born again or he will never see the kingdom of God.

> "Jesus answered and said unto him, Verily, verily, I say unto thee, Except a man be born again, he cannot see the kingdom of God. Nicodemus saith unto him, How can a man be born when he is old?

> can he enter the second time into his mother's womb, and be born? Jesus answered, Verily, verily, I say unto thee, Except a man be born of water and of the Spirit, he cannot enter into the kingdom of God. **That which is born of the flesh is flesh; and that which is born of the Spirit is spirit**" (John 3:3-6).

Jesus said a man must have two births in order to enter God's kingdom (Jn. 3:5-6). Water refers to the first or natural birth, and Spirit refers to the second or spiritual birth. This is clear in the context. Consider verse 6: *"That which is born of the flesh is flesh; and that which is born of the Spirit is spirit."* Baptismal regenerationists insert baptism in this passage but baptism is never mentioned, and when Jesus explained in the same passage how to be born again He didn't mention baptism (John 3:14-18).

Since Jesus compared the natural birth with the new birth, consider two important lessons. *First, both are real events that happen at a certain time.* Salvation is not a process. *Second, both are dramatic events that can be seen by others.* Salvation changes a person's life. "Therefore if any man be in Christ, he is a new creature: old things are passed away; behold, all things are become new" (2 Cor. 5:17).

How is one born again? Jesus explained this in the same passage.

> "And as Moses lifted up the serpent in the wilderness, even so must the Son of man be lifted up: That whosoever believeth in him should not perish, but have eternal life. For God so loved the world, that he gave his only begotten Son, that whosoever believeth in him should not perish, but have everlasting life" (John 3:14-16).

The new birth comes by believing that Jesus came into the world to die on the cross for my sins, by acknowledging that I am a guilty sinner deserving of God's judgment and that Jesus is the only way of salvation from this predicament.

Jesus likened salvation to Moses lifting up the serpent in the wilderness, which refers to the event described in Numbers 21.

"And they journeyed from mount Hor by the way of the Red sea, to compass the land of Edom: and the soul of the people was much discouraged because of the way. And the people spake against God, and against Moses, Wherefore have ye brought us up out of Egypt to die in the wilderness? for there is no bread, neither is there any water; and our soul loatheth this light bread. And the LORD sent fiery serpents among the people, and they bit the people; and much people of Israel died. Therefore the people came to Moses, and said, We have sinned, for we have spoken against the LORD, and against thee; pray unto the LORD, that he take away the serpents from us. And Moses prayed for the people. And the LORD said unto Moses, Make thee a fiery serpent, and set it upon a pole: and it shall come to pass, that every one that is bitten, when he looketh upon it, shall live. And Moses made a serpent of brass, and put it upon a pole, and it came to pass, that if a serpent had bitten any man, when he beheld the serpent of brass, he lived" (Numbers 21:4-9).

Consider the following lessons that we learn from this comparison: *First, in Numbers 21 the people sinned and were judged by God.* Likewise, the Bible says that all have sinned and come short of the glory of God (Rom. 3:23) and the wages of sin is death (Rom. 6:23). There is no salvation unless a person plainly acknowledges that he is a sinner like the Bible says he is. Even our very righteousnesses are as filthy rags before a thrice-holy God (Isaiah 64:6). *Second, God provided the means of salvation.* God instructed Moses to make the serpent and lift it up for the people to see. It was His gift of love. Likewise, it is love that motivated God to send His only begotten Son to die for man's sin. *Third, there was only one way of salvation.* Likewise, the Bible says there is no salvation apart from faith in Jesus Christ. Compare John 14:6; Acts 4:12. *Fourth, the way of salvation was lifted up for all to see.* Compare Mark 16:15, where Christ commanded that the gospel be preached to every person. *Fifth, those that lifted their eyes to the serpent and believed were healed.* The word "believe" is repeated eight times in John chapter 3. Saving faith is not mere mental assent, such as believing a historical fact. Compare James 2:19. *"Thou believest that there is one God; thou doest well: the devils also believe, and tremble."* Saving faith means to put one's trust in Christ, to rely upon Him, to come to Him and to know Him personally. Saving faith must also be in the right thing. One cannot be saved by putting his faith in baptism or the church or sacraments or "the Christian faith" or Mary or one's religious heritage or sincerity or goodness or works. Further, saving faith is exclusive faith. It cannot be in Christ *plus* anything else. *Sixth, the healing was complete.* When the Jew that had been bitten looked at the serpent lifted up on the cross, he was entirely healed. Likewise salvation in Christ is perfect and eternal. Christ provides everything the sinner needs to be right with God and live eternally in glory.

Why did God require Moses to make an image of a serpent? This signified the fact that Jesus would take our sin upon himself on the cross. God the Father forsook Jesus because He was bearing the sin of the world. *"All we like sheep have gone astray; we have turned every one to his own way; and the LORD hath laid on him the iniquity of us all"* (Isaiah 53:6). *"For he hath made him to be sin for us, who knew no sin; that we might be made the righteousness of God in him"* (2 Corinthians 5:21).

These three things--repentance, the Gospel, and the New Birth--are absolutely necessary for salvation, yet multitudes of professing Christians have never repented and believed the gospel and been born again.

A foundational error of the emerging church is to neglect or misunderstand salvation.

LIBERAL EMERGING CHURCH ERROR #3 A NON-DOGMATIC APPROACH TO DOCTRINE

The liberal emerging church is flexible, tolerant, and non-dogmatic. They are rethinking theology. They believe there are many possible "theologies." They "are under no compulsion to stand up and fight for truth" (*Emerging Churches*, p. 124).

The Emergent Village web site says, "... you won't find a traditional statement of faith or dogmatic truth claims coming from Emergent Village per se. ... Whereas statements of faith and doctrine have a tendency to stifle friendships, we hope to further conversation and action around the things of God."

In a paper on the Emergent Village presented to the National Council of Churches on March 17, 2007, Dwight Friesen emphasized that "we diligently resist self-definition in propositional terms which tend to exclude" and "we value humility more than correctness, hospitality more than being set apart, curiosity more than tradition; in fact THEOLOGICAL AGREEMENT IS NOT A PRIMARY GOAL FOR US" (http://dwightfriesen.blog.com/1616648/).

Jonathan Campbell of Seattle, author of *The Way of Jesus*, says, "We no longer need religion with its ... dogmas" (*Emerging Churches*, p. 47).

Peter Rollins of ikon in Belfast, Northern Ireland, says: "I was worried about the evangelical churches' way of reading the Bible as a singular book with one voice rather than as a book with many voices and many ways of interpreting" (*Emerging Churches*, p. 70).

In his analysis of the emerging church, Andy Crouch says:

> "Frankly, the emerging movement loves ideas and theology. It just doesn't have an airtight system or statement of faith. We believe the Great Tradition offers various ways for telling the truth about God's redemption in Christ, but WE DON'T BELIEVE ANY ONE THEOLOGY GETS IT ABSOLUTELY RIGHT. Hence, a trademark feature of the emerging movement is that we believe all theology will remain a conversation about the Truth who is God in Christ through the Spirit, and about God's story of redemption at work in the church. NO SYSTEMATIC THEOLOGY CAN BE FINAL. ... It turns its chastened epistemology against itself, saying, 'This is what I believe, but I could be wrong. What do you think? Let's talk'" ("Five Streams of Emerging Church," *Christianity Today*, February 2007).

Observe that emergents want to have it both ways. They want to say that they love truth on one hand, but they claim that we cannot know and define absolute truth on the other hand. This is a typical emergent contradiction, and contradictions bother them not in the least.

Instead of coming to a settled doctrinal understanding of Scripture and then rejecting that which is contrary to it as heresy, the emerging church is uncertain about theology and opts for dialogue rather than dogmatism.

Brian McLaren says the emerging approach is "less rigid, more generous" (*A Generous Orthodoxy*, p. 190), and it is "conversational, never attempting to be the last word, and thus silence other voices" (p. 169). He says it "doesn't claim too much; it admits it walks with a limp" (p. 171). He says, "To be a Christian in a generously orthodox way is not to claim to have the truth captured, stuffed, and mounted on the wall" (p. 293). He likens doctrinal dogmatism to smoking cigarettes, saying that "it is a hard-to-break Protestant habit that is hazardous to spiritual health" (p. 217). In *A New Kind of Christian* McLaren says all doctrines and theologies are non-absolute, that we need to approach the Bible "on less defined terms" (p. 56).

Rob Bell, founder of Mars Hill Bible Church in Grand Rapids, Michigan, admits that he and his wife have been powerfully influenced toward non-dogmaticism by McLaren's *A New Kind of Christian*. "The Bells started questioning their assumptions about the Bible itself--'discovering the Bible as a human product,' as Rob puts it, rather than the product of divine fiat. 'The Bible is still in the center for us,' Rob says, 'but it's a different kind of center. We want to embrace mystery, rather than conquer it'" ("The Emergent Mystique," *Christianity Today*, Nov. 2004).

Bell says the practice of going to the Bible alone to "just take it for what it really says" is "warped and toxic" because "the assumption is that there is a way to read the Bible that is agenda- and perspective-free" (*Velvet Elvis*, p. 53). He rejects this "assumption."

Bell's wife, Kristen, says: "I grew up thinking that we've figured out the Bible, that we knew what it means. Now I have no idea what most of it means, and yet I feel like life is big again--like life used to be black and white, and now it's in color" (Kristen Bell, quoted in "The Emergent Mystique," *Christianity Today*, Nov. 2004, p. 38).

Kristen Bell told *Christianity Today* that their "lifeboat" out of the "black and white" dogmaticism of old biblical Christianity was Brian McLaren's *A New Kind of Christian*.

Brad Cecil of Axxess in Arlington, Texas, says: "We are not foundational empiricists who feel that we have reduced our faith to the point of irreducible certainty" (Gibbs and Bolger, *Emerging Churches*, p. 123).

Debbie Blue of House of Mercy in St. Paul, Minnesota, says: "We are not very oriented toward apologetics. ... We are comfortable with having a lot of unanswered questions. ... We think it's more honest than providing a lot of answers, abstract notions of truth" (*Emerging Church*, p. 124).

Karen Ward likens theology to a "potluck" meal in which people contribute their favorite dishes (*Listening to the Beliefs of Emerging Churches*, p. 168). She says, "As we gather we will continue to simmer our little theologies and share holy food and Scripture around a common fire" (p. 181).

Andy Crouch says that emergents "are looking for a faith that is colorful enough for their culturally savvy friends, deep enough for mystery, big enough for their own doubts. To get there, they are willing to abandon some long-defended battle lines" ("The Emergent Mystique," *Christianity Today*, Nov. 2004).

Thus they want a Christianity that is worldly enough to attract those who love the world and non-dogmatic enough to allow doubts and heresies.

Spencer Burke has made up the term "spiritual McCarthyism" to define his complaint about Christians who carefully test things by the Bible and who refuse to allow heresy to be taught in their midst ("From the Third Floor of the Garage: The Story of TheOOze," a chapter from Burke's book *Stories of Emergence*, 2003, http://www.spencerburke.com/pdf/presskit.pdf). He doesn't believe you should come to the place where "you believe that you alone have a lock on spiritual truth." He says we should be free to question whether homosexuality is a sin or whether baptism should only be by immersion for believers.

Burke's website, TheOOZE.com, is so named because it is an "ooze-y community [that] tolerates differences and treats people with opposing views with great dignity." He says, "**To me that's the essence of the emerging church**."

None of the emerging leaders are more relativistic and vague about doctrinal truth than Leonard Sweet. For him everything is experiential. He acknowledges that "revelation has occurred" but this revelation only gives us "universal moral truths" and even these broad truths cannot be dogmatically understood because "knowledge about these truths is socially constructed" (*Postmodern Pilgrims*, p. 146). He says, "Objectivity can no longer be the sole objective of the pursuit of truth" (p. 146). Sweet quotes Lorraine Code as saying that "subjectivity--however conflicted and multiple--becomes part of the conditions that make knowledge possible" (p. 149). Sweet is supportive of the poet Robert Bly who said that he had no idea of the meaning of the ending of one of his own poems (p. 149). Sweet says: "For Jesus truth was not propositions or the property of sentences. Rather, truth was what was revealed through our participation and interaction with him, others, and the world" (*Postmodern Pilgrims*, p. 157).

David Foster says, "We must move the conversation from certainty to mystery and back again. By doing so, we will switch from strict one-way communication to open, winsome, two-day dialogue. We will assert and affirm without becoming aggressive and dogmatic" (*A Renegade's Guide to God*, p. 195).

Doug Pagitt of Solomon's Porch in Minneapolis epitomizes the non-dogmatic approach. Pagitt says: "... the truth is we are a community making up the answers as we go along. We are a community brought together more by asking similar deep-seated questions than by all having the same answers. Though answers are useful, we desire not simply to apply the well-grounded answers to previous questions, but to be captured by the pursuit of new wonderings" (*Church Re-imagined*, p. 56). Solomon's Porch's "Bible discussion groups" are not led by any one person but are occasions for each participant to share his or her thoughts.

The sermons at Solomon's Porch "are not lessons that precisely define belief so much as they are stories that welcome our hopes and ideas and participation" (*Church Re-imagined*, p. 166). Pagitt rejects "the Bible says it, I believe it, that settles it" approach (*Listening to the Beliefs of Emerging Churches, p. 44)*. He is concerned when someone holds doctrinal views that do "not seem to be changing or changeable" (p. 43) and claims that "even our most firmly held beliefs were formed in a certain context and situation, and therefore are perspectival" (p. 43).

Dustin, one of the members at Solomon's Porch, admits that the relativistic Bible studies haven't helped him to understand the book of Daniel and concludes, "I can't possibly understand what is 'right' or not in the world" (p. 114). This is the pathetic position in which people find themselves when they explore the emerging church. Jesus promised that the individual that continues in His Word *"shall know the truth, and the truth shall make you free"* (John 8:31-32), but the emerging church says that such a thing is proud legalistic dogmatism.

Tim Condor, pastor of Emmaus Way and member of the coordinating team for Emergent Village, says the emergents have created "safe places for theological inquiry and exploration" and says there must be a "climate of theological openness" (*An Emergent Manifesto of Hope*, p. 106). He is opposed to "theological hazing" that precedes the ordination of pastors or the selection of lay leaders. He is opposed to requiring church staff members to commit to "doctrinal affirmations."

Adam Cleaveland says: "Those involved in the emerging church movement are not black-or-white thinkers. We strive to seek alternative visions and third ways beyond the polarities that have so dramatically seeped into our culture and our faith" (*An Emergent Manifesto of Hope*, p. 125).

Troy Bronsink says emergents are not "prisoners of some exclusive ideology" but "are artists freed like the romantics, gifted to sketch in participation with God, inspired by the breath of God..." (*An Emergent Manifesto of Hope*, p. 67).

Emergents like the strange term **ORTHOPARADOXY** to describe their position. It is a combination of the terms "orthodoxy" and "paradoxy" and it describes the idea that you can hold two opposite positions (two definitions of orthodoxy, two things that are seeming opposites) in harmony. It refers to the strange idea that orthodox theology can actually be many contradictory things at one time.

Dwight Friesen defines "orthoparadoxy as "a hermeneutic for seeing connection [between contradictory views] and a theology of wisely holding what at first glance may appear to be irreconcilable" ("Emergent Village and Full Communion," http://dwightfriesen.blog.com/1616648/).

In other words, if someone believes in a literal virgin birth and someone else believes that the virgin birth was merely "spiritual" or "poetic," the emerging church attempts to view both positions sympathetically and not to reject either one. It embraces contradictions, and that in itself is a grave contradiction! Black and white, light and darkness, yes and no, true and false, dogmatism and relativism, holy and unholy, war and peace, Catholic and Protestant, conservatism and modernism, all have a home in the emerging church!

Tony Campolo is a king of orthoparadoxy. In a review of Campolo's 2006 book *Letters to a Young Evangelical*, David Noebel observes:

> "So much of Campolo's book is decidedly ambiguous, one might even say it is flatly contradictory ... He claims to be a Fundamentalist and not to be a Fundamentalist; to be pro-life and not to be pro-life; to be anti-gay marriage and not to be anti-gay marriage; to be conservative and not to be conservative; to be anti-capitalist and not to be anti-capitalist; to be liberal and not to be liberal; to believe in universal salvation and not to believe in universal salvation; to denigrate America's middle class values and to admit being middle class himself; to hate the rapture and not to hate the rapture..." (David Noebel, "Tony Campolo, Jim Wallis: The Marxist Delusion and a Christian Evangelist," *Christian Worldview Network*, Feb. 19, 2008).

When asked to define "evangelical" in an interview in 2005, Campolo replied:

> "... an evangelical has a very high view of scripture THOUGH NOT NECESSARILY INERRANCY" ("On Evangelicals and Interfaith Cooperation," *Crosscurrents*, Spring 2005, http://findarticles.com/p/articles/mi_m2096/is_1_55/ai_n13798048).

That is a typical emerging church position. Only someone brainwashed by heresy can say that one can have a high view of Scripture without believing it is inerrant. Those are incompatible terms, but Campolo joyfully holds these contradictory views in "unity."

I experienced this up close and personal in an interview with Campolo in January 2008 at the Celebration of a New Baptist Covenant in Atlanta, Georgia. I was representing the Fundamental Baptist Information Service and was wearing my media badge, so Campolo knew my doctrinal position and in the interview he sounded like a die-hard fundamentalist! I had read at least four of Campolo's books before the interview and had heard him speak at other forums, so I knew the rank liberalism of his stance. As we will see in this book, Campolo has stated many times that he believes that those who do not have personal faith in Jesus Christ might be saved, yet in my interview he said that it is imperative to put one's faith in Christ and refused to allow for the possibility of salvation apart from that! Campolo has often ridiculed dispensationalism and its doctrine of an imminent Rapture, but in my interview he said that he believes in an imminent coming of Christ! My co-laborer and cameraman for that interview, Brian Snider, likened him to a chameleon, and the same can be said for the liberal emerging church overall.

The emergents even claim that the Bible itself is contradictory.

> "The Bible is not a textbook of systematic theology. ... Much of our theology therefore must emerge from a negotiated balance between texts, some of which contradict one another. Consequently, deciding on doctrine is messy work, filled with more uncertainties than you'd realize from the dogmatic manner of some Christians" (Donald McCullough, *If Grace Is So Amazing Why Don't We Like It*, pp. 222-223).

In this matter of holding contradictions, the emerging church has borrowed a page from Hinduism.

> "The Hindu religion of today comprises many different metaphysical systems and viewpoints, some of them mutually contradictory. The individual opts for whichever belief or practice suits him and his particular inclinations the best. Hinduism has no formal creed, no universal governing organization" (Lisa Choegyal, *Insight Guides Nepal*, 1994, p. 99).

Recently my wife was talking to a Hindu priest in Nepal who said (translated from Nepali), "Our gods are guiltless and guilty, holy and unholy." At the heart of Hinduism is the most radical ecumenism and syncretism, the ability to hold together in one religion the most extreme contradictions. The emerging church is nothing new!

Orthoparadoxy in the emerging church means not only do different men within the movement hold different and conflicting doctrines but also the same man will hold conflicting doctrines! We have seen that this is true for Tony Campolo.

Another example is Donald McCullough. He discusses the issue of universal salvation in his book *If Grace Is so Amazing, Why Don't We Like It?* and tries to hold both to universalism and to eternal judgment! He says the New Testament contains "two streams of tradition." On the one hand it warns that "unbelief leads to eternal death," while on the other hand (so he says) "universal salvation may remain a desire" (p. 224). He does not care that the doctrine of universal salvation is diametrically opposed to the doctrine that unbelief leads to eternal death.

Consider another example. Donald Miller wrote two entire books (*Blue Like Jazz* and *Searching for God Knows What*) in which he speaks repeatedly against systematized theology and claims that we cannot be dogmatic in theology. The very thesis of *Blue Like Jazz* is that the Christian faith is vague and non-resolving like jazz.

Miller calls doctrinal statements "formulas" and says they are "created by their authors to help us, but they do more hindering than helping" (*Searching for God Knows What*, p. 206). He criticizes the "formulaic methodology" (p. 217). He wonders if all the time spent developing doctrine from the Bible would "be better spent painting or writing or singing or learning to speak stories" (p. 217).

But then in a little blurb at the back of *Searching for God Knows What* Miller says, "... some thinkers may contend I believe systematic theology is the enemy, but this is not true. I find it a helpful guide and certainly recommend the study of systematic theology to enhance and explain, but not to replace, the human story" (p. 233).

This type of contradictory stand is right at home in the emergent church.

Because of the practice of "orthoparadoxy," emerging church writings can, therefore, be very confusing. What a writer seems to believe on one hand is contradicted on the other. THE READER CAN BE LULLED INTO THINKING THAT THE WRITER ACTUALLY HOLDS TO A SOUND BIBLE FAITH ON SOME ISSUE WHEN HE MIGHT ACTUALLY HOLD TO CONTRADICTORY HERESIES AT THE SAME TIME.

Getting back to the non-dogmatic stance of the emerging church, the thesis of the book *Velvet Elvis* by Rob Bell is that Christianity is a never-completed art project. He begins by describing a painting of Elvis Presley that he has in his basement, and says that since no portrait of Elvis can be thought of as the final word, likewise no doctrinal statement can be thought of as absolute. He says that Christianity is an endless process of rethinking the Bible and likens his non-dogmatic theological position to jumping on a trampoline. He says that doctrine should be elastic and flex and stretch like a trampoline (p. 22).

Barry Taylor suggests that we "consider the past two thousand years as an evolution of faith and not as something that has been static and fixed" (*An Emergent Manifesto of Hope*, p. 167). He claims that "faith lives in inquiry and fluidity" and says, "We should consider letting go of our obsession with certainty" (p. 168).

Emerging churches prefer "storytelling to preaching. "Services tend to be interactive and narrative--with A FOCUS ON STORYTELLING rather than a structured presentation" ("Young Pastors Explore New Forms of Worship," *Christian Science Monitor*, Oct. 31, 2002).

Tony Campolo says: "Rather than making theological statements, we need to tell each other our stories. Jesus would tell stories and then say, 'What do you make of this story?'" ("On Evangelicals and Interfaith Cooperation," *Cross Currents*, Spring 2005).

A "story" is non-threatening and non-dogmatic. You can interact with it and take it or leave it, accepting part of it or rejecting the entire thing.

WHAT DOES THE BIBLE SAY?

The Bible, on the other hand, teaches us that doctrine is settled, sure, and absolute. God's people are charged with keeping the pure doctrine of Scripture without spot and passing it along from generation to generation. This is a major emphasis in the New Testament. Consider some key passages:

MARK 4:10-12 -- "*And when he was alone, they that were about him with the twelve asked of him the parable. And he said unto them, Unto you it is given to know the mystery of the kingdom of God: but unto them that are without, all these things are done in parables: That seeing they may see, and not perceive; and hearing they may hear, and not understand; lest at any time they should be converted, and their sins should be forgiven them.*"

The view that Jesus spoke in stories as a way of being somewhat vague and non-dogmatic after an emergent church fashion is very popular, but it is false. In fact, Christ told parables to hide the truth from those who refused to believe. Jesus was a very plain spoken and direct preacher of the truth and oftentimes offended His audience. See, for example, Matthew 13:57; 15:12; John 6:60-61.

ACTS 2:42 -- "*And they continued stedfastly in the apostles' doctrine and fellowship, and in breaking of bread, and in prayers.*"

A major characteristic of the early churches was their unwavering commitment to apostolic doctrine. They did not question the apostles' doctrine or modify it or re-interpret it or ignore it; they continued stedfastly in it, and this is the divine pattern for every church.

MATTHEW 28:19-20 -- *"Go ye therefore, and teach all nations, baptizing them in the name of the Father, and of the Son, and of the Holy Ghost: Teaching them to observe all things WHATSOEVER I HAVE COMMANDED YOU: and, lo, I am with you alway, even unto the end of the world. Amen."*

Christ commanded that the gospel be preached to all nations and that everything He has commanded be passed along to and observed by each succeeding generation of believers. This is to continue until the end of the age. As we have seen in the previous studies on the inspiration of Scripture, Christ promised that the Holy Spirit would lead the apostles into all truth (John 16:13) and that is exactly what happened with the completion and canonization of Scripture. Otherwise, it would be impossible for us to obey Christ's command to teach and observe whatsoever He taught. Notice that Jesus promised that He would be with the churches as they carried out this Commission. This is why we can be sure that the truth has been passed along safely from generation to generation to our day. It is the resurrected Christ who guarantees the preservation of Scripture and the perpetuity of the truth.

ROMANS 6:17 -- *"But God be thanked, that ye were the servants of sin, but ye have obeyed from the heart that form of doctrine which was delivered you."*

Here we see that even salvation is contingent upon believing the right doctrine about the gospel. That doctrine was delivered by divine inspiration through the apostles and prophets of old, inscripturated, canonized, and preserved by the Holy Spirit.

ROMANS 16:17 -- *"Now I beseech you, brethren, mark them which cause divisions and offences contrary to the doctrine which ye have learned; and avoid them."*

The sole standard for truth is the doctrine that we have learned from the apostles and prophets who wrote the Scriptures. On the basis of this doctrine we are to judge all teaching and reject that which is heretical.

ROMANS 16:25-26 -- *"Now to him that is of power to stablish you according to my gospel, and the preaching of Jesus Christ, according to the revelation of the MYSTERY, which was kept secret since the world began, But now is made manifest, and by the scriptures of the prophets, according to the commandment of the everlasting God, made known to all nations for the obedience of faith."*

The emerging church misuses the biblical term "mystery" in its zeal to prove that doctrine should not be settled. Emergents say that doctrine has a "mysterious" element and we cannot therefore be dogmatic. Dan Kimball, for example, says that "we are supposed to approach theology more with a sense of wonder, awe, and mystery than like trying to solve a mathematical puzzle" (*Listening to the Beliefs of Emerging Churches*, p. 91). A *Christianity Today* article about the emerging church says that emergents "are looking for a faith that is colorful enough for their culturally savvy friends, deep enough for mystery, big enough for their own doubts" (Andy Crouch, "The Emergent Mystique," *Christianity Today*, Nov. 2004).

This is the opposite of the meaning of the biblical term "mystery." It is used 22 times in the New Testament, and it refers to something that was hidden in the Old Testament dispensation but is revealed in the New. This is obvious from Romans 16:25-26. A mystery is something that *"was kept secret since the world began, but now is made manifest."* See also Ephesians 3:3-5 and Colossians 1:26-27. A biblical mystery is not something that is mysterious and difficult to understand; it is something that has been revealed in Scripture and should therefore be dogmatically believed.

The Bible was not given so that we would be mystified; it is not mysterious; it is divine REVELATION. It is not shadow but LIGHT.

1 CORINTHIANS 13:12 -- *"For now we see through a glass, darkly; but then face to face: now I know in part; but then shall I know even as also I am known."*

This is another verse that is misused by the emerging church to support the principle that we cannot be dogmatic about theological issues. They say, "In this present world we only see theology darkly and not perfectly," but this is not the meaning of the verse. Paul is not saying that the teaching of Scripture can be understood only imperfectly or that it contains an imperfect revelation. He said elsewhere that the Scripture is given by divine inspiration and is able to make the man of God perfect (2 Timothy 3:16-17) and that the Scripture contains the deep things of God (1 Corinthians 2:9-13). 1 Corinthians 13:12 refers both to the completion of the canon of Scripture and to the perfection of knowledge in Glory, but it lends no support whatsoever to the emerging church idea that we cannot be dogmatic about doctrine in this present time.

1 TIMOTHY 1:3 -- *"As I besought thee to abide still at Ephesus, when I went into Macedonia, that thou mightest charge some that they teach NO OTHER DOCTRINE."*

Paul instructed Timothy to hold fast to the doctrine that he had received from the apostle and not to allow any other doctrine to be taught to the people under his watchcare. That is the very strictest, most dogmatic and intolerant position on doctrine imaginable.

1 TIMOTHY 4:16 -- *"Take heed unto thyself, and unto the doctrine; continue in them: for in doing this thou shalt both save thyself, and them that hear thee."*

Timothy was instructed to take heed to and continue in the doctrine that he had been taught by the apostle. This was to be his sole and sufficient standard of truth, and it would save him and those who heeded his instruction.

1 TIMOTHY 6:13-14 -- *"I give thee charge in the sight of God, who quickeneth all things, and before Christ Jesus, who before Pontius Pilate witnessed a good confession; that thou keep this commandment WITHOUT SPOT, unrebukeable, until the appearing of our Lord Jesus Christ."*

As Paul completed his first epistle to Timothy, he again charged the young preacher to be careful about the doctrine that he had been taught. He was to keep it in every detail, without spot. He was to be mindful of the fact that he would be required to give account unto Christ at His appearing. This proves that a super abbreviated "statement of faith" such as the Nicene Creed and the so-called Apostles' Creed is insufficient. Timothy was instructed to keep *everything* that the apostles taught. The theme of 1 Timothy is church truth. *"But if I tarry long, that thou mayest know how thou oughtest to behave thyself in the house of God, which is the church of the living God, the pillar and ground of the truth"* (1 Tim. 3:15). In this epistle Paul taught doctrine pertaining to things such as prayer (1 Timothy 2:1-6), the woman's role in the ministry (1 Timothy 2:9-15), the qualifications for church officers (chapter 3), dietary matters (1 Tim. 4:3-5), treatment of widows (1 Tim. 5:3-16), treatment of elders (1 Tim. 5:17-22), servant-master relationships (1 Tim. 6:1-5), and the believer's relationship to money and material possessions (1 Tim. 6:6-10). This is the type of teaching that is typically considered non-essential by the emerging church, yet Timothy was instructed to keep it "without spot" until Jesus appears. And the last time I checked, Christ had not yet returned!

2 TIMOTHY 2:2 -- *"And the things that thou hast heard of me among many witnesses, THE SAME commit thou to faithful men, who shall be able to teach others also."*

Timothy was instructed to teach the same doctrine that he had learned from Paul, and those he taught were, in turn, to teach the same doctrine to others. This is the process by which sound doctrine is to be passed along from generation to generation until Jesus comes. We do not have any authority to abridge it.

2 TIMOTHY 3:7 -- *"Ever learning, and never able to come to the knowledge of the truth."*

The Bible warns that the apostasy at the end of the age will be characterized by an educational process that is unable to come to a position of settled truth. A more apt description of the emerging church could not be written. In fact, they claim that it is impossible to come to a settled doctrine, because all interpretation is tainted by human imperfection.

2 TIMOTHY 3:16-17 -- *"All scripture is given by inspiration of God, and is profitable for doctrine, for reproof, for correction, for instruction in righteousness: That the man of God may be perfect, throughly furnished unto all good works."*

The very first purpose for Scripture is doctrine, not story-telling or some other vague thing. It is profitable for doctrine with the objective of making the man of God perfect. Obviously the doctrine must be pure in order to accomplish such an exalted task, and since God has ordained that the Scripture accomplish this task it is equally obvious that He will enable man to arrive at pure doctrine.

2 TIMOTHY 4:2 -- *"Preach the word; be instant in season, out of season; reprove, rebuke, exhort with all longsuffering and doctrine."*

The Word of God is to be preached with doctrine, and the doctrine is to come from the Word of God. The preacher is tasked with preaching God's Word, not philosophy and tradition, not stories. The word translated "preach" is *kerusso*, which means to proclaim or herald. To proclaim the Word necessitates theological dogmatism!

2 TIMOTHY 4:3-4 -- *"For the time will come when they will not endure sound doctrine; but after their own lusts shall they heap to themselves teachers, having itching ears; and they shall turn away their ears from the truth, and shall be turned unto fables."*

One of the hallmarks of the apostasy that is prophesied in many New Testament passages is that there will be a rejection of sound doctrine. If it were not possible for us to know what doctrine is true, this warning would make no sense. Paul assumes that there is one true New Testament doctrinal faith and warns that many will turn away from it. They will prefer teachers who scratch their ears with a new kind of Christianity, one built upon fables and designed to allow people to fulfill their lusts. That is a perfect description of the emerging church!

TITUS 1:9 -- *"Holding fast the faithful word as he hath been taught, that he may be able by sound doctrine both to exhort and to convince the gainsayers."*

It is by sound doctrine that the pastor is able to refute false teachers. If there were no such thing as absolute, settled doctrine it would be impossible even to know who the false teachers are, let alone refute them.

TITUS 2:7 -- *"In all things shewing thyself a pattern of good works: in doctrine shewing uncorruptness, gravity, sincerity."*

Titus is warned that his doctrine must be uncorrupt. Obviously, then, it was possible for him to know for certain what constituted sound doctrine and to follow it.

1 JOHN 2:26-27 -- *"These things have I written unto you concerning them that seduce you. But the anointing which ye have received of him abideth in you, and ye need not that any* man teach you: but as the same anointing teacheth you of all things, and is truth, and is no lie, and even as it hath taught you, ye shall abide in him."

John warned about the false teachers that were even then plaguing the churches. He stated that the true believer has the indwelling Holy Spirit as his teacher and thus is able to know truth from error in a certain and dogmatic sense. John also taught that we abide in Christ by Spirit-led doctrine.

2 JOHN 9-10 -- *"Whosoever transgresseth, and abideth not in the doctrine of Christ, hath not God. He that abideth in the doctrine of Christ, he hath both the Father and the Son. If there come any unto you, and bring not this doctrine, receive him not into your house, neither bid him God speed:"*

John again warned about false teachers and stated that the apostolic doctrine of Christ is the sole and absolute standard for the truth. Those who left that doctrine left Christ. Those who taught another doctrine were to be rejected. This refutes the idea that we should focus on knowing Christ rather than knowing doctrine. Christ is known through correct doctrine, not through mystical "centering"!

JUDE 3 -- *"Beloved, when I gave all diligence to write unto you of the common salvation, it was needful for me to write unto you, and exhort you that ye should earnestly contend for the faith which was once delivered unto the saints."*

Here we see that the New Testament faith was once delivered to the saints during the days of the apostles. It was finished and settled and certain. It is the one final Christian faith. From then until Jesus comes, each believer and each church is responsible to keep it and to defend it with vigor against everything that is contradictory. Note that nothing is to be added to this once-delivered faith. The "faith" is not something that has evolved throughout the church age. It was once delivered, and having been delivered and recorded in Scripture it is the sole authority for faith and practice.

REVELATION 2:14-15 -- *"But I have a few things against thee, because thou hast there them that hold the doctrine of Balaam, who taught Balac to cast a stumblingblock before the children of Israel, to eat things sacrificed unto idols, and to commit fornication. So hast thou also them that hold the doctrine of the Nicolaitans, which thing I hate."*

Christ reproved the church at Pergamos for refusing to take doctrine seriously enough and for entertaining those that taught false doctrines, such as the Balaamites and the Nicolaitans. Christ said He hated those false doctrines. These are strong words. The emerging church often mocks those who have a strong biblicist mindset, but this is the pattern given to us by Christ Himself. The psalmist also testified, *"Therefore I esteem all thy precepts concerning all things to be right; and I hate every false way"* (Psalm 119:128).

This biblical position on doctrine refutes the emerging church heresy.

It is important to understand that the emerging church undermines absolute truth even when it has a right-sounding doctrinal statement. It does this in the following ways:

First, the emerging church undermines absolute truth by redefining terms. Robert Schuller is a prime example of this. In his book *Self-Esteem: The New Reformation*, he gives biblical terms new meaning. He says that *born again* means "to be changed from a negative to a positive self-image" (p. 68), *sin* "is any act or thought that robs myself or another human being of his or her self-esteem" (p. 14), and *Hell* "is the loss of pride that naturally follows separation from God" (p. 14). The emerging church tendency to give biblical and theological terms new meaning has led some to conclude that they are speaking sound doctrine when they aren't.

Second, the emerging church undermines absolute truth by the principle that only the most "cardinal" doctrines of Scripture are essential. The liberal emerging church likes to use the "Apostles Creed" as a basis for unity, but this is ridiculously insufficient. If God had only wanted us to believe a handful of ill-defined truths, why did He give us the entire Bible?

Third, the emerging church undermines absolute truth by contradicting its own doctrine. We have given examples of this. It is the practice of "orthoparadoxy." The emerging church might say something that sounds right on one hand, but it will often contradict this by other statements.

Fourth, the emerging church undermines absolute truth by saying that we should recognize that there is a "mystery" about doctrine that cannot be dogmatically fathomed. Dan Kimball is described like this: "Dan represents a branch of the emerging church that questions a 'we have an answer to everything' mentality. He calls us to remain true to THE ESSENTIALS of the Christian faith, such as the Trinity, the authority of Scripture, the atonement, the resurrection, the second coming, and the summary of faith in the Nicene Creed. BUT HE ADVOCATES 'MYSTERY' EVEN IN THAT WHICH IS AFFIRMED..." (Robert Webber, *Listening to the Beliefs of Emerging Churches*, p. 17).

Thus, on the one hand the emerging church might sound as if it were committed to sound doctrine, while on the other hand it undermines this with its principle that all doctrine has a mysterious quality, an unknowable element, and that we shouldn't therefore be too dogmatic.

LIBERAL EMERGING CHURCH ERROR #4
GLORIFYING DOUBT OVER FAITH

The glorification of doubt and questioning is part of the deconstruction aspect of the liberal emerging church. They aim to deconstruct traditional theology with the objective of reconstructing something different, something allegedly more fitting for "these times."

Rob Bell says that God gives men "the invitation to follow Jesus with all our doubts and questions right there with us" (*Velvet Elvis*, p. 28). He says, "We sponsored a Doubt Night at our church awhile back. People were encouraged to write down whatever questions or doubts they had about God and Jesus and the Bible and faith and church" (p. 29). He says, "Questions bring freedom" (p. 30), and, "Questions, no matter how shocking or blasphemous or arrogant or ignorant or raw, are rooted in humility" (p. 30).

Tim Condor, pastor of Emmaus Way and member of the coordinating team for Emergent Village, says there must be a "climate of theological openness" to allow people to express their doubts (*An Emergent Manifesto of Hope*, p. 106). He says there should never be a punitive consequence or exclusion for expressions of doubt and questioning of even the most cardinal of doctrinal truths.

Adam Cleaveland says that churches should be "open to critique and deconstruction" (*An Emergent Manifesto of Hope*, p. 125). He says there should be safe places "where people can come and be involved in the process of deconstructing ideas and practices, all while remaining open to the new movements and new waves of the Spirit."

Barry Taylor says, "Christian faith is open to discussion. Historically it always has been. It can be questioned and reinterpreted. In fact I would argue that it is meant to be questioned and reinterpreted" (*An Emerging Manifesto of Hope*, p. 167).

Brian McLaren says that we should welcome "the disillusioned and the doubters" (*A Generous Orthodoxy*, p. 172).

WHAT DOES THE BIBLE SAY?

The emerging church's position on doubt/questionings is refuted by the Bible's distinction between sincere and foolish questions.

Believers should entertain honest questions from seekers, but foolish questions are to be rejected.

> "But foolish and unlearned questions avoid, knowing that they do gender strifes" (2 Timothy 2:23).

> "But avoid foolish questions, and genealogies, and contentions, and strivings about the law; for they are unprofitable and vain" (Titus 3:9).

We wholeheartedly support the idea of giving unbelievers "space" for expressing their questions and doubts as they are coming to the Lord. The man who led me to Christ spent a few entire days with me patiently teaching me the Bible and answering my questions. I was chocked full of Humanism, New Age, Hinduism, Christian Science, and other errors, and I had a lot of questions and challenges to what the Bible taught. I believed there were many ways to God, that reincarnation was true, that a man can find the truth by following his heart, that God would not send people to Hell if they had never heard the gospel, that Christ had learned wisdom in Egypt during the "hidden years," and many other false things. The man who led me to Christ knew little to nothing about the things I believed at the time, but he did know the Scripture, and as I expressed my views to him, including my doubts about the Bible, he patiently listened and then replied with Scripture.

In our church planting work in South Asia, many unbelievers visit our public meetings and home Bible studies and village meetings, and we deal with their many questions and doubts. Sometimes their questions are as ridiculous as whether or not we baptize people in cow's blood (some of the Hindus have actually said this behind our backs) or as substantial as why we believe that Jesus Christ is the only Saviour and why He died on the cross. As we deal with their questions, sometimes they go on to saving faith in Christ and sometimes they turn away, but we deal as best as we can with their all of their issues.

After people are saved, they still have many doctrinal questions, of course. I thank the Lord for those who patiently taught me the Scriptures and set my thinking straight when I was a young believer. For example, soon after I was saved I found a book by a Seventh-day Adventist at the public library and became confused about the sabbath and whether or not people go to Heaven or Hell at death and such things. The pastor of the church where I was a member showed me what the Bible said and his help and my own prayerful Bible study resolved those doubts. The same thing happened in regard to Pentecostal-Charismatic doctrine. Having been led to Christ by a Pentecostal, I was confused about whether tongues-speaking is for today and such things, but by studying the Bible privately and receiving help from sound teachers, those issues were resolved. I asked sincere questions and received honest Bible answers and the problem was settled. I recall my late friend and former pastor, Gary Prisk. He had lived a roving lifestyle before he was saved, hitchhiking, using drugs, and he didn't know anything about the Bible. Not long after he came to Christ he went to Bible College, and one day soon after arriving he saw a book with the title "Is Jesus God?" He thought to himself, "No, God is God." He wasn't a heretic; he was simply ignorant; and after he was taught what the Bible says about Christ's divinity he accepted it readily and defended it for the rest of his life.

Foolish questions, on the other hand, are not to be entertained. A "foolish question" is *a question that is asked insincerely by a heretic with the goal of confusing people and leading them astray from sound doctrine.* This is the immediate context of Titus 3:9-10. A heretic is someone who is self-willed and has rejected sound doctrine in favor of his own opinions and perversions of the truth. The terms "heretic" and "heresy" refer to the willful choice of false doctrine, a willful alignment with error. The heretic is not content with the plain teaching of Scripture but pursues his own agenda. This is exactly what we find in emerging church circles. A foolish question is one that is used in an attempt to overthrow plain Bible teaching, such as questions about the Trinity or Christ's bodily Resurrection and virgin birth or biblical inspiration or the eternal suffering of Hell or separation from the world.

It is good to ask sincere questions in the honest search for the truth, but it is evil to entertain questions that deny Bible truth. If the Bible says all unbelievers will suffer conscious eternal torment in fire, which it does, we must not entertain questions that speculate if this is a just punishment. If the Bible claims to be the infallible Word of God, which it does, we are not to question how this could be possible. If the Bible says we are not to love this world, which it does, we are not to question whether this might be a narrow, "legalistic" position.

Our questions must be controlled by the Bible, not the Bible by our questions. *"The secret things belong unto the LORD our God: but those things which are revealed belong unto us and to our children for ever, that we may do all the words of this law"* (Deut. 29:29).

A foolish question is also *a question that produces strife and contention* among Bible-believing Christians. Titus 3:9 associates foolish questions with "contentions and strivings," and 2 Timothy 2:23 says foolish questions "gender strifes." When someone only wants to argue with the Word of God, he stirs up strife and doubt and confusion among others and causes trouble in the churches.

A heretic is not a person who is merely ignorant of sound doctrine. A true believer can be ignorant of sound doctrine, but the evidence that he is not a heretic will be seen when he responds to sound doctrine and rejects the error.

The mouths of heretics are stopped *by refuting their questions and by putting them out of the assemblies* (Titus 3:10-11).

It is impossible to keep the truth without separating from false doctrine and maintaining church discipline. False teachers must be dealt with and not ignored, and the scriptural way to deal with them is to put them out of the assemblies and to separate the believers from them.

The heretic is to be admonished two times (Titus 3:10). An effort is to be made to reclaim the heretic from his error. It is possible that he is not truly a heretic but that he is only teaching out of ignorance, but the effort is not to be long and drawn out. The heretic is to be admonished *only* two times (Titus 3:10). When it is obvious that he is set in his false ways, he must be rejected and put out of the assembly. Otherwise, he will corrupt others. *"A little leaven leaveneth the whole lump"* (Gal. 5:9).

The heretic condemns himself by his self-willed commitment to error. *"Knowing that he that is such is subverted, and sinneth, being condemned of himself"* (Titus 3:11). There is something wrong in the heretic's heart. "Subverted" is from the Greek word "ekstrepho," which means to be twisted or turned inside out. Something has perverted that person's heart so that he loves heresy rather than the truth. "Such a one is subverted or perverted--a metaphor from a building so ruined as to render it difficult if not impossible to repair and raise it up again. Real heretics have seldom been recovered to the true faith: not so much defect of judgment, as perverseness of the will, being in the case, through pride, or ambition, or self-willedness, or covetousness, or such like corruption, which therefore must be taken heed of" (Matthew Henry).

Consider an example of how to deal with a foolish question from Jesus' earthly ministry in Luke 20:1-8 and 20:20-26. Observe that Jesus did not argue with the Pharisees, nor did He waste time giving detailed replies to their insincere questions. He answered with statements that got to the root of the matter and shut their mouths!

If a person asks a sincere question, it should be answered from the Bible, but if he is asking a question to try to spread rebellion and promote false doctrine and draw people away from the truth, it is not profitable to answer it.

Therefore, our first point is that we must make a clear distinction between sincere and foolish questions.

The emerging church's position on doubt/ questionings is refuted by the Bible's requirements for church membership.

There are Bible qualifications for church members, and one of those is that they continue stedfastly in sound apostolic doctrine. This is the pattern that was set in the first church.

> "Then they that gladly received his word were baptized: and the same day there were added unto them about three thousand souls. And they continued stedfastly in the apostles' doctrine and fellowship, and in breaking of bread, and in prayers" (Acts 2:41-42).

Those who were saved and added to the church at Jerusalem on the day of Pentecost were Jews who were steeped in Judaism, but here we see that through the power of the indwelling Holy Spirit they committed themselves to the teaching of the apostles and continued therein.

I am sure they had a thousand and one questions, but the teaching of the apostles settled every issue for them. This is the way it should be in every church.

If a church member asks a question about the deity of Christ or Hell or the sabbath, he should be taught in a patient and compassionate manner. If, though, he refuses to accept the Bible's teaching and persists in his doubt and unbelief and chooses heresy over the truth, he must be put out of the church.

Thus, there are doubts that an unbeliever can express to us in our evangelistic work that a church member is not allowed to hold.

The emerging church's position on doubt/ questionings is refuted by the Bible's exaltation of faith.

The Bible exalts faith over doubt. *"But without faith it is impossible to please him: for he that cometh to God must believe that he is, and that he is a rewarder of them that diligently seek him"* (Heb. 11:6). Jesus rebuked those who doubted (Mat. 6:30; 8:26; 14:31; 16:8) and praised those who had faith (Mat. 8:10; 15:28). He taught that faith is one of the weightier matters of the law (Mat. 23:23) and instructed the people to have faith in God (Mk. 11:22). Zacharias was judged for doubting (Luke 1:20). James says those who doubt can receive nothing from the Lord (James 1:6-8). Christian men are exhorted to praise God *without doubting* (1 Tim. 2:8). To doubt is sin (Rom. 14:23).

The Bible teaches that we must come to terms with doubt; it must be dealt with; it must be resolved. The Psalmist momentarily doubted in Psalm 73, but his doubt was resolved in the same Psalm and he saw himself as a foolish beast for doubting God. John the Baptist doubted when he was in prison, but Jesus settled his doubt by doing Messianic miracles and thus reminding John that He is the One who was promised and also warning that it is those who are *not* offended in him that are blessed (Luke 7:19-22). On the cross, Jesus cried, "My God, my God, why hast thou forsaken me?" (Mat. 27:46), but this was not unresolved doubt; the question He asked is clearly resolved in Scripture. God the Father forsook the Son on the cross because He was bearing the sins of the world (Isaiah 53:5-6; 2 Corinthians 5:21; Galatians 1:4). Jesus' question was answered.

The emerging church's position on doubt/ questionings is refuted by the Bible's teaching on the source of faith.

Faith does not come through contemplative practices or ecumenical dialogue; it comes by God's Word. *"So then faith cometh by hearing, and hearing by the word of God"* (Rom. 10:17).

True faith, being founded upon God's inspired revelation has substance and evidence (Hebrews 11:1). The believer's faith is founded upon *"many infallible proofs"* (Acts 1:3). There is nothing blind about it.

LIBERAL EMERGING CHURCH ERROR #5 CONTEMPLATIVE MYSTICISM

"There is intoxication in the waters of contemplation"
--Thomas Merton

Contents of this section

What Is Mysticism?..117
The Taize Approach..120
The Emerging Church's Love for Mysticism...................121
A Description of the Contemplative Practices................129
The History & Error of Catholic Monasticism................166
Further Warnings about Contemplative Mysticism........187

The liberal emerging church style of "spirituality" is highly mystical. The room might be dimly lit with ambient music playing in the background. The influence of Roman Catholicism and Greek Orthodoxy is very evident, with candles and incense and crosses and statues and labyrinths and Stations of the Cross and icons. There is silence and meditation and chanting and liturgy and artistic endeavors such as dancing and finger painting and poetry.

A contemplative mysticism permeates everything. The Lighthouse Trails ministry, which has done groundbreaking research into this new mysticism, made the following important observation in their newsletter:

> "Some books and several articles have now been written about the emerging church, and interestingly, nearly all of them lack the most important element--the emerging church ... is a conduit for mysticism and is heading right into the arms of Catholicism and eventually a universal interfaith church. THE EMERGING CHURCH IS FUNDAMENTALLY MYSTICAL as can easily be seen by the leaders who feed the emerging movement a steady diet of contemplative spirituality" ("Emerging Church Confusion," *Coming from the Lighthouse*, Oct. 16, 2007).

This is exactly right. Mysticism is at the very heart and soul of the emerging church.

Roger Oakland observes that "wind is to a sail boat what contemplative prayer is to the emerging church" (*Faith Undone*, p. 81).

Emerging church leader Leonard Sweet says:

> "Mysticism, once cast to the sidelines of the Christian tradition, is now situated in postmodernist culture near the center. ... In the words of one of the greatest theologians of the twentieth century, Jesuit philosopher of religion/dogmatist Karl Rahner, 'The Christian of tomorrow will be a mystic, one who has experienced something, or he will be nothing'" (*Quantum Spirituality*, 1991, pp. 11, 76).

In fact, mysticism is permeating Christianity at every level. Ursula King observes that "recent years have seen a greater interest and fascination with the mystics of all ages and faiths than any previous period in history" (*Christian Mystics*, p. 22).

WHAT IS MYSTICISM?

I want to emphasize, first, what mysticism is *not*. It is not merely a desire to know Christ intimately and to be filled with the Spirit and to walk in God's perfect will. It is not merely a life of worship and devotion to God and fruitful Bible study. Mysticism goes far beyond this.

Mysticism is an attempt to commune with God experientially and to find spiritual understanding beyond the pages of the Bible by means of Roman Catholic monastic practices.

Mysticism emphasizes a direct experience of God.

Leonard Sweet defines mysticism as an "*experience* with God" in the metaphysical realm that is achieved through "mindbody experiences" (*Quantum Spirituality*, 1991, p. 11).

Anthony de Mello said: "... we are, all of us, endowed with a mystical mind and mystical heart, a faculty which makes it possible for *us to know God directly*, to grasp and intuit him in his very being..." (*Sadhana: A Way to God*, p. 29).

Ursula King says, "Mystics seek *participation in divine life, communion and union* with God" (*Christian Mystics*, p. 4).

Chamber's Dictionary defines mysticism as "the habit or tendency of religious thought and feeling of those who seek *direct communion with God* or the divine."

Mysticism also emphasizes finding spiritual insight beyond thought and doctrine.

It is focused on experience, feeling, emotion, intuition, and perception.

Leonard Sweet says, "Mysticism begins in experience; it ends in theology" (*Quantum Spirituality*, 1991, p. 76).

Anne Bancroft, author of *Twentieth-Century Mystics and Sages*, defined a mystic as someone who feels "a need to go beyond words and to experience the truth about themselves" (p. vii).

Thomas Merton defined mysticism as an experience with wisdom and God *apart from words*.

Anthony de Mello said:

"The head is not a very good place for prayer. ... You must learn to move out of the area of thinking and talking and move into the area of feeling, sensing, loving, intuiting" (*Sadhana: A Way to God*, p. 17).

"Contemplation for me is communication with God that makes a minimal use of words, images, and concepts or dispenses with words, images, and concepts altogether. This is the sort of prayer that John of the Cross speaks of in his *Dark Night of the Soul* or the author of *The Cloud of Unknowing* explains in his admirable book" (p. 29).

Christianity Today says there are many young evangelicals who are tired of "traditional Christianity" and want "a renewed encounter with God" that goes BEYOND "DOCTRINAL DEFINITIONS" ("The Future Lies in the Past," *Christianity Today*, Feb. 2008).

This is a good definition of mysticism. It is an attempt to experience God beyond the interpretation of Scripture, beyond doctrine, beyond theology.

Spencer Burke of the OOze in Newport Beach, California, says: "A move away from intellectual Christianity is essential. We must move to the mystical" (*Emerging Churches*, p. 230).

Observe that he contrasts mysticism with the intellect. Mysticism tries to reach beyond that which can be understood with the mind, beyond the teaching of Scripture.

Consider this description of centering prayer, which requires putting aside conscious thoughts:

"For in this darkness we experience an intuitive understanding of everything material and spiritual without giving special attention to anything in particular" (*The Cloud of Unknowing*, chapter 68).

This is pure mysticism, and *The Cloud of Unknowing* is a primary resource for the contemplative movement.

Tony Campolo describes contemplative spirituality as mystical stillness and communing with God *without words*:

"I get up in the morning a half hour before I have to and spend time in absolute stillness. I don't ask God for anything. I just simply surrender to His presence and yield to the Spirit flowing into my life. ... An interviewer once asked Mother Teresa, 'When you pray, what do you say to God?' She said, 'I don't say anything. I just listen.' So the interviewer asked, 'What does God say to you?' She replied, 'God doesn't say anything. He listens.' That's the kind of prayer I do in the morning" (*Outreach Magazine*, July/ August 2004, pp. 88, 89).

Mysticism accepts extra-scriptural dreams and visions and insights as revelations from God and, in fact, expects them as a natural product of the contemplative experience.

Richard Foster says, "Christian meditation, very simply is the ability to hear God's voice and obey his word" (*Celebration of Discipline*, 1998, p. 17), and he is not talking here about hearing God's voice through Scripture alone.

In the book *Prayer: Finding the Heart's True Home*, Foster, quoting Thomas Merton, says that contemplative prayer "offers you an understanding and light, which are like nothing you ever found in books or heard in sermons."

The "spiritual insights" that the practitioner obtains through contemplative meditation becomes truth to him that is at least equal in authority to Scripture.

The Catholic "saints" who developed the contemplative practices received countless extra-biblical revelations.

This is the mystical approach that is fast becoming the acceptable means of "spirituality" in all branches of Christianity, including the emerging church.

THE TAIZÉ APPROACH

The mystical movement is strongly influenced by Taizé (pronounced teh-zay), and we find Taizé mentioned frequently in emerging church writings. This is a religious community that was formed in southeastern France during World War II by Roger Schutz, a Swiss Protestant pastor who went by the name of "Brother Roger" and who led the community until his death in 2005. Its goal is to work for world peace and ecumenical unity. The Taizé monastic order includes some 100 allegedly "celibate brothers" from different countries and denominations, including Roman Catholic, Lutheran, Anglican, and Reformed. While the Taizé community itself is very small, the Taizé philosophy has influenced churches throughout the world.

Taizé is a major force for non-doctrinal ecumenism. Each year tens of thousands of people make a pilgrimage to Taizé. These include Christians, Jews, Buddhists, and the unaffiliated. The Roman Catholic connection is very strong. Schutz participated in the Catholic Vatican II Council, and Pope John Paul II visited Taizé in October 1986. Since Schutz's death, Taizé has been led by a Roman Catholic priest named Alois Loeser.

The Taizé services are non-dogmatic and non-authoritative. There is no preaching. "It does not dictate what people must believe. No confessions of faith are required. No sermons are given. No emotional, evangelical-style testimonials are expected. Clergy are not required."

Schutz described the philosophy of Taizé as, "Searching together--not wanting to become spiritual masters who impose; God never imposes. We want to love and listen, we want simplicity" ("Taizé," *Religion and Ethics Newsweekly*, Sept. 20, 2002).

Taizé's non-doctrinal ecumenical Christianity is fueled by mysticism. A "shadowy medieval" atmosphere is shaped by the use of such things as candles, icons, and incense (*Vancouver Sun*, April 14, 2000). The goal is to bring the "worshipper" into a meditative state, "to a place beyond words, a place of just being." There is a lot of repetition, with "one-line Taizé harmonies repeated up to 15 times each."

With its mystical, non-dogmatic, ecumenical philosophy, it is obvious why the emerging church is drawn to Taizé.

The Taizé community is also heavily involved in the same type of "social-justice" issues that are popular with the emerging church.

THE WIDESPREAD INFLUENCE OF MYSTICISM IN THE EMERGING CHURCH

As we have mentioned, mysticism is at the very heart and soul of the emerging church.

The Emerging Village web site makes the following statement:

> "We embrace many historic spiritual practices, including prayer, meditation, contemplation, study, solitude, silence, service, and fellowship..." (Emerging Village web site, http://www.emergentvillage.org/about-information/values-and-practices).

These "historic spiritual practices" come from Rome's wretched past rather than from the Bible. The liberal emerging church is a rejection of the Protestant and Baptist focus on "Scripture alone" and a return to a Roman Catholic perspective that downgrades Scripture and exalts tradition and mystical revelation.

Brian McLaren's 2008 book, *Finding Our Way Again: The Return of the Ancient Practices*, is a complete capitulation to Roman Catholic mysticism.

Mars Hill Graduate School is a proponent of contemplative mysticism. Dan Allender, the president, is described as "an expert in the subject of contemplative prayer." He draws on the writings of Thomas Merton. Mars Hill's course TCE 527 ("The Kingdom of God") and its spiritual formation course use textbooks by Thomas Keating and "Catholic proponent" Michael Downey ("*Christian Post* Says Mark Driscoll 'Ditches' Emergent but Evidence Proves Otherwise," Lighthouse Trails, Feb. 9, 2008).

Emerging leader Tony Jones' *The Sacred Way: Spiritual Practices for Everyday Life* explores spiritual practices from Roman Catholicism and Greek Orthodoxy and offers suggestions on how emergents can use them. He recommends *lectio divina*, silence, centering prayer, Stations of the Cross, icons, the sign of the cross, pilgrimages to Catholic shrines, and the labyrinth. He recommends Catholic mystics such as Gregory of Sinai, John of the Cross, Thomas Merton, Teresa of Avila, Julian of Norwich, and Theresa of Lisieux. He promotes the spiritual practices of Benedict, the founder of the Dominican order, and Ignatius of Loyola, the founder of the Jesuits. Jones describes visits to the Jesuit Communication Center in Dublin, the Monastery of the Ascension in Idaho, the Ava Maria Center in Minnesota, St. Peter's Basilica in Rome, Taizé in France, and a monastery in San Antonio. He recommends putting oneself under the spiritual direction of Catholic nuns.

Fuller Seminary professors Eddie Gibbs and Ryan Bolger, in their sympathetic study of the emerging church, say:

"Whereas the Reformation removed many rituals from the worship service, postmodern worship restores these activities. The reformation focused on the spoken word, while postmodern worship embraces the experienced word. Thus, emerging church worshipers may respond with the sign of the cross, more often associated with Catholic worship, and they receive the deep mystical aspects of communion, candles, and incense. They may retrieve ancient rituals and create new ones involving the body; they may dance in different venues" (*Emerging Churches*, p. 78).

Solomon's Porch in Minneapolis, led by Doug Pagitt, uses labyrinths, celebrates Ash Wednesday by putting ashes on the forehead, practices silent prayer and prayer dancing, makes the sign of the cross, and uses the Stations of the Cross (*Church Re-imagined*, pp. 86, 101, 102). This emerging church also practices pagan and New Age forms of mysticism such as yoga, acupuncture, and massage therapy (pp. 85, 86, 105, 106). Pagitt endorses yoga in his book *Body Prayer: The Posture of Intimacy with God*. Marlene, the church's message therapist, says, "Now I realize that much of Eastern medicine is closer to the holistic model of faith I believe in than Western medicine" (p. 106). An acupuncturist told one of the church members that he had "a lot of heat" in him and it is "drying up his blood." "So the plan is to try to bring the heat down by bringing my ying back into harmony with my yang" (p. 98). This is pagan mystic occultism.

House of Mercy in St. Paul, Minnesota, claims to be "rooted in the Baptist tradition" but it has confessions, celebrates the Eucharist, uses incense, appoints a thurifer (the person who swings an incense pot), and uses candles (*Emerging Churches*, pp. 224, 225).

Quest in Seattle has retreats at a Catholic priory and is coached by nuns (*Emerging Churches*, p. 231).

Rob Bell, pastor of Mars Hill Bible Church in Michigan, invited a Roman Catholic nun from the Dominican Center at Marywood to speak at a church service in March 2006. Ray Yungen remarks: "The Dominican Center has a Spirituality center, which offers a wide variety of contemplative opportunities, including Reiki, a Spiritual Formation program, a Spiritual Director program, labyrinths, Celtic Spirituality, and more. Bell stated in this service how much this sister had taught him in his spiritual walk" (*A Time of Departing*, p. 178). Reiki involves channeling spiritual energy and communicating with spirit guides.

Tony Campolo claims that Roman Catholic mystics such as Francis of Assisi, Ignatius of Loyola, Teresa of Avila, and Catherine of Siena are supersaints that we should emulate (*The God of Intimacy and Action*, pp. 9, 10).

The emerging church is at the forefront of a "new monasticism." *The Boston Globe* reports:

> "There is now a growing movement to revive evangelicalism by reclaiming parts of Roman Catholic tradition--including monasticism. Some 100 groups that describe themselves as both evangelical and monastic have sprung up in North America, according to Rutba House's [Jonathan] Wilson-Hartgrove. Many have appeared within the past five years. Increasing numbers of evangelical congregations have struck up friendships with Catholic monasteries, sending church members to join the monks for spiritual retreats. St. John's Abbey, a Benedictine monastery in Minnesota, now makes a point of including interested evangelicals in its summer Monastic Institute" ("The Unexpected Monks," *The Boston Globe*, Feb. 3, 2008).

Karen Sloan "can often be found praying in Catholic churches" and "hanging around the Dominican order and monastic life" (*An Emergent Manifesto*, p. 260). She authored *Flirting with Monasticism: Finding God on Ancient Paths*.

The late Robert Webber viewed mysticism as a key to the "ancient future" ecumenism that he promoted. He recommended a slew of Catholic mystics, including Thomas à Kempis, Meister Eckhart, Teresa of Avila, Augustine, Bernard of Clairvaux, John of the Cross, and Thomas Merton, calling their works "essential," "a great treasure," and "indispensable." He warned that "we dare not avoid the mystics" and even said that "those who neglect these works do so to their harm" (*Ancient-Future Faith*, p. 135).

The emerging church is even experimenting with *DRUM CIRCLES*.

Mike Perschon is the associate pastor of Holyrood Mennonite Church in Edmonton, Alberta, Canada. He teaches contemplative practices at youth retreats. Writing for the Youth Specialties web site in 2004, Perschon described entire nights "devoted to guided meditations, drum circles, and 'soul labs'" ("Desert Youth Worker: Disciplines, Mystics and the Contemplative Life," Youth Specialties, www.youthspecialties.com/articles/topics/spirituality/desert.php). This was part of the church's "alternative spiritual expressions."

In 2004 the Cameron United Methodist Church in Denver, Colorado, hosted a community drum circle night entitled "drumming up the spirits" (Christine Stevens, "Drumming Up the Spirits," *Christian Sound & Song*, Issue 9, 2005, http://www.ubdrumcircles.com/article_spirits.html). This was "a kick-off to future church based drumming programs" and since then the women's spirituality group has taken up drumming. This church is led by a husband-wife pastor team. Stevens says: "Drumming is happening in churches across America. It is being used in children's programs, worship services, family events, and men's and women's groups."

The group Rhythm Praise is dedicated to hosting drum circles and "rhythm events." It is said to "open up a dialog within a community where communication, shared values, self-esteem and unity can be attained" (http://www.rhythmpraise.org/). It is "a vehicle to break down barriers between people and to foster healing," which sounds very emergent.

The Church of the Holy Comforter of Richmond, Virginia, founded by Regena Stith, uses drum circles. Stith first experienced the drums in the late 1990s during a yoga retreat (Roger Oakland, *Faith Undone*, p. 70). She said that during the drumming "you move out of your head."

Roger Oakland writes:

> "Even though some in the emerging church might consider the drumming at the Church of the Holy Comforter in Richmond a bit extreme, it is growing in popularity and use in the postmodern religious scene. And according to proponents, drumming is a doorway for ecumenical harmony" (*Faith Undone*, p. 70).

Oakland quotes Zachary Reid who says drumming "can transcend denominational and cultural boundaries" ("Feeling the Beat: The Spiritual Side of Drum Circles," *Richmond Times Dispatch*, March 10, 2007).

Oakland also sites an article by Asher Main at the Calvin Institute of Christian Worship web site (March 2005), that says, "It would be to our advantage as worshippers to harness this resource that we see in secular world culture and adapt it and bring it into the church."

I have a niece who was heavily involved in drum circles when she was using hallucinogenic drugs. The weekly drum circle became her "church." She would dance for hours in a trance-like state, caught up in the power of rhythm. After she repented and got right with the Lord she realized that she had been communicating with devils.

Can you imagine the Lord Jesus and Peter and John sitting by the Lake of Galilee pounding away on drums in an attempt to have a mystical experience with God!

The "conservative emerging church" has almost the same enthusiasm for contemplative practices as the "liberal" branch.

In his book *The Emerging Church* Dan Kimball says that it is to their hurt that evangelicals "have neglected so many of the disciplines of the historical church [Catholic Church], including weekly fasting, practicing the silence, and *lectio divina*" (p. 223).

On page 93 Kimball recommends *Soul Shaper: Exploring Spirituality and Contemplative Practices* by Tony Jones. This book advocates many Roman Catholic practices, including silence, stations of the cross, centering prayer, and the labyrinth.

Kimball recommends the Taizé style of worship (*Emerging Worship*, pp. 83, 89). His Vintage Faith Church features candles, incense, crucifixes, artwork, chanting, ambient music, a "multisensory approach," and liturgy (*Emerging Worship*, pp. 78-85, 92, 93).

In October 2001, Kimball wrote an article entitled "A-mazeing Prayer: The Labyrinth Offers Ancient Meditation for Today's Hurried Souls." He describes how that he and his wife first walked a labyrinth for an hour in a darkened hall at the National Pastors Conference in San Diego, and how that they were so impressed that he led his own church to build a labyrinth for its annual art event that year. They transformed one of the church's rooms into a "medieval prayer sanctuary," complete with art on the walls and candles placed "all around the room to create a visual sense of sacred space."

Mark Driscoll is the president of the Acts 29 church planting network. Its "Recommended Reading List" includes many works promoting Roman Catholic contemplative spirituality, including books by Richard Foster, Dallas Willard, St. John of the Cross, Thomas Merton, Teresa of Avila, and Ignatius of Loyola.

Portland's Imago Dei's School of Theology has a course called "Spiritual Formation in the Outdoors" and the required reading includes Henri Nouwen's books *Reaching Out* and *The Way of the Heart*.

Mysticism is spreading throughout Evangelicalism as well as society at large

In the book *Contemplative Mysticism: A Powerful Ecumenical Glue* we have documented the rapid spread of mysticism throughout society at large as well as throughout evangelical Christianity.

Everywhere we look evangelicals are turning to Roman Catholic styles of contemplative spirituality.

The cover story for the February 2008 issue of *Christianity Today* was "The Future Lies in the Past: Why Evangelicals Are Connecting with the Early Church as They Move into the 21st Century." It describes the "lost secrets of the ancient church" that are being rediscovered by evangelicals. The ancient church in question happens to be the Roman Catholic.

Christianity Today recommends that evangelicals "stop debating" and just "embody Christianity." Toward this end they should "embrace symbols and sacraments" and dialogue with "Catholicism and Orthodoxy"; they should "break out the candles and incense," pray the "lectio divina," and learn the Catholic "ascetic disciplines" from "practicing monks and nuns."

The article ends with these amazing words:

> "This is the road to maturity. That more and more evangelicals have set out upon it is reason for hope for the future of gospel Christianity. That they are receiving good guidance on this road from wise teachers is reason to believe that Christ is guiding the process. And THAT THEY ARE MEETING AND LEARNING FROM FELLOW CHRISTIANS IN THE OTHER TWO GREAT CONFESSIONS, ROMAN CATHOLIC AND EASTERN ORTHODOX, IS REASON TO REJOICE IN THE POWER OF LOVE."

What *Christianity Today* sees as evidence of spiritual revival, we see as apostasy. This is a no holds barred invitation to Catholic mysticism, and it will not lead to light but to the same darkness that has characterized Rome throughout its history, and it will lead beyond Rome to the paganism from which Rome originally borrowed its "contemplative practices."

Contemplative spirituality is a broad road today, and on it you can find Mennonites, Lutherans, Southern Baptists, American Baptists, Methodists, Presbyterians, Vineyards, Nazarenes, Willow Creekers, Contemporary Christian rockers, Navigators, you name it. It is recommended by Rick Warren, Bill Hybels, Chuck Swindoll, David Jeremiah, Larry Crabb, Michael W. Smith, and a host of other influential voices.

Mysticism is also at the heart of the New Age philosophy that is permeating western society today. We have documented this in the book *The New Age Tower of Babel*.

Indeed, mysticism is a powerful end-time ecumenical-interfaith glue!

A DESCRIPTION OF THE CONTEMPLATIVE PRACTICES

Following is a description of some of the popular "Christian" contemplative practices. All of these were borrowed from Rome.

Centering Prayer

Centering prayer involves emptying the mind of conscious thoughts about God with the objective of entering into a non-verbal experiential union with God in the center of one's being.

Thomas Keating, one of the modern fathers of centering prayer, claims that "the simplest way to come into contact with the living God is to go to one's center and from there pass into God" (*Finding Grace at the Center*, p. 28).

Here is how he describes it:

> "Then we move in faith to God, Father, Son, and Holy Spirit, dwelling in creative love in the depths of our being. This is the whole essence of the prayer. ... All the rest of the method is simply a means to enable us to abide quietly in this center, and to allow our whole being to share in this refreshing contact with its Source" (*Finding Grace at the Center*, 2002, p. 32).
>
> "... savor the silence, the Presence..." (p. 35).
>
> "As soon as we move in love to God present in our depths, we are there ... we simply want to remain there and be what we are" (p. 39).
>
> "We might think of it as if the Lord Himself, present in our depths, were quietly repeating His own name, evoking His presence and very gently summoning us to an attentive response. We are quite passive. We let it happen" (p. 39).
>
> "... to enter into our Christ-being in the depths" (p. 42).
>
> "... we want immediate contact with God Himself, and not some thought, image, or vision of him..." (p. 42).
>
> "... open yourself interiorly to the mystery of God's enveloping presence" (p. 48).
>
> "... our theme is the center, that is, the place of meeting of the human spirit and the divine Spirit" (p. 80).

The practice is called "this union" (p. 15), this "face-to-face encounter" (p. 15), "passive meditation" (p. 20), "a fourth state of consciousness" (p. 34), "savoring the silence" (p. 35), "this nothing" (p. 49), "the deep waters of silence" (p. 52), "deep tranquility" (p. 54).

Centering prayer requires entering into a non-thinking mode. The 14th century book *The Cloud of Unknowing,* which is quoted extensively in the contemplative movement, describes this at length. The very title refers to the practice of entering a mystical state beyond knowledge. It is called "the blind experience of contemplative love," "this darkness," "this nothingness," "this nowhere."

Note the following statements:

> "Do all in your power to forget everything else, keeping your thoughts and desires free from involvement with any of God's creatures or their

> affairs whether in general or in particular ... pay no attention to them" (*The Cloud of Unknowing*, edited by William Johnston, Image Books, 1973, chapter 3, p. 48).

> "Thought cannot comprehend God. And so, I prefer to abandon all I can know, choosing rather to love him whom I cannot know. ... By love he may be touched and embraced, never by thought. ... in the real contemplative work you must set all this aside and cover it over with a cloud of forgetting" (chapter 6, pp. 54, 55).

> "... dismiss every clever or subtle thought no matter how holy or valuable. Cover it over with a thick cloud of forgetting because in this life only love can touch God as he is in himself, never knowledge" (chapter 8, pp. 59, 60).

> "So then, you must reject all clear conceptualizations whenever they arise, as they inevitably will, during the blind work of contemplative love. ... Therefore, firmly reject all clear ideas, however pious or delightful" (chapter 9, p. 60).

The Book of Privy Counseling, written by the author of *The Cloud of Unknowing*, says:

> "Reject all thoughts, be they good or be they evil" (*The Cloud of Unknowing* and *The Book of Privy Counseling*, edited by William Johnston, Image Books, 1973, chapter 1, p. 149).

A *MANTRA* is the key to entering the non-thinking mode. The practitioner is taught to choose "a sacred word" such as love or sin or God and repeat it until the mind is carried by that practice into a non-thinking communion with God at the center of one's being.

> "... the little word is used in order to sweep all images and thoughts from the mind, leaving it free to love with the blind stirring that stretches out toward God" (William Johnston, *The Cloud of Unknowing*, introduction, p. 10).

The practitioner is taught that he must not think on the meaning of the word.

> "... choose a short word ... a one-syllable word such as 'God' or 'love' is best. ... Then fix it in your mind so that it will be your defense in conflict and in peace. Use it to beat upon the cloud of darkness above you and to subdue all distractions, consigning them to the cloud of forgetting beneath you. ... If your mind begins to intellectualize over the meaning and connotations of this little word, remind yourself that its value lies in its simplicity. Do this and I assure you these thoughts

will vanish" (*The Cloud of Unknowing*, chapter 7, p. 56).

"... focus your attention on a simple word such as sin or God ... and WITHOUT THE INTERVENTION OF ANALYTICAL THOUGHT allow yourself to experience directly the reality it signifies. Do not use clever logic to examine or explain this word to yourself nor allow yourself to ponder its ramifications ... I DO NOT BELIEVE REASONING EVER HELPS IN THE CONTEMPLATIVE WORK. This is why I advise you to leave these words whole, like a lump, as it were" (*The Cloud of Unknowing*, chapter 36, p. 94).

The attempt to achieve a mindless mystical condition through a mantra can produce a mild hypnotic state and open one to demonic activity. Even if you don't consciously try to lose the meaning of the word, it quickly becomes lost to the mind. Ray Yungen, who has done extensive and excellent research into the New Age, explains:

"When a word or phrase is repeated over and over, after just a few repetitions, those words lose their meaning and become just sounds. ... After three or four times, the word can begin to lose its meaning, and if this repeating of words were continued, normal thought processes could be blocked, making it possible to enter an altered state of consciousness because of hypnotic effect that begins to take place. It really makes no difference whether the words are 'You are my God' or 'I am calm,' the results are the same" (*A Time of Departing*, p. 150).

Catholic contemplative master Anthony de Mello agrees with Yungen. He says:

"A Jesuit friend who loves to dabble in such things ... assures me that, through constantly saying to himself 'one-two-three-four' rhythmically, he achieves the same mystical results that his more religious conferees claim to achieve through the devout and rhythmical recitation of some ejaculation. And I believe him" (*Sadhana: A Way to God*, pp. 33, 34).

Centering prayer is so similar to the mystical practice of pagan religions that they recognize it as their own. In his introduction to *The Cloud of Unknowing*, William Johnston says the Catholic author of this 14th century work "speaks a language that Buddhists understand" (p. 11).

Practitioners of eastern religions recognize the power of the mantra in entering the meditative state. Hindu gurus say, "One thorn is removed by another." They are referring to the fact that the mind must be occupied with something; therefore, one word or thought can be used to drive away all others.

Deepak Chopra, a New Age Hindu who believes in the divinity of man, recommends *The Cloud of Unknowing*. He considers the Catholic centering prayer techniques to be the same as Hindu yoga.

> "There is no doubt that people resist the whole notion of God being an inner phenomenon. ... Yet its importance is stated eloquently in the medieval document known as 'The Cloud of Unknowing,' written anonymously in the fourteenth century. ... The writer informs us that ANY THOUGHT IN THE MIND SEPARATES US FROM GOD, because thought sheds light on its object. ... Even though the cloud of unknowing baffles us, it is actually closer to God than even a thought about God and his marvelous creation. We are advised to go into a 'cloud of forgetting' about anything other than the silence of the inner world. For centuries this document has seemed utterly mystical, but it makes perfect sense once we realize that the restful awareness response, WHICH CONTAINS NO THOUGHTS, is being advocated. ...
>
> "We aren't talking about the silence of an empty mind ... But the thought takes place against a background and nonthought. Our writer equates it with KNOWING SOMETHING THAT DOESN'T HAVE TO BE STUDIED. The mind is full of a kind of knowing that could speak to us about anything, yet it has no words; therefore we seek this knowingness in the background" (Chopra, *How to Know God*, 2000, pp. 94, 95, 98).

In this same book, Chopra says, "I believe that God has to be known by looking in the mirror" (p. 9). Thus Chopra is describing meditative methods whereby the individual can allegedly come into contact with his "higher self" or divinity, yet he is using Catholic mysticism to get there!

That the same manual (*The Cloud of Unknowing*) is also popular with contemplative *evangelicals* and that they teach the same techniques as this New Age Hindu guru is a loud warning to those who have ears to hear.

Richard Foster says, "Christian meditation is an attempt to empty the mind in order to fill it" (*Celebration of Discipline*, 1978, p. 15). He says, "[W]e must be willing to go down into the recreating silences..." (p. 15). He says the goal of contemplative prayer is "a pure relationship where we see 'nothing'" (*Prayer: Finding the Heart's True Home*, p. 155).

The result of centering prayer is supposed to be mystical knowledge obtained through communion with God in one's being.

> "For in this darkness we experience an intuitive understanding of everything material and spiritual without giving special attention to anything in particular" (*The Cloud of Unknowing*, chapter 68, p. 137).
>
> "He will let you glimpse something of the ineffable secrets of his divine wisdom..." (*The Cloud of Unknowing*, chapter 27, p. 84).
>
> "Often meditation will yield insights ... More than once I have received guidance ... it is far more common to be given guidance in dealing with ordinary human problems ... It tells us that God is speaking in the continuous present and wants to address us" (Richard Foster, *Celebration of Discipline*, 1978, pp. 17, 19).
>
> "... we learn that our willingness to listen in silence opens up a quiet space in which we can hear His voice, a voice that longs to speak and offer us guidance for our next step" (Ruth Barton, "Beyond Words," *Discipleship Journal*, Sept-Oct. 1999).

Catholic mystics claim that centering prayer is based on the example of Mary in Luke 10:38-42. William Johnson says:

> "Mary turned to Jesus with all the love of her heart, unmoved by what she saw or heard spoken and done about her. She sat there in perfect stillness with her heart's secret, joyous love intent upon *that cloud of unknowing* between her and her God. ... Jesus is present; he is the divine center to which Mary's love is directed. But she has no regard for clear cut images of his beautiful mortal body, no ears for the sweetness of his human voice. She has gone beyond all this to a deeper knowledge, a deeper love and a deeper beauty" (pp. 17, 18; see also *The Cloud of Unknowing*, chapter 17, p. 71).

This is an example of how Catholic contemplatives twist the Scripture. In reality, Mary was not practicing mystical contemplation. She did not empty her mind; she was not going beyond words to a deeper knowledge. She simply sat and listened to Christ speak. *"And she had a sister called Mary, which also sat at Jesus' feet, and heard his word"* (Luke 10:39). She was not trying to achieve union with God through mystical means. She knew that the Son of God was there in human flesh and that she did not have to know anything beyond Him. To know Christ is to know God! Rather than a "cloud of unknowing," Mary had perfect Revelation in the Person of Christ and in His spoken words, and so do we. *"God, who at sundry times and in divers manners spake in time past unto the fathers by the prophets, Hath in these last days spoken unto us by his Son..."* (Hebrews 1:1-2). *"For God, who commanded the light to shine out of darkness, hath shined in our hearts, to give the light of the knowledge of the glory of God in the face of Jesus Christ"* (2 Corinthians 4:6).

Centering prayer is actually a blind leap into the dark with no biblical authority.

Visualization or Imaginative Prayer

Visualization or imaginative prayer is becoming popular throughout evangelicalism.

Jesuit priest Anthony de Mello calls it "fantasy prayer" and says that many of the Catholic saints practiced it (*Sadhana: A Way to God*, pp. 79, 82, 93). Francis of Assisi imagined taking Jesus down from the cross; Anthony of Padua imagined holding the baby Jesus in his arms and talking with him; Teresa of Avila imagined herself with Jesus in His agony in the garden.

This type of thing is an integral part of the spiritual exercises of Ignatius of Loyola. The practitioner is instructed to walk into biblical and extra-biblical historical scenes through the imagination and bring the scene to life by applying all the senses, seeing the events, hearing what people are saying, smelling, tasting, and touching things--all within the realm of pure imagination. He is even to put himself into the scene, talking to the people and serving them. Ignatius encourages practitioners, for example, to imagine themselves present at Jesus' birth and crucifixion.

Consider some excerpts from Ignatius' *Spiritual Exercises*:

> "Imagine Christ our Lord present before you upon the cross, and begin to speak with him ..." (First Week, 53).
>
> "Here it will be to see in imagination the length, breadth, and depth of hell. ... to see in imagination the vast fires, and the souls enclosed ... to hear the wailing ... with the sense of smell to perceive the smoke ... to taste the bitterness ... to touch the flames" (First Week, fifth exercise, 65-70).
>
> "I will see and consider the Three Divine Persons, seated on the royal dais or throne of the Divine Majesty ... I will see our Lady and the angel saluting her. ... [I will see] our Lady, St. Joseph, the maid, and the Child Jesus after His birth. I will make myself a poor little unworthy slave, and as though present, look upon them, contemplate them, and serve them..." (Second Week, 106, 114).
>
> "While one is eating, let him imagine he sees Christ our Lord and His disciples at table, and consider how He eats and drinks, how He looks, how He speaks, and then strive to imitate Him" (Third Week, 214).

Thomas Merton gave an example of this in his book *Spiritual Direction and Meditation*. He said the individual can use this technique to communicate with the infant Jesus in His nativity.

> "In simple terms, the nativity of Christ the Lord in Bethlehem is not just something that I make present by fantasy. Since He is the eternal Word of God before whom time is entirely and simultaneously present, the Child born at Bethlehem 'sees' me here and now. That is to say, I 'am' present to His mind 'then.' It follows that I can speak to Him as to one present not only in fantasy but in actual reality. This spiritual contact with the Lord is the real purpose of meditation" (p. 96).

Merton claimed that this type of thing is not "fantasy," but it is nothing else but fantasy. It is true that Christ is eternal, but nowhere are we taught by the Lord or His apostles and prophets that we should try to imagine such a conversation.

Richard Foster recommends visualizing prayer in his popular book *Celebration of Discipline*:

> "Imagination opens the door to faith. If we can 'see' in our mind's eye a shattered marriage whole or a sick person well, it is only a short step to believing that it will be so. ... I was once called to a home to pray for a seriously ill baby girl. Her four-year-old brother was in the room and so I told him I needed his help to pray for his baby sister. ... He climbed up into the chair beside me. 'Let's play a little game,' I said. 'Since we know that Jesus is always with us, let's imagine that He is sitting over in the chair across from us. He is waiting patiently for us to center our attention on Him. When we see Him, we start thinking more about His love than how sick Julie is. He smiles, gets up, and comes over to us. Then let's both put our hands on Julie and when we do, Jesus will put His hands on top of ours. We'll watch and imagine that the light from Jesus is flowing right into your little sister and making her well. Let's pretend that the light of Christ fights with the bad germs until they are all gone. Okay!' Seriously the little one nodded. Together we prayed in this childlike way and then thanked the Lord that what we 'saw' was the way it was going to be" (*Celebration of Discipline*, 1978, p. 37).

This is not biblical prayer; it is occultism. New Agers have practiced this type of visualization for a century.

Foster recommends that parents pray for their sleeping children after this fashion:

> "Imagine the light of Christ flowing through your hands and healing every emotional trauma and hurt feeling your child experienced that day. Fill him or her with the peace and joy of the Lord. In sleep the child is very receptive to prayer since the conscious mind which tends to erect barriers to God's gentle influence is relaxed" (p. 39).

Foster describes "flash prayers" and "swish prayers" as follows:

> "Flashing hard and straight prayers at people is a great thrill and can bring interesting results. I have tried it, inwardly asking the joy of the Lord and a deeper awareness of His presence to rise up within every person I meet. Sometimes people reveal no response, but other times they turn and smile as if addressed. In a bus or plane we can fancy Jesus walking down the aisles touching people on the shoulder and saying, 'I love you...' Frank Laubach has suggested that if thousands of us would experiment with 'swishing prayers' at everyone we meet and would share the results, we could learn a great deal about how to pray for others. ... 'Units of prayer combined, like drops of water, make an ocean which defies resistance'" (*Celebration of Discipline*, p. 39).

This depicts prayer as an occultic entity rather than a simple communication addressed to God.

Visualization prayer has become very popular within the modern contemplative movement, but it is heretical.

First of all, visualization prayer is disobedience. The Bible contains everything we need for faith and practice. It is able to make the man of God *"perfect, throughly furnished unto all good works"* (2 Timothy 3:16-17). The Bible contains everything we need to learn how to pray correctly, and it says nothing whatsoever about imagination prayer. This is not the type of prayer that Jesus taught us to pray (Matthew 6:9-15).

Second, visualization prayer is vain and foolish because it is pure fantasy. We can't imagine Jesus' birth beyond the simple facts described in Scripture. We don't know what Mary or Joseph or baby Jesus or the room or the manger or the angels or the shepherds or the wise men looked like. We don't know what they said to one another. We don't know the temperature or the exact smells and tastes. If I try to imagine such things I am entering into the realm of vain fantasy.

Third, visualization prayer is not faith. Faith is not based on imagination; it is based on Scripture. *"So then faith cometh by hearing, and hearing by the word of God"* (Romans 10:17). God has given us everything we need in Scripture and our part is to believe what God says. *"But these are written, that ye might believe that Jesus is the Christ, the Son of God; and that believing ye might have life through his name"* (John 20:31). We have everything we need to know about Christ for the present in the Scripture, and we accept it by faith. "Whom HAVING NOT SEEN, ye love; in whom, THOUGH NOW YE SEE HIM NOT, yet believing, ye rejoice with joy unspeakable and full of glory" (1 Peter 1:8).

Fourth, visualization prayer is presumptuous because it goes beyond divine Revelation. Deuteronomy 29:29 says, *"The secret things belong unto the LORD our God: but those things which are revealed belong unto us and to our children for ever, that we may do all the words of this law.*" By going beyond what the Bible says and trying to delve into history through the imagination, I am leaving the revealed things and entering the secret things.

Fifth, visualization prayer is dangerous. It is dangerous because it adds to Scripture. If I get in the habit of visualizing Bible scenes, I can easily think that my visualizations are authoritative. I can fall into Rome's error of accepting extra-biblical revelations. It is also dangerous because demonic entities can involve themselves in my vain imaginings. Satan influenced Peter's thinking (Mat. 16:22-23), and he can certainly influence mine if I venture into forbidden realms.

Consider an example given by emerging church leader Tony Jones in his book *The Sacred Way*. His friend Mike King made John 1:37-39 the focus of contemplative practices at a spiritual retreat. While practicing the Ignatian exercise of imaginative prayer he put himself into the biblical scene. He imagined himself sitting around John's breakfast fire with the disciples, listening as they carried on an imaginative conversation. He imagined seeing Jesus approach and embrace John and hearing them tell stories of their childhood. He imagined them laughing. Then he imagined Jesus getting up and leaving, with John's disciples following. He imagined them walking into the desert and coming to a clearing, when suddenly the imagined Jesus turned around and began interacting with him.

> "When Jesus turned around, the two disciples of John whom I was following parted like the Red Sea and Jesus came right up to me, face to face. Jesus looked past my eyes into my heart and soul: 'Mike, what do you want?' I fell at the feet of Jesus and wept, pouring my heart out" (*The Sacred Way*, p. 79).

Notice that the imaginative prayer practitioner feels at liberty to go far beyond the words of Scripture to fantasize about the passage, creating purely fictional scenes. And observe that the *Jesus* that he imagines (which is certainly *not* the Jesus of the Bible because we do not know what that Jesus looks like and nowhere are we instructed to imagine seeing him) takes on a life of its own and interacts with him. This is either pure mental fiction and therefore absolutely meaningless, or it is a demonic visitation akin to a vision of Mary.

King says that he was powerfully affected by this imagined event. "That day changed me profoundly and is something I will have for the rest of my life, for Jesus said, 'Come, and you will see…'

He thus pretends that Jesus actually said this directly to him, when in fact he only imagined it in a purely fictitious sense.

Following is an example from Youth Specialties, a large evangelical youth ministry. They encourage young people to imagine a conversation with Jesus along the following line:

> It's a normal day like any other. You're busy doing what you do. But as you go about your daily routine, you sense someone wanting to spend time with you. He wants you to come to him. He wants you to be with him. You definitely recognize his voice, but it's been a while since you've spent any real time together. Doesn't he know how busy your life can be? After all, you've been busy doing what you do.
>
> He sits there, hunkered down in the corner of your room waiting for you. He's certainly not pushing himself on you, but you can definitely tell he longs to spend some time with you. You tell him that you don't think you'll have time to meet with him today as you head out the door again.
>
> When you get back from your day, he's there again, waiting for you. He smiles at you as you come in the door and asks you how your day has been. He invites you to sit down and rest for a while. You can tell he wants to hear about your day and everything else you've got going on in your life. He seems very proud of who you are becoming. He asks you about what seems to be pressing in on you and weighing you down. You can tell he genuinely cares about you. He wants what's best for you. So you finally decide to sit down for a few minutes to talk with him.
>
> You start by telling him that you can't talk long because you still have a lot to do before bedtime. But after a few minutes of talking together, your whole world and all the worries of your day seem to simply melt away. You haven't felt this relaxed in a long time. You find yourself pouring your heart out to him. And then he looks you right in the eyes

and tells you how proud he is of you. He tells you how much he loves you and enjoys spending time together.

At that moment you realize this friend who has been waiting to talk with you day after day is Jesus. He has never made you feel guilty about blowing him off day after day. He looks at you and smiles. Its' at that moment that you can tell for the first time in your life that you have a true friend who cares about you for who you are. The time seems to fly by as you continue talking together late into the night ("Something for Your Heart: Guided Meditation," Youth Specialties Student Newsletter #330, Feb. 25, 2008).

This is heretical foolishness. The Lord Jesus Christ is not hunkered down in someone's bedroom. He is enthroned in Heaven at the right hand of the Father. He is not a non-judgmental Big Buddy who exists to build up my self-esteem. He is the Lord of Glory. He is kind and compassionate, but He does not exist to pamper me; I exist to glorify Him!

Observe that this guided meditation mentions nothing about the confession of sin or repentance from sin, nothing about the necessity of obedience and walking in the fear of God and separation from evil in order to maintain fellowship with Christ. The Bible, though, says:

> "If we say that we have fellowship with him, and walk in darkness, we lie, and do not the truth. But if we walk in the light, as he is in the light, we have fellowship one with another, and the blood of Jesus Christ his Son cleanseth us from all sin. If we say that we have no sin, we deceive ourselves, and the truth is not in us. If we confess our sins, he is faithful and just to forgive us our sins, and to cleanse us from all unrighteousness" (1 John 1:6-9).

Calvin Miller claims that "imagination stands at the front of our relationship with Christ."

> "I drink the glory [of Christ's] hazel eyes ... his auburn hair. ... What? Do you disagree? His hair is black? Eyes brown? Then have it your way. ... His image must be real to you as to me, even if our images differ. The key to vitality, however, is the image" (*The Table of Inwardness*, InterVarsity Press, 1984, p. 93).

Each individual can therefore have the christ of his own making through the amazing power of imagination!

The Jesus Prayer

The Jesus Prayer originated within Eastern Orthodox mysticism.

In its most ancient and simple form it consists of repeating the name "Jesus" with every breath.

In another form it consists of repeating, "Lord Jesus Christ, have mercy upon me," or, "Lord Jesus Christ, Son of God, have mercy on me a sinner."

This is to be repeated throughout the day. J.P. Moreland and Klaus Issler recommend saying the Jesus Prayer 300 times a day (*The Lost Virtue of Happiness*, p. 90).

The ancient monastic contemplative manuals suggest that it be said from 3,000 to 12,000 times a day (Tony Jones, *The Sacred Way*, p. 60).

This is supposed to keep one's mind centered on Christ and sensitive to His will.

> "As you do, something will begin to happen to you. God will begin to slowly begin to occupy the center of your attention" (*The Lost Virtue of Happiness*, pp. 90, 92, 93).

Commonly the practitioner is taught not to think on the words but to allow them to speak to him "intuitively."

> "Trying to mentally grasp the meaning of each word of the prayer as we pray it would be mentally confusing. This would be a distraction from prayer. Rather, the full meaning of the Jesus Prayer is best grasped when intuited on the level of spirit beyond the senses, the emotions, or the mind" (Talbot, *The Way of the Mystics*, p. 192).

John Michael Talbot says that the practitioner should "go into the heights of contemplation beyond all concepts and knowledge" (*Come to the Quiet*, p. 176).

This is always the real mystical objective.

The Breath Prayer

The Breath Prayer, which is recommended by Richard Foster in his book *Prayer: Finding the Heart's True Home*, consists of picking a single word or short phrase and repeating it in conjunction with breathing.

John Talbot recommends using the Jesus prayer as a breath prayer. He says his own practice is to say "Lord, Jesus Christ, Son of God" as he breathes in and "have mercy on me, a sinner" as he breathes out (*Come to the Quiet*, p. 175).

Lectio Divina

The term "lectio divina" is Latin and means divine or sacred reading. It is a Catholic monastic method of reading the Scripture in a mystical way.

Upon its face, *lectio divina* might not appear very different from a traditional devotional time that involves reading and meditating on Scripture in communion with the Holy Spirit. Where it differs is as follows:

First, lectio divina does not refer to "meditation" in a Scriptural sense.

Proponents of *lectio divina* point to passages of Scripture that refer to "meditation" (e.g., Joshua 1:8; Psalm 1:2) and the uninformed reader would be led to believe that they are describing a Scriptural practice. In fact, they are describing something very different.

Consider a description of *lectio divina*. The practitioner is taught to begin with deep breathing exercises and repetition of a "prayer word" *to enter into a contemplative state*. This refers to a mantra. The goal is to "become interiorly silent" (Luke Dysinger, "Accepting the Embrace of God: The Ancient Art of Lectio Divina," *Valyermo Benedictine*, Spring 1990). Having prepared himself, the practitioner reads a portion of Scripture slowly and repeatedly, three or four times. He slowly repeats a word or phrase from the passage, allowing it to interact with his "inner world of concerns, memories and ideas." Next he converses with God about the text. Finally, he rests in silence before God. Catholic priest Luke Dysinger says, "Once again we practice SILENCE, LETTING GO OF OUR OWN WORDS; this time simply enjoying the experience of being in the presence of God."

Notice how Thomas Merton describes the meditation performed in *lectio divina* and other Catholic contemplative practices:

> "Meditation is ... a series of interior activities which prepare us for union with God" (*Spiritual Direction and Meditation*, 1960, p. 54).
>
> "Meditation is more than mere practical thinking" (p. 55).
>
> "... the fruitful silence in which words lose their power and concepts escape our grasp is perhaps the perfection of meditation" (p. 57).
>
> "More often than not, we can be content to simply rest, and float peacefully with the deep current of love, doing nothing of ourselves, but allowing the Holy Spirit to act in the secret depths of our soul" (pp. 101, 102).

Richard Foster, who has had a far-reaching influence on the emerging church's contemplative practices, quotes Catholic mystic Madame Guyon as follows:

> "Once you sense the Lord's presence, THE CONTENT OF WHAT YOU READ IS NO LONGER IMPORTANT. The scripture has served its purpose; it has quieted your mind; it has brought you to him. ... You should always remember that YOU ARE NOT THERE TO GAIN AN UNDERSTANDING OF WHAT YOU HAVE READ; rather you are reading to turn your mind from the outward things to the deep parts of your being. YOU ARE NOT THERE TO LEARN OR TO READ, BUT YOU ARE THERE TO EXPERIENCE THE PRESENCE OF YOUR LORD!" (*Devotional Classics*).

Thelma Hall's book on *lectio divina* is titled *Too Deep for Words*. This describes the ultimate objective of the mystical practice.

Robert Webber, late Wheaton College professor, confirms the transcendental aspect of *lectio divina*:

> "The goal of *Lectio Divina* is union with God through a meditative and contemplative praying of Scripture. ... All such attempts at verbalizing the experience necessarily fail to express the reality for the simple reason that CONTEMPLATION TRANSCENDS THE THINKING AND REASONING of meditation ... *Contemplatio* shifts praying the Scripture into a new language (SILENCE). This silence does not ask us to do anything, it is a call to being. Thomas Merton says, 'THE BEST WAY TO PRAY IS: STOP'" (*The Divine Embrace: Recovering the Passionate Spiritual Life*, 2006, pp. 209, 210).

John Michael Talbot says that *lectio divina* must move the practitioner "into a Reality BEYOND IMAGE AND FORM" (*Come to the Quiet*, p. 49). He says, "If God grants it, allow the reality of the sacred text to pass over to pure spiritual intuition in his Spirit," and, "... allow yourself to pass over into contemplation BEYOND WORDS" (pp. 53, 62).

It is obvious that meditation and prayer after the *lectio divina* fashion is far removed from simply contemplating on the Scripture before the Lord and seeking better understanding of it and talking with God about it and applying it to one's life.

Second, lectio divina associates one with centuries-old heresy.

Lectio divina was invented by the heretic Origen in the third century and was adopted as a Roman Catholic practice in the Dark Ages. Origen is a dangerous man to follow. Among other heresies, he denied the infallible inspiration of Scripture and the literal history of the early chapters of Genesis, taught baptismal regeneration and universalism and believed that Jesus was a created being.

The practice of *lectio divina* was incorporated into the rules of Rome's dark monasticism. It was systematized into four steps in the 12th century by Guido II, a Carthusian monk, in "The Ladder of Four Rungs" or "The Monk's Ladder." The four steps are reading, meditation, prayer, and contemplation, which are supposed to be the means by which one "can climb from earth to heaven" and learn "heavenly secrets."

Thus, *lectio divina* is intimately associated with Roman Catholicism and its false gospel. Modern *lectio divina* gurus such as Thomas Merton and Thomas Keating follow in the footsteps of ancient Catholic heretics by intertwining the practice with the heresies of Rome. Merton, for example, associates *lectio divina* with the Mass (which he describes as a "living and supremely efficacious re-presentation of Christ's sacrifice"), baptismal regeneration, meriting union with God, prayers to Mary, and salvation through works (*Spiritual Direction and Meditation*, pp. 62, 71, 72, 74, 108).

Bible believers have maintained rich devotional practices throughout the church age without resorting to something invented by heretics and developed in the bosom of the Harlot Church.

Third, lectio divina is typically used as a means of receiving personal revelation and mystical experiences beyond the words of Scripture.

Youth Specialties' *Youth Worker Journal* says of *lectio divina*, "THE GOAL ISN'T EXEGESIS OR ANALYSIS, but allowing God to speak to us through the word" (quoted from Brian Flynn, "Lectio Divina--Sacred Divination").

This refers to a mystical knowing and a transcendental revelation that supposedly exists beyond conscious thought.

Brian Flynn makes an important observation:

> "The concept of allowing God to speak through His Word is perfectly legitimate. I experience that when I read or meditate on the Bible. However, in the context of this [Youth Specialties'] article the purpose is not to contemplate the meaning of a Bible verse by thinking about it but is rather meant to gain an experience from it."

Thomas Keating says: "The early monks ... would sit with that sentence or phrase ... just listening, repeating slowly the same short text over and over again. This receptive disposition enabled the Holy Spirit to expand their capacity to listen" ("The Classical Monastic Practice of Lectio Divina").

The danger of the *lectio divina* method is illustrated by the fact that its practitioners are taught heresy by this means. Consider a revelation that Basil Pennington said he received through *lectio divina*. He said that he chose Christ's words "I am the way" from John 14:6 and repeated them during his meditation and throughout the day. At the end of the day when he was tired and wasn't looking forward to singing evening prayers at the monastery he says the Lord spoke to him and said, "Oh yes, you are the way," so he "went and sang Vespers and had a great time" (interview with Mary NurrieStearns published on the Personal Transformation website, http://www.personaltransformation.com/Pennington.html). Note that "the Lord" allegedly took the declaration that Christ is the way and applied it to Pennington, instructing him that he, too, is the way, which is rank heresy.

We believe strongly in studying Scripture and seeking God's illumination of it, but this is done through a process of interpretive Bible study and active contemplation rather than through a mystical process that seeks to go beyond the Bible's words and is intimately associated with heresy.

Former psychic Brian Flynn warns:

> "By taking passages of Scripture, which have an intended meaning, and breaking them down into smaller, separate segments, often for the purpose of chanting over and over, the true meaning of the passages are lost. Rather a form of occult mysticism is practiced--with the hope and intention of gaining a mystical experience that God never intended when He gave the inspired words to His servants" (*Running against the Wind*, p. 136).

Fourth, the traditional practice of lectio divina involves the search for a "deeper" meaning of Scripture.

This refers to Origen's spiritualized meaning that is beyond the literal. Origen claimed the Scripture has four levels of meaning and he emphasized the "allegorical" sense above all others. This error leaves the interpretation of Scripture up to the imagination of the reader, because if the Bible does not mean exactly what it says when interpreted by the normal-literal method, then we cannot know for certain what it does mean. This is one of the foundational errors of Roman monasticism, and it is being adopted today by the emerging church.

Thomas Keating says: "By 'ruminating' I mean sitting with a sentence, phrase or even one word that emerges from the text, allowing the Spirit to expand our listening capacity and to OPEN US TO ITS DEEPER MEANING; in other words, TO PENETRATE THE SPIRITUAL SENSE of a scripture passage" ("The Classical Monastic Practice of Lectio Divina").

It is obvious that this "deeper meaning" carries one beyond the true meaning of Scripture, since it is a practice that is loved by Roman Catholics. For centuries Catholic monks and nuns have "meditated" on the Scripture via the method of *lectio divina* but they have never come to the knowledge of the truth! It has only confirmed them in their commitment to Rome's heresies.

Fifth, the practice of lectio divina does not include a strong warning about the potential for spiritual delusion and the danger of receiving "doctrines of devils."

Priest Luke Dysinger says, "Rejoice in the knowledge that God is with you in both words and silence, in spiritual activity and inner receptivity" ("Accepting the Embrace of God: The Ancient Art of Lectio Divina"). If Dysinger, who is a modern monk, would practice biblical devotion in true communion with the Spirit of truth he would recognize that Romanism is heresy and would flee from it, but he is practicing contemplative practices from a position of spiritual blindness and unknowing openness to deception.

Brian Flynn gives an important warning about this practice when he says:

> "I was having a discussion over lunch with a pastor who taught *Lectio Divina* at a local seminary, and he attempted to defend the practice.

He stated that in the process of reading a page of scripture over and over again a word will 'jump out' at you. He said that the Holy Spirit chooses this word for you. However, how do I know that this concept is true? First, there is no reference to *Lectio Divina* in the Bible. Secondly, how do I know what this word is supposed to mean to me? If it were 'love', does that mean I should concentrate on love for self, God, the world, sister, mother, brother? There is no way of knowing other than using my own imagination or desire. ... BY USING THIS PRACTICE, WE ARE TURNING THE BIBLE INTO A MYSTICAL DEVICE FOR PERSONAL REVELATIONS RATHER THAN A SOURCE OF KNOWLEDGE. By taking passages of Scripture, which have an intended meaning, and breaking them down into smaller, separate segments, often for the purpose of chanting over and over, the true meaning of the passages are lost" ("Lectio Divina--Sacred Divination").

Sixth, the practice of lectio divina is contrary to the Bible's instruction about Scripture study.

The New Testament does not instruct the believer to sit in silence before God or to put himself into a contemplative-receptive state. It does not instruct us to use the Scripture to try to "experience God." It instructs us to study as a workman (2 Tim. 2:15). This is an active process rather than a passive one. In the proper practice of Bible study, the mind is fully in gear; the spirit is aggressively seeking God's wisdom and is wary of deception; one is prayerful, seeking divine help; he knows that it is dangerous to isolate Scripture, so he carefully analyzes the context and compares Scripture with Scripture. The wise Bible student does not depend upon his own intuitions about the meaning of Scripture exclusively but consults trusted men of God and carefully uses godly dictionaries and commentaries.

The Stations of the Cross

The Stations of the Cross is a Roman Catholic practice that combines mysticism and heresy. The 14 Stations allegedly depict Christ's trial and crucifixion, and the practitioner seeks to enter mystically into Christ's passion by meditating on each scene.

Beyond the fact that this is not faith but sight and the pictures of Jesus are fictional and are forbidden by Scripture, some of the 14 Stations are purely legendary. Jesus supposedly falls down three times, meets Mary on the way to the cross, has His face wiped by a woman named Veronica, and is taken down from the cross and laid in Mary's arms. None of this is supported by Scripture.

The Mass

The Mass or Eucharist is the highpoint of mysticism in the Roman Catholic Church. As we shall see, it was the very heart and soul of ancient Catholic monastic mysticism and it remains so today. The monks and nuns center their lives on the Mass.

What could be more mystical than touching God with your hands and taking Him into your very being by eating him in the form of a wafer? In the Mass the strangely-clothed, mysterious priest (ordained after the order of Melchisedec) pronounces words that mystically turn a wafer of unleavened bread into the very body of Jesus. The consecrated wafers are eaten by the people. One larger wafer, called the host (which means victim or sacrifice), is placed in a monstrance to be worshipped ("adored") as God. Eventually the host is placed in its own little tabernacle as the center of worship between Masses.

This highly mystical ritual is multisensory, involving touch (dipping the finger into holy water), sight (the splendor of the church and the priestly garments and the instruments of the Mass), smell (incense), hearing (chanting, bells), and taste (eating the wafer).

The Mass is even said to bring man into "divine union" like other forms of contemplative mysticism (Thomas à Kempis, *The Imitation of Christ*, Book IV, chap. 15, 4, p. 210).

The Second Vatican Council reaffirmed the centrality of the Mass in Catholic life:

"The celebration of the Mass ... is the centre of the whole Christian life for the universal Church, the local Church and for each and every one of the faithful. For therein is the culminating action whereby God sanctifies the world in Christ and men worship the Father as they adore him through Christ the Son of God" (Vatican II, "The Constitution on the Sacred Liturgy, General Instruction on the Roman Missal," chap. 1, 1, p. 159).

The Catholic Mass is not a mere remembrance of Christ's death; it is a re-sacrifice of Christ, and the consecrated host IS Christ.

"The victim is one and the same: the same now offers through the ministry of priests, who then offered himself on the cross; only the manner of offering is different. And since in this divine sacrifice which is celebrated in the Mass, the same Christ who offered himself once in a bloody manner on the altar of the cross is contained and offered in an unbloody manner... this sacrifice is truly propitiatory" (Council of Trent, *Doctrina de ss. Missae sacrificio*, c. 2, quoted in *Catechism of the Catholic Church*, 1367).

"For in the sacrifice of the Mass Our Lord is immolated when 'he begins to be present sacramentally as the spiritual food of the faithful under the appearances of bread and wine.' ... For in it Christ perpetuates in an unbloody manner the sacrifice offered on the cross, offering himself to the Father for the world's salvation through the ministry of priests" (Vatican II, "The Constitution on the Sacred Liturgy," Instruction on the Worship of the Eucharistic Mystery, Introduction, C 1,2, p. 108).

"By the consecration the transubstantiation of the bread and wine into the Body and Blood of Christ is brought about. Under the consecrated species of bread and wine Christ himself, living and glorious, is present in a true, real and substantial manner: his Body and his Blood, with his soul and his divinity" (*New Catholic Catechism*, 1314).

"The Council of Trent summarizes the Catholic faith by declaring "... by the consecration of the bread and wine there takes place a change of the whole substance of the bread into the substance of the body of Christ our Lord and of the whole substance of the wine into the substance of his blood. This change the holy Catholic Church has fittingly and properly called transubstantiation" (*New Catholic Catechism*, 1376).

"Because Christ himself is present in the sacrament of the altar he is to be honoured with the worship of adoration" (*New Catholic Catechism*, 1418).

> "The sacrifice of Christ and the sacrifice of the Eucharist are one single sacrifice ... 'In this divine sacrifice which is celebrated in the Mass, the same Christ who offered himself once in a bloody manner on the altar of the cross is contained and offered in an unbloody manner' (*New Catholic Catechism*, 1367)

> "In the liturgy of the Mass we express our faith in the real presence of Christ under the species of bread and wine by, among other ways, genuflecting or bowing deeply as a sign of adoration of the Lord. ... reserving the consecrated hosts with the utmost care, exposing them to the solemn veneration of the faithful, and carrying them in procession" (*New Catholic Catechism*, 1378).

The consecrated host is therefore worshipped as Christ. At the completion of the Mass the host is placed in a little box called a tabernacle and left there to be worshipped.

> "The faithful should therefore strive to worship Christ our Lord in the Blessed Sacrament. ... Pastors [priests] should exhort them to this, and set them a good example. ... The place in a church or oratory where the Blessed Sacrament is reserved in the tabernacle should be truly prominent. It ought to be suitable for private prayer so that the faithful may easily and fruitfully, by private devotion also, continue to honour our Lord in this sacrament" (Vatican II, "The Constitution on the Sacred Liturgy, Instruction on the Worship of the Eucharistic Mystery," Chap. 3, I B, p. 132).

It is obvious that the Mass is not a Scriptural practice. The apostle Paul, under divine inspiration, taught the churches the significance of the Lord's Supper (1 Corinthians 11:17-34), and he did not say that it is a repetition of Christ's sacrifice. It is not Christ becoming a piece of bread. It is not an occasion to eat Christ or partake of him "sacramentally." It is a simple memorial meal, a time of remembrance and confession and worship.

> "For I have received of the Lord that which also I delivered unto you, That the Lord Jesus the same night in which he was betrayed took bread: And when he had given thanks, he brake it, and said, Take, eat: this is my body, which is broken for you: this do IN REMEMBRANCE OF me. After the same manner also he took the cup, when he had supped, saying, This cup is the new testament in my blood: this do ye, as oft as ye drink it, IN REMEMBRANCE OF me" (1 Corinthians 11:23-25).

Paul said that he received this teaching directly from the Lord. It is authoritative. He is the divinely-chosen apostle of the Gentiles, and he praised the churches for keeping the ordinances that he delivered to them (1 Corinthians 11:2).

Speaking for all Catholic nuns and priests, Mother Teresa said that her Jesus is the consecrated wafer of the Mass. In her speech at the Worldwide Retreat for Priests, October 1984, in the Paul VI Audience Hall at Vatican City, she made the following statements:

> "At the word of a priest, THAT LITTLE PIECE OF BREAD BECOMES THE BODY OF CHRIST, the Bread of Life. Then you give this living Bread to us, so that we too might live and become holy" (Mother Teresa, cited in *Be Holy: God's First Call to Priests Today*, edited by Tom Forrest, C.Ss.R., foreword by Msgr. John Magee, South Bend, Indiana: Greenlawn Press, 1987, p. 108).

> "I remember the time a few years back, when the president of Yemen asked us to send some of our sisters to his country. I told him that this was difficult because for so many years no chapel was allowed in Yemen for saying a public mass, and no one was allowed to function there publicly as a priest. I explained that I wanted to give them sisters, but the trouble was that, without a priest, without Jesus going with them, our sisters couldn't go anywhere. It seems that the president of Yemen had some kind of a consultation, and the answer that came back to us was, 'Yes, you can send a priest with the sisters!' I was so struck with the thought that ONLY WHEN THE PRIEST IS THERE CAN WE HAVE OUR ALTAR AND OUR TABERNACLE AND OUR JESUS. ONLY THE PRIEST CAN PUT JESUS THERE FOR US. ... Jesus wants to go there, but we cannot bring him unless you first give him to us" (Mother Teresa, *Be Holy*, pp. 109, 111).

> "One day she [a girl working in Calcutta] came, putting her arms around me, and saying, 'I have found Jesus.' ... 'And just what were you doing when you found him?' I asked. She answered that after 15 years she had finally gone to confession, and received Holy Communion from the hands of a priest. Her face was changed, and she was smiling. She was a different person because THAT PRIEST HAD GIVEN HER JESUS" (Mother Teresa, *Be Holy*, p. 74).

Some Catholics have charged me with misrepresenting their church, but surely the Second Vatican Council and the *New Catholic Catechism* and Mother Teresa are authentic voices. Mother Teresa plainly stated that her Jesus was the wafer of the Mass.

In the 1990s I visited a cloistered nunnery in Quebec. A pastor friend took me with him when he visited his aunt who had lived there for many decades. He and his wife wanted to show the nun their new baby. The nun wasn't allowed to come out into the meeting room to see us; she had to stay behind a metal grill and talk to us from there. The nuns pray in shifts before the consecrated host in the chapel. That is their Jesus and the object of their prayers. At the entrance of the chapel there was a sign that said, "YOU ARE ENTERING TO ADORE THE JESUS-HOST." Nuns were sitting in the chapel facing the host and praying their rosaries and saying their prayers to Mary and their "Our Fathers" and other repetitious mantras that are contrary to Scripture, vainly and sadly wiling away their lives in ascetic apostasy.

We will see that the Catholic saints, who are so exalted today by contemplatives, worshipped the Jesus-host of the Mass.

Many modern converts to Romanism mention the power of the Mass in their conversion. There is doubtless a true occultic power in this ritual.

It is no wonder that the emerging church is so enthralled with the "eucharist." It is a mystical powerhouse.

The Labyrinth

The labyrinth is a circle with a twisting path that winds its way to the center and is used for prayer and meditation. The International Labyrinth Society says it is a "tool for personal, psychological and spiritual transformation."

Used by pagan religions for centuries before the coming of Christ, the labyrinth was "Christianized" by the Roman Catholic Church as part of its desperate search for spirituality apart from the Bible.

Native Americans called it the Medicine Wheel; Celts called it the Never Ending Circle; it is called the Kabala in mystical Judaism (http://www.gracecathedral.org/labyrinth).

The most famous labyrinth was built into the floor of the Roman Catholic Chartres Cathedral in France in the 13th century. This has been duplicated at the Riverside Church in New York City and Grace Cathedral (Episcopal) in San Francisco, both hotbeds of theological liberalism and New Age philosophy.

The three stages of the labyrinth testify to its pagan origins. (This is from the Grace Cathedral web site.) The stages are *Purgation* ("a time to open the heart and quiet the mind"), *Illumination* ("a place of meditation and prayer"), *Union* ("joining God, your Higher Power, or the healing forces at work in the world").

Ray Yungen observes that the practice is associated with centering prayer:

> "Those walking the labyrinth will generally engage in centering or contemplative prayer by repeating a chosen word or phrase while they walk, with the hope that when they reach the center of the labyrinth, they will have also centered down and reached the divinity within" (*A Time of Departing*, p. 179).

Lauren Artress, a canon at Grace Cathedral, founded Veriditas, The World-Wide Labyrinth Project, with the goal "to facilitate the transformation of the Human Spirit." Observe that Human Spirit is capitalized, testifying to the New Age view that man finds divinity within himself. Artress says that she discovered the labyrinth in 1991 through Jean Houston's Mystery School, a New Age organization. The following quote by Houston leaves no doubt as to her philosophy:

> "As we encounter the archetypal world within us, a partnership is formed whereby WE GROW AS DO THE GODS AND GODDESSES WITHIN US" ("The Odyssey of the Soul," http://www.thinking-allowed.com/2jhouston.html).

Exercises at her Mystery School Network include psychospiritual exploration, energy resonance, and altered states of consciousness (http://www.jeanhouston.org).

Artress says:

> "My passion for the labyrinth has never let up! I think this is because I get so much from it. I also can teach everything I want to teach through the labyrinth: meditation, finding our soul assignments, unleashing our creativity, spiritual practice, psycho-spiritual healing; you name it! .... IT HAS THE EXACT COSMIC RHYTHMS EMBEDDED WITHIN IT. I sense that this design was created by great masters of Spirit, who knew the pathway to integrating mind, body and spirit" (Interview with Arts and Healing Network, September 2003).

It is obvious that the labyrinth is an effective tool for New Age occultic experience. That the same pagan-derived practice would be adopted by evangelicals is a loud testimony of evangelicalism's apostasy and its frightful communion with "doctrines of devils."

There is, of course, nothing like a labyrinth in the Bible.

THE HISTORY AND ERROR OF CATHOLIC MONASTICISM

Catholic monasticism, as practiced by its monks and nuns since the time of the "desert fathers," is built upon a foundation of doctrinal heresy, such as the following: that man contributes to his own salvation, that spiritual purification comes through ascetic practices, that "celibacy" is a holier state than marriage, that Mary can hear and answer prayers, and that the Mass is a transubstantiation of bread into Jesus Christ.

The term "ascetic" is from the Greek word "askesis," meaning training or exercise. It usually refers to self denial, renunciation of worldly pursuits, and abstinence from sensual pleasures such as food, sleep, marriage, comfortable and clean clothing, human society, and personal possessions.

Monasticism" means solitary. *Monk* means "one who lives alone."

The objective of Catholic ascetism is to save the soul, to overcome sin and purify the heart and mind, and to encounter God in an experiential way.

It was founded in early centuries after the apostles and was developed particularly in Egypt, which was a hotbed of theological heresy.

The so-called Desert Fathers doubtless borrowed contemplative practices from the pagan east.

> "The meditation practices and rules for living of these earliest Christian monks bear strong similarity to those of their Hindu and Buddhist renunciate brethren several kingdoms to the East ... the meditative techniques they adopted for finding their God suggest either a borrowing from the East or a spontaneous rediscovery" (Ray Yungren, *A Time of Departing*, p. 42).

Bede Griffiths, a Benedictine monk who is influential in the contemplative movement today, said the "neoplatonism" of the Desert Fathers "is the nearest equivalent in the West of the Vedantic tradition of Hinduism in the East" (*Christian Mystics*, p. 59).

Ursula King, in her history of Christian mysticism, traces its origin to Alexandria, Egypt, where "members of the new Jesus movement ... desired to combine their faith with the insights of Greek philosophy" (*Christian Mystics*, p. 27). She observes that all of the founders of monastic mysticism synthesized pagan philosophy with the Bible (pp. 27, 30, 31, 54).

The writings of Clement of Alexandria (115-215), Origen (185-254), Jerome (340-420), Augustine (354-430), and Dionysius the Areopagite (c. 500) paved the way for mystical ascetism.

CLEMENT OF ALEXANDRIA (Titus Flavius Clement), who is called "the first writer on mystical theology" (Ursula King, *Christian Mystics*, p. 29), was "deeply influenced by Greek philosophy" (p. 30). He appropriated mystical themes from Plato. His doctrine of Christ and God was heretical. Clement was one of the fathers of the allegorical method of interpreting the Bible, foisting wild-eyed "spiritual" meanings on the passages. He was one of the fathers of the heresy of purgatory, held to baptismal regeneration, and taught that most men will be saved. He believed that men could become God. He wrote, "I say, the Logos or God became man so that you may learn from man how man may become God" (*Christian Mystics*, p. 32). He also wrote: "That which is true is beautiful; for it, too, is God. Such a man becomes God because God wills it. Rightly, indeed, did Heraclitus say: 'Men are gods, and gods are men; for the same reason is in both'" (W.A. Jurgens, *The Faith of the Early Fathers*).

ORIGEN taught baptismal regeneration and salvation by works. He believed the Holy Spirit was possibly a created being of some sort. He believed in a form of purgatory and universalism, denying the literal fire of Hell and believing that even Satan would be saved eventually. He taught that men's souls are preexistent and that even stars and planets possibly have souls. He believed that Jesus was a created being and not eternal. He denied the bodily resurrection, claiming that the resurrection body is spherical, non-material, and does not have members. (For documentation of these heresies see *Faith vs. the Modern Bible Versions*, which is available from Way of Life Literature.)

Origen believed in the supremacy of celibacy and even castrated himself.

He allegorized the Bible saying, "The Scriptures have little use to those who understand them literally."

JEROME was "a vocal champion of Christian asceticism" and had "a profound influence on the development of clerical celibacy and monasticism in the West" ("Jerome," VirtualReligion.net). The first work he published was a biography of Paul the Hermit. Jerome lived for five years as a hermit in the desert southwest of Antioch doing "ascetic penance," and he spent the last years of his life in a "hermit's cell" near Bethlehem. He believed the state of virginity to be spiritually superior to that of marriage and demanded that church leaders be unmarried. He said, "I praise marriage, but it is because they give me virgins" (Jerome's Letter XXII to Eustochium, section 20). Historian James Heron observed that "no single individual did so much to make monasticism popular in the higher ranks of society" (Heron, *The Evolution of Latin Christianity*, 1919, p. 58).

Jerome "took a leading and influential part in 'opening the floodgates' for the invocation of saints," teaching "distinctly and emphatically that the saints in heaven hear the prayers of men on earth, intercede on their behalf and send them help from above" (Heron, pp. 287, 88). Jerome promoted veneration of holy relics and bones; he taught that Mary was instrumental in salvation and is a perpetual virgin. He taught that Mary was the counterpart of Eve as Christ was the counterpart of Adam, and that through her obedience Mary became instrumental in helping to redeem the human race (Heron, p. 294). Jerome was vicious toward those with whom he disagreed (calling them dogs, maniacs, monsters, stupid fools, two-legged asses, madmen). He laid the groundwork for the Catholic inquisition by arguing for "heretics" to be persecuted and even put to death (Heron, p. 323). Historian Philip Schaff said Jerome had "an intolerant and persecuting spirit" (*History of the Christian Church*, III, p. 206).

AUGUSTINE was also a persecutor. The historian Augustus Neander observed that Augustine's teaching "contains the germ of the whole system of spiritual despotism, intolerance, and persecution, even to the court of the Inquisition" (*General History of the Christian Religion*, 1847). Augustine instigated persecutions against the Bible-believing Donatists who were striving to maintain pure churches after the apostolic pattern. He interpreted Luke 14:23 ("compel them to come in") to mean that Christ requires the churches to use force against heretics.

Augustine was the father of a-millennialism, allegorizing Bible prophecy and teaching that the Catholic Church is the kingdom of God. He taught that the sacraments are the means of saving grace. He was one of the fathers of infant baptism, teaching that baptism took away their sin and calling those who rejected infant baptism "infidels" and "cursed." He taught that Mary did not commit sin and promoted her veneration. He believed Mary played a vital role in salvation (Augustine, Sermon 289, cited in Durant, *The Story of Civilization*, 1950, IV, p. 69). He believed in purgatory. He accepted the doctrine of "celibacy" for "priests," supporting the decree of "Pope" Siricius of 387 that ordered that any priest that married or refused to separate from his wife should be disciplined. He exalted the authority of the church over that of the Bible, declaring, "I should not believe the gospel unless I were moved to do so by the authority of the Catholic Church" (quoted by John Paul II, *Augustineum Hyponensem*, Apostolic Letter, Aug. 28, 1986, www.cin.org/jp2.ency/augustin.html). He believed that the true interpretation of Scripture was derived from the declaration of church councils (Augustin, *De Vera Religione*, xxiv, p. 45).

Augustine interpreted the early chapters of Genesis figuratively (*Debating Calvinism: Five Points, Two Views* by Dave Hunt and James White, 2004, p. 230). He taught the heresy of apostolic succession from Peter (Hunt, p. 230). He taught that God has pre-ordained some for salvation and others for damnation and that the grace of God is irresistible for the elect. By his own admission, John Calvin in the 16th century derived his TULIP theology on the "sovereignty of God" from Augustine. Calvin said: "If I were inclined to compile a whole volume from Augustine, I could easily show my readers, that I need no words but his" (Calvin, *Institutes of the Christian Religion*, Book III, chap. 22).

DIONYSIUS THE AREOPAGITE (also called Pseudo-Dionysius) was an anonymous Syrian monk who lived in the sixth century and whose writings have had a vast influence on Roman Catholic monasticism. His works were translated into Latin in the ninth century. "The influence of his writings --*Celestial Hierarchy*, *Ecclesiastical Hierarchy*, *Divine Names*, and *Mystical Theology*--on Christian mystical thought can hardly be exaggerated. ... Considered as authoritative, his writings greatly stimulated Christian theology and spirituality. They also influenced much of religious life" (*Christian Mystics*, pp. 55, 58).

Like Clement, Origen, Jerome, and Augustine, Dionysius "fused Christian and Greek thought into a synthesis of mystical doctrines" (*Christian Mystics*, p. 54). This illegitimate synthesis created a false Christianity. The apostle Paul, by divine inspiration, had issued strenuous warnings against this error. *"Beware lest any man spoil you through philosophy and vain deceit, after the tradition of men, after the rudiments of the world, and not after Christ"* (Colossians 2:8).

Dionysius taught that God cannot be known perfectly through Scripture but must be experienced directly *beyond* Scripture, *beyond* doctrine, through mindless mysticism, a blind leap into the dark.

> "According to Dionysius, there are two ways in which man can know God: one is the way of reason; the other is the way of mystical contemplation. ... mystical knowledge is greatly superior ... Dionysius speaks much of the transcendence of God, stressing the fact that by reasoning we know little about him. ... WHEN THE FACULTIES ARE EMPTIED OF ALL HUMAN KNOWLEDGE THERE REIGNS IN THE SOUL A 'MYSTIC SILENCE' LEADING IT TO THE CLIMAX THAT IS UNION WITH GOD AND THE VISION OF HIM as he is in himself" (William Johnston, *The Cloud of Unknowing*, introduction, pp. 25, 27).

> "He says that God cannot be known at all in the ordinary sense, but he can be experienced, he can be reached and found if he is sought on the right path. Mystical Theology ... focuses entirely on the utter unity of God, the undivided Ultimate Reality and GODHEAD THAT LIVES IN COMPLETE DARKNESS BEYOND ALL LIGHT. Dionysius writes that the 'unchangeable mysteries of heavenly Truth lie hidden in the dazzling obscurity of the secret Silence, outshining all brilliance with the intensity of their darkness.' God is TOTALLY BEYOND THE

POWER OF THE INTELLECT; contemplation is the only way to 'divine darkness,' which can NEVER BE GRASPED BY THE HUMAN MIND. ... THOSE WHO SEEK THE PATH OF CONTEMPLATION MUST LEAVE ALL ACTIVITIES OF THE SENSE AND THE MIND BEHIND. ... The soul yearns for that 'union with Him whom neither being nor understanding can contain,' who is 'Darkness which is beyond Light,' and whose vision can only be attained through the loss of all sight and knowledge" (Ursula King, *Christian Mystics*, pp. 55-56).

It is obvious that this is not biblical Christianity, yet it is the Christianity of Catholic monastic mysticism. The true and living God dwells in light not in darkness, and He has revealed Himself in the Scripture, which contains the deep things of God (1 Corinthians 2:9-13). God is revealed perfectly in Christ (John 1:18; 14:9; 2 Corinthians 4:4, 6; Colossians 1:15; Hebrews 1:3). Thank God, we don't have to try to find Him through blind mysticism or attempt to achieve salvation through works and sacraments; He has already revealed Himself in Scripture and purchased full eternal salvation for us through the blood of His own Son.

The original Christian hermits lived solitarily in huts or caves in the Egyptian desert. One of these was **PAUL OF THEBES** (also known as Saint Paul the First Hermit or Paul the Anchorite). He lived in a cave for nearly 100 years.

Another influential early hermit was **ANTHONY** (called St. Anthony the Great by Rome) who spent 20 years in complete solitary, not seeing the face of a man, and 40 or 50 more years in seclusion and near solitary, part of that time living in a tomb. Anthony lived near Alexandria, Egypt. Much of the surviving record of Anthony's life pertains to his supposed battles with the devil. One account says the devil beat him unconscious, which again shows the heretical foolishness of the Desert Fathers. Nowhere in Scripture do we find that the devil has that kind of power over a true child of God. (I am not assuming that Anthony was a child of God.) At other times the devil is said to have taken the form of wild beasts. Anthony lived in extreme asceticism, subsisting for six months on a small quantity of bread. He allegedly had visions of angels and heard voices. He would perform vain, obsessive rituals such as standing repeatedly to pray while he was weaving mats, claiming that he learned this from a vision.

By the fourth century the hermits formed communities or monasteries, with each monk living in a separate cell. Eventually there were thousands of hermits, both male and female. This developed gradually into the monastic systems of the Middle Ages.

THE MONASTERY RULES were very strict and legalistic. The *Rule of St. Benedict*, for example, directed every aspect of the monk's life, his clothing, relationships, travel, duties, schedule, meals, worship, reading, habitat, sleep. The monks were forbidden to own anything or to associate with anyone except by permission of the abbot.

> "We mean that, without an order from the abbot, no one may presume to give, receive or retain anything as his own, nothing at all--not a book, writing tablets or stylus--in short, not a single item, especially since monks may not have the free disposal even of their own bodies and wills. For their needs, they are to look to the father of the monastery, and are not allowed anything which the abbot has not given or permitted. ... But if anyone is caught indulging in this most evil practice, he should be warned a first and a second time. If he does not amend, let him be subjected to punishment" (*The Rule of Saint Benedict*, edited by Timothy Fry, 1981, p. 36).
>
> "A generous pound of bread is enough for a day, whether for only one meal or for both dinner and supper" (p. 41).
>
> "Monks should diligently cultivate silence at all times" (p. 43).
>
> "In no circumstances is a monk allowed, unless the abbot says he may, to exchange letters, blessed tokens or small gifts of any kind with his parents or anyone else, or with a fellow monk. He must not presume to accept gifts sent him even by his parents without previously telling the abbot" (pp. 52, 53).
>
> "To provide for laundering and night wear, every monk will need two cowls and two tunics, but anything more must be taken away as superfluous" (p. 53).
>
> "For bedding the monks will need a mat, a woolen blanket and a light covering, as well as pillow. The beds are to be inspected frequently by the abbot, lest private possessions be found there. A monk discovered with anything not given him by the abbot must be subjected to very severe punishment" (p. 54).

> "No one should presume to relate to anyone else what he saw or heard outside the monastery, because that causes the greatest harm. If anyone does so presume, he shall be subjected to the punishment of the rule. So too shall anyone who presumes to leave the enclosure of the monastery, or go anywhere, or do anything at all, however small, without the abbot's order" (p. 66).
>
> "Every precaution must be taken that one monk does not presume in any circumstance to defend another in the monastery or to be his champion, even if they are related by the closest ties of blood" (p. 67).

This is the type of legalistic Christianity that Paul condemned and refuted in the epistles of Romans, Galatians, and Colossians. The Catholic Desert Fathers and Monastics added works to the grace of Christ (see Galatians 1:6-9) and exalted their own tradition to the same level of authority as Scripture.

This is also the asceticism that Paul condemned in Colossians 2:20-23.

> "Wherefore if ye be dead with Christ from the rudiments of the world, why, as though living in the world, are ye subject to ordinances, (Touch not; taste not; handle not; Which all are to perish with the using;) after the commandments and doctrines of men? Which things have indeed a shew of wisdom in will worship, and humility, and neglecting of the body; not in any honour to the satisfying of the flesh."

This is a warning against the gnostic ascetism that was tempting the early churches. These practices are described by Paul as *"the rudiments of the world"* and *"the commandments and doctrines of men."* In other words, they were man-made traditions without Scriptural authority. They were practices such as *"touch not; taste not; handle not."*

The Essenes, for example, lived apart from society, required celibacy, never ate before sundown, ate nothing that was pleasant to the taste, and drank only water.

> "These errorists taught that matter is evil and the body is the source of sin and therefore they treated the body harshly. They denied honor to the body but it was for their own satisfaction of the flesh" (Frank Gaebelein, *The Annotated Bible*).

This is exactly what the Roman Catholic Desert Fathers believed.

In Colossians 2 Paul shows that Christ is the believer's justification, life, and spiritual victory.

Asceticism is a path of error that cannot deliver what it promises.

> "Asceticism is utterly powerless to effect the object aimed at: it does not, it cannot sanctify the flesh. It has a show of wisdom. It is extravagant in its pretensions and loud in its promises. But it never fulfills them. The apostle here declares that it has no value against the indulgence of the flesh (2:23). It, rather, stimulates the appetites and passions it is meant to extirpate. Asceticism has often proved to be a hotbed of vice. Some of the vilest men have been found among those who advocated the strictest austerities. They denounced the holiest of human associations, and branded as sensual the purest relations. Marriage was degraded, celibacy glorified, the family disparaged, domestic life despised. And some of these foes of truth have been canonized! Asceticism does not touch the seat of sin. All its strength is exerted against the body. Sin is of the soul, has its seat in the soul. So long as the heart is corrupt, no bodily restraints will make the life holy. There is one remedy alone for human sin, one that reaches to its roots, that ultimately will totally destroy it, viz., the blood of Christ" (1 John 1:7) (W.A. Moorhead).

THE ERRORS OF ROMAN CATHOLIC MONASTICISM

CONTENTS OF THIS SECTION

Its False Gospel...166
Its Rejection of the Bible as the Sole Authority..............170
Its Adoration of the Host of the Mass...........................175
Its Veneration of Mary..177
Its Belief in Purgatory..180
Its Doctrine of Celibacy..181
Its Ascetism 182

(For more on the errors of Roman Catholic monasticism, see the book *Contemplative Mysticism: A Powerful Ecumenical Glue*.)

A foundational error of Roman monastic mysticism is its false gospel.

According to Rome, salvation is a "treasure" that was purchased by Christ and is increased by the merits of the Saints, particularly Mary. This treasure was given to Peter and the Catholic Church to distribute through its sacraments.

According to the Vatican II Council, God the Father "willed that the work of salvation ... should be set in train through the sacrifice and sacraments" ("Constitution on the Sacred Liturgy," Chap. 1). The "sacrifice" is the Mass.

Salvation, according to Catholicism, thus begins with baptism and is fed by participation in the other six sacraments, with the Mass being the heart and soul of the sacramental system.

Note the following official declarations of the authoritative Second Vatican Council. It was held in the mid-1960s and attended by more than 2,400 Catholic bishops under the headship of Pope John XXIII and Pope Paul VI.

The following quotes are from *Vatican Council II--The Conciliar and Post Conciliar Documents* (imprimatur: Walter P. Kellenberg, D,D., Bishop of Rockville Centre, Aug. 12, 1975; "imprimatur" is the official Catholic stamp of approval and means "let it be printed").

> "For God's only-begotten Son ... has won a treasure for the militant Church ... he has entrusted it to blessed Peter, the key-bearer of heaven, and to his successors who are Christ's vicars on earth, so that they may distribute it to the faithful for their salvation. ... The merits of the Blessed Mother of God and of all the elect ... are known to add further to this treasury'" (ellipsis are in the original) (*Vatican Council II*, "Constitution on the Sacred Liturgy," Apostolic Constitution on the Revision of Indulgences, Chap. 4, 7, p. 80).

> "For it is the liturgy through which, especially in the divine sacrifice of the Eucharist, 'the work of our redemption is accomplished,' and it is through the liturgy, especially, that the faithful are enabled to express in their lives and manifest to others the mystery of Christ and the real nature of the true Church" (Vatican II, "Constitution on the Sacred Liturgy," Introduction, para. 2).

The Desert Fathers were not just trying to gain a deeper level of spirituality; they were trying to gain salvation.

When Abba Arsenius, who lived in the desert and was a disciple of Anthony, asked God how he could be saved, a voice answered him, "Arsenius, flee from the world and you will be saved," and, "Arsenius, flee, be silent, pray always, for these are the source of sinlessness" (Henri Nouwen, *The Way of the Heart*, p. 15).

Consider the vow that was required of novices who entered Shenouda the Archimandrite's monasteries in the fifth century. Shenouda is one of the most renowned "saints" of the Coptic Orthodox Church.

> "I vow before God in His Holy Place, the word which I have spoken with my mouth being my witness; I will not defile my body in any way, I will not steal, I will not bear false witness, I will not lie, I will not do anything deceitful secretly. If I transgressed what I have vowed, I will see the Kingdom of Heaven, but will not enter it. God before whom I made the covenant will destroy my soul and my body in the fiery hell because I transgressed the covenant I made" (Besa, *Life of Shenoute*, translated by D. H. Bell, Cistercian Publications, 1983, pp. 9-10).

This is a gospel of works.

The *Ladder of Divine Ascent,* which was written by John Climacus in the 7th century, depicts the Christian life as a 30-step ladder that reaches to God. This book is still read every year in Orthodox monasteries during Lent and is depicted in icons and paintings. "It shows the spiritual father ushering the monks to the foot of the ladder, with good angels assisting them to ascend, while evil angels are trying to pull them off, dropping them into the gaping jaws of hell" (*Christian Mystics*, pp. 199, 200).

This obviously describes a works gospel.

The Rule of Benedict, which has guided Catholic monasticism since the sixth century, opens with the statement that the monasteries are a "school for the Lord's service" in which "the way to salvation" is taught (Prologue 45, 48). This way of salvation is works. It says that by persevering in the monastic system until death the monks "through patience share in the passion of Christ that [they] may deserve also to share in his Kingdom" (Prol. 50). Chapter 7 of the Rule presents a 12-step ladder of virtue and asceticism that "leads to heaven." These steps include repression of self-will, submission to superiors, confession, stifling laughter, and speaking only when asked a question.

Catherine of Siena taught that the bridge to Heaven is composed of Christ AND the stones of true and sincere virtues (*Christian Mystics*, p. 85).

The Cloud of Unknowing teaches salvation through the sacraments. The author says that baptism cleanses of original sin (chapter 10, p. 61), that the Sacrament of Penance purifies the conscience and "rubs away the great rust of deadly sin" (chapter 15, p. 68; chapter 28, p. 85), and that the practice of contemplation "will eventually heal you of all the roots of sin" (chapter 12, p. 64).

In his book *The Triple Way*, Bonaventure set out the three-fold path of Catholic contemplation, *purgative* (asceticism), *illuminative*, and *unitive* (mystical union with God). He said: "As soon as the soul has mastered three, it becomes holy ... Upon the proper understanding of these three states are founded both the understanding of all scriptures and THE RIGHT TO ETERNAL LIFE" (Talbot, *Come to the Quiet*, p. 93).

That is a works gospel that Paul condemned as cursed of God (Galatians 1:6-9), and Catholic monasticism is built upon this wretched foundation.

Biblical salvation is not in any wise through one's efforts and virtuous works. All *"our righteousnesses are as filthy rags"* before a thrice holy God (Isaiah 64:6). The biblical gospel is salvation through Christ alone by grace alone through faith alone without works of any kind (Romans 3:21-24; 4:1-8; Ephesians 2:8-10). The Bible says that if grace is mixed with works then grace is destroyed, thus Rome's gospel of grace plus works is impossible. Paul wrote: *"And if by grace, then is it no more of works: otherwise grace is no more grace. But if it be of works, then is it no more grace: otherwise work is no more work"* (Romans 11:6). In Christ alone the sinner finds perfection before God, and he receives this full and free salvation directly from Christ without any intermediary such as a human priest or church or sacramental ritual. The believer has everything in Christ. *"But of him are ye in Christ Jesus, who of God is made unto us wisdom, and righteousness, and sanctification, and redemption"* (1 Corinthians 1:30). Through faith in Christ we are cleansed and declared righteous and there is no need to move into a monastery and attempt to purify ourselves through ascetism. We are free to go forth into the world to preach the gospel as Christ commanded and to serve God with a joyful heart.

I have read many books by the Catholic contemplative writers and not once have I read a biblical testimony of salvation.

Ignatius of Loyola was converted through a vision of Mary and the infant Jesus. Angela of Foligno was converted by seeing Francis of Assisi in a dream. John Michael Talbot was converted through a vision of Christ and defines being reborn as a process that includes many things, including contemplative meditation (*Come to the Quiet*, p, 49; also pages 68, 113). This is the Roman Catholic perspective that salvation is a process.

Another foundational error of Rome's monastic mysticism is its rejection of the Bible as the sole authority for faith and practice.

Rome has set up her own tradition as equal in authority to the Bible.

> "Sacred Tradition and sacred Scripture, then, are bound closely together, and communicate one with the other. For both of them, flowing out from the same divine well-spring, come together in some fashion to form one thing, and move towards the same goal ... Thus it comes about that the Church does not draw her certainty about all revealed truths from the holy Scriptures alone. Hence, both Scripture and Tradition must be accepted and honoured with equal feelings of devotion and reverence" (*Vatican Council II: The Conciliar and Post-Conciliar Documents*, edited by Walter Kellenberg, "Dogmatic Constitution on Divine Revelation," Chap. 2, 9, p. 682).
>
> "As a result the Church, to whom the transmission and interpretation of Revelation is entrusted, does not derive her certainty about all revealed truths from the holy Scriptures alone. Both Scripture and Tradition must be accepted and honoured with equal sentiments of devotion and reverence" (*New Catholic Catechism*, 82).

Catholic mystics have always operated in an atmosphere in which the Bible is encrusted with Rome's tradition and interpreted by Rome's authority.

The author of *The Cloud of Unknowing* warned about those who "reject the common doctrine and guidance of the Church" (chapter 56, p. 120). He calls them "the disciples of Anti-Christ" (p. 121). He says that using references from Scripture to prove a doctrine is "a vain fad in conceited intellectual circles" (chapter 70, p. 139).

Teresa of Avila said:

> "The soul always tries to act in conformity with the Church's teaching ... no imaginable revelation, even if it saw the heavens open, would cause it to swerve an inch from the doctrine of the Church" (*The Life of Saint Teresa of Avila by Herself*, chap. 25, p. 178).

In describing the practice of *lectio divina* John Michael Talbot urges his readers to lean on the official teaching of the Catholic Church and not to try to interpret Scripture apart from this. He only recommends that the student study the Bible for himself if he is grounded in "its proper interpretation through the Fathers and magisterium of the Church" (*Come to the Quiet*, p. 48). He even says, "If we ignore the authority of the Church, then we destroy the authority of scripture" (p. 45).

In reality, we destroy the Scripture by submitting it to Rome's tradition.

Not only is Catholic mysticism encrusted with the darkness of tradition and dogma, but it is also open to extra-scriptural revelations. The writings of the mystic saints are absolutely filled with descriptions of how God allegedly spoke to them in visions and voices.

The Bible is used by Rome. It is quoted in the Mass and chanted throughout the day in her monasteries, but it is so encrusted with human tradition that its light does not shine in clarity.

The same situation existed in ancient Israel.

> "But their minds were blinded: for until this day remaineth the same vail untaken away in the reading of the old testament; which vail is done away in Christ. But even unto this day, when Moses is read, the vail is upon their heart. Nevertheless when it shall turn to the Lord, the vail shall be taken away" (2 Corinthians 3:14-16).

Though the Bible is read in the Catholic Church, it is read through the thick veil of tradition and sacerdotalism (priestcraft) and papalism and sacramentalism and saint worship.

The Bible cannot be understood properly apart from the new birth whereby the sinner repents of his sin and puts his faith in Jesus' blood and is consequently cleansed and indwelt by the Holy Spirit, but Rome teaches men to trust in baptism and the other sacraments.

In fact, when discussing the Catholic mystics' rejection of the Bible as the sole authority for faith in practice, we should not forget to document the fact that they usually didn't even have a personal Bible. Very few Christians today are aware of this.

John Talbot describes how that Francis of Assisi gave the monks' only Bible to a poor woman because he believed "the gift of it will be more pleasing to God than our reading from it" (*The Lover and the Beloved*, p. 15).

At the height of her power from the 13th to the 18th century, Rome did not allow "the laity" to have the Bible, particularly in their own common languages. The Council of Toulouse, in 1229, forbade the laity to possess the books of the Old and New Testaments in their languages.

> "We prohibit the permission of the books of the Old and New Testament to laymen, except perhaps they might desire to have the Psalter, or some Breviary for the divine service, or the Hours of the blessed Virgin Mary, for devotion; expressly forbidding their having the other parts of the Bible translated into the vulgar tongue" (Pierre Allix, *Ecclesiastical History*, II, 1821, p. 213).

The Catholic authorities at Toulouse specifically condemned the Waldensian translation known as the Romaunt version (P. Marion Simms, *The Bible from the Beginning*, 1929, p. 153). The Waldensians were persecuted so fiercely and their Scriptures destroyed so thoroughly by Catholic authorities that only seven copies of their New Testaments have survived from the 13th to the 16th centuries. (I have had the privilege of examining two of these, one at Trinity College Dublin and one at Cambridge University.)

Referring to the Inquisition that was permanently established by the Council of Toulouse, William Blackburn says:

> "No legalized institution has ever done more to crush intellectual and religious liberty, or added more to the unspoken miseries of the human race. EVERY LAYMAN DARING TO POSSESS A BIBLE, NOW FIRST FORBIDDEN TO THE LAITY BY THIS COUNCIL, WAS IN PERIL OF THE RACK, THE DUNGEON, AND THE STAKE" (*History of the Christian Church*, 1880, p. 309).

What Rome allowed were only small portions of Scripture, usually from the Psalms and Gospels but not from Paul's Epistles. Further, Catholic Scripture portions were published together with apocryphal and legendary stories in which Mary was commonly exalted higher than Jesus Christ.

Consider, for example, the rightly named *GOLDEN LEGEND*. This was written in the late 13th century by Jacopo of Varazze, a Dominican, and published widely in Europe and England prior to the Reformation. Alleged to be excerpts from the Bible, it was actually filled with legends about the "saints" and "the Bible scraps are lost in a sea of fiction" (David Daniell, *The Bible in English*, p. 108).

Consider the *MIRROR OF THE BLESSED LIFE OF OUR LORD JESUS CHRIST*. This Latin work was translated into English by Nicholas Love and went through eight editions from 1484 to 1530. Alleged to be an "expanded gospel harmony," it was actually filled with Catholic legend and had little to do with the Bible. "The book is not long, but it is padded out with long meditations by and about the Blessed Virgin Mary, who has the overwhelming presence. Although half the book is on the Crucifixion, the Gospels' narrative is only just visible, overtaken by the Virgin Mary's long accounts of her own suffering at that event" (Daniell, p. 161).

It sounds like the original for Mel Gibson's movie *The Passion of the Christ*!

This was the type of "Scripture" that Rome allowed people to have in their own languages.

Wherever the Bible appeared in the common tongue of the people, wherever it was proclaimed unencumbered with Rome's traditions, Rome sought to extinguish the light it brought to benighted men. The Catholic authorities did not mind so much when the Scripture was available in Latin, as this language had ceased to be spoken by the common people. It was the translation of Scripture into the native tongues that particularly raised their ire. We have documented this extensively in the book *Rome and the Bible*, which is available from Way of Life Literature.

For example, in England Rome did everything possible to keep the Bible from being translated into the English language, and after it was translated she did everything possible to keep it out of the hands of the people. Rome bitterly persecuted John Wycliffe, the translator of the first English Bible at the end of the 14th century, and tried to have him arrested and put to death, but failing in that (partially because the papal schism was in full swing and the popes were too busy hurling curses at one another to give their full attention to the Bible translator) Wycliffe was formally condemned at the Council of Constance and his bones were dug up and burned. When William Tyndale translated the first English Bible from Greek and Hebrew in the early 1500s, he had to do it while on the run from the Catholic authorities. Before he was able to complete the Old Testament he was arrested and after a long imprisonment burned at the stake. Rome put to death many other Bible translators, as we have documented in *Rome and the Bible*.

Even the priests and monks and nuns in the monasteries had personal Bibles only in exceedingly rare circumstances. They had breviaries and portions of Scripture selected for them by Rome for use in their repetitious devotions and masses, but typically they did not have their own Bibles and they did not pursue systematic Bible study.

As late as the 19th century, priests in Italy did not have their own Bibles. Alexander Robertson, who long resided in Italy, made the following observation:

> On May 18, 1849, some three thousand copies of the New Testament, according to the Martini version, were seized and destroyed in Tuscany. Priests have told me that even they were not allowed to possess a Martini Bible without the Papal consent, and that the very fact of applying for such consent would bring them under suspicion, and so damage their prospects in the Church. Therefore, they said, 'WE HAVE NO BIBLES.'
>
> A daily newspaper in giving an account of a discussion being carried on between a layman and a clerical in regard to the falsification of the Ten Commandments by the Church, which omits the Second Commandment entirely, and divides the Tenth Commandment into two to make up the number [relates that] 'IN A VILLAGE OF THREE THOUSAND INHABITANTS NO BIBLE COULD BE FOUND'
>
> Students are not taught the Bible in the Papal seminaries. They have many text-books--Alfonso de Liguori's especially--but no Bible. Count Campello, ex-Canon of St. Peter's, was trained in the Academy of Noble Ecclesiastics, the highest training college in Rome (to which once only men of noble birth were admitted, but into which now not one such can be induced to enter), and yet DURING ALL HIS YEARS OF STUDY HE NEVER EVEN SAW A BIBLE (Alexander Robertson, *The Roman Catholic Church in Italy*, 1903, pp. 211-215).

This is the benighted condition in which the Catholic mystic "saints" lived. To say that they were not Bible-centered Christians is a gross understatement, and any possible exception does not disprove the rule.

Another foundational error of Roman monastic mysticism is its adoration of the host of the Mass.

At the heart of monastic mysticism is the Catholic Eucharist or Mass. The "saints" centered their lives around it.

Catherine of Siena lived at times only on the wine and wafer of the Mass.

Catherine of Genoa was so devoted to the Mass that she received it daily.

Julian of Norwich could observe only one thing from the lone little window in her cell, and that was the Mass.

Many of the mystics claimed to have had wonderful experiences during the Mass. Beatrijs of Nazareth, a 13th century Cistercian nun, claims that she saw Jesus on the altar with His arms outstretched and was united with Him, "heart to heart."

Teresa of Avila was also devoted to the Mass, calling it the "Most Holy Sacrament" and believing that the consecrated wafer is Christ. Many of her visions and raptures occurred during Mass.

As we have seen, the Catholic Mass is not a mere remembrance of Christ's death; it is a re-sacrifice of Christ, and the consecrated host of the Mass IS Christ. Christ is therefore worshipped as the host, and this forms a major part of Catholic monastic spirituality.

Consider the following quotes from Thomas Merton's autobiography:

> "And I saw the raised Host--the silence and simplicity with which Christ once again triumphed, raised up, drawing all things to Himself ... Christ, hidden in the small Host, was giving Himself for me, and to me, and, with Himself, the entire Godhead and Trinity..." (*The Seven Storey Mountain*, 1998 edition, pp. 245, 246).
>
> "I fixed my eyes on the monstrance, on the white Host. ... I looked straight at the Host, and I knew, now, Who it was that I was looking at, and I said: 'Yes, I want to be a priest, with all my heart I want it. If it is Your will, make me a priest'..." (*The Seven Storey Mountain*, pp. 279, 280).
>
> "Then ... there formed in my mind an awareness, an understanding, a realization of what had just taken place on the altar, at the Consecration: a realization of God made present by the words of Consecration in a way that made Him belong to me. ... a sudden and immediate contact had been established between my intellect and the Truth Who was now physically really and substantially before me on the altar" (pp. 310, 311).

Another error of Roman monastic mysticism is its veneration of Mary.

The ancient Catholic spirituality that is praised so widely today in evangelical and Baptist circles is intimately associated with rank idolatry and gross heresy. According to Rome, Mary was conceived immaculately (without sin), participated in Christ's suffering for man's sin, ascended to heaven bodily, was crowned Queen of Heaven, and intercedes for mankind. Consider some statements from the Second Vatican Council:

> "Joined to Christ the head and in communion with all his saints, the faithful must in the first place reverence the memory of the glorious ever Virgin Mary, Mother of God and of our Lord Jesus Christ ... Because of the gift of sublime grace she far surpasses all creatures, both in heaven and on earth. ... The Immaculate Virgin preserved free from all stain of original sin, was taken up body and soul into heavenly glory, when her earthly life was over, and exalted by the Lord as Queen over all things" ("Dogmatic Constitution on the Church," chap. 8, I, 52, 53; II, 59, pp. 378, 381- 382).

> "As St. Irenaeus says, she being obedient, became the cause of salvation for herself and for the whole human race. Hence not a few of the early Fathers gladly assert with him in their preaching ... 'death through Eve, life through Mary' ... This union of the mother with the Son in the work of salvation is made manifest from the time of Christ's virginal conception up to his death" ("Dogmatic Constitution on the Church," chap. 8, II, 56, pp. 380-381).

> "Taken up to heaven she did not lay aside this saving office but by her manifold intercession continues to bring us the gifts of eternal salvation. By her maternal charity, she cares for the brethren of her Son, who still journey on earth surrounded by dangers and difficulties, until they are led into their blessed home. Therefore the Blessed Virgin is invoked in the Church under the titles of Advocate, Helper, Benefactress, and Mediatrix [Mediator]" ("Dogmatic Constitution on the Church," chap. 8, II, 62, pp. 382-383).

The book *Saints Who Saw Mary* by Raphael Brown describes the centrality of Mary worship among the Catholic saints. The author documents the Mary visitations experienced by Francis of Assisi, Catherine of Siena, Teresa of Avila, John of the Cross, Ignatius of Loyola, and Bernard of Clairvaux.

Francis of Assisi said:

> "I therefore command all my Brothers, those living now and those to come in the future, to venerate the Holy Mother of God, whom we always implore to be our Protectress, to praise her at all times, in all circumstances of life, with all the means in their power and with the greatest devotion and submission" (*Rule of the Friars Minor*).

Bonaventure said:

> "No one can enter into heaven except through Mary, as entering through a gate" (*On St. Luke's Gospel*).

Bernard authored *Homilies in Praise of the Virgin Mother*.

The anonymous author of the 14th century contemplative prayer manual *The Cloud of Unknowing* speaks of praying to "OUR LADY." He said that "our Lady, St. Mary, was full of grace at every moment" (chapter 3, p. 51). This is a blasphemous statement, since the Bible uses the description "full of grace" only for the Son of God (John 1:14).

Ignatius' *Spiritual Exercises* are filled with Mary veneration. The practitioner is instructed to pray the *Hail Mary* many times and to ask Mary for grace. Ignatius also recommended praying *Hail Holy Queen* ("Three Methods of Prayer," 258). This blasphemous prayer addresses Mary as holy Queen, the Mother of Mercy, our life, our love, our hope, and most gracious advocate.

John of the Cross is said to have lived "in intimate union with God AND HIS MOTHER" ("St. John of the Cross," Doctors of the Catholic Church web site).

Teresa of Avila even claimed to have seen Mary ascend to Heaven.

> "Once, on the Feast of the Assumption of Our Lady, the Queen of the Angels, the Lord was pleased to grant me this favour. In a rapture, I saw a representation of her ascent from heaven, of the joy and solemnity with which she was received, and of the place where she now is" (*The Life of Saint Teresa of Avila by Herself*, chap. 39, p. 305).

Teresa was also devoted to Joseph, and she claimed that Mary was so pleased with this, that both of them appeared and clothed her in a "robe of great whiteness and clarity," after which Mary took her by the hands and "told me that I was giving her great pleasure by serving the glorious St. Joseph, and promised me that my plans for the convent would be fulfilled" (*The Life of Saint Teresa*, chap. 33, p. 247).

Gethsemani Abby in Kentucky, where Thomas Merton lived, is dedicated to Mary. Every evening at 7 pm, seven days a week, the monks and priests pray the Rosary.

Merton was a great venerator of Mary. The first time he visited Gethsemani Abbey he described it as "the Court of the Queen of Heaven" (John Talbot, *The Way of the Mystic*, p. 221). His autobiography is filled with passionate statements about Mary. He calls her Our Lady, Glorious Mother of God, Queen of Angels, Holy Queen of Heaven, Most High Queen of Heaven, Mediatrix of All Grace, Our Lady of Solitude, Immaculate Virgin, Blessed Virgin, and Holy Queen of souls and refuge of sinners. He dedicated himself to her and prayed to her continually.

> "People do not realize the tremendous power of the Blessed Virgin. They do not know who she is: that it is through her hands all graces come because God has willed that she thus participate in His work for the salvation of men. ... She is the Mother of the supernatural life in us. Sanctity comes to us through her intercession. God has willed that there be no other way" (*The Seven Storey Mountain*, p. 251).

Anthony de Mello dedicated his book on contemplation to "the Blessed Virgin Mary," urging his readers to "seek her patronage and ask for her intercession before you start out on this way" (*Sadhana: A Way to God*, pp. 8, 9).

John Michael Talbot said, "I am also feeling the presence of Mary becoming important in my life. ... I feel that she really does love me and intercedes to God on my behalf" (*Contemporary Christian Music Magazine*, November

1984, p. 47). He says that praying the Rosary is one of the most powerful meditative tools.

Another error of Roman monastic mysticism is its belief in purgatory.

The Catholic doctrine of purgatory says that believers must suffer for their sins after death in a place of purgation or purifying, and all of the mystic saints believed in it. Some, such as Catherine of Siena, had visions of it. They believed that the living could help the dead escape purgatory through purchasing masses and indulgences, the worship of saints, even through contemplative practices.

The author of *The Cloud of Unknowing* claimed that through mystical contemplation "the souls in purgatory are touched, for their suffering is eased by the effects of this work" (chapter 3, p. 48).

Catherine of Genoa wrote a *Treatise on Purgatory*. She said that purgatory is a place where souls are separated from God (chapter III) and "endure a pain so extreme that no tongue can be found to tell it" (chapter II), and where the stain of sins are removed before the soul can approach God (chapter VIII).

Teresa of Avila claimed that many souls were brought out of purgatory through her intercession.

> "As for rescuing souls from purgatory and such notable acts, the Lord has granted me so many favours of this kind that I should exhaust myself and my readers if I were to describe them all" (*The Life of Saint Teresa of Avila by Herself*, chap. 39, p. 296).

The doctrine of purgatory denies the perfect sufficiency of Christ's atonement. The place where sin is purged is the cross of Jesus Christ. *"Neither by the blood of goats and calves, but by his own blood he entered in once into the holy place, having obtained eternal redemption for us"* (Hebrews 9:12). He obtained full redemption through His own blood for those who believe. The Bible teaches that as soon as the believer is absent from the body he is present with Christ (2 Corinthians 5:8). The fire of the judgment seat of Christ does not touch the believer himself; it tests his works (1 Corinthians 3:13).

Another error of Roman monastic mysticism is its doctrine of celibacy.

The idea behind Rome's celibacy requirement for priests and nuns is the doctrine that the state of celibacy is more spiritual than marriage and that the priests and nuns are married to Christ. The Catholic Church attempts to find support for this doctrine in Paul's teaching in 1 Corinthians 7, but he never forbade marriage (1 Cor. 7:9, 28, 35). In fact, Paul required that pastors and deacons be married men (1 Timothy 3:2, 5, 11). And the needy women that are supported by the churches are women that have been married (1 Timothy 5:9-10).

There is not a hint in the New Testament of a Catholic-style monastic system with an enforced celibacy.

The "desert fathers" were so zealous for this heresy that some of them castrated themselves. Origen, one of the fathers of the monastic system, was of this number. Many others abandoned wives and husbands, in direct disobedience to the Bible, in order to live "celibate" as monks and nuns.

The Council of Elvira (300-306) and the Council of Carthage (390) demanded that married bishops and priests "keep away from their wives." This was in brazen contradiction to the Bible's exhortation in 1 Corinthians 7:3-5.

> "Let the husband render unto the wife due benevolence: and likewise also the wife unto the husband. The wife hath not power of her own body, but the husband: and likewise also the husband hath not power of his own body, but the wife. Defraud ye not one the other, except it be with consent for a time, that ye may give yourselves to fasting and prayer; and come together again, that Satan tempt you not for your incontinency."

Another error of Roman monastic mysticism is its ascetism.

The Desert Fathers and mystic "saints" practiced extreme ascetism. Many doubtless put themselves into an early grave. Hildegard's "strict practices of fasting and self-punishment, resulted in a lifetime of health problems and migraine headaches" (Talbot, *The Way of the Mystics*, p. 55). John of the Cross so abused his body that, according to the *Catholic Encyclopedia*, "twice he was saved from certain death by the intervention of the Blessed Virgin."

After a diligent study of the desert monastics, we tend to agree with Edward Gibbon, the famous historian of the Roman Empire. He described the typical desert monk as a "distorted and emaciated maniac ... spending his life in a long routine of useless and atrocious self-torture, and quailing before the ghastly phantoms of his delirious brain." Gibbon said, "They were sunk under the painful weight of crosses and chains; and their emaciated limbs were confined by collars, bracelets, gauntlets, and greaves of massy and rigid iron" (*Decline and Fall of the Roman Empire*).

The ascetic practices have many purposes, but none of them are scriptural.

They were thought to be necessary for salvation and sanctification. Pio of Pietrelcina said: "Let us now consider what we must do to ensure that the Holy Spirit may dwell in our souls. ... The mortification must be constant and steady, not intermittent, and it must last for one's whole life. Moreover, the perfect Christian must not be satisfied with a kind of mortification which merely appears to be severe. He must make sure that it hurts" ("Mortification of the Flesh," Wikipedia).

Ascetic practices are also thought to be necessary as part of the path to ecstatic union with God. We have seen that self denial and self injury was the first step in the three-step path to mystical union.

Ascetic practices are also thought to be necessary as penance for sin. In his *Spiritual Exercises* Ignatius of Loyola taught that penance requires "chastising the body by inflicting sensible pain on it" through "wearing hairshirts, cords, or iron chains on the body, or by scourging or wounding oneself, and by other kinds of austerities" (*The Spiritual Exercises of St. Ignatius*, First Week, Vintage Spiritual Classics, p. 31). Pope John XXIII wrote: "But the faithful must be encouraged to do outward acts of penance, both to keep their bodies under the strict control of reason and faith, and to make amends for their own and other people's sins" (*Paenitentiam Agere*, July 1, 1962). Yet we know that the believer's sin is forgiven through the blood of Christ and not through his own self-effort and sacrifice (1 John 1:9).

Ascetic practices are further thought to be necessary because the body and its physical pleasures are evil. John of the Cross, one of the most acclaimed of the Catholic mystical theologians, considered physical existence, with all its attendant needs and desires, as inherently sinful (Talbot, *The Way of the Mystics*, p. 148). Francis of Assisi called his own body "Brother Ass." This error goes back to the Platonic and gnostic philosophy that was imbibed by the Desert Fathers and Church Fathers.

Some of the common ascetic practices of the monastic mystics were as follows:

Extreme fasting

For part of her life Catherine of Siena lived exclusively on the wine and wafer of the Mass. Peter of Alcantara, who was Teresa of Avila's spiritual director, ate only once in three days at the most. The diet in many monasteries is meager. Consider the Order of Cistercians of the Strict Observance.

The monks subsist on a small amount of food for part of the year and are never allowed to eat meat, fish, or eggs.

Self-flagellation

Dominic Loricatus (995-1060), a Benedictine monk, lashed himself 300,000 times with a whip in one six-day period (Edward Gibbon, *The History of the Decline and Fall of the Roman Empire*, vol. V). He did this while reciting the Psalms, 100 lashes for each psalm. Catherine of Siena scourged herself three times a day with an iron chain. Theresa of the Child Jesus "scourged herself with all the strength and speed of which she was capable, smiling at the crucifix through her tears."

Hairshirts

A hairshirt was something uncomfortable worn next to the skin. Commonly it was made of some uncomfortable fabric but some were made of metal. Dominic Loricatus and Ignatius of Loyola wore a coat of chain mail as a hairshirt. Henry Suso devised an undergarment studded with 150 sharp brass nails that pierced his skin.

Bindings

Ignatius had the habit of binding a cord below the knee. The seers of Fatima wore tight cords around their waists. Catherine of Siena wrapped a chain with crosses around her body so tightly that it caused her to bleed; it is described as an "iron spiked girdle." "Her self-punishment left her body covered with gaping wounds, which she blithely referred to as her 'flowers'" (Talbot, *The Way of the Mystics*, p. 81).

Foregoing hygiene

Anthony never bathed his body nor even washed his feet. Henry Suso didn't take a bath in 25 years. For awhile Ignatius of Loyola lived in a cave and begged for food. He didn't bathe, wore rags, and let his hair and nails grow "wildly out of control." In the Order of Cistercians of Strict Observance, Thomas Merton's order, monks are allowed to wash their robes only once a month and they can take showers only by permission of the abbot.

Sleep depravation

Catherine of Siena allowed herself only one-half hour of sleep every other day. No wonder she had strange visions! Peter of Alcantara slept sitting up with his head against a piece of wood and slept only one and a half hours a day for 40 years.

Silence and solitude

Silence is a big part of Catholic monastic ascetism. The hermit Theon, one of the "desert fathers," kept silent for thirty years. Abbot Moses told a young man who asked for guidance, "Go, sit in your cell, and your cell will teach you everything" (*The Way of the Mystics*, p. 24). Romuald, the founder of the Camaldolese order, says the hermit must "sit in his cell like a chick, and destroy himself completely" (Talbot, *Come to the Quiet*, p. 22). Cistercian monks take vows of silence and communicate among themselves only by sign language.

Separation from relatives

Many of the monasteries and convents disallowed the monks and nuns to associate with their relatives. Teresa of Lisieux and her four sisters were nuns in Carmelite convents, and when their father had a series of strokes that left him severely handicapped, they were not allowed to visit him.

The ascetics find biblical support for their practices in Paul's statement in 1 Corinthians 9:27 -- "*But I keep under my body, and bring it into subjection: lest that by any means, when I have preached to others, I myself should be a castaway.*"

Nowhere does Paul say that he performed the type of asceticism that was practiced by the Catholic monastics. He listed many things that he suffered, but for the most part they were things that he was subjected to by outside forces and by dint of the performance of his preaching ministry (2 Corinthians 11:23-27). Paul was not beating and punishing his body and ruining his health through mindless ascetism. In the New Testament, fasting is not a way of punishing oneself; it is a means of spiritual victory over demonic powers (Matthew 17:19-21).

Further, Paul was not talking about his salvation or his sanctification but about his ministry. Paul was concerned that he would be castaway in the sense that he would be put on a shelf in this life so that he could no longer exercise his ministry or that his service would be rejected or disapproved at the judgment seat of Christ. The same Greek word is translated "rejected." Paul was not afraid that he would be lost. In the same epistle he taught that Christ preserves the believer (1 Cor. 1:7-9). What Paul feared was falling short of God's high calling for his life. The context makes this plain. He is talking about running a race and winning a prize.

To confuse this passage with salvation is to misunderstand the Gospel of Jesus Christ. Salvation is not a reward for faithful service. The Bible plainly states that salvation is by grace, and grace is the free, unmerited mercy of God (Eph. 2:8-9). Anything that is merited or rewarded, is not grace (Romans 11:6). On the other hand, after we are saved by the marvelous grace of God, we are called to serve Jesus Christ. We are created in Christ Jesus "unto good works" (Eph. 2:10). If a Christian is lazy and carnal, he will be chastened by the Lord (Heb. 12:6-8), and if he does not respond, God will take him home (Rom. 8:13; 1 Cor. 11:30; 1 John 5:16).

FURTHER WARNINGS ABOUT CONTEMPLATIVE SPIRITUALITY

Contents of This Section:

Error # 1: It downplays the centrality of the Bible in the Christian life.
Error # 2: It is not found in the Bible.
Error # 3: It ignores the Bible's definition of faith.
Error # 4: It ignores Jesus' warning against vain repetition.
Error # 5: It ignores the fact that multitudes of professing Christians are not born again.
Error # 6: It exchanges the God of the Bible for a blind idol.
Error # 7: It ignores the Bible's warnings against associating with heresy and paganism.
Error # 8: It does not encourage one to test everything carefully by Scripture.
Error # 9: It downplays the danger of spiritual delusion.
Error # 10: It produces rotten fruit.
Error # 11: It is not necessary.

Having looked at the errors of Catholic monasticism, we will now consider the errors of contemplative mysticism in general, including its incarnation within evangelicalism and the emerging church. *"To the law and to the testimony: if they speak not according to this word, it is because there is no light in them"* (Isaiah 8:20).

Contemplative Spirituality Error # 1: It downplays the centrality of the Bible in the Christian life.

Contemplative spirituality is supposedly a way to commune with God, but the proper way to do this is not by sitting in silence or repeating a mantra or trying to find an altered state of consciousness or by visualizing an encounter with biblical characters. The proper way to commune with God is to first hear His voice through careful, prayerful Bible study and thoughtful meditation on Scripture and then to communicate with Him in verbal worship and prayer.

I have read dozens of books on contemplative spirituality, and most of them make no mention whatsoever that the Bible is to be central to the Christian life and ministry.

The Catholic mystics had no such belief. As we have seen, they were committed to Rome's heresy that the Bible is only one of many authorities, including Catholic tradition, official councils, the voice of the pope speaking *ex-cathedra*, its doctors, and extra-biblical visions and revelations.

Emerging church leader Tony Jones admits that Catholic practices were rejected by the Protestant Reformation because they are contrary to the doctrine of the primacy of Scripture (p. 81). That is reason enough to reject them!

Eddie Gibbs and Ryan Bolger, in their study of the emerging church, say, "THE REFORMATION FOCUSED ON THE SPOKEN WORD, WHILE POSTMODERN WORSHIP EMBRACES THE EXPERIENCED WORD" (*Emerging Churches*, p. 78).

Tony Campolo co-authored a book with Mary Darling that promotes contemplative spirituality. Observe how that he downplays and ridicules traditional "piety" and biblical absolutes and exalts mysticism as a way to move beyond the pages of Scripture.

> "We finally decided to use the term 'mystical Christianity' to distinguish the kind of spirituality we are advocating from other forms known in the Christian community. For instance, using the word mystical makes it clear that the Christian spirituality that we are discussing here is not to be confused with the kind used as a synonym for personal piety, which too often comes with destructive legalism, or scholastic Christianity, WHICH CAN REDUCE FAITH TO THEOLOGICAL PROPOSITIONS. ... This book is about tapping into the love and reality that GOES BEYOND WHAT RULES AND REASON ALONE CAN APPREHEND. We want to show how daily moments marked by mystical revelations of God's love reveal the limits of propositional truth" (*The God of Intimacy and Action*, pp. 3, 4).

This, my friends, is pure and dangerous heresy. The business about "destructive legalism" and "scholastic Christianity" is a smokescreen. An emphasis upon the Scripture is neither legalism nor scholasticism. It is the emphasis of the New Testament itself. There is no instruction there about pursuing some mystical experience beyond the written Word. Jesus said that those who are His true disciples are those who continue in His Word (John 8:31-32). He prayed that His disciples would be sanctified with the Word (John 17:17).

We are taught that the Scripture is infallibly inspired (2 Timothy 3:16; 2 Peter 1:19-21), living and powerful (Hebrews 4:12), and that it is able to build us up (Acts 20:32), grow us up (1 Pet. 2:2), protect us from the devil (Eph. 6:17), and make us *"perfect, throughly furnished unto all good works"* (2 Tim. 3:17).

If the Bible is able to provide spiritual perfection, which it boldly claims, what more could we need? The answer is that we don't need anything else. Peter described his own experience when he saw Jesus glorified and heard God's voice speaking from Heaven, but he said that we have *"a more sure word of prophecy"* in the Scripture (2 Peter 1:16-21). The apostle exalted the Scripture above all mystical experiences.

The Lord Jesus condemned the Pharisees because they put their tradition on the same level of authority as Scripture (Mark 7:6-7).

God has given us a complete revelation in Scripture and we must honor it by making it the sole authority for faith and practice. And to emphasize the sole authority of Scripture refutes every type of mysticism, whether pagan, New Age, Catholic, Orthodox, charismatic, evangelical, or emerging.

The mystic of every variety rejects the sole authority of Scripture. He doesn't want to be bound by it. He wants to go beyond it. He doesn't want to put God "in a box." And therein lies mysticism's foundational error.

Contemplative Spirituality Error # 2: It is not found in the Bible.

There is no biblical example of the sign of the cross, the Stations of the Cross, pilgrimages, centering prayer, Jesus prayer, breath prayer, imagining conversations with biblical characters, chanting, labyrinths, meditating before icons, statues, and crucifixes, and such things.

Biblical prayer is not mystical contemplation. New Testament prayer is always verbal, conscious communion with God. Jesus gave the model prayer not as something to be repeated by rote but as a lesson on how to pray, and His prayer is distinctly NOT contemplative (Matthew 6:6-13). Jesus condemned vain repetitions and taught us to pray verbally. He did not even hint at contemplative practices such as centering prayer or visualization prayer. Further, Christ taught us to pray to the Father. This is contrary to centering prayer that directs one's attention to "Christ within."

The apostle Paul taught the same thing. His doctrine and practice of prayer can be found in the following passages: Romans 1:8-10; Ephesians 1:15-19; 6:18-20; Philippians 1:3-4,8-11; 4:6-7; Colossians 1:9-12; 2:1-2; 4:2-4; 1 Thessalonians 3:9-13; 5:17; 2 Thessalonians 1:11-12; 3:1-2; 1 Timothy 2:1-6.

According to Paul, prayer is composed of supplications, intercessions, and giving of thanks (1 Timothy 2:1). This is the example he demonstrates in his own prayers (Romans 1:8-10).

New Testament prayer consists of verbal praise, verbal petition, and verbal intercession. Such prayer is the means of obtaining mercy and finding grace to help in time of need (Hebrews 4:16). It is the means of achieving spiritual victory and fruitfulness (Ephesians 6:18-19).

Bible-believing Christians have communed sweetly and effectively with God by the Bible method for 2,000 years without the help of Catholic practices. Hymns such as "Sweet Hour of Prayer" and "In the Garden" describe this communion.

Rome replaced New Testament spirituality, which is a living relationship with Jesus Christ through the new birth and the guidance of the indwelling Holy Spirit and the study of Scripture, with its sacraments, false tradition, and sensual worship. It is sad to see men who profess to be Baptists and evangelical Protestants going back to this vain ritualism.

The attempt by contemplatives to find a biblical basis for their practices is pathetic.

We have seen that they use the example of Mary sitting at Jesus' feet in Luke 10, but Mary didn't sit in silence; she wasn't practicing thoughtless contemplation; she was listening to Christ speak words and the believer can do the same thing today by reading the Bible in communion with the indwelling Spirit.

They point to Christ arising early and going apart to a solitary place to pray (Mark 1:35), but the Bible does not say that He went to a solitary place to practice centering prayer or silent meditation or chanting a mantra or some such thing!

Contemplatives point to Psalm 46:10, *"Be still, and know that I am God,"* but the psalm does *not* say, "Be silent and seek God in your innermost being"! It simply exhorts us to meditate on the fact that God is God and that He is exalted and will be exalted. The rest of the verse says, *"I will be exalted among the heathen, I will be exalted in the earth."* The psalmist was simply saying, "Be patient and know that God is in charge; trust Him; don't fret."

Contemplatives point to Psalm 62:1, *"Truly my soul waiteth upon God: from him cometh my salvation,"* but this simply refers to trusting in the Lord and has nothing to do with meditating in silence and looking within oneself for union with God.

Contemplatives also point to 1 Kings 19:11-12.

> "And he said, Go forth, and stand upon the mount before the LORD. And, behold, the LORD passed by, and a great and strong wind rent the mountains, and brake in pieces the rocks before the LORD; but the LORD was not in the wind: and after the wind an earthquake; but the LORD was not in the earthquake: And after the earthquake a fire; but the LORD was not in the fire: and after the fire A STILL SMALL VOICE" (1 Kings 19:11-12).

Again, this passage does *not* describe Catholic contemplative practices. Elijah was not meditating in silence. He was not sitting in a cave controlling his breathing and chanting mantras to put himself into a mindless contemplative mode to enter the "cloud of unknowing." God spoke to Elijah in a voice, in words, not by some means that is "beyond thought."

We agree with the following statement:

> "If God had wanted us to encounter Him through mystical practices such as contemplative prayer, why did He not say so? Why did He not give examples and instructions? How could the Holy Spirit inspire the writing of the Scriptures yet forget to include a chapter or two on mysticism, spiritual exercises and mediation of the Eastern variety? Are we to believe that all of this is a great oversight, a huge 'oops' on God's part to have left out such vital instructions on an indispensable experience that is absolutely essential to Christian spirituality? Then, having realized what He had done, are we to believe God, centuries later, revealed this missing ingredient of Christian living to Roman Catholic monks, where it was rejected by the Reformers, only to have Richard Foster reintroduce it all to the twentieth century? This is a bit hard to swallow, but apparently is being accepted by many today" (Gary Gilley, "Mysticism").

God has given His people many "mystical" experiences (e.g., Moses' encounter with God on Mount Sinai, Ezekiel's visions, Paul's experience on the road to Damascus, John's visions on the Isle of Patmos), but in each case God gave the experience according to His sovereign will and nowhere does the Bible instruct men to seek after such things. Jesus warned, *"An evil and adulterous generation seeketh after a sign"* (Mat. 12:29).

Contemplative Spirituality Error # 3: It ignores the Bible's definition of faith.

Mysticism makes much of faith, but it is a blind faith, a leap in the dark. The words "blind" and "darkness" are used dozens of times in *The Cloud of Unknowing*.

True faith is simply believing and obeying the Scripture.

> "So then faith cometh by hearing, and hearing by the word of God" (Romans 10:17).

> "But these are written, that ye might believe that Jesus is the Christ, the Son of God; and that believing ye might have life through his name" (John 20:31).

Hebrews 11 is God's Hall of Faith. Noah believed God's warning and built the ark (Heb. 11:7). Abraham believed God's promise and *"obeyed; and he went out, not knowing whither he went"* (Heb. 11:8). The same was true for all of the people mentioned in Hebrews 11. Their faith consisted of believing God's Word and acting on it, nothing more and nothing less.

True faith does not seek after an experience; it is content with believing God's Word regardless of what its experience happens to be; but contemplative spirituality lusts after an experience.

Centering prayer, for example, is all about achieving an experiential communion with God in the depths of one's being. M. Basil Pennington says, "... we want immediate contact with God Himself, and not some thought, image, or vision of him" (*Finding Grace at the Center*, p. 42).

John Caddock rightly warns:

> "The result of this mystical practice is that the practitioner becomes less interested in objective spiritual knowledge found in the Bible and more interested in the subjective experience which is found through centering prayer" ("What Is Contemplative Spirituality?" *Grace Evangelical Society Journal*, Autumn 1997).

Contemplative Spirituality Error # 4: It ignores Jesus' warning against vain repetition.

The Lord Jesus Christ warned against repetitious prayer.

> "But when ye pray, use not vain repetitions, as the heathen do: for they think that they shall be heard for their much speaking. Be not ye therefore like unto them: for your Father knoweth what things ye have need of, before ye ask him" (Matthew 6:7-8).

Yet repetitious prayer and chanting forms a large part of mystical spirituality.

As we have seen, the Jesus Prayer and the Breath Prayer consist of saying one word or one short phrase repeatedly, even hundreds and thousands of times per day.

Centering prayer also involves repeating a mantra such as "God" or "love," and the practitioner is even instructed not to think about the meaning of the word. If that is not "vain repetition," it is difficult to know what it could be.

Those who chant pagan mantras describe the same spiritual benefits as Christian contemplatives: unity with God, spiritual power, enlightenment, bliss. In a 1982 interview, George Harrison, the late Beatle, told how that he once chanted the Hare Krishna mantra (*Hare Krishna, Hare Krishna, Krishna Krishna, Hare Hare, Hare Rama, Hare Rama, Rama Rama, Hare Hare*) for 23 hours, all the way from France to Portugal, nonstop. He said that he found his way even though he couldn't speak French, Spanish, or Portuguese, because "once you get chanting, then things start to happen transcendentally" ("Hare Krishna Mantra-- There's Nothing Higher," George Harrison Interview, 1982, http://www.krishna.org/Articles/2000/08/00066.html).

Contemplative Spirituality Error # 5: It ignores the fact that multitudes of professing Christians are not born again.

Contemplative practices are recommended for Christians indiscriminately, without regard to genuine salvation. I have read dozens of books on contemplative spirituality, and none of them include a clear exhortation to biblical salvation.

In fact, these are Roman Catholic practices and Rome teaches that salvation is through baptism and the sacraments. As we have seen, the Catholic saints who developed contemplative mysticism did not have a biblical testimony of salvation.

M. Basil Pennington is typical when he says, "We have been made sharers in the divine nature by baptism" (*Finding Grace at the Center*, p. 34).

We have seen that the participants in the liberal emerging church rarely have a biblical testimony of salvation.

Centering prayer is the practice of supposedly communing with God in the center of one's being, but how can that be possible if the individual has never been born again and is not, therefore, indwelt by the Holy Spirit? It is impossible, of course. The only thing that the unbeliever can commune with in the center of his being is sinful darkness and deception. *"The heart is deceitful above all things, and desperately wicked: who can know it?"* (Jeremiah 17:9).

No wonder they describe centering prayer as "darkness"!

Contemplative Spirituality Error # 6: It exchanges the God of the Bible for a blind idol.

To reject conscious thinking and biblical reasoning with the objective of finding God beyond a "cloud of unknowing" in "darkness" and "nothingness" -- which is how they describe their own practice -- is to exchange the God of the Bible for a blind idol.

God is not hidden behind a cloud of unknowing. He has revealed Himself in the Bible and in the incarnate Son of God. To say that the Divine Revelation is insufficient and to try to go beyond it is presumption. It is to trade the light for darkness. It is to turn one's back on the truth to enter a lie. It makes space for the creation of a false god that is not defined by Scripture but is perceived and "intuited" through blind mystical experience.

Benedictine priest Willigis Jager says the aim of Christian prayer is transcendental contemplation in which the practitioner enters a deeper level of consciousness. This requires emptying the mind, which is achieved by focusing on the breathing and repeating a mantra. This "quiets the rational mind," "empties the mind," and "frustrates our ordinary discursive thinking" (James Conner, "Contemplative Retreat for Monastics," *Monastic Interreligious Dialogue Bulletin*, Oct. 1985). Jager draws particularly from Johannes Tauler, Meister Eckhart, John of the Cross, Teresa of Avila, and *The Cloud of Unknowing*.

He says that as the rational thinking is emptied and transformed, one "SEEMS TO LOSE ORIENTATION" and must "go on in blind faith and trust." He says that there is "nothing to do but surrender" to "this pure blackness" where "no image or thought of God remains."

This is idolatry. To be dissatisfied with the Revelation God has given of Himself and to attempt to find Him beyond this Revelation through mysticism is to trade the true and living God for an idol.

In *The New Seeds of Contemplation*, Thomas Merton made the following statement:

> "In the end the contemplative suffers the anguish of realizing that HE NO LONGER KNOWS WHAT GOD IS. He may or may not mercifully realize that, after all, this is a great gain, because 'God is not a what,' not a 'thing.' This is precisely one of the essential characteristics of contemplative experience. It sees that there is no 'what' that can be called God" (p. 13).

This is a blatant denial of the Bible as divine revelation. Though it is true that God is not a *thing* in the sense that He is a created being, He *is* a *thing* in the sense that He is a God that can be understood and known by His own revelation.

Seeking God beyond the Bible in thoughtless mysticism opens the practitioner to demonic delusion. He is left with no divinely-revealed authority by which he can test his mystical experiences and intuitions. He is left with an idol of his own vain imagination (Jeremiah 17:9) and a doctrine of devils.

No wonder that pagan mystic practitioners such as Hindu yogis and Zen Buddhists recognize Catholic contemplatives as fellow travelers.

Contemplative Spirituality Error # 7: It ignores the Bible's warnings against associating with heresy and paganism.

To practice contemplative spirituality is to ignore the Bible's warnings about separation because it puts one into intimate contact wit Roman Catholicism, Eastern Orthodoxy, and beyond that with pagan religions.

Though separation is repudiated by the contemplative movement, it is a doctrine that is clearly taught in Scripture.

> "Regard not them that have familiar spirits, neither seek after wizards, to be defiled by them: I am the LORD your God" (Leviticus 19:31).

> "There shall not be found among you any one that maketh his son or his daughter to pass through the fire, or that useth divination, or an observer of times, or an enchanter, or a witch, Or a charmer, or a consulter with familiar spirits, or a wizard, or a necromancer. For all that do these things are an abomination unto the LORD: and because of these abominations the LORD thy God doth drive them out from before thee" (Deuteronomy 18:10-12).

"But were mingled among the heathen, and learned their works. And they served their idols: which were a snare unto them" (Psalms 106:35-36).

"Therefore thou hast forsaken thy people the house of Jacob, because they be replenished from the east, and are soothsayers like the Philistines, and they please themselves in the children of strangers" (Isaiah 2:6).

"Thus saith the LORD, Learn not the way of the heathen..." (Jeremiah 10:2).

"But when ye pray, use not vain repetitions, as the heathen do: for they think that they shall be heard for their much speaking" (Matthew 6:7).

"For I know this, that after my departing shall grievous wolves enter in among you, not sparing the flock. Also of your own selves shall men arise, speaking perverse things, to draw away disciples after them. Therefore watch, and remember, that by the space of three years I ceased not to warn every one night and day with tears" (Acts 20:29-31).

"Now I beseech you, brethren, mark them which cause divisions and offences contrary to the doctrine which ye have learned; and avoid them" (Romans 16:17).

"Wherefore, my dearly beloved, flee from idolatry" (1 Cor. 10:14).

"Ye cannot drink the cup of the Lord, and the cup of devils: ye cannot be partakers of the Lord's table, and of the table of devils. Do we provoke the Lord to jealousy? are we stronger than he?" (1 Cor. 10:21-22).

"Be not deceived: evil communications corrupt good manners" (1 Cor. 15:33).

"Be ye not unequally yoked together with unbelievers: for what fellowship hath righteousness with unrighteousness? and what communion hath light with darkness? And what concord hath Christ with Belial? or what part hath he that believeth with an infidel? And what agreement hath the temple of God with idols? for ye are the temple of the living God; as God hath said, I will dwell in them, and walk in them; and I will be their God, and they shall be my people. Wherefore come out from among them, and be ye separate, saith the Lord, and touch not the unclean thing; and I will receive you, and will be a Father unto you, and ye shall be my sons and daughters, saith the Lord Almighty" (2 Corinthians 6:14-18).

"And have no fellowship with the unfruitful works of darkness, but rather reprove them" (Ephesians 5:11).

"Brethren, be followers together of me, and mark them which walk so as ye have us for an ensample. (For many walk, of whom I have told you often, and now tell you even weeping, that they are the enemies of the cross of Christ: Whose end is destruction, whose God is their belly, and whose glory is in their shame, who mind earthly things" (Philippians 3:17-19).

"Beware lest any man spoil you through philosophy and vain deceit, after the tradition of men, after the rudiments of the world, and not after Christ" (Colossians 2:8).

"Having a form of godliness, but denying the power thereof: from such turn away" (2 Timothy 3:5).

"And we know that we are of God, and the whole world lieth in wickedness. And we know that the Son of God is come, and hath given us an understanding, that we may know him that is true, and we are in him that is true, even in his Son Jesus Christ. This is the true God, and eternal life. Little children, keep yourselves from idols. Amen" (1 John 5:19-21).

"If there come any unto you, and bring not this doctrine, receive him not into your house, neither bid him God speed: For he that biddeth him God speed is partaker of his evil deeds" (2 John 10-11).

"And I heard another voice from heaven, saying, Come out of her, my people, that ye be not partakers of her sins, and that ye receive not of her plagues" (Revelation 18:4).

We see that the doctrine of separation is not based on one or two verses, but it is woven throughout Scripture. Israel was forbidden to associate with her idolatrous neighbors and when she disobeyed she was corrupted by idolatry and lost her holy place and favor with God. Likewise, believers in the New Testament dispensation are forbidden to associate with evil and idolatry. By associating with paganism we become confused in our thinking and corrupt in our ways, and we come under God's judgment.

Yet the contemplative practices that are used by the emerging church come from Roman Catholicism and Greek Orthodoxy, and the fact that these "churches" preach a sacramental gospel that mixes grace with works and are loaded down with heresies and idolatry is ignored. We have documented these in the chapter on "The Error of Catholic

Monasticism." And in the book *Contemplative Mysticism: A Powerful Ecumenical Glue*, we document the heresies and outright insanities associated with Rome's mystic "saints."

Further, many are using Christian contemplative practices as an interfaith bridge to eastern religions, openly promoting the integration of pagan practices such as Zen Buddhism and Hindu yoga.

In the book *Spiritual Friend* (which is highly recommended by the "evangelical" Richard Foster), Tilden Edwards says:

> "This mystical stream is THE WESTERN BRIDGE TO FAR EASTERN SPIRITUALITY" (*Spiritual Friend*, 1980, pp. 18, 19).

Since Eastern "spirituality" is idol worship and the worship of self and thus is communion with devils, what Edwards is unwittingly saying is that contemplative practices are a bridge to demonic realms.

The Roman Catholic contemplative gurus that the evangelicals and emergents are following have developed intimate relationships with pagan mystics.

Jesuit priest Thomas Clarke admits that the Catholic contemplative movement has "BEEN INFLUENCED BY ZEN BUDDHISM, TRANSCENDENTAL MEDITATION, OR OTHER CURRENTS OF EASTERN SPIRITUALITY" (*Finding Grace at the Center*, pp. 79, 80).

THOMAS MERTON, the most influential Roman Catholic contemplative of this generation, was "a strong builder of bridges between East and West" (*Twentieth-Century Mystics*, p. 39). The *Yoga Journal* makes the following observation:

> "Merton had encountered Zen Buddhism, Sufism, Taoism and Vedanta many years prior to his Asian journey. MERTON WAS ABLE TO UNCOVER THE STREAM WHERE THE WISDOM OF EAST AND WEST MERGE AND FLOW TOGETHER, BEYOND DOGMA, IN THE DEPTHS OF INNER EXPERIENCE. ... Merton embraced the spiritual philosophies of the East and integrated this wisdom into (his) own life through direct practice" (*Yoga Journal*, Jan.-Feb. 1999, quoted from the Lighthouse Trails web site).

Merton was a student of Zen master Daisetsu Suzuki and Buddhist monk Thich Nhat Hanh. In fact, he claimed to be both a Buddhist and a Christian. The titles of his books include *Zen and the Birds of the Appetite* and *Mystics and the Zen Masters*.

He said: "I see no contradiction between Buddhism and Christianity. The future of Zen is in the West. I intend to become as good a Buddhist as I can" (David Steindl-Rast, "Recollection of Thomas Merton's Last Days in the West," *Monastic Studies*, 7:10, 1969, http://www.gratefulness.org/readings/dsr_merton_recol2.htm).

Merton defined mysticism as an experience beyond words. In a speech to monks of eastern religions in Calcutta in October 1968 he said: "... the deepest level of communication is not communication, but communion. IT IS WORDLESS. IT IS BEYOND WORDS, AND IT IS BEYOND SPEECH, and it is BEYOND CONCEPT" (*The Asian Journal of Thomas Merton*, 1975 edition, p. 308).

Personally, what Merton found in meditation was the same as what Mother Teresa found: darkness. He said:

> "God, my God, God who I meet in darkness, with you it is always the same thing, always the same question that nobody knows how to answer. I've prayed to you in the daytime with thoughts and reasons, and in the nighttime. I've explained to you a hundred times my motives for entering the monastery, and you have listened and said nothing. And I have turned away and wept with shame. Perhaps the most urgent and practical renunciation is the renunciation of all questions, because I have begun to realize that you never answer when I expect" (*Soul Searching: The Journey of Thomas Merton*, 2007, DVD).

The Bible warns that "*evil communications corrupt good manners*" (1 Cor. 15:33), and it is not surprising, then, that Merton was deeply and negatively influenced by his intimate association with pagan religions. Eventually he denied the God of the Bible, the reality of sin, the separation of man from God because of sin, the necessity of Christ's Atonement, the bodily resurrection, and Hell.

He adopted the belief that within every man is a pure spark of divine illumination, and that men can know God through a variety of paths:

> "At the center of our being is a point of nothingness which is untouched by sin and by illusion, a point of pure truth, a point or spark which belongs entirely to God. It is like a pure diamond blazing with the invisible light of heaven. It is in everybody. I have no program for saying this. It is only given, but the gate of heaven is everywhere" (*Soul Searching: The Journey of Thomas Merton*, 2007, DVD).

In 1969 Merton took the trip of his dreams, to visit India, Ceylon, Singapore, and Thailand, to experience the places where his beloved eastern religions were born. He said he was "going home."

In Sri Lanka he visited a Buddhist shrine by the ocean and contemplated before the idols barefoot. He described this as an experience of great illumination, a vision of "inner clearness." He said, "I don't know when in my life I have ever had such a sense of beauty and spiritual validity running together in one aesthetic illumination" (*The Asian Journal*, p. 235).

Actually it was a demonic delusion.

Six days later Merton was electrocuted in a cottage in Bangkok by a faulty fan switch. He was there to attend a dialogue of contemplative mystics, both Catholic and Buddhist. He was fifty-three years old.

Merton has many disciples in the Roman Catholic Church, including David Steindle-Rast, William Johnston, Henri Nouwen, Philip St. Romain, William Shannon, and James Finley.

Benedictine monk **JOHN MAIN**, who is a pioneer in the field of contemplative spirituality, studied under a Hindu guru. Main syncretized contemplative practices with yoga and in 1975 began founding meditation groups in Catholic monasteries. These spread outside of the Catholic Church and grew into an ecumenical network called the World Community for Christian Meditation (WCCM). He taught the following method:

> "Sit still and upright, close your eyes and repeat your prayer-phrase (mantra). Recite your prayer-phrase and gently listen to it as you say it. DO NOT THINK ABOUT ANYTHING. As thoughts come, simply keep returning to your prayer-phrase. In this way, one places everything aside: INSTEAD OF TALKING TO GOD, ONE IS JUST BEING WITH GOD, allowing God's presence to fill his heart, thus transforming his inner being" (*The Teaching of Dom John Main: How to Meditate*, Meditation Group of Saint Patrick's Basilica, Ottawa, Canada).

THOMAS KEATING is heavily involved in interfaith dialogue and promotes the use of contemplative practices as a tool for creating interfaith unity. He says, "It is important for us to appreciate the values that are present in the genuine teachings of the great religions of the world" (*Finding Grace at the Center*, 2002, p. 76).

Keating is past president of the Monastic Interreligious Dialogue (MID), which is sponsored by the Benedictine and Cistercian monasteries of North America. Founded in 1977, it is "committed to fostering interreligious and intermonastic dialogue AT THE LEVEL OF SPIRITUAL PRACTICE AND EXPERIENCE." This means that they are using contemplative practices and yoga as the glue for interfaith unity to help create world peace. MID works in association with the Pontifical Council for Interreligious Dialogue. Consider one of the objectives of the MID:

> "The methods of concentration used in other religious traditions can be useful for removing obstacles to a deep contact with God. THEY CAN GIVE A BETTER UNDERSTANDING OF THE ONENESS OF CHRIST AS EXPRESSED IN THE VARIOUS TRADITIONS and CONTRIBUTE TO THE FORMATION OF A NEW WORLD RELIGIOUS CULTURE. They can also be helpful in the development of certain potencies in the individual, for THERE ARE SOME ZEN-HINDU-SUFI-ETC. DIMENSIONS IN EACH HEART" (Mary L. O'Hara, "Report on Monastic Meeting at Petersham," *MID Bulletin 1*, October 1977).

Keating and Richard Foster are involved in the Living Spiritual Teachers Project, a group that associates together Zen Buddhist monks and nuns, universalists, occultists, and New Agers. Members include the Dalai Lama, who claims to be the reincarnation of an advanced spiritual entity; Marianne Williamson, promoter of the occultic *A Course in Miracles*; Marcus Borg, who believes that Jesus was not virgin born and did not rise from the grave; Catholic nun Joan Chittister, who says we must become "in tune with the cosmic voice of God"; Andrew Harvey, who says that men need to "claim their divine humanity"; Matthew Fox, who believes there are many paths to God; Alan Jones, who calls the gospel of the cross a vile doctrine; and Desmond Tutu, who says "because everybody is a God-carrier, all are brothers and sisters."

M. BASIL PENNINGTON, a Roman Catholic Trappist monk and co-author of the influential contemplative book *Finding Grace at the Center*, calls Hindu swamis "our wise friends from the East" and says, "Many Christians who take their prayer life seriously have been greatly helped by Yoga, Zen, TM, and similar practices..." (25th anniversary edition, p. 23).

In his foreword to **THOMAS RYAN'S** book *Disciplines for Christian Living*, Henri Nouwen says:

> "[T]he author shows A WONDERFUL OPENNESS TO THE GIFTS OF BUDDHISM, HINDUISM, AND MOSLEM RELIGION. He discovers their great wisdom for the spiritual life of the Christian and does not hesitate to bring that wisdom home."

ANTHONY DE MELLO readily admitted to borrowing from Buddhist Zen masters and Hindu gurus. He even taught that God is everything:

> "Think of the air as of an immense ocean that surrounds you ... an ocean heavily colored with God's presence and God's being. ... While you draw the air into your lungs you are drawing God in" (*Sadhana: A Way to God*, p. 36).

De Mello suggested chanting the Hindu word "om" (p. 49) and even instructed his students to communicate with inanimate objects:

> "Choose some object that you use frequently: a pen, a cup ... Now gently place the object in front of you or on your lap and speak to it. Begin by asking it questions about itself, its life, its origins, its future. And listen while it unfolds to you the secret of its being and of its destiny. Listen while it explains to you what existence means to it. Your object has some hidden wisdom to reveal to you about yourself. Ask for this and listen to what it has to say. There is something that you can give this object. What is it? What does it want from you?" (p. 55).

Some of the Roman Catholic contemplative priests have pursued their interfaith venture so far that they have become Hindu and Zen Buddhist monks. Following are some examples:

JULES MONCHANIN and **HENRI LE SAUX**, Benedictine priests, founded a Hindu-Christian ashram in India called Shantivanam (Forest of Peace). They took the names of Hindu holy men, with le Saux calling himself Swami Abhishiktananda (bliss of the anointed one). He stayed in Hindu ashrams and learned from Hindu gurus. In 1968 le Saux became a hermit in the Himalayas, living there until his death in 1973. His books *Prayer: Hindu-Christian Meeting Point* and *Saccidananda: A Christian Approach to Advaitic Experience* continue to be published.

The Shantivanam Ashram was subsequently led by **ALAN GRIFFITHS** (1906-93). He called himself Swami Dayananda (bliss of compassion), went barefoot, and was clothed in an orange-colored robe after the fashion of a Hindu monk. Through his books and lecture tours Griffiths had a large influence in promoting the interfaith philosophy in Roman Catholic monasteries in America, England, Australia, and Germany. He wrote 12 books on interfaith dialogue, the most popular being *Marriage of East and West*.

WAYNE TEASDALE (1945-2004) was a Roman Catholic lay monk whose writings are influential in the contemplative movement. As a student in a Catholic college in Massachusetts, he began visiting St. Joseph's Abbey near Spencer and came under the direction of Thomas Keating, one of the founders of the centering prayer movement. This eventually led him into an intimate association with pagan religions and the adoption of Hinduism. Teasdale visited Shantivanam Ashram and lived in a nearby Hindu ashram for two years, following in Alan Griffiths' footsteps. In 1989 he became a "Christian" *sanyassa* or a Hindu monk. Teasdale was deeply involved in interfaith activities, believing that what the religions hold in common can be the basis for creating a new world, which he called the "Interspiritual Age" -- a "global culture based on common spiritual values." He believed that mystics of all religions are in touch with the same God. He helped found the Interspiritual Dialogue in Action (ISDnA), one of the many New Age organizations affiliated with the United Nations. (Its UN NGO sponsor is the National Service Conference of the American Ethical Union.) It is committed "to actively serve in the evolution of human consciousness and global transformation."

WILLIGIS JAGER, a well-known German Benedictine priest who has published contemplative books in German and English, spent six years studying Zen Buddhism under Yamada Koun Roshi. (*Roshi* is the title of a Zen master.) In 1981 he was authorized as a Zen teacher and took the name Ko-un Roshi. He moved back to Germany and began teaching Zen at the Munsterschwarzach Abbey, drawing as many as 150 people a day.

In February 2002 he was ordered by Cardinal Joseph Ratzinger (currently Pope Benedict XVI) to cease all public activities. He was "faulted for playing down the Christian concept of God as a person and for stressing mystical experience above doctrinal truths" ("Two More Scholars Censured by Rome," *National Catholic Reporter*, March 1, 2002).

Thus, Ratzinger tried to stem the tide of eastern mysticism that is flooding into the Catholic monastic communities, but he was extremely inconsistent and ultimately ineffectual.

Jager kept quiet for a little while, but soon he was speaking and writing again. In 2003 Liguori Press published *Search for the Meaning of Life: Essays and Reflections on the Mystical Experience,* and in 2006 Liguori published *Mysticism for Modern Times: Conversations with Willigis Jager*

Jager denies the creation and fall of man as taught in the Bible. He denies the unique divinity of Christ, as well as His substitutionary atonement and bodily resurrection. He believes that the universe is evolving and that evolving universe is God. He believes that man has reached a major milestone in evolution, that he is entering an era in which his consciousness will be transformed. Jager believes in the divinity of man, that what Christ is every man can become. He believes that all religions point to the same God and promotes interfaith dialogue as the key to unifying mankind.

Jager learned these heretical pagan doctrines from his close association with Zen Buddhism and his blind mysticism. He says that the aim of Christian prayer is transcendental contemplation in which the practitioner enters a deeper level of consciousness. This requires emptying the mind, which is achieved by focusing on the breathing and repeating a mantra. This "quiets the rational mind," "empties the mind," and "frustrates our ordinary discursive thinking" (James Conner, "Contemplative Retreat for Monastics," *Monastic Interreligious Dialogue Bulletin*, Oct. 1985).

There is also an intimate and growing relationship between the Catholic contemplative movement and the New Age.

The aforementioned Thomas Keating is past president of the Temple of Understanding, a New Age organization founded in 1960 by Juliet Hollister. The mission of this organization is to "create a more just and peaceful world." The tools for reaching this objective include interfaith education, dialogue, and experiential knowledge (mystical practices).

Thomas Merton spoke at a Temple of Understanding conference in Calcutta, India in 1968. He praised the interfaith atmosphere and his fellow religionists:

> "There were good papers by two rabbis, one from New York and one from Jerusalem, and by Dr. Wei Tat, a Chinese scholar from Taiwan, on the I Ching. Also by Sufis, Jains, and others. The warmth of the Ramakrishna monks, alert and quiet. ... I was ... invited tonight to supper at the house of the Birlas, supporters of the Temple of Understanding. In the jeep I had a fine conversation with Judith Hollister, warm, lovely, simple, sincere. ... Vatsala Amin, the young Jain laywoman from Bombay who presented the Jain message at the Temple of Understanding Conference, is an extremely beautiful and spiritual person. ... She meditates on a picture of her guru ... I on my part am impressed by her purity and perfection" (*The Asian Journal of Thomas Merton*, 1975 edition, pp. 34, 35).

Shambhala Publication, a publisher that specializes in Occultic, Jungian, New Age, Buddhist, and Hindu writings, also publishes the writings of Catholic mystics, including *The Wisdom of the Desert* by Thomas Merton, *The Writings of Hildegard of Bingen*, and *The Practice of the Presence of God* by Brother Lawrence.

Sue Monk Kidd, who believes in the divinity of mankind and considers herself a goddess, was asked to write recommendations to two Catholic contemplative books. She wrote the foreword to the 2006 edition of Henri Nouwen's *With Open Hands* and the introduction to the 2007 edition of Thomas Merton's *New Seeds of Contemplation*.

New Ager Caroline Myss (pronounced mace) has written a book based on Teresa of Avila's visions. It is entitled *Entering the Castle: Finding the Inner Path to God and Your Soul's Purpose*. Myss says, "For me, the spirit is the vessel of divinity" ("Caroline Myss' Journey," *Conscious Choice*, September 2003).

On April 15, 2008, emerging church leaders Rob Bell and Doug Pagitt joined the Dalai Lama for the New Age Seeds of Compassion InterSpiritual Event in Seattle. It brought together Episcopalians, Roman Catholics, Buddhists, Sikhs, Muslims, and others. The event featured a dialogue on "the themes common to all spiritual traditions." The Dalai Lama said, "I think everyone, ultimately, deep inside [has] some kind of goodness" ("Emergent Church Leaders' InterSpirituality," *Christian Post*, April 17, 2008). On the Seeds of Compassion web site, the Dalai Lama says, "[Compassion] is my simple religion. There is no need for temples; no need for complicated philosophy. OUR OWN BRAIN, OUR OWN HEART IS OUR TEMPLE; the philosophy is kindness." The Seeds of Compassion's "Seven Compassion Practices" begins with a "morning ritual" whereby the individual meditates on compassion and makes a positive confession about it.

In his book *Velvet Elvis*, Bell gives a glowing recommendation of the New Age philosopher Ken Wilber. Bell recommends that his readers sit at Wilber's feet for three months!

> "For a mind-blowing introduction to emergence theory and divine creativity, set aside three months and read Ken Wilber's *A Brief History of Everything*" (*Velvet Elvis*, p. 192).

Brian McLaren also recommends Wilber's work, and the aforementioned Catholic monk Wayne Teasdale conducted a *Mystic Heart* seminar series with Wilber. In the first one Teasdale said, "You are God; I am God; they are God; it is God" ("The Mystic Heart: The Supreme Identity," http://video.google.com/videoplay?docid=-7652038071112490301&q=ken+Wilber).

Roger Oakland remarks:

> "Ken Wilber was raised in a conservative Christian church, but at some point he left that faith and is now a major proponent of Buddhist mysticism. His book that Bell recommends, *A Brief History of Everything*, is published by Shambhala Publications, named after the term, which in Buddhism means the mystical abode of spirit beings. ...

Wilber is perhaps best known for what he calls integral theory. On his website, he has a chart called the Integral Life Practice Matrix, which lists several activities one can practice 'to authentically exercise all aspects or dimensions of your own being-in-the-world' Here are a few of these spiritual activities that Wilber promotes: yoga, Zen, centering prayer, kabbalah (Jewish mysticism), TM, tantra (Hindu-based sexuality), and kundalini yoga. ... *A Brief History of Everything* discusses these practices (in a favorable light) as well. For Rob Bell to say that Wilber's book is 'mind-blowing' and readers should spend three months in it leaves no room for doubt regarding Rob Bell's spiritual sympathies. What is alarming is that so many Christian venues, such as Christian junior high and high schools, are using *Velvet Elvis* and the *Noomas*" (*Faith Undone*, p. 110).

In *Up from Eden: A Transpersonal View of Human Evolution* (1981, 2004), Ken Wilber calls the Garden of Eden a "fable" and the biblical view of history "amusing" (pp. xix, 3). He describes his "perennial philosophy" as follows:

"... it is true that there is some sort of Infinite, some type of Absolute Godhead, but it cannot properly be conceived as a colossal Being, a great Daddy, or a big Creator set apart from its creations, from things and events and human beings themselves. Rather, it is best conceived (metaphorically) as the ground or suchness or condition of all things and events. It is not a Big Thing set apart from finite things, but rather the reality or suchness or ground of all things. ... the perennial philosophy declares that the absolute is One, Whole, and Undivided" (p. 6).

Wilber says that this perennial philosophy "forms the esoteric core of Hinduism, Buddhism, Taoism, Sufism, AND CHRISTIAN MYSTICISM" (p. 5).

Thus, this New Ager recognizes that Roman Catholic mysticism, which spawned the contemplative movement within Protestantism, has the same esoteric core faith as pagan idolatry!

Contemplative Spirituality Error # 8: It does not encourage one to test everything carefully by Scripture.

The Bible warns repeatedly about the possibility of spiritual delusion, and the only sure way to avoid deception is by carefully testing everything by Scripture, yet this is a principle that is grossly neglected in contemplative writings.

We are to "prove all things" (1 Thess. 5:21). We are to "try the spirits" (1 John 4:1). We are to judge all preaching (1 Cor. 14:29). We are to beware of false prophets which cloak themselves in sheep's clothing (Mat. 7:15-17).

The Bereans were commended for doing this (Acts 17:11), but the emerging church thinks it has a better way.

Spencer Burke tells how he was led into Roman Catholic mysticism:

> "I remember going on a three-day silent retreat with Brennan Manning while I was still at Mariners. To my horror, BRENNAN TOLD US WE SHOULD NOT READ ANY BOOKS DURING THIS TIME--EVEN THE BIBLE. Instead, we should just sit and let God speak to us. I remember going to Brennan and telling him I felt like a phony. I even wrote a poem about it-how I was a mockingbird that didn't have any authentic voice. He nodded then asked why I was so angry at God. Angry? Was I angry? You know, I was. Lisa and I had just lost two kids early in pregnancy and nothing seemed to be going right. I was angry that God had robbed me of being a dad and mad that the evangelical program hadn't worked for me. I mean, I'd done everything I was supposed to and this is what I got? Brennan encouraged me to go back outside and meet Jesus. I was incensed. And yet as I sat there fuming, a strange thing happened. I felt like I could see Jesus standing there asking to come and be with me. In my anger, I refused. I could barely even look at him. Still, there he stood. When I finally relented, he sat down next to me and gently wrapped his arms around me. He didn't say anything, he just held me in my pain. In that moment, I think I realized that God could handle severe honesty. Authenticity, in all its messiness, was not offensive to him. There was room for doubt and anger and confusion. ...
>
> "THAT EXPERIENCE SEEMED TO MARK A TURNING POINT IN MY FAITH. SHORTLY AFTERWARD, I stopped reading from the approved evangelical reading list and BEGAN TO DISTANCE MYSELF FROM THE EVANGELICAL AGENDA. I DISCOVERED new authors and NEW VOICES at the bookstore--Thomas Merton, Henri Nouwen and St. Teresa of Avila. The more I read, the more intrigued I became. Contemplative spirituality seemed to open up a whole new way for me to understand and experience God. I was deeply moved by works like *The Cloud of Unknowning*, *The Dark Night of the Soul* and the *Early Writings of the Desert Fathers*" ("From the Third Floor of the Garage: The Story of TheOOze," http://www.spencerburke.com/pdf/presskit.pdf).

Observe that Brennan Manning taught Burke that he should try to communicate with God WITHOUT THE BIBLE and should accept the experiences that came from this method as authentic. This is blind mysticism.

Manning mocks those who are Bible-oriented. In *The Signature of Jesus* he says:

> "I am deeply distressed by what I only can call in our Christian culture THE IDOLATRY OF THE SCRIPTURES. For many Christians, the Bible is not a pointer to God but God himself. In a word--bibliolatry. God cannot be confined within the covers of a leather-bound book. I develop a nasty rash around people who speak as if mere scrutiny of its pages will reveal precisely how God thinks and precisely what God wants" (pp. 188-89).

This is a ridiculous and false statement. It is a strawman. I don't know any Bible-believing Christians who consider the Bible their God. We do not worship the Bible; we worship the God of the Bible; but we honor the God of the Bible by accepting the Bible as His very Word, as an infallible light in a dark world, which it most definitely claims to be. The Bible *DOES* tell us precisely how God thinks and what He wants. Jesus said, *"He that is of God heareth God's words: ye therefore hear them not, because ye are not of God"* (John 8:47).

Manning's heretical thinking is right at home in the contemplative spirituality movement.

The practice of centering prayer requires being non-judgmental about one's experience.

> "Take everything that happens during the periods of centering prayer peacefully and gratefully, WITHOUT PUTTING A JUDGMENT ON ANYTHING, and just let the thoughts go by" (Pennington and Keating, *Finding Grace at the Center*, pp. 58, 59).
>
> "YOU MUST BE NON-JUDGMENTAL about particular experiences of this prayer" (p. 60).

To the contrary, if everything is not carefully tested by Scripture there is no way to know if something is true or authentically from God. False teachers hide themselves in sheep's clothing (Matthew 7:15). The devil is very subtle, transforming himself into an angel of light, and his ministers appear as ministers of righteousness (2 Corinthians 11:14-15).

Emergents and contemplatives give lip service to honoring the Bible, *but in practice they do not*. Consider Tony Campolo. On the one hand he says we should exercise discernment, but in true emerging church fashion he contradicts this on the other hand:

> "We must pay serious attention to mystical happenings, and discern, in the context of biblical understanding in Christian community, whether or not we believe they are of God. Discernment is crucial to mystical spirituality. Without it, anything goes. On the other hand, WE MUST LEARN TO DOUBT OUR DOUBTS if we are going to be open to the work of the Spirit in our lives" (p. 11).

To "doubt our doubts" cancels out effective biblical discernment!

Contemplative Spirituality Error # 9: It downplays the danger of spiritual delusion.

The Bible repeatedly warns about the danger of spiritual delusion and exhorts believers to be very careful. Consider the following:

> "Beware of false prophets, which come to you in sheep's clothing, but inwardly they are ravening wolves" (Matthew 7:15).

> "And Jesus answered and said unto them, Take heed that no man deceive you. For many shall come in my name, saying, I am Christ; and shall deceive many" (Matthew 24:4-5).

> "For there shall arise false Christs, and false prophets, and shall shew great signs and wonders; insomuch that, if *it were* possible, they shall deceive the very elect" (Matthew 24:24).

> "But I fear, lest by any means, as the serpent beguiled Eve through his subtilty, so your minds should be corrupted from the simplicity that is in Christ. For if he that cometh preacheth another Jesus, whom we have not preached, or if ye receive another spirit, which ye have not received, or another gospel, which ye have not accepted, ye might well bear with him" (2 Corinthians 11:3-4).

"For such are false apostles, deceitful workers, transforming themselves into the apostles of Christ. And no marvel; for Satan himself is transformed into an angel of light. Therefore it is no great thing if his ministers also be transformed as the ministers of righteousness; whose end shall be according to their works" (2 Corinthians 11:13-15).

"That we henceforth be no more children, tossed to and fro, and carried about with every wind of doctrine, by the sleight of men, and cunning craftiness, whereby they lie in wait to deceive" (Ephesians 4:14).

"Beware lest any man spoil you through philosophy and vain deceit, after the tradition of men, after the rudiments of the world, and not after Christ" (Colossians 2:8).

"Therefore let us not sleep, as do others; but let us watch and be sober" (1 Thessalonians 5:6).

"Now the Spirit speaketh expressly, that in the latter times some shall depart from the faith, giving heed to seducing spirits, and doctrines of devils" (1 Timothy 4:1).

"But evil men and seducers shall wax worse and worse, deceiving, and being deceived" (2 Timothy 3:13).

"Be sober, be vigilant; because your adversary the devil, as a roaring lion, walketh about, seeking whom he may devour" (1 Peter 5:8).

"Beloved, believe not every spirit, but try the spirits whether they are of God: because many false prophets are gone out into the world" (1 John 4:1).

To be sober means to be in control of one's mind, to be spiritually and mentally alert. It means to be on guard against danger. It is the opposite of emptying one's mind and letting's one's imagination run wild and using a mantra to keep one's thoughts at bay.

The Bible warns that demons transform themselves into angels of light (2 Cor. 11:13-15). It warns of false christs and false spirits (Mat. 24:4-5; 2 Cor. 11:3-4).

When emergents see "Jesus" in their contemplations, how can they be certain that it is the Jesus of the Bible and not a false christ or a demonic delusion? The only way to be certain is by making the Bible the central authority and carefully testing everything by it, but mysticism does not provide such certainty.

In Scripture, error is often referred to in terms of cunning deception. We are warned that wolves hide in sheep's clothing (Mat. 7:15). See Matthew 24:11, 24; 2 Corinthians 4:2; 11:13; Ephesians 4:14; Colossians 2:4, 8; 2 Thessalonians 2:9-10; 2 Timothy 3:13.

In light of these warnings, we see the danger and folly of the contemplative practices.

Some of the contemplative practices, such as **CENTERING PRAYER**, attempt to shut down the mind. The very title of the popular 14th century meditative book *The Cloud of Unknowing* refers to the practice of blotting out conscious thoughts in the attempt to enter into the depths of silent meditation and transcendental communion with God.

> "I urge you to dismiss every clever or subtle thought no matter how holy or valuable. Cover it with a thick cloud of forgetting because in this life only love can touch God as He is in Himself, never knowledge" (*The Cloud of Unknowing,* chapter 8).

The *Cloud of Unknowing* instructs the contemplative practitioner to choose a one-syllable word and to repeat it as a mantra to "beat down every kind of thought under the cloud of forgetting" (chapter 7, p. 56).

The practitioner is instructed NOT to focus his attention on the meaning of the word or to use "logic to examine or explain this word ... nor allow yourself to ponder its ramifications" (chapter 36, p. 94).

It also says, "Have no fear of the evil one, for he will not dare come near you" (chapter 34, p. 92).

Centering Prayer involves "moving beyond thinking into a place of utter stillness" (*The Sacred Way*, p. 71).

Note the following excerpts from *Finding Grace at the Center* by Pennington and Keating, which emphasize the unthinking aspect of centering prayer:

> "It is best when this word is wholly interior without a definite thought or actual sound" (p. 39).
>
> "We are quite passive. We let it happen" (p. 39).
>
> "As it goes beyond thought, beyond image, there is nothing left by which to judge it" (p. 43).
>
> "By turning off the ordinary flow of thoughts ... one's world begins to change" (p. 48).
>
> "Go on with this nothing, moved only by your love for God" (p. 49).
>
> "The important thing is not to pay any attention to them [thoughts]. They are like the noise in the street..." (p. 51).
>
> "Any thought will bring you out [of the deep waters of silence]" (p. 52).
>
> "[Centering prayer] leads you to a silence beyond thought and words..." (p. 53).
>
> "Firmly reject all clear ideas, however pious or delightful" (p. 54).
>
> "As soon as you start to reflect, the experience is over" (p. 56).

In light of the Bible's warnings about the great potential for spiritual deception and the necessity of constant sobermindedness, I cannot imagine a more dangerous spiritual practice than centering prayer.

Another very dangerous practice in contemplative spirituality is the use of **MENTAL VISUALIZATION**. The spiritual practices of Ignatius of Loyola require imagining oneself living in a biblical scene and having a personal encounter with Christ.

Then there is **DISCURSIVE MEDITATION**, which is usually guided. A leader will instruct the meditators to get comfortable and after a couple of minutes of silence to do something like the following:

"Imagine yourself walking down a road. It's the path of your life. Imagine what the path looks like. Is it curvy? Or straight? Hilly? Flat? Is it wide or narrow, surrounded by trees or by fields? You look down. Is the path rocky? Sandy? Is it dirt? Maybe it's paved. What does it feel like under your feet? And up ahead, what's in your path? Does it look clear or are there hurdles in your way? Something is in your hands. You've been carrying it a long time--it's something you brought with you, in your spirit, up to camp. Look at it. What does it look like? What does it feel like in your hands? Is it hot? Cold? Warm? Is it smooth? Prickly? Sharp? Rough? Is it heavy or light?

"Now look up ahead. A figure is moving toward you. You can't quite make out who it is, but he seems to know you and his pace quickens as he recognizes you. Now you can see--it's Jesus! He's coming closer. What's the expression on his face as he walks toward you? How do you feel? He says a word of greeting to you. What does he say? How do you feel? Do you say anything back?

"Now Jesus is standing in front of you. What does he say? Now he's holding his hands out--he wants you to put what's in your hands into his hands. How does it feel as the object leaves your hands? Do you say anything to Jesus?

"Now you and Jesus start to walk together--he's holding the object of yours. As the two of you walk along, what do you talk about? Imagine the conversation" (Tony Jones, *The Sacred Way*, pp. 83, 84).

This is either pure fantasy and therefore of no value, or it moves into the realm of the occult. We can't imagine a real encounter with Jesus. We don't know what He looks like. The only thing we know about Him is found in the Scripture, and to go beyond that is presumption and disobedience.

> "The secret things belong unto the LORD our God: but those things which are revealed belong unto us and to our children for ever, that we may do all the words of this law" (Deuteronomy 29:29).

In his book *Sacred Pathways*, Gary Thomas recommends dancing with God in one's mind. This is not only ridiculous, it is very dangerous. When we go beyond the Bible in such a fashion, the devil is ready to meet us there as an "angel of light."

Richard Foster even warns that contemplative prayer is "entering deeply into the spiritual realm" and there is the possibility of meeting dark powers. He recommends that practitioners ask "God to surround us with the light of His protection" (*Celebration of Discipline*, 1978, p. 23) and pray this prayer: "All dark and evil spirits must now leave" (*Prayer: Finding the Heart's True Home*, 1992, p. 157). Foster says that not everyone is ready and equipped to enter into the "all embracing silence" of contemplative prayer (p. 156).

In response, Roger Oakland wisely observes:

> "I wonder if all these Christians who now practice contemplative prayer are following Foster's advice. Whether they are or not, they have put themselves in spiritual harm's way. Nowhere in Scripture are we required to pray a prayer of protection before we pray. The fact that Foster recognizes contemplative prayer is dangerous and opens the door to the fallen spirit world is very revealing. What is this--praying to the God of the Bible but instead reaching demons? Maybe contemplative prayer should be renamed contemplative terror. ... Foster admits that contemplative prayer is dangerous and will possibly take the participant into demonic realms, but he gives a disclaimer saying not everyone is ready for it. My question is, *who* is ready, and how will they know they *are* ready? What about all the young people in the emerging church movement? Are they ready? Or are they going into demonic altered states of consciousness completely unaware?" (*Faith Undone*, pp. 99, 100).

The Roman Catholic contemplative monk John Michael Talbot gives an even stronger warning about the potential danger of contemplative prayer. He says:

> "IT CAN BE MOST DESTRUCTIVE IF USED UNWISELY. I CAN ALMOST PROMISE THAT THOSE WHO UNDERTAKE THIS STUDY ALONE WITHOUT PROPER GUIDANCE, AND GROUNDING IN CATHOLIC CHRISTIANITY, WILL FIND THEMSELVES QUESTIONING THEIR OWN FAITH TO THE POINT OF LOSING IT. SOME MAY FIND THEMSELVES SPIRITUALLY LOST. IT HAS HAPPENED TO MANY. For this reason, we do not take the newer members of The Brothers and Sisters of Charity through this material in any depth as part of their formation, but stick squarely to overt Catholic spirituality and prayer teachings. I would not recommend too much integration of these things without proper guidance for those newer to the Catholic or Christian faith" (Talbot, "Many Religions, One God," Oct. 22, 1999, http://www.johnmichaeltalbot.com/Reflections/index.asp?id=135).

Talbot thus recognizes the extreme danger of contemplative practices, yet he thinks he is capable of using them without being harmed by them. He should listen to the words of Scripture: *"Be not deceived: evil communications corrupt good manners"* (1 Corinthians 15:33).

I am convinced that those who participate in such things open themselves up to demonic influence.

David Hunt sounds an important warning about visualizing prayer. He gives the example of a man who visualized Jesus and was then surprised when "Jesus" began to interact with him.

> "I began to visualize myself as a boy of eight. 'Now see if you can imagine Jesus appearing,' [the seminar leader] instructed. 'Let Him walk toward you.' Much to my amazement Jesus moved slowly toward me out of that dark playground. He began to extend His hands toward me in a loving, accepting manner. I NO LONGER WAS CREATING THE SCENE. The figure of Christ reached over and lifted the bundle from my back. And He did so with such forcefulness that I literally sprang from the pew" (Robert L. Wise, "Healing of the Memories: A Prayer Therapy for You," *Christian Life*, July 1984, pp. 63-64).

Hunt observes:

> "That this was more than imagination is clear. The one who originally visualized the image of 'Jesus' was surprised when it suddenly took on a character of its own and he realized that he was no longer creating the image. This 'Jesus' had its own life and personality. There can be no doubt that real contact had been made with the spirit world. We may be equally certain that this being was not the real Jesus Christ. No one can call Him from the right hand of the Father in heaven to put in a personal appearance. The entity could only have been a demonic spirit masquerading as 'Jesus'" (*The Occult Invasion*, "Imagination and Visualization").

Tony Jones describes how that Jesus allegedly appeared to him during one such episode and spoke to him face to face (*The Sacred Way*, p. 79).

Al Dager of Media Spotlight gives a discerning warning about the extreme danger of contemplative practices:

> "Unfortunately, all these exercises serve to do is open the person up to demonic influences that assuage his or her conscience with a feeling of euphoria and even 'love' emanating from the presence that has invaded their consciousness. This euphoria is then believed to validate that the person is on the right spiritual path. It may result in visions, out-of-body experiences, stigmata, levitation, even healings and other apparent miracles."

The guided prayer techniques are exactly the same as the techniques I was taught by disciples of the Hindu guru Paramahansa Yogananda before I was converted. We were supposed to use these techniques to view events in our past lives. The yogic meditation led me into dark realms farther and farther from the holy God of the Bible, the God who is light and in whom *"is no darkness at all"* (1 John 1:5). I repented of it completely after I came to Christ. I wrote to the Self-Realization Fellowship Society, testified to them of my Christian conversion, and asked them to drop my name from their rolls.

Emergent leader Nanette Sawyer unwittingly gives a frightful testimony along this line. She said that she is a Christian (of the liberal brand) because she was taught meditation techniques by a Hindu. She said that while "sitting in meditation, in a technique similar to what Christians call Centering Prayer, I encountered love that is unconditional, yet it called me to responsible action in my life" (*An Emergent Manifesto of Hope*, p. 44). This occurred AFTER she had rejected biblical Christianity and the gospel that Jesus died for our sins (p. 43). She said that she found love and Jesus through Hindu meditation, but it was not the Jesus of the Bible nor was it the love of God as described in the Bible. It was another gospel, another Jesus, and another spirit (2 Cor. 11:4). John warned, *"Beloved, believe not every spirit, but try the spirits whether they are of God: because many false prophets are gone out into the world"* (1 John 4:1), and the only sure way to try the spirits is to test them by the Bible. As for true love, John defined that, too. *"For this is the love of God, that we keep his commandments: and his commandments are not grievous"* (1 John 5:3).

The fact that its practitioners call contemplative spirituality "darkness" is a loud warning to those who have ears to hear.

Brennan Manning calls centering prayer a "GREAT DARKNESS" (*The Signature of Jesus*, p. 145) and an entire chapter of his book is devoted to "Celebrate the Darkness." He claims that the darkness of centering prayer is caused by the human ego being broken and spiritual healing being achieved, but since the practice is not supported by Scripture that is presumption and not faith.

The sixth century Syrian monk who called himself Dionysius the Areopagite said that asceticism and mystical practices can penetrate the mystery of God's "DARK NO-THINGNESS." This man, known as Pseudo-Dionysius, has had a major influence on Catholic mysticism.

The Cloud of Unknowing uses the terms "BLIND" and "DARKNESS" and "NOTHING" repeatedly.

Jesuit priest Anthony de Mello calls centering prayer "DARK CONTEMPLATION" and descending "into THE DARKNESS" (*Sadhana: A Way to God*, pp. 32, 33). He says those who practice centering prayer "expose themselves, in BLIND FAITH, to THE EMPTINESS, the DARKNESS, the idleness, THE NOTHINGNESS" (p. 31).

Catholic monk William Johnston says that meditation is the art of passing from one layer to the next in an inner or downward journey to the core of the personality where dwells the great mystery called God ... WHO DWELLS IN THICK DARKNESS" (*The Inner Eye of Love: Mysticism and Religion*, 1981, p. 127).

God did hide Himself in thick darkness in the Old Testament era because of man's sin and the fact that Christ's atonement had not yet been made (Exodus 20:21), but in reality God is light and not darkness. *"This then is the message which we have heard of him, and declare unto you, that God is light, and in him is no darkness at all"* (1 John 1:5). It is sin that separates the sinner from God and His glorious light. The people in Moses' day had to stand away from Mt. Sinai when God gave the Law and God wrapped Himself in darkness, because the Law of Moses can only reveal sin and cannot justify the sinner (Romans 3:19-20). The Old Testament temple signified this separation. God dwelt in the holy of holies, and no man could enter except the high priest and that only one time a year, on the Day of Atonement. There was a thick veil that barred the way into the holy of holies.

But when Jesus Christ came and died on the cross and shed His blood to make the atonement for man's sin, the veil was rent from top to bottom, signifying that man now has free entrance into God's very presence if he comes through faith in Christ (Mat. 27:50-51).

If a mystic encounters darkness in his mystical journey, that darkness is not God; it is sin and the devil. The darkness of this world is the devil's domain, but God has turned the believer *"from darkness to light, from the power of Satan unto God"* (Acts 26:18). He has *"delivered us from the power of darkness"* (Col. 1:13) and called us *"out of darkness into his marvellous light"* (1 Pet. 2:9). Now we are *"children of light, and the children of the day: we are not of the night, nor of darkness"* (1 Thess. 5:5).

Pierre Teilhard described his practice of meditation as "going down into my innermost self, to THE DEEP ABYSS" (*The Divine Milieu*, p. 76). He said: "At each step of the descent a new person was disclosed within me of whose name I was no longer sure, and who no longer obeyed me." At the end of the journey he found "a bottomless abyss at my feet."

This is a loud warning to those who have ears to hear. Though the mystic believes that he is touching light and truth through contemplative practices, in reality he is fellowshipping with darkness and lies and demons. Who were these "persons" who were distinct from Teilhard himself and who did not obey him? From a biblical perspective, we have to conclude that the man was communicating with demons. This is why he taught such demonic doctrines as evolution and a "cosmic" christ that is something different than the person of Jesus.

John Michael Talbot recommends the use of eastern religious practices such as yoga but, as we have seen, he admits that such experiences "can be most destructive if used unwisely." He even says: "SOME MAY FIND THEMSELVES SPIRITUALLY LOST. IT HAS HAPPENED TO MANY" (Talbot, "Many Religions, One God," Oct. 22, 1999, http://www.johnmichaeltalbot.com/Reflections/index.asp?id=135).

Anything with that type of power for evil and spiritual destruction should be avoided like the plague!

Philip St. Romain, the Catholic lay minister who wrote *Kundalini Energy and Christian Spirituality* (1990), has experienced many strange things while practicing centering prayer. After he "centered down" into silence, gold lights would appear and swirl in his mind, forming themselves into captivating patterns. He felt prickly sensations that would continue for days. "Wise sayings" popped into his mind as if he were "receiving messages from another." He became dependent on his "inner adviser" and "inner eye" that allowed him to see in a spiritual manner. After studying eastern religions he came to the conclusion that he was dealing with kundalini energy, and we have no doubt that he was, because mindless centering prayer brings one into the same dark realm as Hindism's yoga. The "inner adviser" that one encounters through centering prayer is demonic.

Even the heathen practitioners of kundalini warn about its dangers. *The Ayurveda Encyclopedia* says, "Those who awaken their kundalini without a guru can lose their direction in life ... they can become confused or mentally imbalanced ... more harm than good can arise" (p. 336). The book *Aghora II: Kundalini* warns many times that "indiscriminate awakening of the Kundalini is very dangerous" (p. 61). It says, "Once aroused and unboxed Kundalini is not 'derousable'; the genie will not fit back into the bottle. 'After the awakening the devotee lives always at the mercy of Kundalini'" (p. 20). In fact, the book says that "some die of shock when Kundalini is awakened, and others become severely ill" (p. 61).

There is no doubt that the practice of kundalini yoga is demonic to the core.

St. Romain has come to depend upon the voices that he hears in contemplative prayer.

> "I cannot make any decisions for myself without the approbation of THE INNER ADVISER, whose voice speaks so clearly in times of need ... there is a distinct sense of an inner eye of some kind 'seeing' with my two sense eyes" (St. Romain, *Kundalini Energy*, p. 39).

The man is communing with demons and he got there, not through Hindu yoga, but through Catholic contemplative mysticism, the same kind of mysticism promoted by the Quaker Richard Foster and the Southern Baptist Rick Warren.

The Ayurveda Encyclopedia explains that one can encounter internal voices through yogic mediation, and the practitioner is instructed to listen to the voices and follow their counsel.

> "Just as with all spiritual experiences that are out of the norm of supposed societal acceptance, THE HEARING OF INNER SOUNDS OR VOICES (nada) has generally been associated with mental illness. Spiritual counseling reassures a person that their experiences and feelings are spiritual--not abnormal. Understanding nada helps persons feel comfortable when hearing any inner sounds. ... If a sound is heard, listen to it. If many sounds exist, listen to those in the right ear. The first sound heard is to be followed. Then, the next sound heard is also to be followed" (p. 343).

I have never read a more effective formula for demon possession, and "contemplative" practices such as centering prayer and visualization and guided imagery are no different in character than Hindu yoga. In fact, many contemplative practitioners admit this. John Michael Talbot says:

> "For myself, after the moving meditations of Hinduism and Taoism, and the breath, bone-marrow, and organ-cleansing of Taoism, I move into a Buddhist seated meditation, including the Four Establishments of Mindfulness. I do all of this from my own Christian perspective..." (*Come to the Quiet*, p. 237).

Meditation practitioner W.E. Butler, in *Lords of Light*, says that mystical contemplation "brings with it a curious kind of knowing that there is somebody else there with you; you are not alone" (p. 164).

Indeed, but that "somebody else" that the unsaved meditation practitioner encounters is certainly not Almighty God.

Tony Jones admits that the practice of silence often results in spiritual oppression. He mentions "the dark night of the soul" which comes through meditation and says, "It seems one cannot pursue true silence without rather quickly coming to a place of deep, dark doubt" (*The Sacred Way*, pp. 41, 82). He quotes Thomas Merton as follows: "The hermit, all day and all night, beats his head against a wall of doubt. That is his contemplation" (p. 41).

We are reminded of Mother Teresa, who was called a living saint by Catholics and Protestants alike during her lifetime and is on the fast track for canonization in the Catholic Church. She practiced a very serious level of contemplative spirituality all her life, but she found only darkness. This is documented in the shocking book *Mother Teresa: Come Be My Light, the Private Writings of the Saint of Calcutta* (2007), which contains statements made by the nun to her Catholic confessors and superiors over a period of more than 65 years.

In March 1953 she wrote to her confessor: "... THERE IS SUCH TERRIBLE DARKNESS WITHIN ME, as if everything was dead. It has been like this more or less from the time I started 'the work.'" Over the years she had many confessors, and she continually referred to her spiritual condition as "my darkness" and to Jesus as "the Absent One."

In 1962 she wrote: "IF I EVER BECOME A SAINT -- I WILL SURELY BE ONE OF 'DARKNESS,'" and again, "How cold -- how empty -- how painful is my heart. -- Holy communion -- Holy Mass -- all the holy things of spiritual life -- of the life of Christ in me -- are all so empty -- so cold -- so unwanted" (*Mother Teresa: Come Be My Light*, p. 232).

In 1979 she wrote: "The silence and the emptiness is so great -- that I look and do not see, -- Listen and do not hear."

Her private statements about the spiritual darkness she encountered in contemplative prayer continued in this vein until her death, and they are the loudest possible warning about the danger of contemplative mysticism.

The contemplative practices are vehicles for coming into contact with demons.

Contemplative practices have even led some to goddess worship.

This is what happened to **SUE MONK KIDD** (b. 1948), and her experience is a loud warning about flirting with Catholic mysticism.

She was raised in a Southern Baptist congregation in southwest Georgia. Her grandfather and father were Baptist deacons. Her grandmother gave devotionals at the Women's Missionary Union, and her mother was a Sunday School teacher. Her husband was a minister who taught religion and was a chaplain at a Baptist college. She was not a nominal Christian but was very involved, teaching Sunday School and attending church Sunday morning and evening and Wednesday. She describes herself as the person who would have won a contest for "Least Likely to Become a Feminist."

She was inducted into a group of women called the Gracious Ladies, the criterion for which was "one needed to portray certain ideals of womanhood, which included being gracious and giving of oneself unselfishly." She was also a Christian writer and contributing editor to *Guideposts* magazine.

But for years she had felt a spiritual emptiness and lack of contentment. Prayer was "a fairly boring mental activity" (Kidd's foreword to Henri Nouwen's *With Open Hands*, 2006, p. 10). She says,

> "I had been struggling to come to terms with my life as a woman--in my culture, my marriage, my faith, my church, and deep inside myself" (*The Dance of the Dissident Daughter*, p. 8).

She was thirty years old, had been married about 12 years and had two children.

Instead of learning how to fill that emptiness and uncertainty with a know-so salvation and a sweet walk with Christ in the Spirit and a deeper knowledge of the Bible, she began dabbling in Catholic mysticism. A Sunday School co-worker gave her a book by the Roman Catholic monk Thomas Merton. She should have known better than to study such a book and should have been warned by the brethren, but the New Evangelical philosophy that controls the vast majority of Southern Baptist churches created an atmosphere in which the reading of a Catholic monk's book by a Sunday School teacher was acceptable.

Kidd began to practice Catholic forms of contemplative spirituality and to visit Catholic retreat centers and monasteries.

> "... beginning in my early thirties I'd become immersed in a journey that was rooted in contemplative spirituality. It was the spirituality of the 'church fathers,' of the monks I'd come to know as I made regular retreats in their monasteries. ... I thrived on solitude, routinely practicing silent meditation as taught by the monks Basil Pennington and Thomas Keating. ... For years, I'd studied Thomas Merton, John of the Cross, Augustine, Bernard, Bonaventure, Ignatius, Eckhart, Luther, Teilhard de Chardin, *The Cloud of Unknowing*, and others" (pp. 14, 15).

Of Merton's autobiography, *The Seven Storey Mountain*, which she read in 1978 for the first of many times, she says,

> "My experience of reading it initiated me into my first real awareness of the interior life, igniting an impulse toward being ... it caused something hidden at the core of me to flare up and become known" (Kidd's introduction to *New Seeds of Contemplation*, 2007, pp. xiii, xi).

Of Merton's book *New Seeds of Contemplation* she says, "[It] initiated me into the secrets of my true identity and woke in me an urge toward realness" and "impacted my spirituality and my writing to this day."

Merton communicated intimately with and was deeply affected by Mary veneration, Buddhism, Hinduism, and Sufism, so it is not surprising that his writings would create an appetite that could lead to goddess worship.

In *The New Seeds of Contemplation*, Merton made the following frightening statement that shows the great danger of Catholic mysticism:

> "In the end the contemplative suffers the anguish of realizing that HE NO LONGER KNOWS WHAT GOD IS. He may or may not mercifully realize that, after all, this is a great gain, because 'God is not a what,' not a 'thing.' This is precisely one of the essential characteristics of contemplative experience. It sees that there is no 'what' that can be called God" (p. 13).

What Catholic mysticism does is reject the Bible as the sole and sufficient and perfect revelation of God and tries to delve beyond the Bible, even beyond thought of any kind, and find God through mystical "intuition." In other words, it is a rejection of the God of the Bible. It claims that God cannot be known by doctrine and cannot be described in words. He can only be experienced through mysticism. This is a blatant denial of the Bible's claim to be the very Word of God.

This opens the practitioner to demonic delusion. He is left with no perfect objective revelation of God, no divinely-revealed authority by which he can test his mystical experiences and intuitions. He is left with an idol of his own vain imagination (Jeremiah 17:9) and a doctrine of devils.

Kidd's own first two books were on contemplative spirituality --*God's Joyful Surprise* (1988) and *When the Heart Waits* (1990).

The involvement in Catholic contemplative practices led her to the Catholic Mass and to other sacramental associations.

> "I often went to Catholic mass or Eucharist at the Episcopal church, nourished by the symbol and power of this profound feeding ritual" (p. 15).

There is an occultic power in the Mass that has influenced many who have approached it in a receptive, non-critical manner.

She learned dream analysis from a Jungian perspective and believed that her dreams were revelations. One recurring dream featured an old woman. She concluded that this is "the Feminine Self or the voice of the feminine soul" and she was encouraged in her feminist studies by these visitations.

She spent much time with a friend who had a feminist mindset and was "exploring" feminist writings, and she began to read ever more radical feminists, such as Elisabeth Schussler Fiorenza, Elaine Pagels, and Rosemary Radford Ruether.

She says, "I began to form what I called my feminist critique" (p. 59). She learned to see "patriarchy" as "a wounder of women and feminine life" (p. 60).

She determined to stop testing things and follow her heart, rejecting the Bible's admonition to "prove all things" (1 Thessalonians 5:21).

> "I would go through the gate with what Zen Buddhists call 'beginner's mind,' the attitude of approaching something with a mind empty and free, ready for anything, open to everything. ... I would give myself permission to go wherever my quest took me" (p. 140).

She rejected the doctrine that the Bible is the sole authority. In church one day the pastor proclaimed this truth, and she describes the frightful thing that happened in her heart at that moment:

> "I remember a feeling rising up from a place about two inches below my navel. ... It was the purest inner knowing I had experienced, and it was shouting in me no, no, no! The ultimate authority of my life is not the Bible; it is not confined between the covers of a book. It is not something written by men and frozen in time. It is not from a source outside myself. My ultimate authority is the divine voice in my own soul. Period. ... That day sitting in church, I believed the voice in my belly. ... The voice in my belly was the voice of the wise old woman. It was my female soul talking. And it had challenged the assumption that the Baptist Church would get me where I needed to go" (*The Dance of the Dissident Daughter*, pp. 76, 77, 78).

She began to think that the Bible is wrong in its teaching about women and that women should not take the subordinate position described therein. She came to believe that Eve might have been a hero instead of a sinner, that eating the forbidden fruit had actually opened Eve's eyes to her true self. Kidd came to the conclusion that the snake was not evil but "symbolized female wisdom, power, and regeneration" (p. 71). She was surprised and pleased to learn that the snake is depicted as the companion of ancient goddesses, concluding that this is evidence that the Bible is wrong.

She determined that she was willing to lose her marriage if necessary.

> "I would not, could not forfeit my journey for my marriage or for the sake of religious acceptance or success as a 'Christian writer.' I would keep moving in my own way to the strains of feminine music that sifted up inside me, not just moving but embracing the dance. ... I felt the crumbling of the old patriarchal foundation our marriage had rested upon in such hidden and subtle ways. Though both of us would always need to compromise, THERE WAS NO MORE SACRIFICING MYSELF, NO MORE REVOLVING AROUND HIM, NO MORE LOOKING TO HIM FOR VALIDATION, trying to be what I thought he needed me to be. My life, my time, my decisions became newly my own" (pp. 98, 125).

In her case, her husband stayed with her and came to accept her feminist vision, even leaving his job in the Christian college and becoming a psychotherapist, but in many other cases the feminist philosophy has destroyed the marriage. She says, "I've met women who in such circumstances have stayed and others who've left. Such choices are achingly difficult, but I've learned to respect whatever a woman feels she must do." It is amazing how self-deceived a person can become, to the point where they are convinced that it is a righteous thing to renounce a solemn marriage vow that was made before God and man.

She rejected God as Father.

> "I knew right then and there that the patriarchal church was no longer working for me. The exclusive image of God as heavenly Father wasn't working, either. I needed a Power of Being that was also feminine" (*The Dance of the Dissident Daughter*, p. 80).

She came to believe in the divinity of man.

> "There's a bulb of truth buried in the human soul that's 'only God' ... the soul is more than something to win or save. It's the seat and repository of the inner Divine, the God-image, the truest part of us" (*When the Heart Waits*, 1990, pp. 47, 48).

> "When we encounter another person ... we should walk as if we were upon holy ground. We should respond as if God dwells there" (*God's Joyful Surprise*, p. 233).

She began to delve into the worship of ancient goddesses. She traveled with a group of women to Crete where they met in a cave and sang prayers to "the Goddess Skoteini, Goddess of the Dark." She says, "... something inside me was calling on the Goddess of the Dark, even though I didn't know her name" (*The Dance of the Dissident Daughter*, p. 93).

Soon she was praying to God as Mother.

> "I ran my finger around the rim of the circle on the page and prayed my first prayer to a Divine Feminine presence. I said, 'Mothergod, I have nothing to hold me. No place to be, inside or out. I need to find a container of support, a space where my journey can unfold'" (p. 94).

She came to the place where she believed that she is a goddess.

> "Divine Feminine love came, wiping out all my puny ideas about love in one driving sweep. Today I remember that event for the radiant mystery it was, how I felt myself embraced by Goddess, how I felt myself in touch with the deepest thing I am. It was the moment when, as playwright and poet Ntozake Shange put it, 'I found god in myself/ and I loved her/ I loved her fiercely'" (*The Dance of the Dissident Daughter*, p. 136).

> "To embrace Goddess is simply to discover the Divine in yourself as powerfully and vividly feminine" (p. 141).

> "I came to know myself as an embodiment of Goddess" (*The Dance of the Dissident Daughter*, p. 163).

> "When I woke, my thought was that I was finally being reunited with the snake in myself--that lost and defiled symbol of feminine instinct" (p. 107).

She came to believe in the New Age doctrine that God is in all things and is the sum total of all things, that God is the evolving universe and we are a part of God.

> "I thought: Maybe the Divine One is like an old African woman, carving creation out of one vast, beautiful piece of Herself. She is making a universal totem spanning fifteen billion years, an extension of her life and being, an evolutionary carving of sacred art containing humans, animals, plants, indeed, everything that is. And all of it is joined, blended, and connected, its destiny intertwined. ... In other words, the Divine *coinheres* all that is. ... To *coinhere* means to exist together, to be included in the same thing or substance" (pp. 158, 159).

She built an altar in her study and populated it with statues of goddesses, Jesus, a Black Madonna -- and a mirror to reflect her own image.

> "Over the altar in my study I hung a lovely mirror sculpted in the shape of a crescent moon. It reminded me to honor the Divine Feminine presence in myself, the wisdom in my own soul" (p. 181).

She even believes that the world can be saved by the divine mother.

> "I know of nothing needed more in the world just now than an image of Divine present that affirms the importance of relationship--a Divine

Mother, perhaps, who draws all humanity into her lap and makes us into a global family" (p. 155).

Her book ends with the words, "She is in us."

According to Kidd's book *The Dance of the Dissident Daughter*, her daughter, too, has accepted goddess worship.

Sue Monk Kidd is quoted by evangelicals such as David Jeremiah (*Life Wide Open*), Beth Moore (*When Godly People Do Ungodly Things*), and Richard Foster (*Prayer: Finding the Heart's True Home*). Kidd's endorsement is printed on the back of Dallas Willard's book *The Spirit of the Disciplines*. She wrote the foreword to the 2006 edition of Henri Nouwen's *With Open Hands* and the introduction to the 2007 edition of Thomas Merton's *New Seeds of Contemplation*.

Another example of how Catholic contemplative spirituality has led to goddess worship is the sad story of **ALAN RICHARD "BEDE" GRIFFITHS**.

He was born in England and studied at Oxford under C.S. Lewis, who became a lifelong friend. In 1931, while at Oxford he converted from Anglicanism to Catholicism. The next year he joined the Benedictine monastery of Prinknash Abbey near Gloucester and was ordained a priest in 1940. The name *Bede*, meaning prayer, was given to him when he entered the Benedictine order.

He moved to India and became a Hindu monk (while remaining a Catholic priest), calling himself Swami Dayananda (bliss of compassion), going barefoot, and clothing himself in an orange-colored robe.

He accepted the Hindu concept of the interrelatedness of everything and the unity of man with God.

"He loved to quote the Chandogya Upanishad (8,3) [Hindu scriptures] to show that while our body takes up only a small space on this planet, OUR MIND ENCOMPASSES THE WHOLE UNIVERSE: 'There is this city of Brahman (the human body) and in it there is a small shrine in the form of a lotus, and within can be found a small space. This little space within the heart is as great as this vast universe. The heavens and the earth are there, and the sun and the moon and the stars; fire and lightning and wind are there, and all that now is and is not yet--all that is contained within it" (Pascaline Coff, "Man, Monk, Mystic," http://www.bedegriffiths.com/bio.htm).

He rejected the Bible's doctrine that there is good and evil:

"I saw God in the earth, in trees, in mountains. It led me to the conviction that there is no absolute good or evil in this world. We have to let go of all concepts which divide the world into good and evil, right and wrong, and begin to see the complimentarity of opposites which Cardinal Nicholas of Cusa called the *coincidentia oppositorum*, the 'coincidence of opposites'" (1991, http://www.bedegriffiths.com/bio.htm).

At the end of his life he came to believe in a Mother goddess. This was the fruit of his communion with idolatry through contemplative spirituality. In 1990, after a stroke, he began to speak of the awakening of his repressed feminine.

"Intimating it was a mystical experience which could not properly be put into words, Father [Griffiths] used symbolic language to try and express the depth of the experience. The two symbols he used were the Black Madonna and the Crucified Christ. He said these two images summed up for him something of this mysterious experience of the Divine feminine and the mystery of suffering. When he first spoke about THE BLACK MADONNA, he said his experience of her was deeply connected to the Earth-Mother, to the forms of the ancient feminine found in rocks and caves and in the different forms in nature. HE LIKENED IT TO THE EXPERIENCE OF THE FEMININE EXPRESSED IN THE HINDU CONCEPT OF *SHAKTI*--THE POWER OF THE DIVINE FEMININE. Later Father wrote these reflections on the Black Madonna: 'The Black Madonna symbolizes for me the Black Power in Nature and Life, the hidden power in the womb. ... I feel it was this Power which struck me. She is cruel and destructive, but also deeply loving and nourishing.'

"A few months later Father again wrote: 'THE FIGURE OF THE BLACK MADONNA STOOD FOR THE FEMININE IN ALL ITS FORMS. I FELT THE NEED TO SURRENDER TO THE MOTHER, and this gave me the experience of being overwhelmed by love. I realized that surrendering to death, and dying to oneself is surrendering to Total Love.'

"Regarding the image of the Crucified Christ, Father made the statement that his understanding of the crucifixion had deepened profoundly. He wrote: 'On the Cross Jesus surrendered himself to this

> Dark Power. He lost everything: friends, disciples, his own people, their law and religion. ... He had to enter the Dark Night, to be exposed to the abyss. Only then could he become everything and nothing, opened beyond everything that can be named or spoken; ONLY THEN COULD JESUS BE ONE WITH THE DARKNESS, THE VOID, THE DARK MOTHER WHO IS LOVE ITSELF'" (http://www.bedegriffiths.com/bio.htm).

Griffiths had a large influence in promoting interfaith philosophy in Roman Catholic monasteries in America, England, Australia, and Germany through his books and lectures. He wrote 12 books on interfaith dialogue, the most popular being *Marriage of East and West*.

Griffiths' love for the Black Madonna is interesting. Sue Monk Kidd, too, as she traveled from Catholic contemplative practices to goddess worship, experienced a great love for the Black Madonna. Thomas Merton did the same thing in his journey into Roman Catholic mysticism and beyond to Zen Buddhism. The Madonna was originally borrowed from pagan idolatry, from the ancient mother goddess mystery religions that stemmed from Babel.

I would urge my readers in the strongest manner possible not to dabble in contemplative practices. There really is no telling where it might lead. It can lead to Rome or Buddha or even to Artemis.

Contemplative Spirituality Error # 10: It produces rotten fruit.

Those who practice contemplative spirituality claim that it should be tested by its fruit, assuring us that the fruit is good, but from a biblical perspective it is demonically rotten.

First, the fruit of contemplative spirituality is heretical doctrine. That contemplative spirituality produces heretical fruit is obvious from its very history. It came from Rome and it nurtured Rome's heresies. Never did contemplative spirituality teach the Catholic "saints" and mystics to reject Rome's errors. Never did it lead them to the true grace of Christ apart from sacramentalism and priestcraft. Never did it reveal to them the blasphemy of venerating Mary. Never did it enlighten their minds so they could see and accept the "faith which was once delivered to the saints" (Jude 3).

In the 25th anniversary edition of *Finding Grace at the Center*, which promotes centering prayer, Jesuit priest Thomas Clarke says:

> "Bringing theology to the center is like dipping a fabric in a liquid which restores and transfigures its inherent beauty. This is the place where the great doctors of the [Roman Catholic] Church carried on their pondering of the mystery. Only to the degree that theology takes place in the stillness of the Center will it be capable of nourishing the Church" (pp. 92, 93).

Thus, Clarke recognizes that Catholic theology was nurtured by Catholic contemplative practices, and we know that Rome's theology is the doctrine of devils (1 Timothy 4:1-5).

Second, the fruit of contemplative spirituality is ecumenical unity. In fact, together with contemporary praise music, contemplative mysticism is one of the most powerful glues of the ecumenical movement.

Larry Crabb, in the foreword to David Benner's *Sacred Companions*, which has been described as "a who's who of mystical and pantheistic writings," says:

> "The spiritual climate is ripe. Jesus seekers across the world are being prepared to abandon the old way of the written code for the new way of the Spirit" (p. 9).

The term "Jesus seekers" refers to all sorts of professing Christians. Crabb tells us that because of this "new way of the Spirit," referring to contemplative mysticism, all sorts of Christians are giving up the "old way of the written code," referring to the Bible! Crabb says that Christians of all doctrinal persuasions are being drawn together and instructed by Rome's mystical practices. What a powerful warning to those who have ears to hear!

Consider what is happening within "evangelicalism" in general and the emerging church in particular. Contemplative practices are bringing evangelicals into association with the doctrines of devils that Paul warned of in 1 Timothy 4.

> "Now the Spirit speaketh expressly, that in the latter times some shall depart from the faith, giving heed to seducing spirits, and doctrines of devils; speaking lies in hypocrisy; having their conscience seared with a hot iron; forbidding to marry, and commanding to abstain from meats, which God hath created to be received with thanksgiving of them which believe and know the truth" (1 Timothy 4:1-3).

Observe that the doctrines of devils are intimately associated with religious legalism and asceticism, forbidding to marry and requiring abstinence from meats. This type of asceticism is at the very heart of Roman Catholic monastic mysticism. The Gethsemani Cistercian monastery where Thomas Merton lived requires that the monks take a vow of celibacy and forbids them to eat meat! To commune with the Catholic monastics is to commune with demons!

The back-to-Rome movement within evangelicalism is being fed by and hastened along through these contemplative practices. It is one of the important factors in the blending process that is going on. We have already given many examples of this.

Consider the book *The Way of the Mystics*. It was coauthored by a Roman Catholic (John Talbot) and an evangelical Protestant (Steve Rabey) and one of the recommendations on the back cover is by a Pentecostal (Jack Hayford). The glue bringing these three "streams" of Christianity together is mysticism.

The Roman Catholic Church is becoming more evangelical and the evangelicals are becoming more Catholic. In the 376-page book *Evangelicals and Rome*, first published in 1999, we warned:

"Most popular evangelical men and organizations have strong and growing sympathies toward the Roman Catholic Church. In the following chapters we give thorough documentation of this. *Christianity Today*, founded by Billy Graham and other New Evangelical leaders, now has three Roman Catholic editors. Evangelical publishers are busy putting out books sympathetic to Rome and calling for ecumenical relationships."

Zach Roberts, a Baptist pastor and founder of the Dogwood Abbey in Winston-Salem, North Carolina, meets regularly with a Catholic Trappist monk to discuss contemplation. The fruit of his contemplative activities is evident by his own testimony. He has come to see Roman Catholicism as authentic Christianity. He says, "I grew up in a tradition [Southern Baptist] that believes Catholics are pagans. I never really understood that. Now I'd argue against that wholeheartedly" ("The Unexpected Monks," *The Boston Globe*, Feb. 3, 2008).

Another heretical fruit of contemplative spirituality is interfaith syncretism. We have already documented this, but we want to repeat it here by way of emphasis. On the part of contemplatives there is a huge borrowing from Hinduism, Buddhism, Taoism, Sufism, and Native American "spirituality." Contemplative mysticism is a powerful glue for uniting Christianity with paganism.

In a 2005 interview Tony Campolo said:

"Speaking of Francis [of Assisi], here's a wonderful story. I got to meet the head of the Franciscan order. I met him in Washington. He said let me tell you an interesting story. He told me about one of their gatherings, where they bring the brothers of the Franciscan order together for a time of fellowship. About eight years ago they held it in Thailand and out of courtesy, they really felt they needed to show some graciousness to the Buddhists, because they were in a Buddhist country. So they got Buddhist theologians together and Franciscan theologians together and sent them off for three days to talk and see if they could find common ground. They also took Buddhist and Franciscan monastics and sent them off together to pray with each other. On the fourth day they all reassembled. The theologians were fighting with each other, arguing with each other, contending there was no common ground between them. The monastics that had gone off praying together, came back hugging each other. IN A MYSTICAL RELATIONSHIP WITH GOD, THERE IS A COMING TOGETHER OF

PEOPLE WHERE THEOLOGY IS LEFT BEHIND AND IN THIS SPIRITUALITY THEY FOUND A COMMONALITY.

> "It seems to me that when we listen to the Muslim mystics as they talk about Jesus and their love for Jesus, I must say, it's a lot closer to New Testament Christianity than a lot of the Christians that I hear. In other words IF WE ARE LOOKING FOR COMMON GROUND, CAN WE FIND IT IN MYSTICAL SPIRITUALITY, EVEN IF WE CANNOT THEOLOGICALLY AGREE?" ("On Evangelicals and Interfaith Cooperation," *Cross Currents*, Spring 2005).

Mystical experience is being exalted over doctrine, and mysticism is being seen as a key to radical ecumenical and interfaith unity. But if you turn your back to Bible doctrine and try to reach beyond it through mysticism, you are entering the realm of spiritual delusion with no sure light to lighten your path.

Catholic priest Basil Pennington describes how that an unsaved Hindu monk found great satisfaction in the practice of centering prayer.

> "I presented the Centering Prayer in my usual way, wondering what chords of response this call to faith and love might be striking in the Hindu monk. We soon entered into the prayer and enjoyed that beautiful fullness of silence. As we came out of the experience I shot a concerned glance in the direction of our Eastern friend. He had--or, I could almost say, was--a most beautiful smile, a deep, radiant expression of peaceful joy. Gently he gave his witness: 'This has been the most beautiful experience I have ever had.' This was for me on many levels a very affirming experience" (*Centering Prayer*).

That an idol worshipper would find Catholic centering prayer a beautiful experience was "affirming" to Pennington, but to the Bible believer it is a loud and clear warning that the practice is pagan to the core.

Evangelicals who are busy reading and recommending books by the mystics would be wise to take heed to this warning. If they delve into Catholic contemplative practices they are in great danger of being corrupted by this illicit endeavor.

Let me give a couple of examples of how evangelicals are coming into intimate fellowship with paganism through mystical practices.

Richard Foster repeatedly recommends the late Trappist monk Thomas Merton, but Merton, in turn, was in intimate association with Hinduism, Buddhism, and Sufism. Merton said: "I see no contradiction between Buddhism and Christianity. The future of Zen is in the West. I intend to become as good a Buddhist as I can" (David Steindl-Rast, "Recollection of Thomas Merton's Last Days in the West," *Monastic Studies*, 7:10, 1969, http://www.gratefulness.org/readings/dsr_merton_recol2.htm).

The evangelical psychologist Larry Crabb wrote a glowing foreword to David Benner's book *Sacred Companions*. Benner, in turn, highly recommends New Ager John Gorsuch's book *An Invitation to the Spiritual Journey*, which calls Hindu gurus *saints* and promotes Tibetan Buddhist meditations.

Willow Creek Community Church, where Bill Hybels is the senior pastor, featured an article by Keri Wyatt Kent in the fall 2007 issue of its magazine. In the midst of painting a rosy picture of contemplative spirituality she mentions Catholic priest Richard Rohr. He, in turn, wrote the foreword to Paul Coutinho's book *How Big Is Your God*, which promotes interfaith worship between Hindus, Buddhists, and Christians.

This is only a tiny glimpse into the way that contemplative spirituality results in the most radical ecumenism and interfaith compromise, channeling evangelicals toward Catholicism and paganism. Neither Richard Foster nor Larry Crabb nor Willow Creek believe that all religions worship the same God, but their enthusiasm for contemplative practices has brought them and their followers into association with those who do. They are not yet New Age themselves, but they are using the same type of "spiritual" practices that are nurturing the New Age and their thinking is being corrupted by this illicit association.

Another rotten fruit of contemplative spirituality is universalism. Basil Pennington says that through centering prayer we "experience the presence of Christ in each person we meet" and "we sense a oneness with them" (*Finding Grace at the Center*, p. 44).

This is obviously a demon-taught experience, because the presence of Christ is most definitely NOT in every person we meet and the believer does not have oneness with the unbeliever. The apostle John wrote, "*And we know that we are of God, and the whole world lieth in wickedness*" (1 John 5:19).

Yet this is the fruit of Roman Catholic mysticism. Mother Teresa, who was a very serious contemplative practitioner, was taught in her spirit that all men are children of God. Speaking of AIDS sufferers she said, "Each one of them is Jesus in a distressing disguise" (*Time*, Jan. 13, 1986). When she died, her longtime friend and biographer Naveen Chawla said that he once asked her bluntly, "Do you convert?" She replied: "Of course I convert. I convert you to be a better Hindu or a better Muslim or a better Protestant. Once you've found God, it's up to you to decide how to worship him" ("Mother Teresa Touched other Faiths," Associated Press, Sept. 7, 1997).

The liberal emerging church's universalistic tendencies are doubtless coming from the dark self and the demons that they are fellowshipping with through mystical practices.

Tony Campolo says: "The Emergent Church [tends] to reject the exclusivistic claims that many evangelicals make about salvation. They are not about to damn the likes of Gandhi or the Dalai Lama to hell simply because they have not embraced Christianity" ("Growing: Movement is new form of evangelism," *Winston-Salem Journal*, Dec. 6, 2004).

Dallas Willard says, "It is possible for someone who does not know Jesus to be saved" (*Apologetics in Action*).

Spence Burke says, "I don't believe you have to convert to any particular religion to find God" (*A Heretic's Guide to Eternity*, p. 197).

Nanette Sawyer says that emergents don't segregate people into saved/unsaved categories; instead they "embrace the unknowability of a person's eternal status" (*An Emergent Manifesto of Hope*, p. 49).

Brennan Manning says:

> "[T]he god whose moods alternate between graciousness and fierce anger ... the god who exacts the last drop of blood from his Son so that his just anger, evoked by sin, may be appeased, is not the God revealed by and in Jesus Christ. ... HE DOES NOT EXIST" (Brennan Manning, *Above All*, p. 58-59; the foreword to this book is written by Contemporary Christian Music artist Michael W. Smith).

William Shannon, another Roman Catholic contemplative, said almost the same thing:

> "This is a typical patriarchal notion of God. He is the God of Noah who sees people deep in sin, repents that He made them and resolves to destroy them. He is the God of the desert who sends snakes to bite His people because they murmured against Him. ... He is the God who exacts the last drop of blood from His Son, so that His just anger, evoked by sin, may be appeased .This God whose moods alternate between graciousness and fierce anger ... THIS GOD DOES NOT EXIST" (*Silence on Fire*, pp. 109, 110)

Contemplative practices are encouraging the spread of such heresies, and this is a loud warning to those who have ears to hear.

Contemplative Spirituality Error # 11: It is not necessary.

For two millennia Bible-believing Christians have walked in sweet fellowship with God and lived victorious spiritual lives and done God's will without contemplative practices.

The Waldenses did not need such practices to send missionaries out across Europe in the face of Rome's Holy

Office of the Inquisition. I own most of the histories of the Waldenses, and they did not practice Catholic mysticism.

Baptists have not needed contemplative practices to preach the gospel to multitudes and to establish New Testament churches across the world. I own most of the histories of the Baptists, and they did not practice Catholic mysticism.

William Tyndale, Matthew Henry, Charles Spurgeon, Adoniram Judson, Harry Ironside, and countless other men and women of God have lived spiritually rich and fruitful lives without contemplative practices.

We conclude with the following very important statement by former Catholic priest Richard Bennett:

> As Mediator, Christ Jesus is the only means of union between God and man, '*that in the dispensation of the fullness of times he might gather together in one all things in Christ, both which are in heaven, and which are on earth; in him*' (Eph. 1:10). Christ Jesus is exalted to '*the right hand of the Majesty on high*' (Heb. 1:3) as the One Savior. He and His Gospel are objective and real! This Gospel is not an idle tale, nor a piece of incomprehensible mysticism; rather it is the proclamation of the awesome historical work of redemption accomplished by God Himself. The Father appointed Christ Jesus as the guarantee of real salvation. Christ Jesus was glorified in finishing the Father's mightiest work. In Christ's own words, '*I have glorified thee on earth; I have finished the work which thou gavest me to do*' (Jn. 17:4). He had fulfilled all the Father's will and so gloriously honored the Father.
>
> As Savior He is exalted high above '*all principality and power, and might and dominion, and every name that is named, not only in this world, but also in that which is to come*' (Eph. 1:21). He alone, and not some mystic charm of Rome or Buddha, has been given all authority in heaven and in earth. He has been given power over all flesh that He should in His own words, '*give eternal life to as many as thou hast given him*' (Jn. 17:2). He alone has been given a name, which is above every name, '*that at the name of Jesus every knee should bow, of things in heaven, and things in earth, and things under the earth; and that every tongue should confess that Jesus Christ is Lord, to the glory of God the Father*' (Phil. 2:10-11). It is God's commandment that we trust on Christ, '*This is His command, that we should believe on the name of His Son Jesus Christ*' (1 John 3:23).

TRUE FAITH INVOLVES A REPUDIATION OF THE SELF-DECEIT OF EXPERIENTIAL MYSTICAL MEANS OF REACHING GOD, *'for there is one God, and one mediator between God and men, the man Christ Jesus.'* (1 Tim. 2:5). The Lord Jesus stands ready to receive every sinner who will throw away his rebellion and pride and trust in Him alone for salvation! Preaching the real historical Christ and His Gospel is the answer to the mindless adumbrations of Rome and the ecumenical mystics. Thus alone can the true Church, God's People *'go forth fair as the moon, clear as the sun, and terrible as an army with banners'* (Song of Solomon 6:10).

The Gospel is a mighty deliverance from the groveling religious subjectivism of Rome and her pagan mistresses. To know God is life itself to a Christian, in the words of the Lord Himself, *'this is life eternal, that they might know thee the only true God, and Jesus Christ, whom thou hast sent'* (John 17:3). Knowledge of God, and faith in Him, are the means whereby all spiritual supports and comforts are conveyed to the true believers. *'According as his divine power hath given unto us all things that pertain unto life and godliness, through the knowledge of him that hath called us to glory and virtue'* (2 Pet. 1:3) (Bennett, "The Mystic Plague: Catholicism Sets a Spiritualist Agenda," n.d., http://www.bereanbeacon.org/MysticPlague.html).

(For more about contemplative spirituality, see *Contemplative Mysticism: A Powerful Ecumenical Glue*. One of the features of this book is a "Biographical Catalog of Contemplative Mystics" that describes the lives and beliefs of 58 influential voices in this movement.

LIBERAL EMERGING CHURCH ERROR #6 A SOCIAL-JUSTICE, KINGDOM-BUILDING GOSPEL

According to emerging church theology, the object of the church's mission on earth is not the preaching of the gospel but the building of the kingdom of God. It is earth-minded and mocks a heavenly-minded orientation. It gets more excited about solving the "AIDS crisis" and saving polar bears than winning lost souls.

Emerging church writings say very little about the salvation of the soul, but they say a lot about the salvation of society and creation. Their activism runs toward all sorts of very liberal social-justice concerns--environmentalism, animal rights, you name it. If there is any emphasis at all upon the winning of souls, it is a secondary thing.

They use terms such as "missional" and "holistic" to define this agenda.

Brian McLaren has "a strong conviction that THE EXCLUSIVE, HELL-ORIENTED GOSPEL IS NOT THE WAY FORWARD" (*A Generous Orthodoxy*, p. 120, f. 48). In *A New Kind of Christian*, McLaren's postmodern hero rejects the idea that the gospel is about getting individual souls into Heaven, because this "smacked of selfishness" and was unacceptable to postmodern thinking (pp. 82, 83).

McLaren says that Jesus' objective was "holistic reconciliation."

> "I think what Jesus was about ... was a global, public movement or revolution to bring holistic reconciliation, a reconnection with God, with others, with ourselves, with our environment" (*A New Kind of Christian*, p. 73).

McLaren is not referring to what Jesus will do when He returns to establish His kingdom but what He is allegedly doing today. He says that the proper objective of churches is not merely the salvation of souls but renewing the world and saving the planet from destruction (p. 83).

In his books *The Secret Message of Jesus* and *Everything Must Change*, McLaren expands on this theme. He says that "the essential message of Jesus" is the kingdom of God, and this is "not just a message *about* Jesus that focused on the afterlife, but rather the core message *of* Jesus that focused on personal, SOCIAL, AND GLOBAL TRANSFORMATION IN THIS LIFE" (*Everything Must Change*, p. 22). He says THE KINGDOM OF GOD IS "ABOUT CHANGING THIS WORLD" (p. 23).

Eddie Gibbs and Ryan Bolger, in their study on the emerging church, say:

> "Rooted in the work of N.T. Wright, emerging churches embrace the gospel of the kingdom as revealed in Mark 1:15-16. At the outset of the Gospel narrative, THE GOOD NEWS WAS NOT THAT JESUS WAS TO DIE ON THE CROSS TO FORGIVE SINS BUT THAT GOD HAD RETURNED AND ALL WERE INVITED TO PARTICIPATE WITH HIM IN THIS NEW WAY OF LIFE, IN THIS REDEMPTION OF THE WORLD. It is this gospel that the emerging church seeks to recover. As one leader confided privately, 'We have totally reprogrammed ourselves to recognize the good news as a means to an end--that the kingdom of God is here. ... We don't dismiss the cross; it is still a central part. But THE GOOD NEWS IS NOT THAT HE DIED BUT THAT THE KINGDOM HAS COME.' ...
>
> "[Joel McClure of Water's Edge in Michigan says,] 'The gospel is that God wants you to help solve that problem, to participate with God through redeeming acts. THE GOSPEL IS NOT THAT WE AGREE WITH SOME ABSTRACT PROPOSITIONS IN ORDER TO QUALIFY TO GO TO HEAVEN WHEN WE DIE BUT AN INVITATION TO LIVE IN A NEW WAY OF LIFE. Sharing the good news is not only about conversion. It is about inviting someone to walk with you relationally, and it takes a while to demonstrate this gospel.' ...
>
> "THE GOSPEL OF EMERGING CHURCHES IS NOT CONFINED TO PERSONAL SALVATION. IT IS SOCIAL TRANSFORMATION arising from the presence and permeating of the reign of Christ" (*Emerging Churches*, pp. 54, 56, 63).

Rob Bell, author of *Velvet Elvis*, says:

> "The Bible paints a much larger picture of salvation. It describes all of creation being restored. ... Rocks and trees and birds and swamps and ecosystems. God's desire is to restore all of it. ... A Christian is not someone who expects to spend forever in heaven there. A Christian is someone who anticipates spending forever here, in a new heaven that comes to earth. THE GOAL ISN'T ESCAPING THIS WORLD BUT MAKING THIS WORLD THE KIND OF PLACE GOD CAN COME TO. ... To make the cross of Jesus just about human salvation is to miss that God is interested in the saving of everything. Every star and rock and bird. All things" (*Velvet Elvis*, pp. 109, 110, 150, 161).

Bell's church, Mars Hill Bible Church in Grand Rapids, Michigan, has the following statement of purpose:

> "We take great joy in PARTNERING WITH GOD TO CHANGE THE WORLD, embracing the truth that ALL OF LIFE IS SACRED, hope is real and tomorrow can be better than today."

Donald Miller says that one thing that drew him to Imago Dei, an emerging church in downtown Portland, Oregon, was the fact that the pastor didn't see evangelism as "a target on the wall in which the goal is to get people to agree with us about the meaning of life." Rather, "He saw evangelism as reaching a felt need" (*Blue Like Jazz*, p. 114). He liked this because he had always felt guilty for not "telling anybody about Jesus except when I was drunk at a party."

Under the "Activism" section of his web site Miller links to radical leftist organizations such as the ACLU, Greenpeace, and Moveon.org. His note accompanying the links says these organizations are doing the work of God.

Matt Palmer, a member of the emergent church founded by Spencer Burke, says, "Our goal is to be there for each other and try to find activities [through which] we can service our community" ("These Christians Radically Rethink What a Church Is," *Los Angeles Times*, Aug. 14, 2005). "Missional" activities at this church include visiting a Buddhist gathering and discussing it in a non-judgmental manner and setting up an art gallery at a park. The *Los Angeles Times* reported: "On a recent Sunday, the group spread out chicken, salad and fruit on picnic tables at Lions Park in Costa Mesa and invited everyone there to join them. More than 30 did. They also gave out small cardboard cameras, with self-addressed envelopes, and invited people to take 'pictures in celebration of life,' then mail them to Burke's 700-square-foot Huntington Beach 'shack,' his garage that serves as the church's office."

Tony Campolo claims that believers are saved in order to change the world:

> "[Jesus] saved us in order that He might begin TO TRANSFORM HIS WORLD into the kind of world that He willed for it to be when He created it" (Campolo, *It's Friday but Sunday's Coming*, p. 106).

"Our call is to be God's agents, TO RESCUE NOT ONLY THE HUMAN RACE BUT THE WHOLE OF CREATION" (Campolo, "Why Care for Creation," *Tear Times*, Summer 1992).

Campolo claims that believers are commissioned to build the kingdom of God in this world, and he borrows theology from all sorts of heretics to prove his point. In *How to Rescue the Earth without Worshiping Nature* (Thomas Nelson, 1992), he said: "If the Shalom of God and the peaceable kingdom of Isaiah 11 are to become real, then new ways of thinking must be established. With some help from St. Francis and Teilhard de Chardin, we just might make it" (p. 89). Thus, he borrows theology from a Catholic mystic who was committed to a false gospel and a New Age evolutionist who worshipped a "cosmic christ."

In *Red Letter Christians*, Campolo says:

"Red Letter Christians believe that Jesus Christ has already initiated this new Kingdom. ... The Good News is that in Him, what Isaiah prophesied [Isaiah 65:20-25] is even now breaking loose in history. ... This hope for God's Kingdom on earth has been, since Christ, in the process of being actualized. ... both the salvation of individuals *and* the transformation of society are Kingdom non-negotiables" (p. 33).

The mission statement of Ecclesia of Houston, Texas, founded by Chris Seay, says:

"We believe that the church exists for the world and not for herself-- she is to introduce and usher in the Kingdom of God into every part of this world."

Sherry and Geoff Maddock, in their contribution to *An Emerging Manifesto of Hope*, testify how that their thinking about salvation broke "out of old paradigms" (p. 80).

"Many of us were raised with the understanding that salvation is the exact size and shape of a particular soul. This individualization of soteriology seems to fall short of the salvation imagery we find in the biblical drama. ... God's saving work is best understood in terms of cosmic healing, holism, and liberation. ... As we confront the broader issues of systemic injustice, WE EXPAND OUR THINKING ABOUT 'GETTING SAVED.' ... Through practices such as caring for AIDS sufferers, feeding the homeless, protesting the wanton destruction of the environment, or welcoming newly arrived refugees, we find salvation that is closer to the *shalom* of Scripture. ... Not only soul, whole body! Not only whole body, all of the faithful community! Not only all of the faithful community, all of humanity! Not only all of humanity, all of God's creation" (pp. 81, 82).

Leonard Sweet calls the emerging church's objective "quantum spirituality," and calls the practitioners thereof "New Light pastors." He says this type of spirituality "bonds us to all creation" and "entails a radical doctrine of embodiment of God in the very substance of creation" (*Quantum Spirituality*, p. 124). Elsewhere he says, "New Light embodiment means to be 'in connection' and 'information' with all of creation" (*Carpe Manana*, p. 124). He even goes so far as to call the earth part of the "cosmic body of Christ" (Ibid.). Sweet calls for a "New Light movement of 'world-making' faith" that will "CREATE THE WORLD THAT IS TO, AND MAY YET, BE" (http://www.leonardsweet.com/Quantum/quantum-ebook.pdf, p. 12).

The Sojourners mission is "to articulate the biblical call to social justice, inspiring hope and building a movement TO TRANSFORM individuals, communities, the church, and THE WORLD" (http://www.sojo.net/index.cfm?action=about_us.mission).

Doug Pagitt describes the technological and social-justice achievements of the present time and says these "will be carried to extremes beyond our control by our grandchildren," claiming that "these wondrous times are just the beginning" (*An Emergent Manifesto of Hope*, p. 304). Pagitt says, "... the Kingdom of God is synonymous with the creativity of God," and, "When we employ creativity to make this world better, WE PARTICIPATE WITH GOD IN THE RE-CREATION OF THE WORLD" (*Church Re-imagined*, pp. 189, 185).

A member of Pagitt's Solomon's Porch in Minneapolis described her dream for doing "mission" in Guatemala by opening a "healing camp." It would "provide free massage, chiropractic, and bioresonance treatments for several weeks annually to our Guatemalan friends" and at night they would "teach yoga and healthy-cooking classes" (*Church Reimagined*, p. 197).

Donald McCullough says that GOD'S GRACE IN CHRIST "EMBRACES BOTH US AND CREATION" and says that "to despoil creation--polluting oceans, fouling air, decimating forests--is to spit in the face of Jesus Christ" (*If Grace Is So Amazing, Why Don't We Like It*, pp. 207, 208).

WHAT DOES THE BIBLE SAY?

It is important to observe that the emerging church's social-justice gospel is nothing new. It has been the misguided "gospel" of theological liberals for 100 years.

Theological liberalism has always replaced the biblical gospel of redeeming souls with a humanistic gospel of redeeming society. Walter Rauschenbusch (1861-1918), often called the father of the "social gospel," was raised in a conservative family but adopted liberal theological beliefs as a student at Rochester Theological Seminary. Rauschenbusch rejected the inerrancy of Scripture and the substitutionary atonement of Jesus Christ and developed a social-justice kingdom-building program.

> "Rauschenbusch's view of Christianity was that its purpose was to spread a Kingdom of God, not through a fire and brimstone style of preaching but by leading a Christlike life. Rauschenbusch did not view Jesus' death as an act of substitutionary atonement but, in his words, he died 'to substitute love for selfishness as the basis of human society.' He wrote that 'Christianity is in its nature revolutionary' and tried to remind society of that. He explained that the Kingdom of God 'is not a matter of getting individuals to heaven, but of transforming the life on earth into the harmony of heaven'" ("Walter Rauschenbusch," *Wikipedia*).

Rauschenbusch formed a group called the Brotherhood of the Kingdom, which sought to establish the priority of kingdom building as the proper objective of Christianity.

In 1919, the Northern Baptist Convention, the predecessor to the American Baptist Church USA, called Rauschenbusch "the most potent personality in America in the modern revival of the idea of the Kingdom of God" (*Annual of the Northern Baptist Convention*, 1919, pp. 169-71).

The World Council of Churches and the various national councils and the liberal denominations they represent have long maintained an emerging church style social gospel. The National Council of Churches in America (NCC), for example, has had a liberal "social creed" since 1908 when it was called the Federal Council of Churches. In 2008, the old creed was replaced with an updated one that would make the emerging church proud. Proclaiming "a message of hope for a fearful time," the 2008 NCC social creed seeks to transform society through social-justice work and to save the earth through environmental activities. Chief among its tools are interdenominational ecumenism and interfaith dialogue.

In fact, a social-justice emphasis is nothing new within evangelicalism itself. The New Evangelical philosophy, which arose in the late 1940s and spread throughout evangelicalism over the ensuing decades, had an emphasis on social-political work from its inception. Harold Ockenga, the co-founder and first president of Fuller Theological Seminary and editor of *Christianity Today*, claimed to have coined the term "neo-evangelical" for a speech that he gave in 1948. He said, "The summons to social involvement received a hearty response from many evangelicals. ... It [the New Evangelicalism] had a new emphasis upon the application of the gospel to the sociological, political, and economic areas of life" (Harold Ockenga, in the foreword to *The Battle for the Bible* by Harold Lindsell).

In 1966 the Evangelical Foreign Missions Association (an arm of the National Association of Evangelicals) said in its statement on social action: "... we urge all evangelicals to stand openly and firmly for racial equality, human freedom and all forms of social justice throughout the world."

The books *The New Left and Christians Radicalism* (by Arthur Gish, 1970) and *The Christian Revolutionary* (by Dale W. Brown, 1971) influenced many evangelicals in the direction of pacifism, communalism, and leftist social-political activism.

In 1971 a group of students at Trinity Evangelical Divinity School founded the People's Christian Coalition. They moved to Washington, D.C., lived communally, held to pacifistic views, and promoted social-justice issues. The leader, Jim Wallis, published *Sojourners* magazine to propagate this philosophy. He also wrote *Agenda for Biblical People*, which was "the radical evangelicals' foremost manifesto." Wallis has had an emerging church outlook for many decades.

In 1973 the Chicago Declaration of Evangelical Social Concern was published by roughly 50 evangelical leaders, including Carl F. Henry. It called for a more aggressive sociopolitical agenda among evangelicals. A new organization, Evangelicals for Social Action, was formed at that time. Its chairman, Ron Sider, was the author of *Rich Christians in an Age of Hunger*. He claimed that Christians are responsible to help the poor by living sacrificially and also to change the structures of injustice that lead to poverty in this present world. He criticizes American Christians, in particular, for not saving the world and for allegedly hurting the poor in other parts of the world by consuming too much. Sider claims that preaching the death, burial, and resurrection of Christ for the salvation of sinners is not the gospel unless you are also preaching social-justice issues. "If you preach the gospel in all aspects with the exception of the issues which deal specifically with your time, you are not preaching the gospel at all."

(Two books that have taken Sider's position to task are David Chilton's *Productive Christians in an Age of Guilt Manipulators* and Herbert Schlossberg's *Idols for Destruction*.)

In 1974 the Lausanne Covenant, which was drafted by major

evangelical leaders including Billy Graham, stated that "evangelism and socio-political involvement are BOTH part of our Christian duty."

In his 1978 book *The Worldly Evangelicals*, Richard Quebedeaux documented the burgeoning evangelical social gospel movement. The "worldly evangelicals" about whom Quebedeaux wrote were "generally the younger Christians of the evangelical left." He observed that the growing popularity of the social gospel among evangelicals was following hand-in-hand with the liberalizing trend in theology, such as the rejection of biblical inerrancy, and the liberalizing trend in Christian living, meaning the rejection of "old taboos" such as drinking, smoking, dancing, rock & roll, profanity, attending the theater, and dressing sensually. Quebedeaux wrote:

> "... EVANGELICALS ARE SHIFTING THEIR FOCUS FROM THE HEREAFTER TO THE HERE AND NOW, stressing time rather than eternity. ... we can discern very little, if any, reference to heaven and hell (except existentially) in young evangelical publications. Building a just society and developing ethical living here and now seem far more important than preparing people for heaven" (p. 19).
>
> "In the present 'identity confusion' among evangelicals, MANY ARE IN TRANSITION, moving from one stance to another (GENERALLY FROM RIGHT TO CENTER OR LEFT)" (p. 27).
>
> "InterVarsity Press publishes popular and scholarly books of evangelical conviction, an increasing number of which can be rightly termed politically and socially radical" (p. 102).
>
> "In addition to Miquez Bonino, a number of other leading Latin American evangelicals now affirm (though not uncritically) both liberation theology in general and the possibility of Marxist-Christian cooperation in working for social justice and political change in particular. Notable among them are Samuel Escobar, Rene Padilla, and Orlando Costas, author of *The Church and Its Mission*" (p. 112).

In his 1985 book *Partly Right*, Tony Campolo described the same thing. He called it "the prophetic left wing of evangelical Christianity."

> "Those in positions of leadership in this group of evangelicals are sometimes called 'closet Communists' by their New Right critics. They tend to oppose the American military buildup, and they call for a redistribution of wealth, welfare programs for the poor, the abolishment of capital punishment, an end to U.S. intervention in Central American nations, and a host of other concerns that are usually on the liberal political agenda. ... The New Evangelicals argue that those who would become followers of Jesus must recognize that concern for the poor and the oppressed is related to the evangelistic mission which goes with discipleship ... They call for a new economic order" (*Partly Right*, pp. 216, 217).

These descriptions of the "left wing" of evangelicals in the late 1970s and early 1980s are an apt description of the emerging church today, a quarter of a century later.

Thus, the emerging church's social-justice gospel is nothing really new.

The emerging church's social-justice-environmentalist gospel is refuted by the New Testament definition of the gospel.

Paul defined the gospel in Romans 1-3. He told the church at Rome, "*I am ready to preach the gospel to you that are at Rome*" (Rom. 1:15), and said that "*the gospel is the power of God unto salvation*" (Rom. 1:16). He then proceeded to preach the gospel in the first three chapters of the epistle. According to Paul, the gospel begins with the bad news that God is a holy God who judges sin and that all men, being sinners, are thus under God's just condemnation (Rom. 1:18-32; 2:12-16; 3:9-18). Paul then presents the good news that the sinner can be justified or declared righteous by God through faith in the blood atonement of Jesus Christ (Rom. 3:21-25). When preaching the gospel in Romans 1-3, Paul said nothing about saving society or the earth. Such things were not a part of Paul's gospel.

Paul also summarized the gospel in 1 Corinthians 15:

> "Moreover, brethren, I declare unto you the gospel which I preached unto you, which also ye have received, and wherein ye stand; by which also ye are saved, if ye keep in memory what I preached unto

you, unless ye have believed in vain. For I delivered unto you first of all that which I also received, how that Christ died for our sins according to the scriptures; and that he was buried, and that he rose again the third day according to the scriptures" (1 Cor. 15:1-4).

The gospel is the preaching of the cross that is able to save men's souls. It is the message that Christ died for our sins, was buried, and rose again the third day according to Bible prophecy.

The gospel of Jesus Christ is not for the salvation of the world; it is for the salvation of sinners. The term gospel is never used in the New Testament for a social-justice-environmental objective in this present time.

And Paul warned that if anyone preaches a different gospel than the one delivered to the apostles, he is under God's curse (Galatians 1:6-8).

The emerging church's social-justice-environmentalist gospel is refuted by Christ's example.

The Lord Jesus Christ did not come to earth merely to have a good time with sinners, to hang out with them and find out what they were thinking. He did not make any attempt to involve Himself in global social-justice issues and He did not even hint at the necessity of caring for the environment.

Rather, He said, *"For the Son of man is come to seek and to save that which was lost"* (Luke 19:10), and He said this not in the context of saving the world; He said this in the context of saving the sinner Zacchaeus. See Luke 19:1-9.

Paul said, *"This is a faithful saying, and worthy of all acceptation, that CHRIST JESUS CAME INTO THE WORLD TO SAVE SINNERS; of whom I am chief"* (1 Tim. 1:15).

In the inspired record of Jesus' earthly life in the Gospels we see Him dealing with unbelievers about their need for salvation. He led the Samaritan woman and many of her fellow villagers to salvation (John 4:5-42), and in the process He taught the disciples that there is a great urgency about this business and that they should be busy winning people before it is too late.

> "Say not ye, There are yet four months, and then cometh harvest? behold, I say unto you, Lift up your eyes, and look on the fields; for they are white already to harvest. And he that reapeth receiveth wages, and gathereth fruit unto life eternal: that both he that soweth and he that reapeth may rejoice together" (John 4:35-36).

Christ warned often about the danger of hell fire and demanded that people repent (Luke 13:1-5; Mark 9:43-48; John 3:36; 8:24).

Thus, the emerging church's social-justice-environmentalist gospel is refuted by Christ's own example.

The emerging church's social-justice-environmentalist gospel is refuted by Christ's Great Commission.

After the Lord rose from the dead and before He went back to Heaven, He focused the disciples' attention on the thing that was closest to His heart. We call this the Great Commission because it is emphasized so forcefully in the New Testament. It is repeated in Matthew 28:18-20, Mark 16:15-16, Luke 24:46-48, John 20:21, and Acts 1:8.

It is the command to go into all the earth and preach the gospel to every individual in every nation, and as we have seen, the gospel is the message of salvation from sin through faith in the death, burial, and resurrection of Jesus Christ (1 Corinthians 15:3-4).

The Great Commission requires that believers preach the gospel to every single person on earth (Mark 16:15). That is a truly large task, and it will never be done by trying to develop a close relationship with every unbeliever, dialoguing with them at length, and "building trust." It will be done by boldly proclaiming the gospel near and far by every means available.

This is genuine New Testament missionary work.

The emerging church's social-justice-environmentalist gospel is refuted by the example of the apostles and early churches.

We have a divinely-inspired record of the lives and ministries of the apostles and early churches in the book of Acts and the New Testament epistles, and there we see that they did not follow the emerging church program. There is not a hint in the book of Acts that the apostles and early churches pursued any sort of grandiose social-justice agenda. They did not set out to save the environment. They did not organize protests against the many great social-political ills of the Roman Empire. They preached the gospel and lived holy lives and planted churches and discipled believers and loved their neighbors (but not after the manner that this is defined by the emerging church) and looked for the return of Christ.

Paul and his co-laborers went from town to town and preached the gospel publicly to people wherever they were found. They spoke *"boldly in the Lord, which gave testimony unto the word of his grace"* (Acts 14:3).

Paul didn't just hang out with sinners for the sake of making friendships and serving them in some vague sense. He went from place to place preaching the gospel to as many as would listen with the clear and unequivocal objective of winning them to Christ. He said:

> "For though I be free from all men, yet have I made myself servant unto all, that I might gain the more. And unto the Jews I became as a Jew, that I might gain the Jews; to them that are under the law, as under the law, that I might gain them that are under the law; to them that are without law, as without law, (being not without law to God, but under the law to Christ,) that I might gain them that are without law. To the weak became I as weak, that I might gain the weak: I am made all things to all men, that I might by all means save some" (1 Cor. 9:19-22).

Paul wasn't a servant of men simply to be a servant of men; he was a servant of men so that he might gain them to salvation. *"Even as I please all men in all things, not seeking mine own profit, but the profit of many, that they may be saved"* (1 Cor. 10:33).

It is true that believers should have a godly influence in this world. We are light and salt. But that does not add up to the social-justice-environmentalist gospel as spelled out by the emerging church. We agree with the following statement by Jonathan Leeland from the Pastors' and Theologians' Forum on Church and Culture on the 9Marks web site:

> "The church is not called to transform culture, at least not in the sense that most people use that phrase today. If by transform one means 'convert,' then fine. But that's not how the phrase is being used. You cannot transform what is blind except by giving it sight. You cannot transform what is deaf except by giving it hearing. You cannot transform what is stone except by making it flesh. You cannot transform what is dead except by making it alive. How do you 'transform' something that's dead? If you happen to be supernatural, you can make it alive (John 1:13). But you cannot transform it. ... In the same way that Christians are called to live and love like Good Samaritans, we should always be looking for ways to serve our non-Christian neighbors--that they might be given sight, hearing, hearts of flesh, and life!" (Leeland, Pastors' and Theologians' Forum on Church and Culture, http://www.9marks.org/partner/Article_Display_Page/0,,PTID314526|CHID598016|CIID2371850,00.html).

"Having your conversation honest among the Gentiles: that, whereas they speak against you as evildoers, they may by your good works, which they shall behold, glorify God in the day of visitation" (1 Peter 2:12).

"As we have therefore opportunity, let us do good unto all men, especially unto them who are of the household of faith" (Galatians 6:10).

The emerging church's social-justice-environmentalist gospel is refuted by Christ's warnings about always being ready for His return.

> "For they themselves shew of us what manner of entering in we had unto you, and how ye turned to God from idols to serve the living and true God; And to wait for his Son from heaven, whom he raised from the dead, even Jesus, which delivered us from the wrath to come" (1 Thessalonians 1:9-10).

Christ taught that great judgments will come upon the world (Matthew 24; Mark 13; Luke 21) and that believers must be ready at all times for His return. He likened His return to the days of Noah when the people mocked Noah and ignored his warnings up to the very day that he went into the ark, and then the judgment came and the world was destroyed (Mat. 24:36-39).

Christ warned, *"Therefore be ye also ready: for in such an hour as ye think not the Son of man cometh"* (Mat. 24:44).

The doctrine of judgment to come and the imminent return of Christ is not the figment of some novelist's imagination! The New Testament teaches us to expect His return at any time.

> "Let your moderation be known unto all men. The Lord is at hand" (Phil. 4:5).

> "Be ye also patient; stablish your hearts: for the coming of the Lord draweth nigh. Grudge not one against another, brethren, lest ye be condemned: behold, the judge standeth before the door" (James 5:8-9).

> "But the end of all things is at hand: be ye therefore sober, and watch unto prayer" (1 Pet 4:7).

The imminency of Christ's return teaches us that winning people to Christ is an urgent matter. The emerging church idea that it is enough to build relationships with the unsaved without confronting them with the claims of the gospel is not only wrong; it is criminal. We have been provided with a pardon for sinners in the gospel; we are ambassadors for Christ and have been given the responsibility of urging unbelievers to be reconciled with God (2 Cor. 5:20).

It is impossible to accomplish the great work of world evangelism while also trying to build the kingdom of God by involving ourselves in great socio-political endeavors. There is simply not the time or the resources to do both, and history shows us that when Christians try to save society (not to speak of the earth) the gospel of personal salvation gets pushed far to the back of the bandwagon and is soon kicked right off.

Evangelist D.L. Moody had it right when he said: "I look upon this world as a wrecked vessel. God has given me a lifeboat and said to me, 'Moody, save all you can.'"

The emerging church's social-justice-environmentalist gospel is refuted by its ineffectiveness and its inability to address the root problem of this world's ills.

If the emerging church wants to prove its ability to establish the kingdom of God, let them go to Nepal or some place like that and fix the social-justice-environmental issues there. That would be a good testing ground for their theories. If they can't bring peace and righteousness and justice and environmental wholeness and lift up the poor of one little nation, how can they possibly expect to bring it to the entire world?

They might reply that they are only the forerunners of the kingdom of God, but that is not what they actually teach. As we have seen, Sojourners' mission is to "transform the world." Leonard Sweet says that the so-called New Light movement will "create the world that is to be." Chris Seay says the church's job is to "usher in the kingdom of God into every part of the world." Tony Campolo claims that the kingdom prophesied in Old Testament passages such as Isaiah 65:20-25 is "in the process of being actualized." Campolo says, "Our call is to be God's agents, to rescue not only the human race but the whole of creation." Rod Bell says, "The goal isn't escaping this world but making this world the kind of place God can come to." Brian McLaren says that the kingdom of God is "about changing this world." Eddie Gibbs and Ryan Bolger say, "The good news is not that Christ died but that the kingdom has come" and that we are "invited to participate with him in the redemption of the world."

If that is true, then they should prove it, but in reality they can do no such thing. They cannot make the lion lie down with the lamb or the nations beat their swords into plowshares; they cannot solve the Middle East problem; they cannot make the nations bow down before the King of kings. All of the liberal social-justice activity of the past century has not changed the dark character of this world system or solved the world's systemic problems in any substantial way.

This is for the simple reason that they do not have the power to address and fix the root of the world's ills. The root, of course, is man's fallen heart and the devil's position as the god of this world (2 Cor. 4:4) and man's obstinate rebellion against God and His Christ (Psalm 2). Unless the emerging church can subdue and change men's hearts and overthrow the devil from his throne, nothing of lasting substance will be accomplished and the world will continue to be just as dark as it has been for 6,000 years.

The kingdom of God cannot be established even by the most well-meaning and committed believers; it can only be established by the glorious appearance of the Son of God. It will be established through a divine Dictator exercising supernatural power and wielding a rod of iron!

The emerging church's social-justice-environmentalist gospel is refuted by the Bible's teaching that this present creation will be destroyed.

The creation will be "redeemed," to be sure, but it will not be redeemed by evolution and human activity. It will be redeemed by judgment and replacement.

The old creation was good and perfect when it came from God's hand (Gen. 1:31), but it fell under God's curse because of Adam's sin.

> "And unto Adam he said, Because thou hast hearkened unto the voice of thy wife, and hast eaten of the tree, of which I commanded thee, saying, Thou shalt not eat of it: cursed is the ground for thy sake; in sorrow shalt thou eat of it all the days of thy life; thorns also and thistles shall it bring forth to thee; and thou shalt eat the herb of the field; in the sweat of thy face shalt thou eat bread, till thou return unto the ground; for out of it wast thou taken: for dust thou art, and unto dust shalt thou return" (Genesis 3:17-19).

This curse has not been lifted. Every earthly occupant toils under its dark shadow every day of his or her life.

The apostle Paul taught that the *"whole creation groaneth and travaileth in pain together until now"* and the believer is waiting for redemption from this condition (Romans 8:22-23).

The curse upon creation will be lifted when Christ returns; the desert will blossom as a rose and the lion will lie down with the lamb (Isaiah 11:6; 35:1). The curse will be done away with permanently when this present heaven and earth will be burned up and replaced with the new heaven and new earth. The "global warming" that Bible believers should be concerned with is that described in the following passage.

> "But the day of the Lord will come as a thief in the night; in the which the heavens shall pass away with a great noise, and the elements shall melt with fervent heat, the earth also and the works that are therein shall be burned up. Seeing then that all these things shall be dissolved, what manner of persons ought ye to be in all holy

conversation and godliness, looking for and hasting unto the coming of the day of God, wherein the heavens being on fire shall be dissolved, and the elements shall melt with fervent heat? Nevertheless we, according to his promise, look for new heavens and a new earth, wherein dwelleth righteousness" (2 Peter 3:10-13).

The emerging church ignores, rejects, and mocks this doctrine, but wise men take heed.

The emerging church's social-justice-environmentalist gospel is refuted by the Bible's doctrine that the believer is to be heavenly minded.

Paul warned that certain false teachers are characterized by minding the things of this world rather than the things of heaven.

> "Brethren, be followers together of me, and mark them which walk so as ye have us for an ensample. (For many walk, of whom I have told you often, and now tell you even weeping, that they are the enemies of the cross of Christ: Whose end is destruction, whose God is their belly, and whose glory is in their shame, WHO MIND EARTHLY THINGS.) FOR OUR CONVERSATION IS IN HEAVEN; from whence also we look for the Saviour, the Lord Jesus Christ: Who shall change our vile body, that it may be fashioned like unto his glorious body, according to the working whereby he is able even to subdue all things unto himself" (Philippians 3:17-21).

Paul held himself up as the standard for truth, because he was the Lord's apostle and wrote by divine revelation. The false teachers that he exposed were those who minded earthly things. In contrast, the believer's citizenship is in Heaven and we are looking forward to Christ's return and the bodily resurrection.

Paul taught the same thing in Colossians:

> "If ye then be risen with Christ, seek those things which are above, where Christ sitteth on the right hand of God. SET YOUR AFFECTION ON THINGS ABOVE, NOT ON THINGS OF THE EARTH. For ye are dead, and your life is hid with Christ in God. When Christ, who is our life, shall appear, then shall ye also appear with him in glory" (Colossians 3:1-4).

The liberal emerging church identifies itself as heretical by its focus on this world and its rejection of the heavenly perspective.

The emerging church's social-justice-environmentalist gospel is refuted by the Bible's doctrine of the kingdom of God.

Misunderstanding the kingdom of God is a foundational error of all aspects of the emerging church. They believe that "the long-promised kingdom, spoken of by the Hebrew prophets, was *established in provisional form* with the coming of Jesus and the outpouring of His Spirit (*Emerging Churches*, p. 47).

By surveying the Old and New Testaments, we can see the error of this doctrine.

1. In the Old Testament the kingdom of God was God's rule over all creation (Psa. 103:19) and on earth it referred to His kingdom in Israel (1 Chron. 28:5; 2 Chron. 13:8).

That kingdom was destroyed because of Israel's disobedience, but Old Testament prophecies predicted that the kingdom would be re-established on earth by Christ, David's greater Son, and that He will reign in truth and righteousness (Isaiah 9:6-7; Daniel 2:44; 7:14).

2. Christ came to Israel and preached the kingdom.

The gospel of the kingdom is the gospel that Jesus preached when He presented Himself to Israel as the Messiah. Both John the Baptist and Jesus preached, *"Repent: for the kingdom of heaven is at hand"* (Mat. 3:2; 4:17). This was the announcement of the kingdom promised to David's Son (Isaiah 9:6-7). (The kingdom of God and the kingdom of Heaven are largely synonymous in the Gospels. One emphasizes the fact that it is God's kingdom, while the other emphasizes that it is a kingdom that will come from

Heaven.) Christ came to His own people, Israel, but they rejected Him (John 1:11; 19:15), and He warned them that the kingdom would be taken from them because of their rebellion and given to another nation (Mat. 21:42-26). Christ preached a literal glorious kingdom that would be established on earth. Peter, James, and John were given a foreview of it on the Mount of Transfiguration (Lk. 9:27-31). Christ taught His disciples to pray that God's kingdom would come to earth (Luke 11:2). He said Abraham, Isaac, and Jacob would be in the kingdom (Lk. 13:29). He corrected the view of those who thought the kingdom of God was going to be established at that time, saying that the kingdom would not be established until the *"noble man" goes into a far country and then returns"* (Lk. 19:11-27). Christ said the kingdom would be established after the Great Tribulation (Lk. 21:31). He said He would drink the fruit of the vine with His disciples in the kingdom (Lk. 22:18). When the disciples were arguing about who would be great in the kingdom of God, Christ corrected their thinking about the nature of greatness but He also confirmed that the kingdom of God is a literal kingdom that will be established at His return (Lk. 22:24-30). Jesus plainly stated that His kingdom is not of this world NOW (John 18:36). His kingdom will come when He comes in power and glory to establish it.

Jesus came unto His own people, Israel, and was rejected, and this had been prophesied in Scripture. He then turned his focus from Israel and said, *"I will build my church; and the gates of hell shall not prevail against it"* (Mat. 16:18). Christ stopped announcing the kingdom and turned His attention to dying on the cross for man's sin, and after He rose from the dead He sent His disciples forth to preach the gospel to every nation (Acts 1:8). In this present church age Christ is calling out a people for His name from among the Gentiles while Israel is largely blinded, but when this dispensation is finished He will turn His attention back to Israel and fulfill His covenants with them (Rom. 11:25-27).

3. The kingdom of God is in a *mystery* form during this present church age (Mat. 13:10-11).

A "mystery" is truth that was hidden in the Old Testament but revealed in the New (Rom. 16:25-26). The Old Testament did not see the church age in between Christ's two comings.

During the church age, the kingdom takes a strange form not described in Old Testament prophecy. The king is in Heaven and the kingdom is not yet established on earth. Instead, the kingdom of God resides in the small, despised apostolic churches, while the devil's false kingdom grows quickly and spreads throughout the world (Mat. 13:31-32).

4. Believers enter a spiritual kingdom of Christ when they are born again (Col. 1:13).

This is the kingdom comprised of all who submit to God's authority.

5. The kingdom of God will come to earth in its prophetic fullness at the return of Christ. See Acts 14:22; 1 Corinthians 6:9-10; 1 Thessalonians 2:12; 2 Timothy 4:1; James 2:5; 2 Peter 1:11; Revelation 12:10.

Believers are not building the kingdom of God on earth today. They are snatching brands from the coming fire before the day of salvation is finished (1 Cor. 9:19; 10:33; 2 Cor. 5:11, 18-21; 6:2; Jude 23). Today the "whole world lieth in wickedness" (1 John 5:19), and the devil is its god (2 Cor. 4:4). The apostles and prophets in the early churches (as described in the book of Acts and the Epistles) did not band together to accomplish grandiose social-justice projects; they did not pursue artsy activities; they did not try to save the earth; they preached the gospel and shined as lights in this dark world by their holy lives. Christ's Great Commission emphasizes gospel preaching (Mat. 28:18-20; Mk. 16:15; Lk. 24:46-48; Acts 1:8). After Christ rose from the dead and as

He was preparing them for His ascension, the disciples asked Him, *"Lord, wilt thou at this time restore again the kingdom to Israel?"* (Acts 1:6). Jesus' reply is very instructive. He did not correct their understanding of the establishment of a literal kingdom of earth. He told that it was not time for that long-expected kingdom to be established and that our duty in this church age is to preach the gospel to the ends of the earth. *"And he said unto them, It is not for you to know the times or the seasons, which the Father hath put in his own power. But ye shall receive power, after that the Holy Ghost is come upon you: and ye shall be witnesses unto me both in Jerusalem, and in all Judaea, and in Samaria, and unto the uttermost part of the earth"* (Acts 1:7-8). After this, Christ ascended to Heaven and poured out the Holy Spirit upon the disciples to empower them for this great work. This commission of world evangelism will not be abrogated until church age saints are removed from this world and the Lord regenerates Israel and restores them to the front burner of His plan for the ages.

The rod of iron

The Bible says that in the kingdom of God the Law will be enforced with a rod of iron (Rev. 2:26-27; 12:5; 19:15; Psalm 2:7-9). Christ's kingdom will not be a democracy but a divine dictatorship, a theocracy, and no one will be given a choice as to whether to obey Him or not. Christ's law will be established as international law and every individual will be required to obey it, and disobedience will be dealt with quickly and rigorously. Justice and righteousness will reign because injustice and unrighteousness will be punished and punished quickly. If the emerging church is truly building the kingdom of God today, they should be wielding this rod. The very fact that believers are not wielding this rod today is evidence that we are not establishing the kingdom of God on earth. The kingdom of God will be established by supernatural power, not by the feeble efforts of non-empowered saints in this present world in which the devil is god and believers are suffering pilgrims (2 Cor. 4:4).

What about Luke 17:20-21?

> "And when he was demanded of the Pharisees, when the kingdom of God should come, he answered them and said, The kingdom of God cometh not with observation: Neither shall they say, Lo here! or, lo there! for, behold, the kingdom of God is within you."

In interpreting this passage we must first note that there is a sense in which the kingdom of God WILL come with observation, as Jesus stated in verse 24 of this same passage. *"For as the lightning, that lighteneth out of the one part under heaven, shineth unto the other part under heaven; so shall also the Son of man be in his day."* Christ taught the same thing in Luke 19:11-27 and many other places, as we have seen in the previous study on the kingdom.

In what sense, then, is Christ saying that the kingdom of God "cometh NOT with observation" and "the kingdom of God is within you"? These statements are addressed to the Pharisees.

Jesus was saying that the kingdom of God would not come with observation in the sense of searching for it in various places. It would not come by searching. See verse 21 and Matthew 24:26-27. It would also not come with observation in the sense of demand. It would not come by demanding it in that present time. The Pharisees were demanding that Jesus show them the kingdom of God, and their demand would not be fulfilled. They had rejected Him as Messiah, so the kingdom of God was not going to come in that present time.

The kingdom of God was in them in the sense that it was already in their midst because Christ the King was present. The term "kingdom of God" is used repeatedly in this sense in the Gospels, as Christ was presenting Himself as the Messiah of Israel. *"The kingdom of God is come nigh unto you"* (Lk. 10:9). Note the following passages carefully: Luke 10:9, 11; 11:20; 13:28-29; 14:15; 19:11; 21:31; 22:16, 18; 23:51.

Jesus was not saying that the kingdom of God was in the midst of the Pharisees in the sense that it was inside of them in a spiritual sense, because they were not saved. He said elsewhere, *"Ye are of your father the devil, and the lusts of your father ye will do. He was a murderer from the beginning, and abode not in the truth, because there is no truth in him. When he speaketh a lie, he speaketh of his own: for he is a liar, and the father of it"* (John 8:44).

As we have seen, the Bible is clear in its teaching of the kingdom of God, and Jesus made it plain that He was referring to a kingdom that was promised to Him as the Son of David and that would be established at His return. To take Luke 17:20-21, which is a relatively obscure passage, and build one's doctrine of the kingdom primarily upon it and then use it to overthrow the teaching of many plain Scriptures is upside down hermeneutics. This is the way that false teachers (mis)use the Scripture.

What about Romans 8:16-25?

> "The Spirit itself beareth witness with our spirit, that we are the children of God: And if children, then heirs; heirs of God, and jointheirs with Christ; if so be that we suffer with him, that we may be also glorified together. For I reckon that the sufferings of this present time are not worthy to be compared with the glory which shall be revealed in us. For the earnest expectation of the creature waiteth for the manifestation of the sons of God. For the creature was made subject to vanity, not willingly, but by reason of him who hath subjected the same in hope, because the creature itself also shall be delivered from the bondage of corruption into the glorious liberty of the children of God. For we know that the whole creation groaneth and travaileth in pain together until now. And not only they, but ourselves also, which have the firstfruits of the Spirit, even we ourselves groan within ourselves, waiting for the adoption, to wit, the redemption of our body. For we are saved by hope: but hope that is seen is not hope: for what a man seeth, why doth he yet hope for? But if we hope for that we see not, then do we with patience wait for it."

The emerging church uses this passage in support of its doctrine that the kingdom of God is being built on earth today, but in fact it teaches the exact opposite. I was amazed when I first saw this passage used by an emerging church writer, because it actually refutes their position. Paul is contrasting the believer's condition in this present life with his condition in the future. In this present life we are subject to the pain and suffering caused by the fallen state of mankind. Presently we are subject to vanity, to the bondage of corruption, to groaning and travailing, and to waiting for redemption. It is in the future that we will experience the redemption of the body and the glorious salvation promised in the prophecies. This points to the return of Christ and the resurrection of the saints and the supernatural establishment of the kingdom on earth. The redemption described in this passage is something that will occur in the future and is certainly not occurring today! It is something that Christ will accomplish by His infinite power and not something that we can possibly bring about through grandiose socio-political endeavors.

The emerging church's social-justice-environmentalist gospel is refuted by the Bible's command not to yoke together with unbelievers and heretics.

In its socio-political activities, the emerging church develops intimate relationships with unbelievers and heretics. Books such as "Red Letter Christians" by Tony Campolo and "The Great Awakening" by Jim Wallis call for this type of activity.

Wallis' heroes in the social justice faith include the theological modernist Desmond Tutu, the Neo-Orthodox Dietrich Bonhoeffer, the Marxist Nelson Mandela, the Hindu Mahatma Gandhi, and the Catholic Pope John Paul II. Walls displays their pictures in his office (*The Great Awakening*, p. 24).

Holly Rankin Zaher of Three Nails in Pittsburgh, Pennsylvania, says: "We partner with others who seem to embody kingdom values and are doing kingdom work, even if they are not 'orthodox' Christians. We collect cans with Unitarians, work at blues festivals, and work with secular organizations in Pittsburgh" (*Emerging Churches*, p. 43).

In his autobiography Robert Schuller describes a meeting with Islamic leaders and says:

> "Standing before a crowd of devout Muslims with the Grand Mufti [of Jerusalem], I know that WE'RE ALL DOING GOD'S WORK TOGETHER. Standing on the edge of a new millennium, we're laboring hand in hand to repair the breach. ... I'm dreaming a bold impossible dream: that positive-thinking believers in God will rise above the illusions that our sectarian religions have imposed on the world, and that leaders of the major faiths will rise above doctrinal idiosyncrasies, choosing not to focus on disagreements, but rather TO TRANSCEND DIVISIVE DOGMAS TO WORK TOGETHER TO BRING PEACE AND PROSPERITY AND HOPE TO THE WORLD" (*My Journey*, pp. 501, 502).

The following are just a few of the Scriptures that forbid this type of alliance in the ministry of Jesus Christ.

> "Now I beseech you, brethren, mark them which cause divisions and offences contrary to the doctrine which ye have learned; and avoid them" (Rom. 16:17).

> "Be not deceived: evil communications corrupt good manners" (1 Cor. 15:33).

> "Be ye not unequally yoked together with unbelievers: for what fellowship hath righteousness with unrighteousness? and what communion hath light with darkness? And what concord hath Christ with Belial? or what part hath he that believeth with an infidel? And what agreement hath the temple of God with idols? for ye are the temple of the living God; as God hath said, I will dwell in them, and walk in them; and I will be their God, and they shall be my people. Wherefore come out from among them, and be ye separate, saith the Lord, and touch not the unclean thing; and I will receive you, and will be a Father unto you, and ye shall be my sons and daughters, saith the Lord Almighty" (2 Cor. 6:14-18).

> "And have no fellowship with the unfruitful works of darkness, but rather reprove them" (Eph. 5:11).

> "Having a form of godliness, but denying the power thereof: from such turn away" (2 Tim. 3:5).

The emerging church ignores these plain Scriptures to its own spiritual destruction. When light associates with darkness, when truth associates with error, the result is always the corruption of light and truth.

Consider the Christian World Liberation Front (CWLF), which was formed by Campus Crusade for Christ as a means of evangelizing "radical and countercultural students and street people by adopting their dress, language, and basic lifestyles, but not their politics" (Richard Quebedeux, *The Worldly Evangelicals*, p. 151). Instead of evangelizing the radicals, the compromising Christians were evangelized by the radicals! Quebedeux observes, "Unfortunately for Crusade, however, CWLF was itself radicalized politically in the process of its ministry, and now fits in well with Berkeley left more generally" (p. 151).

No other result should have been expected from such an unscriptural venture.

The emergent church's radical environmentalist agenda has no support whatsoever in the Bible.

The emerging church's environmental agenda is not just to keep the air clean and the streams pure; it goes far beyond that to a position that is akin to earth worship.

The Emergent Village says:

> "We see the earth and all it contains as God's beloved creation, and so we join God in seeking its good, its healing, and its blessing" (Emergent Village web site, http://www.emergentvillage.org/about-information/values-and-practices).

Leonard Sweet says:

> "New Light embodiment means to be 'in connection' and 'information' with all of creation. New Light communities extend the sense of connectionalism to creation and see themselves as members of an ecological community encompassing the whole of creation. 'This is my body' is not an anthropocentric metaphor. Theologian/feminist critic Sallie McFague has argued persuasively for seeing Earth, in a very real sense, as much as a part of the body of Christ as humans. We are all earthlings. ... WE CONSTITUTE TOGETHER A COSMIC BODY OF CHRIST" (*Carpe Manana*, p. 124).

> "Quantum spirituality bonds us to all creation as well as to other members of the human family. New Light pastors are what Arthur Peacocke calls 'priests of creation'--earth ministers who can relate the

realm of nature to God, who can help nurture a brother-sister relationship with the living organism called Planet Earth. This entails a radical doctrine of EMBODIMENT OF GOD IN THE VERY SUBSTANCE OF CREATION" (*Quantum Spirituality*, p. 124).

In May 2008 Pastor Jeffrey Whittaker attended Brian McLaren's *Everything Must Change* tour at Goshen College in Indiana, and he witnessed the emerging church's environmental frenzy first hand ("A Pastor Reports on McLaren's Everything Must Change Tour," June 2, 2008, http://herescope.blogspot.com/).

The very first session was titled "Focusing on the Wounds of Our Planet." They sang a song based on Francis of Assisi's poem "Brother Sun, Sister Moon" and watched a DVD by the Sierra Club "exposing the immoral mining techniques used by energy companies in West Virginia." Then they were treated to a song that cried out against "our rape of Mother Earth." The second day's session began with another environmentalist song that said mining is a "scar cut across the face of Mother Earth." They were constantly reminded that "catastrophic consequences due to global warming are upon us." Another session opened with the "Hymn of Remorse," which bewailed the supposed desecration of the earth. "We repent for covering your colorful earth with gray cement ... for cutting down trees ... for scarring your earth ... Lord, have mercy, can we be restored?"

By no stretch of the imagination can such a position be supported by the Bible. From the very beginning God gave man the right to use the earth.

> "And God blessed them, and God said unto them, Be fruitful, and multiply, and replenish the earth, and subdue it: and have dominion over the fish of the sea, and over the fowl of the air, and over every living thing that moveth upon the earth" (Genesis 1:28).

Man has a divine right to subdue the earth and use its resources, to cut its trees and mine its ore and pump its oil. This does not mean he has the right to destroy the earth and make it into a filthy cesspool; no one in his right mind is in support of making the air unbreathable and the water undrinkable and such things. But God has given man the right to use the earth's resources in a responsible manner.

The environmentalist movement is not based on proven science; it is not merely the push for reasonable conservation; it is a blind religious faith. Its most zealous proponents are gullible tools in the hands of one-worlders who intend to use the environmentalist cause to increase their authority at a local, national, and global level. When Marxist globalists get on the environmentalist bandwagon, you have to know that something other than love for a clean earth is driving the program.

Jonah Goldberg has wisely observed:

> "At its core, environmentalism is a kind of nature worship. It's a holistic ideology, shot through with religious sentiment. ... Environmentalism's most renewable resources are fear, guilt and moral bullying" ("The Church of Green," *Los Angeles Times*, Op-Ed, May 20, 2008).

As for "global warming", it is not an established fact. In reality, it is nothing more than a weak theory; and many scientists do not believe it. In March 2008, for example, more than 100 prominent environment scientists presented papers at the International Conference on Climate Change in New York City. They concluded that global warming is a natural process rather than the result of human activity. Joseph Bast, president of the Heartland Institute, said: "The purpose of the conference is to provide a platform for the hundreds of scientists, economists, and policy experts who dissent from the so-called 'consensus' on global warming" ("Scientists Meet in NYC to Challenge Gore, UN," *WorldNetDaily*, March 4, 2008).

Art Robinson, co-founder of the Oregon Institute of Science and Medicine, launched the Petition Project to give a forum for scientists to express their disagreement with the theory of man-made global warming. More than 31,000 scientists (including 9,000 Ph.D.s) have signed their names to the following statement: "There is no convincing scientific evidence that human release of carbon dioxide, methane, or other greenhouse gases is causing or will, in the foreseeable future, cause catastrophic heating of the Earth's atmosphere and disruption of the Earth's climate. Moreover, there is substantial scientific evidence that increases in atmospheric carbon dioxide produce many beneficial effects upon the natural plant and animal environments of the Earth" ("U.N. 'Scaring Planet Earth' into Global Tax," *WorldNetDaily*, June 19, 2008).

Take the frenzy to ban plastic shopping bags.

> "Scientists are attacking the global campaign to ban plastic shopping bags, saying the activists' claim that the modern conveniences are responsible for the deaths of 100,000 animals and one million seabirds is based on a 'typo' in a 2002 report [by the Australian government] and there is no scientific evidence showing the bags pose a direct threat to marine mammals. [The report was derived from a Canadian study in Newfoundland that only sited the death of marine mammals by discarded fishing nets and made no mention of plastic bags!] Researchers and marine biologists have told the *London Times* plastic bags pose, at best, a minimal threat to most marine species, including seals, whales, dolphins and seabirds" ("Anti-plastic Crusaders Stuck Holding the Bag," *WorldNetDaily*, March 9, 2008).

It takes more energy to make and recycle paper shopping bags than plastic ones, but banning plastic bags makes the environmental activists felt better and that is what is really important.

Consider, too, the frenzy to save the polar bears.

> "The U.S. government just put polar bears on the threatened species list because climate change is shrinking the Arctic ice where they live. Never mind that polar bears are in fact thriving--their numbers have quadrupled in the last 50 years. Never mind that full implementation of the Kyoto protocols on greenhouse gases would save exactly one polar bear, according to Danish social scientist Bjorn Lomborg, author of the 2007 book *Cool It!* Yet about 300 to 500 polar bears could be saved every year, starting right now, Lomborg says, if there were a ban on hunting them in Canada. What's cheaper, trillions to trim carbon emissions or paying off the Canadians to stop killing polar bears?" ("The Church of Green," *Los Angeles Times*, May 20, 2008).

The common sense evident in this paragraph is exactly what is often missing in the environmental movement.

The movement is also shot through and through with duplicity. There appears to be a willingness to say anything and ignore any inconvenient fact as long as by so doing you can further your cause.

> "During the 2000 presidential campaign, for example, much was made of Houston becoming the 'smog capital of America.' But Houston's overall air quality was improving at the time. Houston became the nation's smog capital only because Los Angeles's air improved even faster, passing Houston in a race of positives. Perhaps the commentators who spoke as though Houston's air were getting worse did not understand the issue. More likely they did not want to understand-for cleaner air would violate the rule of Good News Bad" (Gregg Easterbrook, "Bad News Good, Good News Bad," Brookings Institute, Spring 2002).

Environmental activists have claimed that more U.S. cities are violating air standards, but what they don't say is that the EPA standards have grown progressively stricter and that the pollution levels have actually gone down dramatically. Data produced by the Environmental Protection Agency shows that between 1976 and 1997, ozone declined 31 percent; sulfur dioxide, 67 percent; and nitrogen oxide, 38 percent. In that same period, the population rose 25 percent, the gross domestic product doubled, and vehicle-miles traveled increased 125 percent! That should be cause for shouting, but the response by environmental activists has been anything but joyful! Doom and gloom is always the name of the game.

Activists have claimed that pollution has risen at runaway levels under President George Bush's watch. "Yet the overall number of bad-air days has actually been falling steadily. In 2001, there were fewer than half as many air-quality warning days across the country as in 1988. Los Angeles has experienced just one Stage 1 ozone warning in the past five years, an incredible decline. During the 1970s, Los Angeles averaged about 100 Stage 1--alert days per year" ("Why Bush

Gets a Bad Rap on Dirty Air," *Time* magazine, May 22, 2003).

Further, environmentalists too often focus their attention on America and other developed countries rather than the countries that are really and truly raping the earth, choking the rivers, and blackening the sky. As for America, its water and air is cleaner than in a generation and its forests more widespread than even in the 19th century. Bald eagles and peregrine falcons are off the endangered list; black bear and coyotes and moose and buffalo and deer and other wildlife are increasing dramatically. The Brookings Institute web site recently observed: "Arguably the greatest postwar achievement of the U.S. government and of the policy community is ever-cleaner air and water, accomplished amidst population and economic growth" (http://www.brookings.edu/articles/2002/spring_energy_easterbrook.aspx).

If an environmental activist wants to spend his energy on saving the earth, let him leave America or England or Switzerland where environmental consciousness is high and the people have plenty of resources to solve the problems, and move to Russia, India, or China, to name some countries that are true environmental disasters, and dedicate his life to solving those problems.

The fact is that the environmental movement's dire predictions have been proven wrong for more than a half century. Since Rachel Carson's "Silent Spring," its theme song has been "The Sky Is Falling," but it has not fallen. There has been no silent spring. During George H.W. Bush's term of office in the early 1990s environmentalists were threatening a "new silent spring" of dead Appalachian forests. In fact, the forests have made a wonderful comeback.

LIBERAL EMERGING CHURCH ERROR #7 REJECTION OF DISPENSATIONAL THEOLOGY AND THE IMMINENCY OF CHRIST'S RETURN

Closely associated with the previous error of a social-justice kingdom-building gospel is the fact that the emerging church rejects the imminent Rapture of New Testament saints.

The emerging church rejects dispensational theology and thus misinterprets Scripture, confusing the church with Israel, interpreting prophecy allegorically, getting its commission from Genesis 1 and Isaiah 2:4 and Matthew 5-7 instead of Acts 1:8.

Brian McLaren mocks the "fundamentalist expectations" of a literal second coming of Christ with its attendant judgments on the world and assumes that the world will go on like it is for hundreds of thousands of years (*A Generous Orthodoxy*, p. 305). He calls the literal, imminent return of Christ "pop-Evangelical eschatology" (*Generous Orthodoxy*, p. 267) and the "eschatology of abandonment" (interview with Planet Preterist, Jan. 30, 2005, http://planetpreterist.com/news-2774.html). McLaren says that the book of Revelation is not a "book about the distant future" but is "a way of talking about the challenges of the immediate present" (*The Secret Message of Jesus*, 2007, p. 176). He says that phrases such as "the moon will turn to blood" "are no more to be taken literally than phrases we might read in the paper today" (*The Secret Message*, p. 178).

Jonny Baker of Grace in London, England, rejects dispensationalism as "escapology theology" and "advocates that Christians need to invest themselves in the current culture, not live on hold until time runs out" (*Emerging Churches*, pp. 78, 79).

Tony Jones says that the emergent church, in contrast to the dispensational viewpoint, is characterized by "an eschatology of hope" (*An Emergent Manifesto of Hope*, p. 130). He says:

> "What I mean is that the folks who hang around the emerging church tend to see goodness and light in God's future, not darkness and gnashing of teeth. While that may seem obvious to some followers of God, pop theology today is facing the other way. ... Those novelists and the theologians who provide them their material take the view that we're in a downward spiral, and when things 'down here' become bad enough, Jesus will return in glory. But those of us represented in this book take the contrary view. God's promised future is good, and it awaits us, beckoning us forward" (p. 130).

N.T. Wright, who has a great influence on the emerging church, warns that the doctrine of an imminent rapture is dangerous because it interferes with kingdom building and environmental activities.

> "If there's going to be an Armageddon, and we'll all be in heaven already or raptured up just in time, it really doesn't matter if you have acid rain or greenhouse gases prior to that. Or, for that matter, whether you bombed civilians in Iraq. All that really matters is saving souls for that disembodied heaven" ("Christians Wrong about Heaven, Says Bishop," *Time*, Feb. 7, 2008).

Tony Campolo believes the same thing. Speaking at the Cooperative Baptist Fellowship's annual meeting in June 2003, Campolo said:

> "Instead of preaching against *Harry Potter* I suggest that you people who are preachers start preaching against those really hot sellers in the Christian community, those 'Left Behind' books. Nobody wants to say it. You are scared to attack the 'Left Behind' books which are false theology and unbiblical to the core. And it is about time you stand up and say so.
>
> "I mean all of this stuff comes out of not only fundamentalism. It comes out of dispensationalism, which is a weird little form of fundamentalism that started like a hundred fifty years ago. ... Augustine doesn't talk about it. Calvin, Luther, none of those people talk about it. Southern Seminary has now enshrined Calvin. Well, if you're going to enshrine Calvin at least accept his eschatology, which would put 'Left Behind' out of business tomorrow. ...
>
> "I think that we need to challenge the government to do the work of the Kingdom of God, to do what is right in the eyes of the Lord. That whole

sense of the rapture, which may occur at any moment, is used as a device to oppose engagement with the principalities, the powers, the political and economic structures of our age" ("Opposition to women preachers evidence of demonic influence," Baptist Press, June 27, 2003).

Thus, Campolo boldly rejects dispensationalism and sees it as an enemy of the truth and of the kingdom of God.

We believe Campolo is right about one thing, and that is if you follow Calvin you might as well follow his eschatology. In fact, the rapid growth of Calvinism among evangelicals has been accompanied by an increase in the popularity of amillennialism.

I should also point out that we don't support the *Left Behind* series, but we reject it not for its dispensational viewpoint but for other reasons that we have delineated in our report "Left Behind: Tolerable Entertainment, Intolerable Theology," http://www.wayoflife.org/fbns/leftbehind.htm.

Campolo says that Protestant leaders such as Luther and Calvin didn't hold to a dispensational approach to Scripture, but that is a meaningless point. Since they were wrong on so many important issues, their views on this are irrelevant. Among other things, the Protestant leaders baptized babies and drowned Baptists! Our authority is not Protestantism or the "church fathers," it is the Bible, and the Bible teaches a literal millennium and a literal and imminent Rapture. We are to be looking for Christ's return at any moment.

> "Watch therefore: for ye know not what hour your Lord doth come. But know this, that if the goodman of the house had known in what watch the thief would come, he would have watched, and would not have suffered his house to be broken up. Therefore be ye also ready: for in such an hour as ye think not the Son of man cometh" (Matthew 24:42-44).

WHAT DOES THE BIBLE SAY?

A consistent application of the literal method of interpretation will result in a dispensational theology.

We agree with the following statement by Charles Ryrie: "If plain or normal interpretation is the only valid hermeneutical principle and if it is consistently applied, it will cause one to be a dispensationalist. As basic as one believes normal interpretation to be, and as consistently as he uses it in interpreting Scripture, to that extent he will of necessity become a dispensationalist" (*Dispensationalism*, revised 1995, p. 20).

This, to me, is the bottom line, because I am convinced that the normal-literal method of Bible interpretation is the only proper method. If a non-literal method is adopted, the mind of the interpreter becomes the real authority.

One of the things that I am most thankful for in my Bible education is having been taught the importance of a normal-literal method of interpretation. I still recall fondly how that this opened up the Scriptures to me when I was a young Christian. I didn't accept it blindly. I had filled my mind and heart with Scripture before I went to Bible School, and I had learned to test all things by it. I was trusting in promises such as John 7:17 and 8:31-32, and the normal-literal method of interpretation rang true to me as soon as I heard it. I knew that it was the truth, and I sensed that it was a very important truth.

The early Christians interpreted prophecy literally.

While it is true that certain forms of dispensationalism, such as Darby dispensationalism, were not taught until more recent times, the early Christians after the apostles taught a type of dispensationalism. Justin Martyr (A.D. 100-165) believed in four phases of history in God's plan: From Adam to Abraham, from Abraham to Moses, from Moses to Christ, and from Christ to the eternal state. Irenaeus (A.D. 120-202) taught something similar, dividing the dispensations into the creation to the flood, the flood to the law, the law to the gospel, the gospel to the eternal state. In *Ages and Dispensations of the Ante-Nicene Fathers,* Larry Crutchfield observes that some of the early church leaders "came very close to making nearly the same divisions modern dispensationalists do."

The early Christians interpreted the Bible prophecy literally and were definitely looking for a literal millennial kingdom and a literal fulfillment of God's covenants with Israel (Acts 3:19-21; Romans 11:25-27). It was not until centuries later that amillennialism and allegoricalism arose.

The New Testament teaches the Rapture in the clearest of terms:

> "But I would not have you to be ignorant, brethren, concerning them which are asleep, that ye sorrow not, even as others which have no hope. For if we believe that Jesus died and rose again, even so them also which sleep in Jesus will God bring with him. For this we say unto you by the word of the Lord, that we which are alive and remain unto the coming of the Lord shall not prevent them which are asleep. For the Lord himself shall descend from heaven with a shout, with the voice of the archangel, and with the trump of God: and the dead in Christ shall rise first: Then we which are alive and remain shall be caught up together with them in the clouds, to meet the Lord in the air: and so shall we ever be with the Lord. Wherefore comfort one another with these words" (1 Thessalonians 4:13-18).

William Newell observes: "The early Church for 300 years looked for the imminent return of our Lord to reign, and they were right" (Newell, *Revelation*).

Lutheran historian Philip Schaff makes the same observation:

> "The most striking point in the eschatology of the ante-Nicene age [before 325 AD] is the prominent chiliasm, or millenarianism, that is the belief of a visible reign of Christ in glory on earth with the risen saints for a thousand years, before the general resurrection and judgment. ... It was indeed ... a widely current opinion of distinguished teachers, such as Barnabas [end of first century], Papias [a disciple of John], Justin Martyr [born about 100 AD], Irenaeus [120-202 AD] the disciple of Polycarp who in turn was the disciple of John, Tertullian [150-220

AD], Methodius [third century], and Lactantius [end of third and beginning of fourth century]" (*History of the Christian Church,* 1884, II, p. 614).

Since the apostles and prophets who wrote the New Testament Scripture are the standard of truth (Romans 16:17), and since the early churches followed this standard, we must follow their teaching and example in the interpretation of prophecy.

When we interpret the Bible dispensationally, we understand that the kingdom of God that Christ proclaimed was the real earthly kingdom promised to David's Son and it will be established when He returns.

We have seen this in the previous study on the kingdom. The believer's job, therefore, is not to build the kingdom of God in this world. The emerging church erroneously replaces the centrality of preaching the gospel and winning souls with the centrality of building the kingdom. A dispensational view of Bible prophecy in general and of the kingdom of God in particular is necessary to rightly divide the Scriptures in this matter and to avoid error (2 Timothy 2:15). The world's swords will be beaten into plowshares and the lion will lie down with the lamb and righteousness and justice will flow as a river WHEN CHRIST RETURNS and not at any time before then.

When we interpret the Bible dispensationally, we understand that God's commission to Adam and Eve in Genesis 1 is different from His commission to believers today.

Christian environmentalists point to Genesis 1:28 to support their agenda. *"And God blessed them, and God said unto them, Be fruitful, and multiply, and replenish the earth, and subdue it: and have dominion over the fish of the sea, and over the fowl of the air, and over every living thing that moveth upon the earth."* In reply to this we would say, first, that, the church's commission is not Genesis 1:28 but Acts 1:8. Christ made that clear when He repeated that commission five times after His resurrection (Mat. 28:19-20; Mk. 16:15; Lk. 24:44-48; Jn. 20:21; Acts 1:8). The church's main program is saving souls rather than saving the earth. Second, Genesis 1:28 commands man to be fruitful and multiply and fill the earth with children, but the emerging church is rarely in support of large families, believing the environmentalist myth that earth's resources are very limited and must be preserved and that small families are therefore to be preferred. Third, Genesis 1:28 commands man to subdue and have dominion over the earth, but most environmentalists of the emerging church variety don't want man to subdue the earth; they want him to leave it alone.

When we interpret the Bible dispensationally, we understand that the church is not Israel, that God's plan for Israel is not His plan for the church, and that the church does not replace Israel.

God has put Israel aside temporarily during this present church age, but He will turn to Israel again and fulfill His covenants with her. Paul makes this clear in Romans 11:25-27:

> "For I would not, brethren, that ye should be ignorant of this mystery, lest ye should be wise in your own conceits; that blindness in part is happened to Israel, until the fulness of the Gentiles be come in. And so all Israel shall be saved: as it is written, There shall come out of Sion the Deliverer, and shall turn away ungodliness from Jacob: For this is my covenant unto them, when I shall take away their sins."

Many things in the Gospels and many things in Christ's earthly ministry and teaching had an emphasis upon Israel rather than upon the church. We have seen this in the previous studies on the kingdom of God in the Bible. The church is NOT Israel and does not fulfill Israel's covenants and we should not confuse its program with hers.

When we interpret the Bible dispensationally, we understand that kingdom prophecies are interpreted literally and not allegorically.

The emerging church takes its commission from Old Testament prophecies that have nothing to do with our day. These prophecies speak of the return of Christ and the establishment of His literal kingdom on earth. For example, the pacifism and anti-war philosophy that permeates the emerging church takes prophecies such as Isaiah 2:4 and applies them to our day. "*And he shall judge among the nations, and shall rebuke many people: and they shall beat their swords into plowshares, and their spears into pruninghooks: nation shall not lift up sword against nation, neither shall they learn war any more.*" But this has nothing whatsoever to do with the church age. The United Nations is built upon this same dispensational confusion. There is a statue outside of the UN headquarters in New York City of a man beating a sword into a plow. The nations will indeed beat their swords into plowshares one day, but it won't be at the instigation of the United Nations or of the misguided emerging church. It will be at the command of Jesus Christ, when He sits as King on the throne of David and His dominion extends from sea to sea (Zechariah 9:10).

When we interpret the Bible dispensationally, we understand that there are many things in the Gospels that are not written directly for the church age and we learn to view the Gospels through the lens of the Epistles rather than the other way around. We understand Christ's Sermon on the Mount in its proper context, which is a future kingdom that will be established when He returns.

Contrary to a proper dispensational interpretation, the emerging church focuses on Christ's earthly life and ministry and teaching as opposed to the teaching of the New Testament epistles. Though they would doubtless say that they do not neglect or slight the epistles, this is exactly what they do in our estimation. The emerging church believes in "the way of Jesus," which is "given verbal expression in the Sermon on the Mount" (*Emerging Churches*, p. 44). Barry Taylor of Sanctuary in Santa Monica, California, says, "I needed to stop reading Paul for a while and instead focus on Jesus" (*Emerging Churches*, p. 48).

Fuller Seminary professor Ryan Bolger describes his course on Church and Mission as follows:

> "In my Church and Mission class this last quarter, we discussed this idea -- continuing the work of Jesus as the primary task of 'church'. We talked about Jesus' central message, the proclamation of the kingdom of God. We talked about how the church finds its true identity when it continues this proclamation, both in their corporate life and in the story they tell about God. We talked about how the kingdom is not an abstract concept -- Jesus' proclamation created a space that included the outcasts and the sinners and invited them into community. It gave voice to the voiceless, the enemy a seat at the table. I asked my very big class (74 students!), what would it look like if our sole mission strategy was to continue Jesus' ministry? And what if it had to stay pretty concrete, staying pretty close to the actual things Jesus did in community with his disciples? WHAT IF THAT WAS THE STUFF WE HAD TO GET RIGHT, THE CENTRAL STUFF, AND THAT THE OTHER STUFF, WHILE IMPORTANT, WAS PERIPHERAL? In our jobs at Starbucks, or in our neighborhood groups, or in our church systems, what if hospitality, including the marginalized, overflowing generosity, giving voice to those without, were the essentials? Could these sorts of communal practices point to God and change the world? In our class, we replaced the church rubric (how many are in or out?) with kingdom rubrics -- how are our practices, anywhere, like the kingdom (or not)? Are our activities that we participate in moving in that direction? How might we foster, through our conversations, positive moves towards the kingdom at Starbucks, in our neighborhoods, and in our church systems?" (http://thebolgblog.typepad.com/thebolgblog/2007/03/continuing_jesu.html).

The list of Jesus' practices that were described in this course included the following: "acts of liberation, healing activities, working for justice (econ, racial, gender), solidarity with those care for the poor, inclusion of the marginalized, redrawing social boundaries."

Observe how that Bolger focuses on Christ's earthly ministry and puts other parts of the New Testament on the periphery.

But a proper understanding of the Gospels teaches us that Christ did not come to earth to be hospitable and to show generosity and to give the marginalized a voice and to care for the poor. He came to announce His Messiahship to Israel, which He did and was rejected. Having accomplished that part of His earthly program, Christ said He came to seek and to save that which was lost (Luke 19:10) and to build the church (Matthew 16:18), and He commissioned the churches to carry forward this specific task above all others (Mark 16:15; Luke 28:46-48; Acts 1:8). *"But ye shall receive power, after that the Holy Ghost is come upon you: and ye shall be witnesses unto me both in Jerusalem, and in all Judaea, and in Samaria, and unto the uttermost part of the earth."*

Further, Christ said that He would send the Holy Spirit to lead the disciples into all truth (John 16:13), and that is exactly what we have in the book of Acts and the New Testament Epistles. God raised up Paul to be the apostle to the Gentiles, and through his teaching we rightly interpret Christ's earthly ministry for this present time (Rom. 11:13; Gal. 1:7-8; 2 Tim. 1:11). Paul's epistles are not in conflict with those of Peter, James, and John, but Paul is especially the apostle to the Gentiles and as such is our chief theologian. If we get our doctrine of the gospel and the purpose of the Christian life and ministry from Paul we will not go astray.

Tony Campolo calls himself a "red-letter Christian" and has written a book by that title.

> "By calling ourselves Red-Letter Christians, we are alluding to the fact that in several versions of the New Testament, the words of Jesus are printed in red. In adopting this name, we are saying that we are committed to living out the things that He said. Of course, the message in those red-lettered verses is radical, to say the least. If you don't believe me, read Jesus' Sermon on the Mount (Matthew 5-7). In those red letters, He calls us away from the consumerist values that dominate contemporary American consciousness. He calls us to be merciful, which has strong implications for how we think about capital punishment. When Jesus tells us to love our enemies, he probably means we shouldn't kill them. Most important, if we take Jesus

seriously, we will realize that meeting the needs of the poor is a primary responsibility for His followers. Figuring out just how to relate those radical red letters in the Bible to the complex issues in the modern world will be difficult, but that's what we'll try to do" (quoted from "Red Letter Christian," Oct. 25, 2007, http://livingintentionally.wordpress.com/2007/10/25/red-letter-christian/).

Jim Wallis says the same thing.

"In Matthew 5, 6, and 7, Jesus offers his Sermon on the Mount, which serves as the manifesto of his new order, the Magna Carta of the new age, the constitution of the kingdom" (*The Great Awakening*, p. 62).

But Bolger, Campolo, and Wallis and other emergents are very selective in their obedience to the Sermon on the Mount. In fact, the Sermon on the Mount clearly refutes emerging church theology.

Christ warned against breaking even the least of God's commandments (Mat. 5:19). This is in contrast to the emerging church's position that only the "cardinal" doctrines are of great significance.

Christ frequently warned about hell fire (Mat. 5:22, 29-30), but this is a subject that emergents grossly neglect and even blatantly deny.

Christ warned about imprisonment for disobedience to God's Word (Mat. 5:25-26), but emergents do not take this literally.

Christ warned strongly against divorce and remarriage (Mat. 5:31-32). In contrast we have the emerging church's tendency to downplay the importance of strict morality. The emerging church is even hesitant to condemn homosexuality, but if it is adultery in God's eyes for a man to divorce his wife and marry another *woman*, except for fornication, how much more is it immoral for a man to sleep with a man or a woman with a woman?

Christ taught against laying up treasures on earth (Mat. 6:19-21), yet Campolo and most other emergents and their churches and organizations have a great many treasures on earth. In an interview with Campolo in February 2008 at the New Baptist Covenant Celebration in Atlanta, Georgia, I asked him if he obeys the Lord's command in the Sermon on the Mount to sell what you have and give alms. He admitted that he is something of a hypocrite in that area. He drives a nice car, lives in a nice house, has nice clothes, heaps of possessions, a retirement fund, etc. There are exceptions, but in general the emergents really don't take this part of Christ's Sermon all that seriously!

Christ taught the people to be heavenly-minded (Mat. 6:19-21), but the emerging church ridicules this mindset and instructs us to be earthly-minded.

Christ said to take no thought about food or clothing (Mat. 6:25, 31), but the emerging church typically takes plenty of thought about this.

Christ said to take no thought for tomorrow (Mat. 6:34), but the emerging church makes detailed plans.

Christ said not to give holy things to dogs (Mat. 7:6), but the emerging church doesn't want to believe that there is a great difference between holy and unholy and does not believe in dividing people into groups and calling some dogs, disliking "judgmentalism" and "labeling."

Christ taught that men are evil (Mat. 7:11), but the emerging church thinks that this is not necessarily true.

Christ taught that the way of salvation is narrow and few are saved (Mat. 7:13-14), but the emerging church claims that the way of salvation is broad and many might be saved, even if they don't have personal faith in Jesus.

Christ taught that we should be on the lookout for false teachers (Mat. 7:15), but the emerging church claims that we should relax and not be uptight about doctrine and error.

Prominently in His teaching on the kingdom of God, Christ commanded men to repent of their sin. *"From that time Jesus began to preach, and to say, Repent: for the kingdom of heaven is at hand"* (Mat. 4:17). Yet the emerging church is exceedingly weak about the business of repentance and is not even certain that homosexuals have anything to repent of!

Further, the Sermon on the Mount reminds us that Christ was a bold and dogmatic preacher, whereas the emerging church doesn't like such preaching, preferring story-telling and "sharing."

Thus, this idea that we should be Red-Letter Christians is not consistently followed even by its own proponents. The Gospels do not present a Christ that looks anything like the emerging church.

Failure to recognize dispensational distinctions such as these is a major error of the emerging church, and they have borrowed this page from Reformed Theology.

LIBERAL EMERGING CHURCH ERROR #8 LOW KEY ABOUT EVANGELISM

In light of the universalistic tendencies of the liberal emerging church and its overwhelming emphasis on a social-justice gospel, it is not surprising that evangelism receives a very low priority and is even looked upon with suspicion by many.

Eddie Gibbs and Ryan Bolger say that "the word *evangelism* has a bad odor" for many of the emerging people (*Emerging Churches*, p. 130).

Emergents have moved "away from an exclusively verbal and often confrontational style of evangelism" and "steer clear of negative aspects of evangelism" (p. 145). They reject the "prepackaged, judgmental, we-have-it-all-together approach of aggressively confronting individuals in a way that lacks respect and sensitivity" (p. 145).

They consider direct evangelism as an "agenda" that would get in the way of developing sincere relationships with the unsaved. Rachelle Mee-Chapman of Thursday PM in Seattle asks: "Can I have an agenda with someone and still be genuine? Can I be truly loving when I want to convert someone?" (*Emerging Churches*, p. 126).

The answer, of course, is that there is nothing more genuinely loving than seeking to win the lost before it is eternally too late, but the confused emerging church mindset does not understand these things.

In his blog for August 29, 2005, Bolger promoted what he calls "hospitality apologetics" --

> "Hospitality apologetics does not focus on the verbal argument at all, in fact it is way down on the list of priorities. Rather than presenting an argument, these communities present a life. THEY DO NOT CONCERN THEMSELVES WITH PRESENTING A GOSPEL FORMULA, but rather their focus is on whether the gospel was demonstrated in the recipients midst. How do they go about that? Primarily, these communities extend hospitality to the recipient, i.e. the outsider becomes an insider, and the outcast is included. THESE ACTS ARE NOT PERFORMED SO THAT THE GOSPEL CAN LATER BE PRESENTED--THESE ACTS CONSTITUTE THE GOSPEL" (http://thebolgblog.typepad.com/thebolgblog/2005/08/hospitality_apo.html).

Karen Ward of the Church of the Apostles in Seattle says: "I no longer believe in evangelism. To be postevangelism is to live our lives in Christ without a strategy but with the compassion and the servant posture of Jesus Christ. We do not do evangelism or have a mission" (p. 135).

Ben Edson of Sanctus1 in Manchester, England, describes how that a visiting speaker talked about evangelism and during the prayer time invited the group to think about one or two friends they could target for evangelism and bring to church. This resulted in an uproar because "people's friends were their friends; they were not targets" and they "would feel dishonest in their friendships if they were aiming to get them into Sanctus1" (*Emerging Churches*, p. 127).

The reason for this strange way of thinking about evangelism is that they don't really believe that every person is lost and Hell-bound without regenerating faith in Jesus Christ. If they did, they would recognize that preaching the gospel is not "targeting" or salesmanship; it is genuine compassionate friendship. Would a true friend allow his friend to go to Hell without trying to stop him?

Chris Matthews of Linden Church in Swansea, England, says: "The concept of friendship evangelism has always been something we have struggled with, as this is hardly unconditional love! We feel the call to serve the community and to be a presence for good, and our prayer is that along the way we will see people find faith. ... Throw us into the midst of culture, and see what happens!" (*Emerging Churches*, pp. 127, 130).

Brad Cecil of Axxess in Arlington, Texas, says: "Axxess is missional but *not* in the sense that we are trying to save all the individuals we are engaged with in the culture so that the kingdom will advance and Christ can work. Instead, we are trying to make our community a place where you can feel the kingdom of God, and we don't think we need to save anyone for this to happen" (*Emerging Churches*, p. 129).

Debbie Blue of House of Mercy in St. Paul, Minnesota, says:

> "We are definitely not out on the streets trying to get people to accept Jesus into their hearts so that they can be saved from hell" (*Emerging Churches*, p. 123).

Simon Hall of Revive in Leeds, England, says, "The people in Revive are very cynical about any evangelistic techniques. My own vision is simply to put the people of God out there in the marketplace and hope that we live a life that attracts people to God" (*Emerging Churches*, p. 130).

The liberal emerging church believes as much in dialogue as in evangelism. They "are prepared to be evangelized in the process" and believe that evangelism is "a two-way process" (*Emerging Churches*, p. 131). They "visit people of other faiths and spiritualities and allow themselves to be evangelized in order to learn more about other walks of life" (p. 132).

Nanette Sawyer of Wicker Park Grace Church in Chicago says they "desire to do evangelism without imperialism; to go into a community and be with them; to become them, knowing their stories, letting them know me, and letting myself be changed by them" (p. 131).

Pete Rollins of ikon in Belfast, Northern Ireland, says: "We deemphasize the idea that Christians have God and all others don't by attempting to engage in open two-way conversations" (p. 132).

Dwight Friesen of Quest in Seattle says: "God has used other religions and other persuasions to draw me to him. God works in these religions in mysterious ways" (p. 132).

Ben Edson says: "We had a guy from the Manchester Buddhist center come to Sanctus1 a couple of weeks ago and talk about Buddhist approaches to prayer. We didn't talk about the differences between our faiths. We didn't try to convert him" (p. 133).

WHAT DOES THE BIBLE SAY?

Jesus commanded us to preach the gospel to every creature (Mk. 16:15). That can never be accomplished in a low-key, "lifestyle" manner. It can only be done through an aggressive program of evangelism that seeks to present the gospel claim to every individual.

The evangelism we see in the book of Acts is an aggressive, confrontational style of evangelism. In the book of Acts and the New Testament Epistles the word "preach" appears 95 times. On the day of Pentecost, Peter boldly preached Christ to the multitude gathered in Jerusalem. When the persecution came, *"they that were scattered abroad went every where preaching the word"* (Acts 8:4). *"Philip went down to the city of Samaria, and preached Christ unto them"* (Acts 8:5). Paul preached to people wherever he found them. *"Paul also and Barnabas continued in Antioch, teaching and preaching the word of the Lord, with many others also"* (Acts 15:35).

According to the emerging church, Christ was non-condemning toward sinners and we should be, as well. In fact, Christ said that the world is condemned already (John 3:18), and He did not overlook man's sin. He exposed the rich young ruler's covetousness (Mat. 19:16-22) and the woman at the well's fornication (John 4:16-18). Christ often warned about eternal, fiery Hell (e.g., Mat. 5:22, 29, 30, 7:19; 10:28; 11:23; 13:40, 42, 50; 23:33; Mark 9:43-48; John 3:36).

The good news of the gospel must begin with the bad news of sin and condemnation. This is how Paul preached the gospel in Romans 1-3. He began with nearly three chapters on man's sinful, condemned condition before a holy God before he got to the good news of what Jesus did on the cross.

According to the emerging church, Christ's love for sinners is *unconditional*, but this is not true. His love is unfathomable but not unconditional. Consider the following statements that the Lord Jesus Christ made: "He that hath my commandments, and keepeth them, he it is that loveth me: and he that loveth me shall be loved of my Father, and I will love him, and will manifest myself to him" (John 14:21). "I am the vine, ye are the branches: He that abideth in me, and I in him, the same bringeth forth much fruit: for without me ye can do nothing. If a man abide not in me, he is cast forth as a branch, and is withered; and men gather them, and cast them into the fire, and they are burned" (John 15:5-6). "Not every one that saith unto me, Lord, Lord, shall enter into the kingdom of heaven; but he that doeth the will of my Father which is in heaven. Many will say to me in that day, Lord, Lord, have we not prophesied in thy name? and in thy name have cast out devils? and in thy name done many wonderful works? And then will I profess unto them, I never knew you: depart from me, ye that work iniquity" (Matthew 7:21-23). "He that believeth on the Son hath everlasting life: and he that believeth not the Son shall not see life; but the wrath of God abideth on him" (John 3:36). "I tell you, Nay: but, except ye repent, ye shall all likewise perish" (Luke 13:3). Repent or perish is not the message of unconditional love!

The emerging church says on the one hand that we are to follow the method of Jesus, but on the other hand they say that evangelism should be low key and should involve more a long-term relationship approach rather than a direct approach. In fact, Christ taught that the disciples were to proclaim the Word of God to every city and if a city refuses their message they were to wipe off the dust of the city as a testimony against them and move on to another place (Luke 9:5; 10:10-12). Thus, true "Red-Letter Christianity" will be very direct in preaching the gospel and will reject those who reject Christ! This is dramatically different from the emerging church approach.

LIBERAL EMERGING CHURCH ERROR #9 WORLDLINESS

One of the messages of the emerging church is that life is a party to be enjoyed. There is little or no call to separate from the evil things of the world.

Mars Hill Graduate School in Seattle says we must "incarnate the gospel through joyful participation in a culture's glory" and become "lovers of language, story, drama, film, music, dance, architecture, and art in order to deepen our love of life and the God of all creativity" (Mars Hill Graduate School, http://www.mhgs.edu/common/about.asp#scpriture).

One of the popular terms for the Christian life in emerging circles is "dancing." Life is a dance, they say; but though there is great joy and blessing in the Christian life, it is never described as a dance or a party in the New Testament epistles this side of the marriage supper of the Lamb in Revelation 19. To deny oneself (Mat. 16:24), to mortify the flesh (Rom. 8:13), to put off the old man (Eph. 4:22), to be in heaviness through manifold temptations (1 Pet. 1:6), to endure chastening (Heb. 12:7), to have on the whole armor of God in order to withstand the forces of evil (Eph. 6:11-18), to be sober and vigilant so as not to be devoured by the devil (1 Pet. 5:8), to serve God with reverence and godly fear (Heb. 12:28) -- these are not dancing, happy-party type of activities!

One of the themes of David Foster's *A Renegade's Guide to God* is his hatred of rules, which is pretty evident even from the title. He claims that Jesus was a "Renegade" and that those who serve Jesus properly (in the emergent way) will be renegades against traditional Bible Christianity. One chapter is entitled "Jesus Is Cool, but Christians Creep Me Out," the theme being it is only traditional churches that have given Jesus a bad name in the world's eyes. Foster says, "Renegades run from religion because they resist being named, revolt at being shamed, and rebel against being tamed" (p. 8). He demands a fun life (p. 9). He says, "We won't be 'told' what to do or 'commanded' how to behave" (p. 10). He says, "Sermons on the evils of smoking, drinking, movie-going, the clothes we shouldn't wear, or the theme parks we should boycott seem insulting" (p. 11). He thinks it's great that women wear "halter tops and short shorts" to "seeker sensitive" churches (p. 264).

Spencer Burke describes how he gave up the doctrine of separation from worldliness:

> "Growing up, I believed in isolationism. I heard lots of people I respected talk about how important it was to come out of the world and be separate. Over time, however, I began to meet people who challenged that belief. ... Over time, I seemed to meet more and more people who didn't fit with the stereotype of the good Christian. By their very lives, these people challenged me to stop speaking the code language of my youth--'Breaker, Breaker. Smoky the Antichrist dead ahead,'--and start engaging with the wider culture around me" ("From the Third Floor of the Garage: The Story of The Ooze," http://www.spencerburke.com/pdf/presskit.pdf).

Chris Seay of Ecclesia in Houston, Texas, says, "I am not an ambassador for morality, nor do I long to see the world become a more moral place" (*Faith of My Fathers*, p. 148), and, "The early church did not jump up and down and say, 'You're immoral.' ... [The Bible] never says to fight for personal morality" (p. 146).

In reply to Seay's challenge about jumping up and down and saying you're immoral, I seem to recall a man named John the Baptist who lost his head because he told the political leader of his day that he was committing adultery! And Ephesians 5:11 commands us not only to have no fellowship with the unfruitful works of darkness, "BUT RATHER REPROVE THEM."

Seay makes the following amazing statement that reveals just how spiritually wrong and dangerous the emergent thinking is:

> "I still think one of the great fallacies of Christian thinking is this kind of garbage in/garbage out mentality. You know, I remember being 16 years old and being taught that kind of thing. 'Stay away from culture because what you think you will absorb. See, your brain is a sponge, you'll absorb whatever you hear and see'" (Chris Seay, "The Dick Staub Interview with Chris Seay," *Christianity Today*, Sept. 1, 2002, http://www.christianitytoday.com/ct/2002/septemberweb-only/9-23-21.0.html).

Seay loves to watch the R-rated *Soprano* television show. He describes the hero of this unclean movie, the mobster Tony Soprano, "cursing up a blue streak, as a throng of naked women with near-perfect bodies crowded around him," yet Seay says that he always turns back to the program ("The Dick Staub Interview with Chris Seay," *Christianity Today*). Seay's mind is so permeated with this filthy TV series that he wrote a book "The Gospel According to Tony Soprano" to "explore the many reasons why the hit series has connected so deeply with viewers, and expose the mysteries of faith, family, life, and God that permeate the show" (from the back cover of the book).

Donald McCullough says, "The way to God, the incarnation tells us, is not to escape into a diaphanous realm, NOT TO DENY THE FLESH, NOT TO SUPPRESS OUR ORDINARY DRIVES AND DESIRES" (*If Grace Is So Amazing, Why Don't We Like It*, p. 47). He says, "The embrace of God's grace includes the whole of human life" and lists among God's gifts such things as drinking and listening to rock & roll (p. 48). He complains about preachers who say, "... don't do that, curb your appetites, reign in desire, discipline and sacrifice yourself" (p. 104). He claims that the grace of God means "we may relax in our humanity" (p. 141).

McCullough's book contains profanity (pp. 9, 92, 113) and is filled with positive references to drinking.

Donald Miller says, "The problem with the Christian community was that we had ethics, we had rules and laws and principles to judge each other against" (*Blue Like Jazz*, p. 215).

Miller describes a house where he lived communally with a group of other single men in Portland in connection with an emerging church there. They called the house Graceland, not because of the grace of God in Christ but because they love filthy Elvis Presley, and Presley's hedonistic mansion was called Graceland (*Blue Like Jazz*, p. 178). One occupant of the emergent household was a communist; another posed nude for the brochure of his advertising agency; another was "a womanizer, always heading down to Kell's for a pint with the lads" (pp. 178, 179). When they played Nintendo, they would "yell profanities at each other."

Rob Bell says it is wrong to "complain about how bad the world is" (*Velvet Elvis*, p. 166). He says this "isn't the kind of voice Jesus wants his followers to have in the world."

Bell's Mars Hill Bible Church in Grand Rapids searched for a bass player for their worship team that could play "in the style of Jimmy Eat World and Coldplay [secular rock bands]" ("The Emergent Mystique," *Christianity Today*, November 2004).

Many of the emerging churches in the United Kingdom are patterned after the club or rave culture, which focuses on all-night, drug-enhanced, sexual dance parties. The Cultural Shift Network is planning "club-culture churches throughout the U.K." (*Emerging Churches*, p. 82). Ian Mobsby of Moot in London says, "It presented a way of being church that was born out of the community vibe of clubs and raves" (*Emerging Churches*, p. 81). The now-defunct Nine O'clock Service began in 1985 and required that "each member listen to dance music, go clubbing, and read club-culture magazines" and "a stylist helped them buy clothes and adopt hairstyles that were indigenous to club culture" (*Emerging Churches*, p. 83). (This particular club-culture church disbanded after the leader "made inappropriate advances among the females of the leadership team," p. 84.)

Adam Cleaveland likens emergents to "artists freed like the romantics" and claims that "because of God's 'Yes' to the world, the world is our canvas" (*An Emergent Manifesto of Hope*, p. 125).

The freedom that the emerging church envisions is freedom to listen to raunchy music, watch raunchy movies, dress as one pleases, frequent bars and filthy rock concerts, dance, drink, gamble, cuss, and commit homosexuality.

WHAT DOES THE BIBLE SAY?

The emerging church position on the world is refuted by Christ's example.

Christ was a friend of sinners in that He came to seek and to save them (Luke 19:10), but He was always an enemy of sin and He never participated in any sinful activity. He was involved socially with sinners, attending their weddings and feasts, but He was not a "party animal." He lived and preached righteousness in every situation. He was a friend of sinners even while being "separate from sinners" (Heb. 7:26) because of His absolute holiness.

Matthew 11:19 says that Christ was *"a man gluttonous, and a winebibber, a friend of publicans and sinners,"* but this was what His enemies said about Him. In fact, He was neither gluttonous nor a winebibber. He was a friend of publicans and sinners not in that He partied with them but in that He loved them and sought to save them.

Christ was *not* "non-judgmental". He reproved sin. He exposed the rich young ruler's covetousness (Mat. 19:16-22) and the woman at the well's fornication (John 4:16-18). Christ often warned about eternal, fiery Hell (e.g., Mat. 5:22, 29, 30, 7:19; 10:28; 11:23; 13:40, 42, 50; 23:33; Mark 9:43-48; John 3:36). His very first message was "repent" (Mat. 4:17), and He warned that those who do not repent will perish (Luke 13:3; John 3:36). He called people evil (Mat. 7:11; 12:34). He looked upon people with anger for their hardness of heart (Mark 3:5). He warned people to stop sinning (John 5:14; 8:11).

None of this sounds very "cool" in a worldly sense, nor would it be an effective way to keep a worldly party hopping!

The emerging church position on the world is refuted by man's fall.

In the beginning man lived in a pristine environment and could do as he pleased and follow every desire of his heart as long as he kept God's one commandment, but man sinned and he and the entire creation fell. God cursed the creation for man's sake.

> "And unto Adam he said, Because thou hast hearkened unto the voice of thy wife, and hast eaten of the tree, of which I commanded thee, saying, Thou shalt not eat of it: cursed is the ground for thy sake; in sorrow shalt thou eat of it all the days of thy life; thorns also and thistles shall it bring forth to thee; and thou shalt eat the herb of the field" (Genesis 3:17-18).

That curse had never been lifted and it won't begin to be lifted until Christ returns and it won't be lifted entirely until the establishment of the new heaven and the new earth. It is in Revelation 22:3, after this present world has passed away, that we read those blessed words, *"And there shall be no more curse..."*

Today the devil is called the god of this world, because it is under his direction and control (2 Corinthians 4:4). The apostle John said *"the whole world lieth in wickedness"* (1 John 5:19). Paul said that those who are without Christ in this world walk *"according to the course of this world, according to the prince of the power of the air, the spirit that now worketh in the children of disobedience"* (Ephesians 2:2).

Thus, God has not presently said "yes" to this world and it is much more like the devil's playground than the believer's "canvas."

The emerging church position on the world is refuted by the Bible's teaching that the believer is not of the world.

> "I have given them thy word; and the world hath hated them, because they are not of the world, even as I am not of the world. I pray not that thou shouldest take them out of the world, but that thou shouldest

keep them from the evil. THEY ARE NOT OF THE WORLD, even as I am not of the world. Sanctify them through thy truth: thy word is truth" (John 17:14-17).

The saint cannot settle down and be comfortable in this world because he is not of the world and is even hated by the world. The believer's citizenship is in Heaven and in this present world he is sanctified unto God through the Scriptures and is therefore different from and misunderstood by the world. The world thinks it *"strange that ye run not with them to the same excess of riot, speaking evil of you"* (1 Peter 4:4).

This is not true for emergents. They are comfortable in the world and are partying along with the world in many ways. They have the same interests as the world, the same loves, and they even share the same views on many social-political issues, such as women's and homosexual rights and environmentalism. The world considers them "cool."

The emerging church position on the world is refuted by the Bible's warnings not to love the world.

As a result of the fall of man and the corruption of the world and the domination of the devil over it, the believer is exhorted not to love it.

Consider the following Scriptures:

> "And be not conformed to this world: but be ye transformed by the renewing of your mind, that ye may prove what is that good, and acceptable, and perfect, will of God" (Romans 12:2).

> "And have no fellowship with the unfruitful works of darkness, but rather reprove them" (Ephesians 5:11).

> "Pure religion and undefiled before God and the Father is this, To visit the fatherless and widows in their affliction, and to keep himself unspotted from the world" (James 1:27).

> "Ye adulterers and adulteresses, know ye not that the friendship of the world is enmity with God? whosoever therefore will be a friend of the

world is the enemy of God" (James 4:4).

> "Love not the world, neither the things that are in the world. If any man love the world, the love of the Father is not in him. For all that is in the world, the lust of the flesh, and the lust of the eyes, and the pride of life, is not of the Father, but is of the world. And the world passeth away, and the lust thereof: but he that doeth the will of God abideth for ever" (1 John 2:15-17).

Every evil thing in the world is to be rejected. We are not to be conformed to any of its unholy ways, and the standard by which the world is to be measured is God's Word. Everything pertaining to the lust of the flesh, and the lust of the eyes, and the pride of life is to be rejected, and that covers a lot of territory in this sin-cursed world! We are to apply this standard to fashion, music, literature, art, movies, photography, you name it. Everything in this world is to be weighed by God's holy standard and everything evil is to be rejected.

Ephesians 5:11 says that not only is the believer to have *no* fellowship with the unfruitful works of darkness, he is also responsible to reprove them. That is the very thing that worldly Christians consider "judgmental" and hateful and decidedly uncool.

Even those things that are questionable are to be rejected, because *"he that doubteth is damned if he eat, because he eateth not of faith: for whatsoever is not of faith is sin"* (Romans 14:23).

But what about Paul's statements "all things are lawful to me" and "I am made all things to all men"? Let's consider these in their proper context:

> "All things are lawful unto me, but all things are not expedient: all things are lawful for me, but I will not be brought under the power of any. Meats for the belly, and the belly for meats: but God shall destroy both it and them. Now the body is not for fornication, but for the Lord; and the Lord for the body" (1 Corinthians 6:12-13).

> "All things are lawful for me, but all things are not expedient: all things are lawful for me, but all things edify not. Let no man seek his own, but every man another's wealth" (1 Corinthians 10:23-24).

These verses are frequently misused today by those who desire liberty to fulfill their carnal desires. They would have us believe that the apostle Paul was saying that the Christian has liberty to wear immodest fashions, watch indecent movies, romp near naked at the beach, listen to sensual rock music, become a beer making expert, and fellowship with anyone that "loves Jesus" regardless of his doctrinal beliefs, etc.

Is that what the statement "all things are lawful" mean? By no means! Obviously there are limitations on the Christian's liberty. The New Testament Scriptures, in fact, put great limits upon our "liberty." We are not free to commit fornication (1 Cor. 6:16-18; 1 Thess. 4:3-6) or to be involved in any sort of uncleanness (1 Thess. 4:7) or to fellowship with the unfruitful works of darkness (Eph. 5:11) or to be drunk with wine (Eph. 5:18) or to allow any corrupt communication to proceed out of our mouths (Eph. 4:29) or to allow any filthiness of the flesh or spirit (2 Cor. 7:1) or to be involved in anything that has even the appearance of evil (1 Thess. 5:22) or to love the things that are in the world (1 John 2:15-17) or to befriend the world (James 4:4) or to dress immodestly (1 Tim. 2:9), etc.

What, then, did the apostle mean? He meant that the Christian has been set free by the blood of Christ, free from the wages of sin, free from the condemnation of the law, free from the ceremonies of the Mosaic covenant, but not free to sin and not free to do anything that is not expedient or edifying.

Paul explains himself perfectly in these passages. In 1 Corinthians 6:12-13, he uses the example of eating meat. In 1 Corinthians 8:1-13 and 10:23-28 he uses the example of eating things that have been offered to idols. In such things, the Christian is free, because these are matters in which the

Bible is silent. There are no dietary restrictions for the New Testament Christian as there were under the Mosaic Law. We do not have to fear idols; we know they are nothing. This is the type of thing Paul is referring to in 1 Corinthians, if we would only allow him to explain himself rather than attempt to foist some strange meaning upon his words that would fill the Bible with contradiction.

Paul addresses the same thing in Romans chapter 14. The Christian is free from laws about eating and keeping holy days (Rom. 14:2-6). We are not to judge one another in such things, because these are matters about which the Bible is silent in this dispensation. This does not mean, though, we are not to judge anything and that we are free to do whatever we please. When the Bible has spoken on any issue, our only *liberty* is to obey, and we have every right to judge on the basis of the Bible's teaching.

> "For though I be free from all men, yet have I made myself servant unto all, that I might gain the more. And unto the Jews I became as a Jew, that I might gain the Jews; to them that are under the law, as under the law, that I might gain them that are under the law; to them that are without law, as without law, (being not without law to God, but under the law to Christ,) that I might gain them that are without law. To the weak became I as weak, that I might gain the weak: I am made all things to all men, that I might by all means save some" (1 Corinthians 9:19-22).

What Paul is saying in this passage is that he was willing to do anything *lawful and proper* in trying to win men to Christ. He looked upon this earthly life as an opportunity to do God's will and to bear spiritual fruit and toward that end he was willing to endure any sacrifice, indignity, and shame. He was exceedingly single-minded in his pursuit of God's will. Paul did everything possible not to *unnecessarily* offend those to whom he was preaching. He knew that many would be offended at the gospel but he didn't want them to be offended at him if there was anything he could do about it. In every culture there are things that an outsider can do to cause unnecessary offense. Paul cared little about his personal liberty; what he cared about the most was not abusing his liberty so that someone would stumble at his action and reject the gospel as a result.

Unto the Jews he became as a Jew, that he might gain the Jews; to them that are under the law, as under the law, that he might gain them that are under the law (1 Cor. 9:20). This means that even though Paul knew that as a believer in Christ he was no longer obligated to keep the Mosaic Law and certainly that he was under no obligation to keep Jewish tradition, he was willing to submit to certain rituals for the sake of reaching the Jews. He did his best not to offend them, as long as by so doing he would not confuse or corrupt the gospel. This is why Paul had Timothy circumcised (Acts 16:1-3). Since Timothy's mother was a Jew, Paul did not want to give unnecessary offense to the Jews to whom he was preaching. On the other hand, Paul did not have Titus circumcised, because he did not have any Jewish blood (Gal. 2:3-4). This is in conformity to the decision that was made in Acts 15. Paul rebuked Peter for separating himself from the Gentiles in order to please the Jews (Gal. 2:11-14). It is important to observe that there is a fine line between adapting wisely to cultural and religious situations and compromising the gospel. We must be very careful in these matters and follow the leadership of the Holy Spirit.

To them that are without law, Paul lived as without law, that he might gain them that are without the law (1 Cor. 9:21). "In innocent things he could comply with people's usages or humours for their advantage. ... he would accommodate himself to all men, where he might do it lawfully, to gain some" (Matthew Henry). If a missionary would be fruitful he must live by Paul's philosophy. He must do everything possible and lawful not to offend those to whom he preaches. If they take their shoes off in the house, he takes his off. If they dress a certain way, he dresses that way insofar as he can do so without acting contrary to the standards of God's Word. If they believe it is wrong to hand you something with the left hand or to cross your legs in such a fashion that one foot is pointing toward another person or some such thing, he honors that custom. If they offer him something to eat or drink that he normally would prefer not eat, he does his best to eat it anyway so as not to offend them. Those are the types of things that Paul was referring to, but he certainly did not mean that he ever lived in a lawless fashion or that he adopted customs that are forbidden in Scripture.

To the weak he became as weak, that he might gain the weak (1 Cor. 9:22). Paul explained this in Romans 14. The weak person is a believer, or at least a professing believer, who has a weak conscience about things that are actually matters of liberty in the Christian life. He thinks that he must abstain from certain food even though the Bible does not command him to do so; he thinks that some days are holier than others. See Romans 14:1-5. Paul was willing to live in such a manner that the weak would not be offended at his actions, even though he knew that he had liberty before the Lord in such things. "If truth offends men, we cannot help it. But in matters of ceremony, and dress, and habits, and customs, and forms, we should be willing to conform to them, as far as can be done, and for the sole purpose of saving their souls" (Barnes).

The emerging church philosophy regarding the believer's relationship with the world is contrary to the entire tenor of the New Testament writings and is an appalling perversion of these passages.

FOUR TESTS FOR CHRISTIAN ACTIVITIES

In 1 Corinthians 6:12-13 and 10:23-24 Paul gives four tests to determine whether the Christian should allow a certain thing in his life:

(1) Does it bring me under its power?
(2) Is it expedient?
(3) Does it edify?
(4) Does it help or hinder my fellow man or does it cause him to stumble?

These are tests that are applied *not* to things which already are forbidden in Scripture, but to things the Bible does not specifically address.

The sincere application of these tests to things commonly allowed in the emerging church would put a quick stop to many practices. Rock music *does* bring people under its addictive power; it does *not* spiritually edify; it *is* influenced by demons (a simple study of the history of rock music will confirm this); it is not therefore expedient for the Christian who is instructed to be sober and vigilant against the wiles of the devil; and it does appeal to the flesh which the Christian is supposed to crucify.

Immodest clothing that is too short or too low or too tight does hinder our fellow man by putting before him a temptation to sin in his thought life; it does not edify those who see us clothed in such a fashion; it does have the potential to cause others to stumble.

The Bible says that we have liberty in Christ, liberty from eternal condemnation, liberty to serve God and to enjoy our unspeakably wonderful salvation. It does not say, though, that we have liberty to do whatever we please with our lives or to do anything that is not expedient or edifying.

The apostle Paul had such a low view of "personal liberty" that he was willing to forego the eating of meat for the rest of his life if he thought that such eating would offend his brother and cause his brother to stumble (1 Cor. 8:13).

Contrast this apostolic view of Christian liberty with that which is so popular today. Those who are consumed with their "liberty" will not forego even highly questionable things for the sake of glorifying Christ and edifying their fellow man. When confronted with such things, they become puffed up and lash out against a straw man they call "legalism."

If you accept the lie that the very concept of drawing a line for Christian standards is "legalistic," that the emphasis of the Christian life should be upon "liberty," you have no boundaries. We have observed repeatedly that those who enter this path are on a downward moral and spiritual slide.

Some women fight for the "liberty" to wear loose pants, but soon they are wearing tight pants. They fight for the "liberty" to wear loose-fitting shorts, but soon they are wearing shorter and tighter ones. Some want the liberty to miss some church services, but soon they are missing many. They want the liberty to listen to jazzy praise music, but soon they are addicted to contemporary hard rock. They want the liberty to watch some questionable videos, but soon they are on a steady diet of R-rated ones or worse. They want the liberty to fellowship with anyone who is "evangelical," but soon they are fellowshipping even with those who have a false gospel. Or at least they become sympathetic with and defensive of those who are doing such things.

You do not lose anything by holding a strict line of biblical standards in this present evil world, but you have much to lose if you loosen those standards. One thing those who let down their standards often lose is their children, to the world.

> "For, brethren, ye have been called unto liberty; ONLY USE NOT LIBERTY FOR AN OCCASION TO THE FLESH, but by love serve one another" (Galatians 5:13).
>
> "As free, and NOT USING YOUR LIBERTY FOR A CLOAK OF MALICIOUSNESS, but as the servants of God" (1 Peter 2:16).
>
> "While they promise them liberty, they themselves are the servants of corruption: for of whom a man is overcome, of the same is he brought in bondage" (2 Peter 2:19).

The emerging church position on the world is refuted by the Bible's warning against idolatry.

The emerging church encourages dialogue with the world and "joyful participation in a culture's glory," but this ignores the fact that the world is given over to idolatry. From America to the Netherlands to India to Kenya to Brazil, this world's cultures are deeply influenced by man's idolatry.

Consider the Bible's sharp warnings about fellowship with idolatry:

> "But that we write unto them, that they abstain from pollutions of idols, and from fornication, and from things strangled, and from blood" (Acts 16:20).

> "Neither be ye idolaters, as were some of them; as it is written, The people sat down to eat and drink, and rose up to play" (1 Corinthians 10:7).

> "Wherefore, my dearly beloved, flee from idolatry" (1 Corinthians 10:14).

> "But I say, that the things which the Gentiles sacrifice, they sacrifice to devils, and not to God: and I would not that ye should have fellowship with devils. Ye cannot drink the cup of the Lord, and the cup of devils: ye cannot be partakers of the Lord's table, and of the table of devils. Do we provoke the Lord to jealousy? are we stronger than he" (1 Corinthians 10:20-22).

> "And what agreement hath the temple of God with idols? for ye are the temple of the living God; as God hath said, I will dwell in them, and walk in them; and I will be their God, and they shall be my people. Wherefore come out from among them, and be ye separate, saith the Lord, and touch not the unclean thing; and I will receive you" (2 Corinthians 6:16-17).

> "Little children, keep yourselves from idols. Amen" (1 John 5:21).

> "But I have a few things against thee, because thou hast there them that hold the doctrine of Balaam, who taught Balac to cast a stumblingblock before the children of Israel, to eat things sacrificed unto idols, and to commit fornication" (Revelation 2:14).

> "But the fearful, and unbelieving, and the abominable, and murderers, and whoremongers, and sorcerers, and idolaters, and all liars, shall have their part in the lake which burneth with fire and brimstone: which is the second death" (Revelation 21:8).

These are not suggestions; they are solemn warnings from a holy and jealous God. *"For thou shalt worship no other god: for the LORD, whose name is Jealous, is a jealous God"* (Exodus 34:14).

The emerging church position on the world is refuted by the Bible's warnings against the deceptive, ensnaring nature of the world, the flesh, and the devil.

The emerging church calls for a rejection of the "garbage in /garbage out mentality" and a more open, non-judgmental approach to the world system and its culture, but this ignores the fact that non-critical participation with the world brings one in danger of being entrapped by the world.

Peter warned, *"Dearly beloved, I beseech you as strangers and pilgrims, abstain from fleshly lusts, which war against the soul"* (1 Peter 2:11). To participate in fleshly lusts, whether through sensual music or raunchy movies or unwholesome video games or Internet surfing or whatever, feeds the fleshly man and weakens the spiritual man. To indulge fleshly lusts weakens the spiritual life.

Paul warned, *"For the flesh lusteth against the Spirit, and the Spirit against the flesh: and these are contrary the one to the other: so that ye cannot do the things that ye would"* (Galatians 5:17). If you feed the flesh you are weakening the influence of the Spirit.

Paul also warned, *"Be not deceived: evil communications corrupt good manners"* (1 Corinthians 15:33). If the believer communicates closely with evil it will have a corrupting influence upon his Christian life. This is a foundational principle. If you put bad apples and good apples into a barrel together, the bad always corrupt the good. Left to themselves, weeds always overrun cultivated flowers. This is why wise parents are very careful about whom they allow their children to associate with and what type of things they allow their children to do.

For this reason, the believer must be exceedingly cautious about what he does and where he goes, but you will look long and hard to find this important warning in the writings of the emergents.

It is not surprising that many of the emergents have become victim to the world, the flesh, and the devil. Mark Driscoll, who was once closely associated with the Leadership Network, admits that many of the emerging church leaders have become disqualified through moral failures.

> "A team of young pastors, including myself, was then formed by Leadership Network, and we flew around the country speaking to other pastors about the emerging culture and the emerging church ... This led to the founding of a number of networks led by young men like me, most of whom were friends and acquaintances and whom the Enemy baited with lust. For example, a young church-planter who had planted a church in Southern California helped launch and direct a well-known network, until a moral failure cost him both his position as senior pastor and his platform. Likewise, a young church-planter in Colorado had helped shape a singles' network, until he too was disqualified for moral failure. Sadly, THERE'S A WHOLE LIST OF OTHER YOUNG PASTORS OF A VARIETY OF NOTE WITH SIMILAR STORIES" (*The Radical Reformission*, pp. 16, 17).

Driscoll enlarges on this admission later in the book:

> "Tragically, I have seen many young pastors undertake reformission without a wise understanding of worldliness, pastors who, rather than converting lost people, were themselves converted and are no longer pastors but instead are adulterers, divorcees, alcoholics, perverts, homosexuals, feminists, and nut jobs" (p. 124).

Yet Driscoll has the audacity to claim that the "garbage in, garbage out" philosophy, that says we are affected by evil things we put into our minds and hearts, is a myth and that he is glad that he rejected the counsel that was given to him as a young Christian to separate himself from secular rock (p. 125). He says that "we must watch films, listen to music, read books, watch television ... and engage in other activities as theologians and missionaries filled with wisdom and discernment" (p. 127). But if even the emergent pastors themselves don't have such wisdom and can't avoid being captured by the world, the flesh, and the devil, as he himself admits, how does he truly expect the average Christian in emergent churches to avoid being corrupted by his flirtation with worldliness?

In order to understand culture and become "reformissional," Driscoll recommends a "cultural-immersion project" during which believers read the worldly magazine *Cosmo Girl*, which is filled with immodest images, tune in to a hardcore rock station, listen to "a sexual talk program like Tom Leykis or Howard Stern," and watch "a movie you normally would not" (pp. 131, 132).

Driscoll and every other emergent leader will be held accountable before God for the spiritual damage that is done through such unscriptural and truly dangerous counsel.

The emerging church position on the world is refuted by the Bible's distinction between holy and profane, clean and unclean.

We are told that "to emerging churches, all of life must be made sacred," and, "... for emerging churches, there are no longer any bad places, bad people, or bad times. All can be made holy. All can be given to God in worship. All modern dualisms can be overcome. ... Instead of profaning the church, secular music becomes holy, and therefore the rest of their lives becomes holy as well" (*Emerging Churches*, pp. 66, 67, 71).

Ben Edson of Sanctus1 in Manchester, England, says: "We try to create bridges that span the secular/sacred divide because we don't make that distinction. We use secular music in worship as well as film and literature" (*Emerging Churches*, p. 67).

This is clearly refuted in Scripture. One of the meanings of the term "profane" in the Bible is to make common or unholy. The Hebrew word "chol," which is translated "profane" in Ezekiel 22:26 and 44:23 is elsewhere translated "common" (1 Sam. 21:4) and "unholy" (Lev. 10:10).

God reproved Israel because her priests refused to make a difference between the holy and the profane.

> "Her priests have violated my law, and have profaned mine holy things: they have put no difference between the holy and profane, neither have they shewed difference between the unclean and the clean, and have hid their eyes from my sabbaths, and I am profaned among them" (Ezekiel 22:26).

This is exactly what the emerging church does. They say, "Everything is spiritual; nothing is profane." They take the holy things of God and make them common and the common things of the world and make them holy. It is confusion and it is a great error.

A major theme of the book of Leviticus is the holiness of God and the distinction between the clean and the unclean. Israel was taught to be very careful about how she lived in order to maintain a holy walk before God and to be acceptable to Him. The key verse is 20:26 -- *"And ye shall be holy unto me: for I the Lord am holy, and have severed you from other people, that ye should be mine."*

Leviticus teaches us that the holy is polluted by the unholy, which is contrary to emerging church doctrine.

> "Or if a soul touch any unclean thing, whether it be a carcase of an unclean beast, or a carcase of unclean cattle, or the carcase of unclean creeping things, and if it be hidden from him; he also shall be unclean, and guilty" (Leviticus 5:2).

If one of God's people touched something that was unclean by God's standard, he did not make the unclean holy; the unclean thing made him unclean.

The New Testament teaches the same thing. To the worldly church at Corinth the apostle wrote: *"Wherefore come out from among them, and be ye separate, saith the Lord, and*

TOUCH NOT THE UNCLEAN THING; and I will receive you" (2 Corinthians 6:17).

The churches today cannot make worldly things holy, but the worldly can make the churches unholy. Rock & roll, for example, does not become holy just because it is used in God's service. To the contrary, since it is inherently sensual and fleshly and worldly it pollutes those who use it. Immodest dress styles do not become sanctified when they are worn by believers; moral pollution is inherent in the styles. If a church shows an R-rated movie that has profanity and cursing and immodestly attired women and such things or it hosts a New Years Eve dance-champagne party, the church does not sanctify the movie or the party; the worldly activities pollute the church.

Over the door of every emerging church could be written, "*Her priests have violated my law, and have profaned mine holy things: they have put no difference between the holy and profane, neither have they shewed difference between the unclean and the clean...*"

Someone might ask, What about Romans 14:14? "*I know, and am persuaded by the Lord Jesus, that there is nothing unclean of itself: but to him that esteemeth any thing to be unclean, to him it is unclean.*"

Scripture must be interpreted by context, and the context of Romans 14 is Christian liberty in things *not addressed by Scripture*. Paul was discussing things such as diet (verses 2-6). Thus, the context is those things that are not clearly addressed in Scripture and about which there is personal liberty. There is no special Christian diet laid out in the New Testament as there was in the Mosaic dispensation, so in matters of diet each believer has liberty. In Christianity, diet is a matter of personal preference and health, not holiness. In such things we are not to judge one another (verse 10). When Paul says in verse 14 that "*there is nothing unclean of itself,*" he was not speaking of life in general; he was speaking about food in particular. He makes this very clear in the next verse. *"But if thy brother be grieved with thy meat, now walkest thou not charitably. Destroy not him with thy meat, for whom Christ died"* (Romans 14:15).

When it comes to life in general there are many unclean things, as other Scriptures so plainly teach, but when it comes to diet, food is neither clean nor unclean in a spiritual sense. It is just food!

The emerging church position on the world is refuted by a biblical definition of "legalism."

The emerging church applies the term "legalism" to a strict biblicist position on doctrine and Christian living. To have rules for dress or music is "legalism," they claim.

True legalism, though, has a two-fold definition in the Word of God.

First, legalism is to mix works with grace for salvation.

This is the theme of the epistle of Galatians. Paul warns the churches against turning from the grace of Christ (Gal. 1:6) and emphasizes that salvation is not by works or law-keeping but by the grace of Christ *alone*. The Judaizers who were trying to mislead the churches in Galatia were legalists who were corrupting the gospel of grace by mixing it with works.

> "Knowing that a man is not justified by the works of the law, but by the faith of Jesus Christ, even we have believed in Jesus Christ, that we might be justified by the faith of Christ, and not by the works of the law: for by the works of the law shall no flesh be justified" (Gal. 2:16).

> "For as many as are of the works of the law are under the curse: for it is written, Cursed is every one that continueth not in all things which are written in the book of the law to do them. But that no man is justified by the law in the sight of God, it is evident: for, The just shall live by faith" (Gal. 3:10-11).

> "Wherefore the law was our schoolmaster to bring us unto Christ, that we might be justified by faith. But after that faith is come, we are no longer under a schoolmaster" (Gal. 3:24-25).

According to this biblical definition, legalists today are any who add works to the grace of Christ for salvation. The Roman Catholic Church does this. So does the Church of Christ and the Worldwide Church of God and the Seventh-day Adventists and the Jehovah's Witnesses and the Mormons and many others.

Second, legalism is to add human tradition to the Word of God.

> "Ye hypocrites, well did Esaias prophesy of you, saying, This people draweth nigh unto me with their mouth, and honoureth me with their lips; but their heart is far from me. But in vain they do worship me, teaching for doctrines the commandments of men" (Mat. 15:7-9).

Jesus rebuked the Pharisees for exalting their own tradition to the same authority as the Scripture. There is one authority for faith and practice, and that is the Bible. Anything that is exalted to a place of authority equal to the Bible is condemned by God.

The Pharisees of old, in committing both of these errors, were true legalists. They rejected the grace of Jesus Christ, teaching that the way of salvation was by the keeping of the law, and they made their own tradition authoritative over people's lives.

The Roman Catholic Church also commits both of these errors. The authoritative Second Vatican Council affirmed salvation by sacraments (works) plus the authority of tradition.

> "For it is the liturgy through which, especially in the divine sacrifice of the Eucharist, 'the work of our redemption is accomplished'" (*Vatican Council II: The Conciliar and Post-Conciliar Documents*, edited by Walter Kellenberg, "Constitution on the Sacred Liturgy," Introduction, para. 2).

> "Sacred Tradition and sacred Scripture, then, are bound closely together, and communicate one with the other. For both of them, flowing out from the same divine well-spring, come together in some fashion to form one thing, and move towards the same goal ... Thus it comes about that the Church does not draw her certainty about all revealed truths from the holy Scriptures alone. Hence, both Scripture

and Tradition must be accepted and honoured with equal feelings of devotion and reverence" (*Vatican Council II,* "Dogmatic Constitution on Divine Revelation," Chap. 2, 9, p. 682).

Many others exalt tradition and extra-biblical revelation to the same authority as God's Word today. Christian Science adds Mary Baker Eddy's writings. Seventh-day Adventism adds Ellen G. White's writings. (Sometimes they try to deny this, but we have documented it in the book *Avoiding the Snare of Seventh-day Adventism.*) Many Pentecostals and Charismatics add (at least in practice) personal revelations and experience.

We must be careful, as we seek to apply the principles of Scripture to Christian living, that we do not go beyond the Bible. For example, to set specific standards of modesty for female church workers that are supported by clear Scriptural principles, such as requiring a certain dress length, is not legalism, because the Bible requires modesty and forbids nakedness, even defining it as showing the leg and thigh (Isa. 47:2-3). But setting standards can become legalism if the requirements go beyond clear Scriptural principles and are set up as authoritative. In drawing lines, we must be very careful that our lines are God's and not our own. I have heard of churches that have forbidden men to wear pink shirts, because it is allegedly "feminine," but this is going far out on a limb. The color pink, while vaguely associated with femininity in some instances, is not so intricately associated with it that we can make a law about it. Other churches have forbidden beards and facial hair. One mission that supports Central American national pastors has this rule, but it is more than ridiculous; it is legalistic, because not only does the Bible not forbid facial hair on men, it encourages it by the example of Old Testament prophets (Ezr. 9:3) and even Jesus Christ Himself (Isa. 50:6). Beards are mentioned 15 times in the Bible and never in a negative sense. Another mission board forbade interracial marriages and adoptions for missionaries, but while there are practical issues that can be addressed pertaining to interracial marriages and adoptions, the Bible nowhere forbids them.

Thus, we must be careful in drawing lines, making sure that our lines are God's and not our own.

Having seen what legalism is, let us now consider what it is not.

For a Bible preacher to urge God's people to obey the details of God's Word by the grace of Christ cannot be legalism, because this is precisely what God requires. Consider the following Scripture very carefully.

> "For by grace are ye saved through faith; and that not of yourselves: it is the gift of God: Not of works, lest any man should boast. For we are his workmanship, created in Christ Jesus UNTO GOOD WORKS, which God hath before ordained that we should walk in them" (Eph. 2:8-10).

Here we see that while the blood-washed saint is saved *by* grace without works, he is also saved *unto* good works. The believer obeys God's Word, not in order to be saved but because he has been saved. It therefore cannot be legalism for a preacher to urge God's people to keep the works of God contained in the New Testament. I count 88 specific commandments in the epistle of Ephesians alone.

Consider this one:

> "And have no fellowship with the unfruitful works of darkness, but rather reprove them" (Eph. 5:11).

This is a far-reaching requirement. The believer must guard every area of his life, every activity, to make sure that he is not having fellowship with the works of darkness. Not only so, but he is to reprove the works of darkness. This is one of the verses that spoke to my heart 35 years ago and convinced me that I had to put rock & roll music out of my Christian life. It is certainly an unfruitful work of darkness, but the requirement does not stop with music. It involves every aspect of the Christian life: dress, companionship, music, entertainment, literature, relationships with churches and professing believers, you name it. To take such commandments of the New Testament faith seriously and to apply them rigorously cannot, therefore, be "legalism."

> "For the grace of God that bringeth salvation hath appeared to all men, teaching us that, denying ungodliness and worldly lusts, we should live soberly, righteously, and godly, in this present world; looking for that blessed hope, and the glorious appearing of the great God and our Saviour Jesus Christ; Who gave himself for us, that he might redeem us from all iniquity, and purify unto himself a peculiar people, zealous of good works. These things speak, and exhort, and rebuke with all authority. Let no man despise thee" (Titus 2:11-15).

Here, again, we see that the grace of Christ does not teach Christians to live carelessly or encourage them to live as close to the world as possible. It teaches them to live in a strict manner concerning holiness. The true grace of God teaches us to deny ungodliness and worldly lusts, which is a far-reaching obligation. It requires that we examine every area of our lives and churches in order to root out ungodliness. It requires that we reject every fashion of worldly lust. It involves every aspect of the Christian life: dress, companionship, music, entertainment, literature, you name it.

Notice in Titus 2:15 that the Spirit of God concludes this passage about avoiding ungodliness with the following exhortation to preachers: *"These things speak, and exhort, and rebuke with all authority. Let no man despise thee."* The preacher has a solemn obligation before God to speak, exhort, and rebuke on the basis of this teaching. It cannot, therefore, be any sort of "legalism" if a preacher takes this obligation seriously and applies the teaching to every area of life, speaking, exhorting, and rebuking about ungodliness and worldly lusts.

> "I charge thee therefore before God, and the Lord Jesus Christ, who shall judge the quick and the dead at his appearing and his kingdom; preach the word; be instant in season, out of season; reprove, rebuke, exhort with all longsuffering and doctrine" (2 Tim. 4:1-2).

Here we see a similar obligation to the one in Titus 2:15. The preacher has a solemn responsibility before God for his preaching and he will give an account to Jesus Christ. He is to preach the Word. What part of it? All of it! He is not only to read the Word; he is to preach it and to apply it to the people's everyday lives. He is to preach it with reproof, with rebuke, and with exhortation. He is to make sure that the Word of God gets down to where the people live. He is to apply it to every aspect of people's lives, to their family lives, their employment, their service for Christ, their companionships, their entertainment, their dress, their music, you name it. The Word of God speaks to every area of life, and the preacher is obligated to follow it wherever it leads. This is definitely not "legalism."

> "Teaching them to observe all things whatsoever I have commanded you: and, lo, I am with you alway, even unto the end of the world. Amen" (Mat. 28:20).

This is part of the obligation of Christ's Great Commission. Those who believe the gospel and are baptized are to be taught to keep ALL things that He has commanded. This is another far-reaching requirement. It means that the churches are to be concerned about all of the New Testament faith and not just some part of it that happens to be popular at the moment or some part that is viewed as "cardinal," and they are to train the people to obey all of it. The churches are obligated, therefore, to teach separation from the world, separation from false teaching, rejection of heretics, church discipline, the reality of eternal Hell, repentance, denial of self, everything that is taught in Scripture. To take Christ's commandment seriously and to seek to be faithful to the whole New Testament faith cannot, therefore, be "legalism."

Strict obedience to God's Word by Christ's grace is the way of liberty, not bondage.

> "Then said Jesus to those Jews which believed on him, If ye continue in my word, then are ye my disciples indeed; and ye shall know the truth, and the truth shall make you free" (John 8:31-32).

Since continuing in Christ's Word is the way to demonstrate true discipleship, it is obvious that strict obedience of the New Testament faith is not legalism.

"For this is the love of God, that we keep his commandments: and his commandments are not grievous" (1 John 5:3).

Since the love of God is to obey His commandments, it is obvious that obedience is not legalism.

The believer does not keep the Word of God in his own power and strength or to his own glory. He keeps it by the power of the indwelling Christ and to His glory. *"I am crucified with Christ: nevertheless I live; yet not I, but Christ liveth in me: and the life which I now live in the flesh I live by the faith of the Son of God, who loved me, and gave himself for me"* (Gal. 2:20).

Nevertheless, keeping all of the New Testament Christian faith is the responsibility of every believer and proclaiming all of it is the responsibility of every preacher, and this is *not* legalism.

The emerging church position on the world is refuted by a proper interpretation of 2 Corinthians 3:6.

"Who also hath made us able ministers of the new testament; not of the letter, but of the spirit: for the letter killeth, but the spirit giveth life."

The emerging church uses this verse to defend the philosophy that we should not be too strict about doctrine and practice. According to the emergent interpretation, 2 Corinthians 3:6 teaches that believers are not obligated to pay attention to the letter or details of God's Word and to the literal meaning of Scripture, because such a position kills. It is the "spirit" of the Scripture that matters, they say, referring to a loose, tolerant position.

In fact, 2 Corinthians 3 has nothing to do with the interpretation of Scripture and gives no support to the idea that the details of the Bible should *not* be taken seriously. Consider the context.

"Not that we are sufficient of ourselves to think any thing as of ourselves; but our sufficiency is of God; Who also hath made us able ministers of the new testament; not of the letter, but of the spirit: for the letter killeth, but the spirit giveth life. But if the ministration of death, written and engraven in stones, was glorious, so that the children of Israel could not stedfastly behold the face of Moses for the glory of his countenance; which glory was to be done away: How shall not the ministration of the spirit be rather glorious? For if the ministration of condemnation be glory, much more doth the ministration of righteousness exceed in glory. For even that which was made glorious had no glory in this respect, by reason of the glory that excelleth. For if that which is done away was glorious, much more that which remaineth is glorious. Seeing then that we have such hope, we use great plainness of speech: And not as Moses, which put a vail over his face, that the children of Israel could not stedfastly look to the end of that which is abolished: But their minds were blinded: for until this day remaineth the same vail untaken away in the reading of the old testament; which vail is done away in Christ. But even unto this day, when Moses is read, the vail is upon their heart. Nevertheless when it shall turn to the Lord, the vail shall be taken away. Now the Lord is that Spirit: and where the Spirit of the Lord is, there is liberty. But we all, with open face beholding as in a glass the glory of the Lord, are changed into the same image from glory to glory, even as by the Spirit of the Lord" (2 Corinthians 3:5-18).

In this passage, Paul shows the dramatic contrast between the Law of Moses and the New Testament faith, between the Old Covenant and the New. He is talking about the Law that was *"written in stones"* (verse 7). That is obviously the Law of Moses that was given on Mt. Sinai (Ex. 31:18). That Old Covenant was a *"ministration of death"* (verse 7) and a *"ministration of condemnation"* (verse 9) because it required perfect obedience from sinful men who are unable to give it and it requires death for every infraction (Galatians 3:10-12). The purpose of the Law of Moses was not to save men but to show them their lost condition before a holy God and to point the way to Christ. It was a "schoolmaster." Compare Romans 3:19-24 and Galatians 3:24-26.

When Paul says that we are *"ministers of the new testament; not of the letter,"* he is saying that we do not preach the Old Covenant but the New. When he says, "... *the letter killeth, but the spirit giveth life,"* he is saying that the Old Covenant brings death but the New Covenant gives life because it is a covenant of grace.

He is not saying that the letters or details of the New Testament should not be respected. Such an interpretation is contrary to the immediate context of the passage as well as to the larger context of the rest of the New Testament.

Elsewhere Paul taught the believers to keep the New Testament commandments *"without spot"* (1 Tim. 6:14) and to keep even the teaching about such things as hair length and the practice of the Lord's Supper exactly as it has been delivered to us (1 Corinthians 11:2ff). That is obviously a very, very strict doctrine of obedience.

In 2 Corinthians 3 Paul was refuting the doctrine of the Judaizers who tried to mingle the grace of Christ with the Law of Moses for salvation. Compare Acts 15:1-29 and Galatians 1:6-9; 2:16-21; 3:1-3, 19-26.

LIBERAL EMERGING CHURCH ERROR #10
LOVING TO DRINK

One thing that is evident in the writings of emerging church leaders is their love for alcoholic drink.

The book *Listening to the Beliefs of Emerging Churches: Five Perspectives*, for example, contains probably a dozen references to the joys of drinking. The contributors are Karen Ward, Mark Driscoll, John Burke, Dan Kimball, and Doug Pagitt. They meet in bars and taverns for theological discussions. They exchange beer-making techniques.

Some members of Spirit Garage meet in an Irish bar in downtown Minneapolis on Wednesday for a weekly Theology Pub, a mix of biblical discussion and beer ("Hip New Churches Pray to a Different Drummer," *New York Times*, Feb. 18, 2004).

Mars Hill Church in Seattle sets up a "champagne bar" at their New Year's Eve parties and attendees are reminded to bring their IDs so they can enjoy the bubbly. Mars Hill also has "beer-brewing lessons" for men.

Riverview Community Church in Holt, Michigan, has a RiverBrew night featuring homebrewed beer and religious discussion. Ministry leader Brett Maxwell says: "It's intimidating for someone to walk into a church having never been there. But if a friend invites them to go hang out, have a brew or two, and hang out with some of the guys from church, that's a much less intimidating environment" ("Holt Ministry Celebrates Its Love of God and Beer," *Lansing State Journal*, Feb. 29, 2008). When asked what Jesus would drink, Maxwell replied, "I believe he would sit down with people in the bar, and he would drink what they were drinking, and he would be happy to do that."

The Journey in St. Louis, Missouri, hosts a "Theology at the Bottleworks" where participants "grab a beer and discuss political or spiritual topics, such as the role of women in society, the legal system, or animal rights" ("Brewing Battle Missouri Baptists Frown on Beer as Evangelistic Hook," *Christianity Today*, June 29, 2007). This outreach is advertised as "grab a brew and give your view."

Damascus Road Church in Marysville, Washington, has a "Men's Bible and Brew" night.

Jim West has written "Drinking with Calvin and Luther" to promote the idea that alcoholic beverages are a gift from God, something not only to be allowed but celebrated. He says, "They reveled in it as a gift of God."

Phyllis Tickle leads a regular Beer and Bible gathering at Kudzu's in Memphis, Tennessee. Tickle says this type of thing is "exactly where religion is going right now" ("Seeking Spirituality Outside of Churches," *Memphis Online*, Sept. 8, 2008). Participant Doug Hardin said that he was raised

Baptist but left it 30 years ago and that he "wouldn't be comfortable joining a church Bible study." Another participant says that he likes the pub approach, because "we don't have to do religion the way we've always done it."

WHAT DOES THE BIBLE SAY?

It is true that some of the Protestant Reformers drank alcoholic beverages, but they are not our authority. They also "baptized" babies and drowned Baptists!

It is true that there are instances in the Old Testament in which God allowed His people Israel to drink alcoholic wine, but there are many things in the O.T. that we do not practice today.

I believe that Christians today should not drink alcoholic beverages for the following three reasons, among others, and I am convinced that these are universally applicable:

The Bible warns that wine and strong drink is a mocker and deceives men.

"Wine is a mocker, strong drink is raging: and whosoever is deceived thereby is not wise" (Prov. 20:1).

To say that alcoholic beverages can be consumed in moderation sounds reasonable, but very few drunks have ever set out to become a lush. It is an irrefutable fact that a man that does not drink at all will never get drunk and will never become a drunkard.

All of the emerging church drinkers admit that the Bible forbids drunkenness, but all of their talk about the delights of drinking and beer making, of "a Guinness" and "a round of imperial pints," makes me wonder if they don't sometimes get a bit tipsy at their drinking confabs, not to say *drunk*! How inebriated does one have to be to be drunk? Do emerging churches ever need to appoint "designated drivers"?

I doubt Noah planned to get drunk and to cause so much trouble for his grandson, trouble that has abiding consequences to this day--but wine is a mocker.

My maternal grandfather came from a long line of drunks, and before my godly grandmother married him she made him promise that he would never touch a drop of liquor, and that is a promise which he made. But one day he and another carpenter were working on a house and the other fellow talked my grandfather into having just a sip "to cool the tongue." They both got roaring drunk and ended up in jail, and my granddad was a deacon in a Baptist church! He was deeply repentant and was restored and never drank another drop as far as anyone knows, but it was a powerful reminder to him that wine is a mocker.

Alcohol has the ability to deceive and corrupt. One can never know if he will control it or it will control him. The instruction in Proverbs 20:1 tells me that the wise man leaves it entirely alone.

The following is a wise statement from *John G. Paton: Missionary to the New Hebrides*, 1891:

> "From observation, at an early age I became convinced that mere Temperance Societies were a failure, and that Total Abstinence, by the grace of God, was the only sure preventive as well as remedy. What was temperance in one man was drunkenness in another; and all the drunkards came, not from those who practised total abstinence, but from those who practised or tried to practise temperance. I had seen temperance men drinking wine in the presence of others who drank to excess, and never could see how they felt themselves clear of blame; and I had known Ministers and others, once strong temperance advocates, fall through this so-called moderation, and become drunkards. Therefore it has all my life appeared to me beyond dispute, in reference to intoxicants of every kind, that the only rational temperance is Total Abstinence from them as beverages, and the use of them exclusively as drugs, and then only with extreme caution, as they are deceptive and deleterious poisons of the most debasing and demoralizing kind."

Consider, too, the following testimony that a reader sent to me on this subject:

> "Brothers and sisters in Christ, I have firsthand knowledge of what drinking just one drink can do to a family. My dad at age 15 was put on a horse behind a neighbor man, rode into the nearby town and took his first drink. From that day forth he was hooked and became an almost lifelong alcoholic. The suffering that our family went/is going through is unspeakable. Dad accepted Christ at age 62, and became a teetotaler. He could not stand for his alcoholic friends to stop by and offer him a drink as they always had in the past. Because of his alcoholism and verbal abuse of my little sister, she will never recover. It has affected our family in a terribly adverse way all of the years. My sincere recommendation is NEVER TOUCH IT, for you know not what the first drink of it will do. It is sort of like the first temptation to take the first bite out of the apple in the garden. Millions of homes are broken and destroyed, souls in hell, and in torment here on earth, as a result of alcohol."

Can the emergents guarantee that they and their drinking buddies will never get even a little drunk? Can they guarantee that their actions will not tempt someone to become an alcoholic? No, they cannot, because "wine is a mocker."

The Bible instructs the believer not to give offense in anything.

> "Give none offence, neither to the Jews, nor to the Gentiles, nor to the church of God: Even as I please all men in all things, not seeking mine own profit, but the profit of many, that they may be save" (1 Cor. 10:32-33).

I personally quit smoking a few months after I was saved and it was not because I thought it was inherently wrong or because I was concerned about my health; it was because I knew that it could offend others. I wanted my testimony to be pure of offence so that God would use me and I would have eternal fruit. I didn't want to be witnessing to someone and have them possibly ignore me or be distracted because they saw a pack of cigarettes in my pocket.

If that is true for smoking, and it is, then it is even truer for drinking alcoholic beverages. It is a fact that many unbelievers think that a believer should not drink. They have higher standards for Christians than some Christians have for themselves. Consider Utah, where even unregenerate

Mormons believe it is wrong to drink alcoholic beverages! How would Mormons look upon non-Mormon Christians who drink?

Even the possibility that someone would be offended because of his drinking should be sufficient for the believer to put it out of his life, and that possibility is very great in modern society. Paul was willing to stop eating meat entirely in this present world if he thought someone would be offended and his testimony hurt (1 Cor. 8:13), and eating meat is a perfectly legitimate activity. How much more should a believer be willing to give up alcoholic beverages, which are highly questionable at best and have the potential in themselves to cause harm (which meat does not)!

The Bible commands the believer to abstain from all appearance of evil (1 Thess. 5:22).

That is a far reaching exhortation. Alcoholic beverages are a great evil and curse in modern society. Consider the automobile wrecks, the ruined health and early graves, the adulteries, the lewdness, the divorces, the neglected children, the abused wives, the waste of money, the gambling, the blasphemy, the pure foolishness. Look at the beer and liquor ads, how they invariably flaunt sensuality and irresponsibility. In January 2005 the Royal College of Physicians in England warned that Britain is suffering from an epidemic of alcohol-related problems that is fuelling violence and illness throughout the country (*The Telegraph*, Jan. 3, 2005). The same epidemic is raging throughout the world.

If anything has the appearance of evil today, it is alcoholic beverages, and the Bible does not merely suggest that we abstain from all appearance of evil; it commands us to do so!

It is also important to understand that there is a dramatic difference between the alcoholic content of wine today and that of Bible times. The following quotes by Norman Geisler and Robert Stein are from *Focus in Missions*, September 1986:

> "Many wine-drinking Christians today mistakenly assume that what the New Testament meant by wine is identical to wine used today. This, however, is false. In fact, today's wine is by biblical definition strong drink, and hence is forbidden in the Bible. ... Even ancient pagans did not drink what some Christians drink today" (Geisler).
>
> "To consume the amount of alcohol that is in two martinis today, by drinking wine containing three parts water to one part wine (the biblical ratio) a person would have to drink over twenty-two glasses" (Stein).

As for the idea that Jesus made and drank alcoholic wine, I would point the reader to the article "Did Jesus Make Alcoholic Wine" by the late Bruce Lackey, which is at the Way of Life web site

LIBERAL EMERGING CHURCH ERROR #11 ECUMENISM

The Emergent Village web site says:

> "We are committed to honoring and serving the church in all its forms-- Orthodox, Roman Catholic, Protestant, Evangelical, Pentecostal, Anabaptist and new forms still being birthed--rather than favoring some forms of the church and critiquing or rejecting others, we see that every form of the church has both weaknesses and strengths, both liabilities and potential. ... We seek to be irenic [promoting peace] and inclusive of all our Christian sisters and brothers, rather than elitist and critical" (Emergent Village web site, http://www.emergentvillage.org/about-information/values-and-practices).

Brian McLaren epitomizes the emerging church's radical ecumenism by calling himself "evangelical, post-protestant, liberal, conservative, mystical, poetic, biblical, charismatic, contemplative, fundamentalist, Calvinist, anabaptist, anglican, Methodist, catholic, green, incarnational, emergent" (*A Generous Orthodoxy*, subtitle to the book).

The fact that these various doctrinal positions are contradictory and irreconcilable does not bother the man one iota. He is fully committed to "orthoparadoxy," being convinced that he can hold contradictions in harmony.

In *A New Kind of Christian*, McLaren says that labels such as Catholic, Protestant, liberal, and evangelical "are about to become inconsequential" in a postmodern Christianity (p. 41).

Seven emerging church leaders proclaimed:

> "... we value dialogue very highly, and we are convinced that open and generous dialogue rather than chilling criticism and censorship offers the greatest hope for the future of the church in the world" ("Our Response to Critics of Emerging," Tony Jones, Doug Pagitt, Spencer Burke, Brian McLaren, Dan Kimball, Andrew Jones, Chris Seay, March 2, 2005, http://emergent-us.typepad.com/emergentus/2005/06/official_respon.html).

The authors who contributed to *An Emergent Manifesto of Hope* include liberal Protestant, Roman Catholic, and Seventh-day Adventist.

Tim Condor, pastor of Emmaus Way, loves theological dialogue" and is opposed to "exclusion" and wants to see fellowship grow "across many of the deepest chasms of Christian tradition" (*An Emergent Manifesto of Hope*, p. 107).

Shane Claiborne has spent time working with the Roman Catholic Missionaries of Charity and praises Mother Teresa as a truly spiritual person, even though she held a false sacramental gospel and worshipped the wafer of the Catholic mass as Christ. Further, she was a universalist and her "sisters" prepare Hindus to die by teaching them to pray to their false gods. None of that bothers emergents. They save their criticism for the man who warns about such false things.

David Foster says:

> "... we welcome the Calvinist and the Armenians, the Charismatics and the Presbyterians, the Baptist and the Methodists. We love High Church, Low Church, and no-church music. We love the

contemplatives and the activitists. ... we don't care what church you attend, or what denominational label you wear" (*A Renegade's Guide to God*, p. 280, 281).

When Mark Batterson was asked what category his church falls under, he replied:

"We're a mix; we're sort of one of those emerging churches. I mean we're reaching emerging generations but the funny thing is, I don't really like labels because labels tend to come with stereotypes. Personally, I'm kind of a denominational mutt. I come from seven different church backgrounds growing up. But I think the Lord's used that in my life to see that nobody has a corner on the Truth, but each of those expressions are kind of one dimension of who God is and if we could learn from each other and love each other, I think we'd be a lot better off than focusing on our differences" ("'Theater Church' Pastor on Positive Church Buzz," *Christian Post*, June 29, 2007).

Emergent Scot McKnight praised Wheaton College professor Alan Jacobs for speaking out against the firing of Joshua Hochschild, after he joined the Roman Catholic Church in 2003. In an article in *First Things*, April 2006, Jacobs called upon Wheaton to open its doors to Catholic professors. In reprinting the article at his web site, McKnight said: "Nice to hear his voice in this matter, and it's a voice that we are in a new day, one in which Catholics and Evangelicals can be much more cooperative" (http://www.jesuscreed.org/?p=891).

The late Robert Webber, who has had a vast influence within the emerging church in particular and evangelicalism at large, called for a broad ecumenism:

"A goal for evangelicals in the postmodern world is to accept diversity as a historical reality, but to seek unity in the midst of it. This perspective will allow us to see Catholic, Orthodox, and Protestant churches as various forms of the one true church..." (*Ancient-Future Faith*, p. 85).

"... evangelicals need to go beyond talk about the unity of the church to experience it through an attitude of acceptance of the whole church and an entrance into dialogue with the Orthodox, Catholic, and other Protestant bodies" (*Ancient-Future Faith*, p. 89).

Chris Seay of Ecclesia in Houston, Texas, believes "it's possible for people to have bad theology and still know Christ" and refuses "to take a noisy stand against their position, showing impatience, showing judgment, and causing division" (*Faith of My Fathers*, p. 86). He says, "As for navigating theological differences, I let most of them go…"

Consider the following quotes from the book *Emerging Churches* by Eddie Gibbs and Ryan Bolger, which demonstrate the broadminded ecumenical philosophy of the emerging church:

> "I guess I don't define myself primarily as evangelical or Protestant … Those things don't seem to matter too much to me as definitions. … Hardly anyone knows what denomination we are or seems to care" (Debbie Blue, House of Mercy, St. Paul, Minnesota, pp. 36, 37).

> "I'm post-Protestant. In many ways, I feel post-charismatic as well. By this I mean that I'm confused" (Roger Ellis of Revelation Church, Chichester, U.K., p. 36).

> "To be honest, not very many in my church would have a clue what they are. … those aware of their past or place in history might say 'Protestant' or 'Catholic'" (Si Johnston, Headspace, London, England, p. 36).

> "Some would definitely see themselves as postevangelical, while others would be more open-evangelical and some are more liberal-Catholic. The issue of denomination is fairly interesting, as we have a mix of people from Plymouth Brethren to Roman Catholic. I sometimes wonder whether we would be better described as postdenominational" (Ben Edson, Sanctus1, Manchester, U.K., p. 37).

> "I like the idea of moving beyond the horizons of old terms and labels … I would like to be more convergent in terms of connecting with the wider body of Christ … The goal is for us to put away labels that exclude" (Andrew Jones, Boaz, U.K., p. 37).

> "I'm not sure we'd agree on a label. None of them seems to fit us as a group. As has been said on our website, 'Let the world be free of labels!'" (Sue Wallace, Visions, York, U.K., p. 38).

> "My main aim for the community is not to be 'post' anything but to be 'and' everything. We are evangelical *and* charismatic *and* liberal *and* orthodox *and* contemplative *and* into social justice *and* into alternative worship" (Simon Hall, Revive, Leeds, U.K., pp. 38, 39).

Rob Bell says, "I am learning that my tradition includes the rabbis and reformers and revolutionaries and monks and nuns and pastors and writers and philosophers and artists and every person everywhere who has asked big questions of a big God" (*Velvet Elvis*, p. 14).

WHAT DOES THE BIBLE SAY?

The ecumenical philosophy is refuted by the Bible's teaching on doctrine.

> "As I besought thee to abide still at Ephesus, when I went into Macedonia, that thou mightest charge some that they teach NO OTHER DOCTRINE" (1 Tim. 1:3).

> "And the things that thou hast heard of me among many witnesses, THE SAME commit thou to faithful men, who shall be able to teach others also" (2 Timothy 2:2).

We have already seen what the Bible teaches about doctrine. There is only one true apostolic Christian faith and we have been given the Holy Spirit so that we can know that faith. We are required to teach that exact faith to the next generation. Thus, the ecumenical philosophy is unscriptural. It is impossible to reconcile a strict stand for Bible doctrine with any sort of ecumenism. It is impossible to stand for all of the doctrine of the Bible and be ecumenical in any sense.

The ecumenical philosophy is refuted by the Bible's command to contend for the faith.

> "Beloved, when I gave all diligence to write unto you of the common salvation, it was needful for me to write unto you, and exhort you that ye should earnestly contend for the faith which was once delivered unto the saints" (Jude 3).

It is impossible to have the mindset of fighting for the one revealed faith and be ecumenical at the same time. These are contradictory programs. Fighting for the faith is a divisive thing that invariably ruins ecumenical harmony!

The ecumenical philosophy is refuted by the Bible's warning of false teachers.

The New Testament is filled with warnings about false teachers. Jesus warned about them during His earthly ministry (Mat. 7:15-17) as well as in His messages to the seven churches following His resurrection and ascension (Rev. 2:2, 6, 14-16, 20-23). The apostle Paul warned about false teachers repeatedly (1 Cor. 15:12; 2 Cor. 11:1-4, 12-15; Gal. 1:6-9; 5:7-12; Phil. 3:17-21; Col. 2:4-8, 20-23; 1 Tim. 4:1-3; 2 Tim. 3:5-13; 4:3-4). Peter warned about them (2 Peter 2). John warned about them (1 John 2:18-27; 4:1-3). Jude warned about them (Jude 3-19). It is impossible to be on the lookout for false teachers as aggressively as the Bible commands and be ecumenical at the same time. To be on the lookout for false teachers and to be diligently comparing every teaching with the Scripture to know whether it is true or false is contrary to the broadminded emerging church philosophy.

The ecumenical philosophy is refuted by the Bible's command to separate from error.

> "Now I beseech you, brethren, mark them which cause divisions and offences contrary to the doctrine which ye have learned; and avoid them" (Romans 16:17).

Not only are we to hold to sound doctrine and contend for it and be on the lookout for false teaching, but we are also to separate from those who teach false doctrine. And what is the standard for judging what is true and what is false? The Bible is the standard, and according to the Bible we can know the truth, and we are responsible to God for doing so.

> "If any man will do his will, HE SHALL KNOW OF THE DOCTRINE, whether it be of God, or whether I speak of myself" (John 7:17).

> "Then said Jesus to those Jews which believed on him, If ye continue in my word, then are ye my disciples indeed; and YE SHALL KNOW THE TRUTH, and the truth shall make you free" (John 8:31-32).

> "Study to shew thyself approved unto God, a workman that needeth not to be ashamed, rightly dividing the word of truth" (2 Timothy 2:15).
>
> "But the anointing which ye have received of him abideth in you, and ye need not that any man teach you: but as THE SAME ANOINTING TEACHETH YOU OF ALL THINGS, and is truth, and is no lie, and even as it hath taught you, ye shall abide in him" (1 John 2:27).

The biblical practice of separation is diametrically opposed to the doctrine of ecumenism. It is impossible to practice both at the same time, and no amount of clever emerging church "orthoparadoxy" can change that fact.

The ecumenical philosophy is refuted by the Bible's definition of true Christian unity.

Let's examine some major passages on Christian unity:

> "That they all may be one; as thou, Father, art in me, and I in thee, that they also may be one in us: that the world may believe that thou hast sent me" (John 17:21).

The modern ecumenical movement has taken John 17:21 as its theme song, claiming that the unity for which Christ prayed is an ecumenical unity of professing Christians that disregards biblical doctrine. The context of John 17 destroys this myth. In John 17 the Lord plainly states that the unity for which He was praying is a unity based on salvation and truth and separation from the world.

> "I have manifested thy name unto the men which thou gavest me out of the world: thine they were, and thou gavest them me; and THEY HAVE KEPT THY WORD. ... For I HAVE GIVEN UNTO THEM THE WORDS WHICH THOU GAVEST ME; AND THEY HAVE RECEIVED THEM, and have known surely that I came out from thee, and they have believed that thou didst send me. ... I HAVE GIVEN THEM THY WORD; AND THE WORLD HATH HATED THEM, because they are not of the world, even as I am not of the world. ... Sanctify them through THY TRUTH: thy word is TRUTH. ... And for their sakes I sanctify myself, that they also might be sanctified THROUGH THE TRUTH" (John 17:6, 8, 14, 17, 19).

This is not a unity of true Christians with false, nominal with genuine, sound doctrine with heresy. It is not a unity that ignores doctrinal differences for the sake of an enlarged fellowship.

In fact, there is nothing in Christ's prayer to indicate that man is to do anything whatsoever to create the unity described herein. John 17 is not a commandment addressed to men; it is a High Priestly prayer addressed to God the Father, and the prayer was answered. It describes a spiritual reality that was created by God among genuine born again saints who are committed to the Scriptures, not a possibility that must be organized by man.

> "Now I beseech you, brethren, by the name of our Lord Jesus Christ, that ye all speak the same thing, and that there be no divisions among you; but that ye be perfectly joined together in the same mind and in the same judgment" (1 Corinthians 1:10).

Observe, first, that biblical unity is a matter of having one mind. This is contrary to the ecumenical "unity in diversity." The type of "unity" that we find in the ecumenical movement is not true unity at all; it is confusion; it is "Babel."

Observe, secondly, that the unity that God requires is in the assembly. This exhortation was addressed to a church. It is possible to have the type of unity described here in the congregation, because doctrine can be agreed upon and enforced through a church covenant. In the church we can have the same doctrine of Christ, Holy Spirit, salvation, spiritual gifts, sanctification, Christian living, prophecy, you name it, because we have a statement of faith and requirements for church membership and we have pastors and discipline; but this is impossible in a broad ecumenical context.

> "I therefore, the prisoner of the Lord, beseech you that ye walk worthy of the vocation wherewith ye are called, with all lowliness and meekness, with longsuffering, forbearing one another in love; endeavouring to keep the unity of the Spirit in the bond of peace. There is one body, and one Spirit, even as ye are called in one hope of your calling; one Lord, one faith, one baptism, one God and Father of all, who is above all, and through all, and in you all" (Ephesians 4:1-6).

In this passage we see true biblical unity and it is far removed from the ecumenical philosophy.

First, true Christian unity is a unity of the Spirit (Eph. 4:3). This means that it is a unity involving those who are regenerated by and led by the Spirit of God. Contrast this with the ecumenical concept of bringing together anyone that names the name of Christ regardless of his or her actual spiritual condition. At a large ecumenical conference in St. Louis in 2000 (the North American Congress on the Holy Spirit & World Evangelization), I asked many of the people who were manning ministry booths, "When were you born again?" Not one gave a scriptural answer. Some said they were born again when they were baptized. Some, when they had a charismatic style experience. Others weren't even familiar with the term. Yet all of these people are intimately involved in leadership within the ecumenical movement.

Second, true Christian unity is a unity of the one faith (Eph. 4:5). Biblical unity is impossible apart from the once-delivered faith taught by the apostles. God's people are called upon to "*earnestly contend for the faith which was once delivered unto the saints*" (Jude 3). There is no unity between those who believe and follow the Bible and those who do not. Note that "the faith" is not divided into cardinal and secondary issues. In Matthew 23:23 Jesus taught that while not everything in Scripture is of equal importance, everything has some importance. Nothing clearly taught in Scripture is to be despised and set aside for the purpose of unity. In 1 Timothy 6:14, Paul taught Timothy to keep the apostolic doctrine "without spot" until the return of Christ. Spots are small, seemingly insignificant things. Paul was teaching Timothy to value everything in Scripture. The theme of 1 Timothy is practical church truth (1 Tim. 3:15). In this epistle Paul dealt with things such as church government (1 Tim. 3) and the woman's role in church work (1 Tim. 2). These are the very things that are typically downplayed in ecumenical ventures, because they are considered of "secondary" importance. Yet Paul taught Timothy to keep all of these things without spot until Jesus comes. Timothy was instructed to allow "no other doctrine" (1 Tim. 1:3). That is the strictest kind of standard for doctrine, and when one holds that standard of doctrine it is impossible to be ecumenical in any sense.

Third, true Christian unity is a unity that is found in the New Testament assembly. The command in Ephesians 4:3 is addressed to the church at Ephesus (Eph. 1:1). It was not addressed to "the worldwide body of Christians." As we have seen, it is possible to practice biblical unity within the assembly because doctrine and righteousness can be enforced and preserved there (1 Corinthians 5; Titus 3:9-11). Outside of the assembly, though, there is no biblical discipline, leadership, or oversight. When Christians attempt to practice interdenominational and parachurch unity, there is always compromise because respect for every aspect of the New Testament faith results in division rather than unity. I am not responsible to maintain a unity with every professing Christian in the world but with the believers in my assembly, in my local body, and with others with whom I am truly likeminded. The Bible says we are to glorify God *"with one mind and one mouth"* (Romans 15:6). That is not a description of any type of ecumenism! This is only possible in the New Testament assembly, where believers can be united together in doctrine and spirit and purpose in a way that is impossible in a broader context.

> "Only let your conversation be as it becometh the gospel of Christ: that whether I come and see you, or else be absent, I may hear of your affairs, that ye stand fast in one spirit, with one mind striving together for the faith of the gospel" (Philippians 1:27).

The teaching of this passage is that, first, biblical unity is a function of the local church. This instruction was addressed to the church at Philippi. True Christian unity is not a parachurch or interdenominational issue.

Second, biblical unity means having one mind. It is not an ecumenical "unity in diversity." Compare Romans 15:5-6; 1 Corinthians 1:10; 2 Corinthians 13:11.

Third, biblical unity requires total commitment to the one apostolic faith. The New Testament faith is not many separate doctrines but is one unified body of truth into which all doctrines fit. It is unscriptural to think that only a few "cardinal" doctrines are necessary while other New Testament teachings and practices are tertiary and can be ignored for the sake of unity. As one wise pastor observed, we will either limit our message or we will limit our fellowship. If you determine to preach everything in Scripture, then you will automatically limit your sphere of fellowship. The choice is clear. If one is faithful to the New Testament faith, it is impossible to have broad fellowship in this apostate hour, and if one is committed to broad fellowship he must be willing to limit his message.

LIBERAL EMERGING CHURCH ERROR #12
TENDING TOWARD UNIVERSALISM

I am using the term "universalism" in a broad sense. In its strictest sense, it means that every person will be saved. Emerging church leaders do not usually believe this, but they do often believe that there is salvation outside of personal faith in Christ. This is why I say that they "tend toward universalism." There is a tendency within the emerging church to broaden salvation far beyond biblical bounds.

Brian McLaren says:

> "Missional Christian faith asserts that Jesus did not come to make some people saved and others condemned. Jesus did not come to help some people be right while leaving everyone else to be wrong. Jesus did not come to create another exclusive religion..." (*A Generous Orthodoxy*, p. 120).

I don't know exactly what *Jesus* McLaren is talking about here, but it is emphatically *not* the Jesus of the Bible!

McLaren says:

> "I don't believe making disciples must equal making adherents to the Christian religion. It may be advisable to many (not all!) circumstances to help people become followers of Jesus and remain within their Buddhist, Hindu, or Jewish contexts" (*A Generous Orthodoxy*, 2004, p. 260).

In *A New Kind of Christian*, McLaren says, "I don't think it's our business to prognosticate the eternal destinies of anyone else" (p. 92) and offers a quote from a C.S. Lewis novel as his authority. In this novel Lewis's character was a soldier who served a false god named Tash all his life, but he was accepted nonetheless by Aslan, who represents Christ.

> "Alas, Lord, I am no son of Thine but the servant of Tash. He answered, Child, all the service thou has done to Tash, I account as service done to me. ... Therefore if any man swear by Tash and keep his oath for the oath's sake, it is by me that he has truly sworn, though he know it not, and it is I who reward him."

According to C.S. Lewis, who is deeply loved by all branches of the emerging church, an individual might be saved even if he follows a false religion in this life and makes no personal profession of faith in Jesus Christ.

McLaren says that the Indian Hindu leader Gandhi "sought to follow the way of Christ without identifying himself as a Christian" (*A Generous Orthodoxy*, p. 189).

McLaren teaches that there is much good in pagan religions and that they have been a good thing for the world.

> "My knowledge of Buddhism is rudimentary, but I have to tell you that much of what I understand strikes me as wonderful and insightful, and the same can be said of the teachings of Muhammad, though of course I have my disagreements. ... I'd have to say that the world is better off for having these religions than having no religions at all, or just one, even if it were ours. ... They aren't the enemy of the gospel, in my mind..." (*A Generous Orthodoxy*, pp. 62, 63).

The man needs to spend a few years living in India or Nepal to see how the Hindu religion has corrupted and debased the people, how it has turned women into chattel, cows and snakes and monkeys into gods, certain classes of people into untouchables, and human life in general into something of little value, how it has encouraged pride and self-centeredness and discouraged humility and compassion and gratitude. Or maybe he should spend a few years in an Islamic country such as Saudi Arabia or Pakistan to see what the Muslim religion has done to the people. Are they better off because they can change their religion only on the pain of death or because a woman has no real rights or because she can be beaten or killed just because she does something that the male members of the family believe is unacceptable?

McLaren says that Buddhism is not the enemy of the gospel, but how can a religion that teaches that Jesus Christ is not God and not the only Saviour of the world NOT be an enemy of the gospel?

Spencer Burke of the Ooze condemns fundamentalists for interpreting John 14:6 in a "narrow and literal" manner. He then says that we don't know that Jesus actually said that and if he did, we don't have an accurate translation of it.

> "So how do I interpret this particular Scripture? First, Christianity as a religion didn't exist when Jesus spoke these words. Compounding this point are two additional facts: no one actually recorded Jesus' words at the time he spoke them, so we have no proof that they are indeed his words, and what he did say, he said in Aramaic, which means that nothing in the Bible as translated into an other language can be taken literally anyway" (*A Heretic's Guide to Eternity*).

If Burke is right here, it would mean that we cannot trust anything in the Bible! (Rick Warren highly recommends Burke's Ooze blog.)

Donald McCullough discusses the issue of universal salvation in his book *If Grace Is so Amazing, Why Don't We Like It*? He says that "universal salvation may remain a desire--even, on the basis of important New Testament texts, a hope that need not be whispered in secret but shouted in public" (p. 224). He says, "Many years ago, I decided that I would rather risk erring on the side of God's grace ... In the Bible, the indisputable movement of God's salvation is toward inclusion rather than exclusion..." (p. 225).

Karen Ward says:

> "I affirm no other Savior than Jesus Christ, yet at the same time, I feel no need to know with certainty the final destination of those of other faiths who either have no knowledge of Christ or who do not accept the Christian claims of the atonement" (*Listening to the Beliefs of Emerging Churches*, p. 46).

This is typical emerging church gibberish. Ward thinks she can hold these contradictions in perfect harmony, but it is impossible. If Jesus Christ is the only Saviour, then we CAN know with certainty the final destination of those who do not receive Him, and that destination is Hell! This is not our judgment; it is Almighty God's as revealed plainly to us in Scripture!

Leonard Sweet says:

> "One can be a faithful disciple of Jesus Christ without denying the flickers of the sacred in followers of Yahweh, or Kali, or Krishna" (*Quantum Spirituality*, p. 130).

What does this mean? Have those "flickers of the sacred" put their adherents into a saving relationship with Almighty God and taken them to Heaven?

Simon Hall of Revive in Leeds, England, says: "... while we recognize God's presence in other religions and in people of no faith, we still see Jesus as the most perfect revelation of God and therefore the SUREST route to God" (Gibbs and Bolger, *Emerging Churches*, p. 123).

The term "surest" is different from "only."

Dave Sutton of New Duffryn Community Church in Newport, England, says:

"I don't take God into somewhere ... You might meet God in some of the people you work with. ... My understanding is that if the kingdom is what God is about, then God might be involved in other faiths" (*Emerging Churches*, pp. 53, 133).

Ben Edson of Sanctus in Manchester, England, says:

"Many evangelicals believe they are taking God to the world. I do not like the dualism associated with that kind of theology" (*Emerging Churches*, p. 53).

Si Johnston of Headspace in London, England, says:

"Our policy as far as I see it is that we are friendly with other faith/religious traditions. We are more about dialogue and discussion with them than about obliterating them with heavy-handed apologetics" (*Emerging Churches*, p. 126).

Donald Miller, in *Blue Like Jazz*, said that "flaming liberals" also love Jesus (p. 110). He said that a group of atheistic, drug-using, fornicating, thieving hippies that he once met were "purely lovely" and they taught him about "goodness, about purity and kindness" (pp. 208, 209). He said that this taught him that there is light and truth outside of Christianity.

The late Henri Nouwen, whose writings are constantly referenced by the emerging church, said:

"Today I personally believe that while Jesus came to open the door to God's house, ALL HUMAN BEINGS CAN WALK THROUGH THAT DOOR, WHETHER THEY KNOW ABOUT JESUS OR NOT. Today I see it as my call to help every person claim his or her own way to God" (*Sabbatical Journey*, New York: Crossroad, 1998, p. 51).

Dallas Willard writes:

"I am happy for God to save anyone he wants in any way he can. IT IS POSSIBLE FOR SOMEONE WHO DOES NOT KNOW JESUS TO BE SAVED. But anyone who is going to be saved is going to be saved by Jesus" (*Cutting Edge* magazine, winter 2001, http://www.dwillard.org/articles/artview.asp?artID=14).

Thus, Willard claims that someone can be saved by Jesus even without putting his faith in Jesus. At first glance it might appear that this honors Christ, but actually it is a blatant denial of His teaching.

Spencer Burke says:

> "In moving into the world of material spirituality, the world of bricolage and quilting, institutional faiths like Christianity have the opportunity once again to offer their threads of what a life with God can be and return to their real purpose--NOT CONTROLLING THE GATES OF HEAVEN but facilitating new life in the people who encounter faith and grace. ... I DON'T BELIEVE YOU HAVE TO CONVERT TO ANY PARTICULAR RELIGION TO FIND GOD" (*A Heretic's Guide to Eternity*, pp. 147, 148, 197).

Burke also writes:

> "It may come as a surprise, but Jesus has never been in the religion business. He's in the business of grace, and GRACE TELLS US THERE IS NOTHING WE NEED TO DO TO FIND RELATIONSHIP WITH THE DIVINE. THE RELATIONSHIP IS ALREADY THERE; we only need to nurture it. Of course, growing up, I had a much different concept of grace. I grew up in an environment where grace was described as 'unmerited favor.' The only problem was that getting this 'unmerited favor' still required doing something--namely, 'asking Jesus in your heart' or praying a prayer" (*A Heretic's Guide to Eternity*).

Burke "celebrates the many ways God is revealed" and "recognizes that the Spirit has been with these people all along" (*Emerging Churches*, p. 132). When a Buddhist family visited Burke's emerging community in Newport Beach, California, instead of proclaiming to them the gospel of Jesus Christ, they all visited a Buddhist temple together and participated in a guided meditation.

Nanette Sawyer said that the doctrine that some people are saved and some are not is wrong and is something that she rejected on her way to an emerging church position (*An Emergent Manifesto of Hope*, p. 43). She said that she is a Christian because of what she was taught by a Hindu meditation master (p. 44). Her personal credo is "I believe that all people are children of God, created and loved by God, and that God's compassionate grace is available to us at all times" (p. 45). She says that Emergents don't segregate people into saved/unsaved categories; instead they "embrace the unknowability of a person's eternal status" (p. 49).

Samir Selmanovic, in his chapter in *An Emergent Manifesto of Hope*, tells the story of a Native American Indian chief who rejected "allegiance to the name of Christ" and instead chose to "be like him" (pp. 190, 191). In other words, this pagan Indian chief was allegedly a follower of Christ even though he rejected the gospel. Selmanovic also tells of a non-Christian friend named Mark who rejected Christianity but in whose life Christ was supposedly embedded "in substance rather than in name" (p. 192). Selmanovic says, "Christ being 'the only way' is not a statement of exclusion but inclusion, an expression of what is universal. ... To put it in different terms, there is no salvation outside of Christ, but there is salvation outside of Christianity" (p. 194). Selmanovic claims that even non-Christian religions as a whole might come under this "reality," because "religions live under the spiritual laws of the kingdom of God" and "God may employ their religious convictions and practices..." (p. 195).

Tony Campolo says:

> "The Emergent Church [tends] to reject the exclusivistic claims that many evangelicals make about salvation. They are not about to damn the likes of Gandhi or the Dalai Lama to hell simply because they have not embraced Christianity" ("Growing: Movement is new form of evangelism," *Winston-Salem Journal*, Dec. 6, 2004).

In January 2007 Campolo told the *Edmonton Journal* (Alberta, Canada) that he is not sure who will go to Heaven. Asked by the paper, "Do you believe non-Christians can go to heaven?" Campolo replied:

> "That's a good question to ask because the way we stand is we contend that trusting in Jesus is the way to heaven. However, we do not know who Jesus will bring into the kingdom and who He will not. We are very, very careful about pronouncing judgment on anybody. We leave judgment in the hands of God and we are saying Jesus is the way. We preach Jesus, but we have no way of knowing to whom the grace of God is extended" ("Canada's Different Evangelicals," *Edmonton Journal*, Jan. 27, 2007).

This is contradictory emerging church gobbly-gook! If we believe that "trusting Jesus is the way to Heaven," then we most definitely DO know who Jesus will bring into the kingdom. He will bring those that trust Him and He will not bring those that do not trust Him. As for pronouncing judgment on people, it is not our judgment. It is God in His infallible Word who has stated such things as, *"He ... that believeth not shall be damned"* (Mark 16:16), and, *"He ... that believeth not the Son shall not see life; but the wrath of God abideth on him,"* (John 3:36), and, *"He ... that hath not the Son of God hath not life"* (1 John 5:12).

In his critique of *Breaking the Missional Code* by Ed Stetzer and David Putman, Fuller Seminary professor Ryan Bolger says:

> "Throughout the work, the authors use a typology of churched and unchurched. I don't believe churched/unchurched is a helpful way to frame reality. It seems to imply that church is inherently good and unchurched is correspondingly bad. Instead of an ecclesiological rubric, however, I think a missiological paradigm might be more helpful. Paul Hiebert, missiologist, writes about centered and bounded sets. WHAT MATTERS IS NOT WHETHER WE ARE IN OR OUT (CHURCHED OR UNCHURCHED), BUT INSTEAD IT IS OUR DIRECTION THAT MATTERS--are we moving closer to the King (or Kingdom) or moving further away?" (http://thebolgblog.typepad.com/thebolgblog/2007/04/breaking_the_mi.html).

This is not a biblical understanding of salvation. A better term than church/unchurched is saved/unsaved! And salvation is not a matter of "moving closer to the King." It is a matter of whether or not you are truly born again. According to 1 John 5:12, you either have the Son or you don't.

Rob Bell says that "the most powerful things happen when the church surrenders its desire to convert people" (*Velvet Elvis*, p. 167). His counsel is that "THE CHURCH MUST STOP THINKING ABOUT EVERYBODY PRIMARILY IN CATEGORIES OF IN OR OUT, SAVED OR NOT, BELIEVER OR NONBELIEVER." He calls Christ's way "the best possible way to live" and says that Jesus did not claim one religion is better than another when he said he was "the way, the truth and the life." Rather, "his way is the way to the depth of reality" ("'Velvet Elvis' Author Encourages Exploration of Doubts," Beliefnet, 2005).

Bell describes a wedding of two pagan unbelievers. They had been living together in fornication and wanted to "make it official" and asked him to perform the ceremony. They told him that "they didn't want any Jesus or God or Bible or religion to be talked about" but "they did want me to make it really spiritual" (*Velvet Elvis*, p. 76). He agreed with this ridiculous request and claims that the wedding "resonated with the peace and harmony of unsoiled nature" because "God made it unspoiled by speaking it into existence" (p. 92). He thus denies the fall of creation. He then says that "in the deepest sense we can comprehend, MY FRIENDS ARE RESONATING WITH JESUS, WHETHER THEY ACKNOWLEDGE IT OR NOT" (p. 92). Thus, he would have us believe that this couple is allegedly blessed of God and resonating with Jesus even though they have rejected Jesus, God, and the Bible!

Shane Hipps, Rob Bell's co-pastor at Mars Hill Church, made the following statement in the first in a series of sermons on the Gospel of John, October 5, 2008:

> "Jesus is the ultimate unifier of these various diverse ways of looking at the world. Having a distinct religious identity marked by some boundaries, knowing how you are different from other religions, isn't a problem. John isn't trying to get rid of that. He is trying to point beyond it. To lose your religious identity is like losing a sail at sea. The sail is like religion. The wind is the spirit. You need a sail to catch the wind, to harness the wind. But you gotta realize that the sail isn't the wind. ... Just because we claim Jesus as the center of our religion does not make us one and the same with the wind of God. It just means we have another sail. ... This is what John is doing, and it is extremely innovative, and it's very unsettling, that he's inviting us beneath and beyond the things that make distinctions between us. ... That's why it says it was the light and life of all people. It didn't say it was the light and life of people who believe in Jesus. This Logos affects everybody, including Osama Ben Laden. As long as he's got breath, in him is the spark of the divine" (http://trinitymennonite.com/audio/TMC-Sermon-2008-10-05.mp3).

Hipps quotes some strange "translation" of John 1:9 or makes up his own, changing the wording from "That was the true Light, which lighteth every man that cometh into the world," to "it was the light and life of all people." In truth, Jesus gives light to every man through creation (Rom. 1:20) conscience (Rom. 2:14-15), and Scripture (Mark 16:15), but this does not add up to the emergent heresies of there being "a divine spark" in every man or every religion being a "sail" for God's Spirit.

Alan Jones says:

> "I am no longer interested, in the first instance, in what a person believes. Most of the time it's so much clutter in the brain. ... I wouldn't trust an inch many people who profess a belief in God. Others who do not or who doubt have won my trust. I want to know if joy, curiosity struggle, and compassion bubble up in a person's life. I'm interested in being fully alive. THERE IS NO OBJECTIVE AUTHORITY..." (Alan Jones, *Reimagining Christianity*, 2005, pp. 79, 83; Brian McLaren's glowing endorsement appears on the back cover).

WHAT DOES THE BIBLE SAY?

The emerging church doctrine of universalism is refuted by the Bible's warnings that those who do not believe in Christ will perish.

Consider the following unequivocal Scriptures:

> "To the law and to the testimony: if they speak not according to this word, it is because *there is* no light in them" (Isaiah 8:20).

> "Howbeit in vain do they worship me, teaching *for* doctrines the commandments of men" (Mark 7:7).

> "And he said unto them, Go ye into all the world, and preach the gospel to every creature. He that believeth and is baptized shall be saved; but he that believeth not shall be damned" (Mark 16:15-16).

> "I tell you, Nay: but, except ye repent, ye shall all likewise perish" (Luke 13:3).

> "Jesus answered and said unto him, Verily, verily, I say unto thee, Except a man be born again, he cannot see the kingdom of God" (John 3:3).

"He that believeth on him is not condemned: but he that believeth not is condemned already, because he hath not believed in the name of the only begotten Son of God" (John 3:18).

"He that believeth on the Son hath everlasting life: and he that believeth not the Son shall not see life; but the wrath of God abideth on him" (John 3:36).

"I said therefore unto you, that ye shall die in your sins: for if ye believe not that I am he, ye shall die in your sins" (John 8:24).

"But ye believe not, because ye are not of my sheep, as I said unto you. My sheep hear my voice, and I know them, and they follow me" (John 10:26-27).

"Neither is there salvation in any other: for there is none other name under heaven given among men, whereby we must be saved" (Acts 4:12).

"And the times of this ignorance God winked at; but now commandeth all men every where to repent: Because he hath appointed a day, in the which he will judge the world in righteousness by that man whom he hath ordained; whereof he hath given assurance unto all men, in that he hath raised him from the dead" (Acts 17:30-31).

"For we are unto God a sweet savour of Christ, in them that are saved, and in them that perish: To the one we are the savour of death unto death; and to the other the savour of life unto life. And who is sufficient for these things?" (2 Corinthians 2:15-16).

"In whom the god of this world hath blinded the minds of them which believe not, lest the light of the glorious gospel of Christ, who is the image of God, should shine unto them" (2 Corinthians 4:4).

"And this is the record, that God hath given to us eternal life, and this life is in his Son. He that hath the Son hath life; and he that hath not the Son of God hath not life" (1 John 5:11-12).

"And we know that we are of God, and the whole world lieth in wickedness" (1 John 5:19).

"Whosoever transgresseth, and abideth not in the doctrine of Christ, hath not God. He that abideth in the doctrine of Christ, he hath both the Father and the Son" (2 John 9).

According to the Bible, there is no salvation apart from faith in Jesus Christ. This is not some sort of "faith" that a person can have and still remain a Buddhist or a Hindu or a Muslim or an Agnostic or a New Age pagan; it is a faith that produces the new birth and makes one a follower of Jesus Christ.

The emerging church doctrine of universalism is refuted by the Bible's teaching that the believers are not part of the world.

According to the Bible, there is the world of the unsaved who live in darkness and there is the world of the saved who live in the light. We pass from darkness to light when we believe on the Lord Jesus Christ in a saving manner, and after that we are no longer of the world.

> "If the world hate you, ye know that it hated me before it hated you. If ye were of the world, the world would love his own: but because ye are not of the world, but I have chosen you out of the world, therefore the world hateth you" (John 15:18-19).

> "I have manifested thy name unto the men which thou gavest me out of the world: thine they were, and thou gavest them me; and they have kept thy word" (John 17:6).

> "I have given them thy word; and the world hath hated them, because they are not of the world, even as I am not of the world. I pray not that thou shouldest take them out of the world, but that thou shouldest keep them from the evil. They are not of the world, even as I am not of the world" (John 17:14-16).

> "To open their eyes, and to turn them from darkness to light, and from the power of Satan unto God, that they may receive forgiveness of sins, and inheritance among them which are sanctified by faith that is in me" (Acts 26:18).

> "Be ye not unequally yoked together with unbelievers: for what fellowship hath righteousness with unrighteousness? and what communion hath light with darkness" (2 Corinthians 6:14).

> "And you hath he quickened, who were dead in trespasses and sins" (Ephesians 2:1).

> "For ye were sometimes darkness, but now are ye light in the Lord: walk as children of light" (Ephesians 5:8).

> "Who hath delivered us from the power of darkness, and hath translated us into the kingdom of his dear Son" (Colossians 1:13).

"Ye are all the children of light, and the children of the day: we are not of the night, nor of darkness" (1 Thessalonians 5:5).

"Ye are of God, little children, and have overcome them: because greater is he that is in you, than he that is in the world. They are of the world: therefore speak they of the world, and the world heareth them. We are of God: he that knoweth God heareth us; he that is not of God heareth not us. Hereby know we the spirit of truth, and the spirit of error" (1 John 4:4-6).

The emerging church doctrine of universalism is refuted by the Bible's teaching about the current condition of the unbeliever.

The condition of the unbeliever who has not been made alive in Christ is described in Ephesians chapter 2.

He is dead in trespasses and sins (Eph. 2:1).
He is under the devil's control (Eph. 2:2).
He is by nature a child of wrath (Eph. 2:3).
He is without Christ, having no hope, and without God in the world (Eph. 2:12).
He is far from God (Eph. 2:13).

Only through being made alive in Christ as described in Ephesians 2:1 can this frightful condition be changed.

The Lord Jesus Christ said that the unbeliever is condemned already (John 3:18). There is nothing that the unbeliever must do to be condemned. Unless he repents and turns to Jesus Christ he will abide under God's condemnation for ever.

"For there is no respect of persons with God. For as many as have sinned without law shall also perish without law: and as many as have sinned in the law shall be judged by the law; (For not the hearers of the law are just before God, but the doers of the law shall be justified. For when the Gentiles, which have not the law, do by nature the things contained in the law, these, having not the law, are a law unto themselves: Which shew the work of the law written in their hearts, their conscience also bearing witness, and their thoughts the mean while accusing or else excusing one another;) In the day when God shall judge the secrets of men by Jesus Christ according to my gospel" (Romans 2:11-16).

The emerging church doctrine of universalism is refuted by the Great White Throne judgment.

> "And I saw a great white throne, and him that sat on it, from whose face the earth and the heaven fled away; and there was found no place for them. And I saw the dead, small and great, stand before God; and the books were opened: and another book was opened, which is the book of life: and the dead were judged out of those things which were written in the books, according to their works. And the sea gave up the dead which were in it; and death and hell delivered up the dead which were in them: and they were judged every man according to their works. And death and hell were cast into the lake of fire. This is the second death. And whosoever was not found written in the book of life was cast into the lake of fire" (Revelation 20:11-15).

The overthrow of the final rebellion described in Revelation 20:7-10 is followed by the Great White Throne Judgment of the unsaved. This is the second resurrection and the second death. The first resurrection pertains to the saved, while the second pertains to the unsaved. The first death is the separation of the spirit from the body, while the second is eternal separation from God in the lake of fire.

They stand before a throne, which describes God's majesty and great authority. This is the throne of the King of kings and Lord of lords, the throne where every yea is yea and every nay is nay, where no man's person is respected and no bribe is accepted, beyond which there is no appeal.

It is a *white* throne, the white signifying holiness and righteousness. This is God's throne of holy judgment against all sin. There is no rainbow as there is in Revelation 4. The rainbow signifies God's covenant of mercy, but at the Great White Throne judgment there is no grace, no mercy, no covenant of hope. In contrast to the believer in Christ, who comes freely and boldly to a *"throne of grace"* of his own accord because of Christ's blood (Heb. 4:16; 10:19), the unbeliever is dragged before a fearful, blazing white throne to obtain unmitigated justice.

> "Who can stand before his indignation? and who can abide in the fierceness of his anger? his fury is poured out like fire, and the rocks are thrown down by him" (Nahum 1:6).

"For the LORD thy God is a consuming fire, even a jealous God" (Deut. 4:24).

"Clouds and darkness are round about him: righteousness and judgment are the habitation of his throne. A fire goeth before him, and burneth up his enemies round about" (Psalm 97:2-3).

"For our God is a consuming fire" (Heb. 12:29).

It is a *great* throne, signifying God's omnipotence. The sinner, who invariably thinks of himself as important and worthy of favor, will be fully aware of his lowly insignificance and vanity and utter sinfulness when he stands before this great throne.

The occupant of this throne is Jesus Christ, to whom the Father has given all judgment (John 5:22). Mankind has said, *"We will not have this man to reign over us"* (Luke 19:14), but now they will stand before Him, the very object of their rebellion, and give account of every thought, word, and deed.

The subjects that stand before the throne are the unsaved. *We know that these are the unsaved, because they are not part of the first resurrection* (Rev. 20:6) and they are judged by their works. *We know, too, that these are the unsaved because their names are not written in the book of life through faith in Jesus Christ.* Compare Revelation 20:15. There are no exceptions mentioned. *We know, further, that these are the unsaved because those who believe in Christ will not be condemned* (John 3:18; 5:24). The judgment of the saved, those who have built their lives upon the foundation of Jesus Christ, is described in 1 Corinthians 3:11-15. It is a judgment of work (singular) rather than works (plural). The believer's judgment is for the purpose of examining his work or service for Christ to determine rewards or loss thereof. The unbeliever's judgment, on the other hand, is for the purpose of examining his *works* (plural) to expose his sin against God's Law and his rejection of God's light and to justify his eternal condemnation. The judgment of the believer's work can result in loss of reward but not loss of salvation (1 Cor. 3:15). The judgment of the unbeliever's works, on the other hand, results in the individual himself being cast into the lake of fire. No exceptions are mentioned.

This will be a judgment of *works*, which means that those who appear here will be condemned, for all are sinners (Romans 3:9-18), and *"we are all as an unclean thing, and all our righteousnesses are as filthy rags"* (Isaiah 64:6). Salvation, on the other hand, is not of works but is by the grace of Christ (Ephesians 2:8-9).

The book of works will be opened. A record is kept of every man's works, including every idle word and every secret thing (Mat. 12:36; Lk. 8:17; Rom. 2:16). Psalm 50:16-21 describes the type of things that will come up at the Great White Throne Judgment.

No sinner can stand before a holy God and be judged for his works without being condemned, so the conclusion of this judgment is foregone. Though there will possibly be degrees of punishment in the lake of fire (compare Matthew 11:20-24), all will be condemned and sent there.

This is Revelation's other "whosoever."

> "And whosoever was not found written in the book of life was cast into the lake of fire" (Rev. 20:15).

> "And the Spirit and the bride say, Come. And let him that heareth say, Come. And let him that is athirst come. And whosoever will, let him take the water of life freely" (Rev. 22:17).

The punishment is eternal conscious suffering. Compare Revelation 20:10, where we are told that the antichrist and the false prophet *"shall be tormented day and night for ever and ever."*

The message of the Great White Throne judgment is that man must trust Christ in this present life or be forever doomed. There is no salvation apart from personal faith in Christ.

The emerging church doctrine of universalism is refuted by the New Jerusalem.

The last two chapters of the book of Revelation describe the New Jerusalem, which is the city of the redeemed. It also describes those who are without and have no part in these things.

"But the fearful, and UNBELIEVING, and the abominable, and murderers, and whoremongers, and sorcerers, and idolaters, and all liars, shall have their part in the lake which burneth with fire and brimstone: which is the second death" (Revelation 21:8).

"And there shall in no wise enter into it any thing that defileth, neither whatsoever worketh abomination, or maketh a lie: but they which are written in the Lamb's book of life" (Revelation 21:27).

"For without are dogs, and sorcerers, and whoremongers, and murderers, and idolaters, and whosoever loveth and maketh a lie" (Revelation 22:15).

Only those whose names are written in the Lamb's book of life will be in the New Jerusalem. Every unbeliever and idolater and practitioner of witchcraft and whoremonger and liar will be in the lake of fire. Notice that everyone that loves a lie will be in the lake of fire. That includes those who love the lie of evolution or the lie or atheism or the lie of humanism or the lie of universalism or the lie of any false religion or philosophy.

What about Matthew 25:31-46?

One of the many passages that are grossly misinterpreted by the emerging church is Matthew 25:31-46. According to the emergent interpretation, there will be a general judgment following Christ's return and He will judge men according to how involved they were in social-justice issues (feeding the poor, caring for the sick, ministering to the imprisoned, etc.). Thus, non-Christians can be accepted by God on the basis of what they do to serve the poor and needy, and Christians should therefore have unity with social-justice minded non-Christians. They generally teach that by helping the poor and sick and imprisoned you are helping Christ.

For example, Tony Campolo says:

> "When it comes to what is ultimately important, the Muslim community's sense of commitment to the poor is exactly in tune with where Jesus is in the 25th chapter of Matthew. That is the description of judgment day. And if that is the description of judgment day what can I say to an Islamic brother who has fed the hungry, and clothed the naked? You say, 'But he hasn't a personal relationship with Christ.' I would argue with that. And I would say from a Christian perspective, in as much as you did it to the least of these you did it unto Christ. You did have a personal relationship with Christ, you just didn't know it. And Jesus himself says: 'On that day there will be many people who will say, when did we have this wonderful relationship with you, we don't even know who you are ...' 'Well, you didn't know it was me, but when you did it to the least of these it was doing it to me'" ("On Evangelicals and Interfaith Cooperation," *Crosscurrents*, Spring 2005, http://findarticles.com/p/articles/mi_m2096/is_1_55/ai_n13798048).

Observe how that Campolo brazenly adds to God's Word, by putting something new into the mouths of those described in Matthew 25:37-39. He claims that they will say, "When did we have this wonderful relationship with you, we don't even know who you are." But Jesus says nothing about relationship, and He does not say that these are people that do not know Him.

The emergent interpretation of Matthew 25:31-36 ignores the context of the passage.

The context of Matthew 25 is the judgment of the nations at the return of Christ at the end of the Great Tribulation and it pertains to how the nations treated Israel.

During the Tribulation, God will regenerate Israel and 144,000 Jewish evangelists will go throughout the world preaching the gospel of the kingdom and announcing the soon coming of Christ; as a result, multitudes will be saved out of every nation and tongue (Revelation 7). Further, the two Jewish witnesses will preach in Jerusalem for three and a half years and perform miracles on the earth (Revelation 11:1-6). This period was described by Jesus in Matthew 24:9-14:

> "Then shall they deliver you up to be afflicted, and shall kill you: and ye shall be hated of all nations for my name's sake. And then shall many be offended, and shall betray one another, and shall hate one another. And many false prophets shall rise, and shall deceive many. And because iniquity shall abound, the love of many shall wax cold. But he that shall endure unto the end, the same shall be saved. And this gospel of the kingdom shall be preached in all the world for a witness unto all nations; and then shall the end come."

Thus, the gospel of the kingdom will be preached throughout the world during the Tribulation in the midst of great persecution and hatred.

The gospel of the kingdom is the gospel that Jesus preached when He presented Himself to Israel as the Messiah. Both John the Baptist and Jesus preached, *"Repent: for the kingdom of heaven is at hand"* (Mat. 3:2; 4:17). This was the announcement of the kingdom promised to David's Son (Isaiah 9:6-7). The Jews rejected their Messiah and His kingdom (John 1:11; 19:15), and He warned them that the kingdom would be taken from them because of their rebellion and given to another (Mat. 21:42-26). Thus John says, *"He came unto his own, and his own received him not. But as many as received him, to them gave he power to become the sons of God, even to them that believe on his name"* (John 1:11-12). Jesus came unto His own people, Israel, and was rejected, and this was prophesied in Scripture (e.g., Isaiah 53:3). He then turned from Israel and said, *"I will build my church; and the gates of hell shall not prevail against it"* (Mat. 16:18). Christ stopped announcing the kingdom and prepared to die on the cross to make atonement for man's sin, and after He rose from the dead He sent His disciples forth to preach the gospel to every nation (Acts 1:8). In this present church age Christ is calling out a people for His name from among the Gentiles while Israel is largely blinded, but when this dispensation is finished God will turn His attention back to Israel and will fulfill His covenants with her.

> "For I would not, brethren, that ye should be ignorant of this mystery, lest ye should be wise in your own conceits; that blindness in part is

happened to Israel, until the fulness of the Gentiles be come in. And so all Israel shall be saved: as it is written, There shall come out of Sion the Deliverer, and shall turn away ungodliness from Jacob: For this is my covenant unto them, when I shall take away their sins" (Rom. 11:25-27).

At the end of the first three and a half years of the Tribulation the antichrist will come to power and reign over the earth with cruelty (Rev. 13:15-18). He will overcome the Jewish evangelists in Jerusalem and they will die and after three and a half days be raised up and ascend to Heaven (Rev. 11:7-12). After this the antichrist will overcome the ancient people Israel (Rev. 13:7-10) and the remnant will flee into the wilderness where they will be protected by God (Rev. 12:12-17). In Daniel the antichrist is called the little horn and a king of fierce countenance and a vile king, and we are told that he will overcome Israel (Dan. 7:21-25; 8:23-25; 11:32-34).

The people of the earth will see these things and will have a choice of whether to help the Jews or curse them, similar to the choice they had during World War II, and at the end of the Tribulation Jesus will judge the people of the nations on that basis. As God said to Abraham, *"And I will bless them that bless thee, and curse him that curseth thee: and in thee shall all families of the earth be blessed"* (Gen. 12:3).

Thus, the context of the judgment described in Matthew 25 is men's treatment of Israel.

The previous chapter makes this clear. In Matthew 24 Jesus described the Great Tribulation and explained that Israel will be at the heart of His program for that time. See Matthew 24:9-20. It is immediately after the Tribulation that Jesus will return (Mat. 24:29-31).

Jesus' words in Matthew 25:40 also make this clear. *"And the King shall answer and say unto them, Verily I say unto you, Inasmuch as ye have done it unto one of the least of these MY BRETHREN, ye have done it unto me."* Christ's brethren don't consist of all people indiscriminately. In this church age His brethren are those who are saved (Rom. 8:29). We become children of God through faith in Christ (John 1:12; Gal. 3:26). In the Great Tribulation Jesus' people will be the converted Jews who receive Him as their Messiah and those who are converted through their preaching.

Thus, when Jesus says, *"I was an hungred, and ye gave me no meat: I was thirsty, and ye gave me no drink: I was a stranger, and ye took me not in: naked, and ye clothed me not: sick, and in prison, and ye visited me not"* (Mat. 25:42-43), He is referring to the persecuted Jews and the Jewish proselytes of the Tribulation period.

James Gray rightly says, "As His own chosen nation, through whom He will reveal Himself to the nations, the Jews hold through all time an official position and have a sacred character, and in the day of their restoration and of the judgment of the nations, the great question will be, how far have the other nations regarded them as His people, and so treated them" (*The Concise Bible Commentary*, p. 416).

Allegorical interpretation of Bible prophecy and the principle of replacement (replacing Israel with the church) is something that the emergents have borrowed from Reformed theology, which in turn borrowed it from the Roman Catholic Church and its "doctors," such as Augustine.

The emergent interpretation of Matthew 25:31-36 ignores what the Bible teaches about the gospel.

According to the gospel, men are not saved by doing good works. They are saved by God's grace. *"For by grace are ye saved through faith; and that not of yourselves: it is the gift of God: Not of works, lest any man should boast"* (Ephesians 2:8-9). Salvation is a free gift that was purchased at great price by Christ's blood. Paul says, *"And if by grace, then is it no more of works: otherwise grace is no more grace. But if it be of works, then is it no more grace: otherwise work is no more work*" (Rom. 11:6). Salvation is either a gift or it is works, but it cannot be both.

The emergent interpretation of Matthew 25:31-36 confuses the effect of salvation with salvation itself.

The Bible teaches us that good works are the effect and fruit of salvation. After Paul explained that salvation is a free gift of God's grace in Ephesians 2:8-9, he showed that works follow after as the natural product thereof. *"For we are his workmanship, created in Christ Jesus unto good works, which God hath before ordained that we should walk in them"* (Eph. 2:10).

Those who submit to the gospel and are saved are converted and live a new kind of life. *"Therefore if any man be in Christ, he is a new creature: old things are passed away; behold, all things are become new"* (2 Cor. 5:17). This is what will happen during the Tribulation.

The emergent interpretation of Matthew 25:31-36 ignores what the Bible teaches about other judgments.

There is no general judgment described in the Bible. In fact, there are at least three judgments.

First, there is the judgment of church age believers at the judgment seat of Christ (1 Cor. 3:11-15). This is a judgment of those who have trusted Christ and built their lives upon that solid foundation. Their ministries for Christ will be examined to see if they will be rewarded or not. Regardless of whether they win or lose rewards, they will be saved. *"If any man's work shall be burned, he shall suffer loss: but he himself shall be saved; yet so as by fire"* (1 Cor. 3:15).

Second, there is the judgment of the nations following the Great Tribulation. This is described in Matthew 25.

Third, there is the judgment of the unsaved at the end of the Millennium. This is described in Revelation 20:11-15. These are judged by their works according to God's holy law and condemned and cast into the lake of fire.

To interpret Matthew 25:31-46 in the emergent way is to contradict massive amounts of clear Scripture.

LIBERAL EMERGING CHURCH ERROR #13
DOWNPLAYING HELL

Closely associated with the emerging church's tendency toward universalism is its denial of or watering down of the doctrine of Hell.

Donald Miller tells about one of his housemates named Stacy who wrote a story of an astronaut who has an accident while working on a space station and has to spend the rest of his life circling the earth in a special space suit and suffering a lingering death. Miller concludes, "Stacy had delivered as accurate a description of hell as could be calculated" (*Blue Like Jazz*, p. 172).

Thus, he describes a "hell" without fire or torment, and a "hell" that has an end.

Rob Bell defines Hell as "a way, a place, a realm absent of how God desires things to be" (*Velvet Elvis*, p. 147). Bell says Hell is "a realm where things are not as God wants them to be; where things aren't according to God's will; where people aren't treated as fully human" (*Sex God*, p. 21). He says it is "disturbing" "when people talk more about hell after this life than they do about hell here and now" (*Velvet Elvis*, p. 148). But the Bible nowhere uses the term Hell to describe something that exists in this present life.

In a podcast interview in January 2006 with Leif Hansen, Brian McLaren said that if the doctrine of Hell is true then the Christ's message and the cross are "false advertising." He said if Hell is true then people can legitimately question God's goodness. This interview is truly amazing in a fearful way. Hansen says that he doubts God's very existence and even casts a profanity at Jesus. And yet the two of them ramble on in a very knowing sort of way, mocking fundamentalists and Calvinists and anyone else who won't accept the emerging church's unbelief. It is a great warning that if you reject the truth you are walking in darkness.

McLaren said:

> "Does it make sense for a good being to create creatures who will experience infinite torture, infinite time, infinite--you know, never be numbed in their consciousness? I mean, how would you even create a universe where that sort of thing could happen? It just sounds--It really raises some questions about the goodness of God. ...
>
> "The traditional understanding says that God asks of us something that God is incapable of Himself. God asks us to forgive people. But God is incapable of forgiving. God can't forgive unless He punishes somebody in place of the person He was going to forgive. God doesn't say things to you--Forgive your wife, and then go kick the dog to vent your anger. God asks you to actually forgive. And there's a certain sense that, A COMMON UNDERSTANDING OF THE ATONEMENT PRESENTS A GOD WHO IS INCAPABLE OF FORGIVING. UNLESS HE KICKS SOMEBODY ELSE. ...
>
> "... one of the huge problems is the traditional understanding of hell. Because if the cross is in line with Jesus' teaching then--I won't say, the only, and I certainly won't say even the primary--but a primary meaning of the cross is that the kingdom of God doesn't come like the kingdoms of this world, by inflicting violence and coercing people. But that the kingdom of God comes through suffering and willing, voluntary sacrifice. But in an ironic way, THE DOCTRINE OF HELL BASICALLY SAYS, NO, THAT THAT'S NOT REALLY TRUE. THAT IN THE END, GOD GETS HIS WAY THROUGH COERCION AND VIOLENCE AND INTIMIDATION AND DOMINATION, just like every other kingdom does. The cross isn't the center then. The cross is almost a distraction and false advertising for God" (McLaren, http://www.understandthetimes.org/mclarentrans.shtml and http://str.typepad.com/weblog/2006/01/brian_mclaren_p.html).

Hansen replies as follows:

> "Oh, Brian, that was just so beautifully said. I was tempted to get on my soap box there and you know--Because as you and I know there are so many illustrations and examples that you could give that show why THE TRADITIONAL VIEW OF HELL COMPLETELY FALLS IN THE FACE OF--IT'S JUST ANTITHETICAL TO THE CROSS. But the way you put it there, I love that. It's false advertising. And here, Jesus is saying, turn the other cheek. Love your enemy. Forgive seven times seventy. Return violence with self-sacrificial love. But if we believe the traditional view of hell, it's like, well, do that for a short amount of time. Because eventually, God's going to get them."

McLaren also said:

> "The church has been preoccupied with the question, 'What happens to your soul after you die?' AS IF THE REASON FOR JESUS COMING CAN BE SUMMED UP IN, 'JESUS IS TRYING TO HELP GET MORE SOULS INTO HEAVEN, AS OPPOSED TO HELL, AFTER THEY DIE.' I JUST THINK A FAIR READING OF THE GOSPELS BLOWS THAT OUT OF THE WATER. I don't think that the entire message and life of Jesus can be boiled down to that bottom line" ("The Emerging Church," Part Two, *Religion & Ethics*, July 15, 2005, http://www.pbs.org/wnet/religionandethics/week846/cover.html).

WHAT DOES THE BIBLE SAY?

The Lord Jesus Christ preached on Hell 14 times in the four Gospels and defined it as a place of fiery eternal judgment for those who reject the truth in this world. If we will be true "Red-Letter Christians," we will follow Christ's example and preach Hell frequently and preach it hot and fearful!

> "But I say unto you, That whosoever is angry with his brother without a cause shall be in danger of the judgment: and whosoever shall say to his brother, Raca, shall be in danger of the council: but whosoever shall say, Thou fool, shall be in danger of hell fire" (Matthew 5:22).

> "Every tree that bringeth not forth good fruit is hewn down, and cast into the fire" (Matthew 7:19).

> "And fear not them which kill the body, but are not able to kill the soul: but rather fear him which is able to destroy both soul and body in hell" (Matthew 10:28).

> "And thou, Capernaum, which art exalted unto heaven, shalt be brought down to hell: for if the mighty works, which have been done in thee, had been done in Sodom, it would have remained until this day" (Matthew 11:23).

"As therefore the tares are gathered and burned in the fire; so shall it be in the end of this world. The Son of man shall send forth his angels, and they shall gather out of his kingdom all things that offend, and them which do iniquity; and shall cast them into a furnace of fire: there shall be wailing and gnashing of teeth" (Matthew 13:40-42).

"So shall it be at the end of the world: the angels shall come forth, and sever the wicked from among the just, and shall cast them into the furnace of fire: there shall be wailing and gnashing of teeth" (Matthew 13:49-50).

"Woe unto you, scribes and Pharisees, hypocrites! for ye compass sea and land to make one proselyte, and when he is made, ye make him twofold more the child of hell than yourselves" (Matthew 23:15).

"Ye serpents, ye generation of vipers, how can ye escape the damnation of hell" (Matthew 23:33).

"Then shall he say also unto them on the left hand, Depart from me, ye cursed, into everlasting fire, prepared for the devil and his angels" (Matthew 25:41).

"And if thy hand offend thee, cut it off: it is better for thee to enter into life maimed, than having two hands to go into hell, into the fire that never shall be quenched: Where their worm dieth not, and the fire is not quenched. And if thy foot offend thee, cut it off: it is better for thee to enter halt into life, than having two feet to be cast into hell, into the fire that never shall be quenched: Where their worm dieth not, and the fire is not quenched. And if thine eye offend thee, pluck it out: it is better for thee to enter into the kingdom of God with one eye, than having two eyes to be cast into hell fire: Where their worm dieth not, and the fire is not quenched" (Mark 9:43-48).

"But I will forewarn you whom ye shall fear: Fear him, which after he hath killed hath power to cast into hell; yea, I say unto you, Fear him" (Luke 12:5).

"And in hell he lift up his eyes, being in torments, and seeth Abraham afar off, and Lazarus in his bosom" (Luke 16:23).

LIBERAL EMERGING CHURCH ERROR #14
WEAK ON THE ISSUE OF HOMOSEXUALITY

Brian McLaren says:

> "Frankly, many of us don't know what we should think about homosexuality. ... We aren't sure if or where lines are to be drawn, nor do we know how to enforce with fairness whatever lines are drawn. ... Perhaps we need a five-year moratorium on making pronouncements" ("Brian McLaren on the Homosexual Question," Jan. 23, 2006, http://blog.christianitytoday.com/outofur/archives/2006/01/brian_mclaren_o.html).

In December 2006, McLaren spoke at the Open Door Community Church in Sherwood, Arkansas. The church's web site said:

> "The leadership at Open Door Community Churches are excited to see gay and non-gay Christians worshiping together as one. We believe that gay and non-gay Christians can and should come to the table of the Lord together, side by side, without labels. We believe that as these two historically separate communities join together at the cross of Jesus Christ a healing and a new understanding of oneness in Christ occurs in both groups. We are part of a growing revival of grace-filled Christians transcending either the terms 'conservative' or 'liberal.' Above all things, we are a GRACE CHURCH! We are a family embracing the full spectrum of race, age, gender, family status, sexual orientation, economic status and denominational background."

Tony Jones, National Coordinator of the Emerging Village, says:

> "I now believe that GLBTQ can live lives in accord with biblical Christianity (as least as much as any of us can!) and that their monogamy can and should be sanctioned and blessed by church and state" (Jones, "How I Went from There to Here: Same Sex Marriage Blogalogue," Nov. 18, 2008, http://blog.beliefnet.com/tonyjones/2008/11/same-sex-marriage-blogalogue-h.html).

On January 18, 2009, Jones wrote: "Adele Sakler, whom I've known for a few years, has started yet another 'hyphenated' group within the emergent network-of-networks. She's calling it 'Qeermergent,' and, as you might guess, it's focused on GLBTQ issues."

Doug Pagitt says:

> "It we have a theology formed in a worldview that sees sexuality as sin, our means, intentions, and explanations of sexuality will be affected" (*Listening to the Beliefs of Emerging Churches*, p. 140).

In an interview Chris Seay said:

> "In your community, are you called to the gospel of Christ, or are you called to be the moral police? Approach homosexuals without condemnation but with God's love and the gospel" ("Shayne Wheeler and Chris Seay on Homosexuals and the Church," ChurchRelevance.com, June 19, 2007).

Spencer Burke believes that "the evangelical church may be wrong about homosexuality" (http://www.zondervan.com/media/samples/pdf/0310253861_samptxt.pdf#search='spencer%20burke%20homosexuality).

Donald McCullough says that "condemning homosexuality feels natural because about 95 percent of us could never imagine engaging in such a practice" but "in a world turned upside down by grace, we must distrust whatever feels natural" (*If Grace Is So Amazing, Why Don't We Like It*, pp. 201, 202).

Donald Miller tells of an experience he had as a guest on a conservative radio talk show program. He was asked what he thought about the homosexuals who are trying to take over the country. Instead of expressing concern about the radical homosexual agenda, Miller naively claimed that he wasn't aware of such a thing and expressed more concern about Christians who oppose homosexuals (pp. 187-189). He said that "morality as a battle cry against a depraved culture is simply not a New Testament idea" (p. 186). He said that if Christians are "using war rhetoric to communicate a battle mentality, we are fighting on Satan's side" (p. 190).

Tony Campolo believes that homosexuals are usually born that way, that it is not a "volitional" problem. Campolo's wife, Peggy, supports homosexual marriage. In fact, she is affiliated with the Association of Welcoming and Affirming Baptists, the mission of which is "to create and support a community of churches, organizations and individuals committed to the inclusion of gay, lesbian, bisexual and transgender persons in the full life and mission of Baptist churches." At the New Baptist Covenant Celebration (AWAB) in Atlanta in January 2008, which I attended with press credentials, I interviewed an AWAB council member named Kathy Stayton. She said that she does not believe the first three chapters of Genesis are literal history, that marriage is a divinely-ordained institution, or that homosexual acts, even outside of "committed relationships," are sinful.

At their booth at the new Baptist Covenant Celebration the AWAB was distributing an article by Peggy Campolo entitled "Some Answers to the Most Common Questions about God's GLBT [gay, lesbian, bisexual, transgendered] Children" from the Summer 2000 edition of *The InSpiriter*. She counsels homosexuals to "ask the Holy Spirit to give you a sense of God's timing" about "coming out" of the closet! She says, "I can celebrate the committed monogamous partnerships of my gay brothers and lesbian sisters."

Jim Wallis, founder of *Sojourner*, says in his book *The Great Awakening* (2008), that "civil rights for gay and lesbian people and equal protection under the law for same-sex couples" is "a justice issue" (p. 229). It appears that he doesn't believe that homosexuality is the moral abomination that the Bible says it is, because it would be difficult to understand why a professing Christian would think that it would be "just" to legalize a moral abomination. He also says that he supports "civil unions" and "spiritual 'blessings' for gay couples."

WHAT DOES THE BIBLE SAY?

The Bible condemns the practice of homosexuality unequivocally.

The Bible teaches that sexual relationships and activities outside of the holy bond of marriage are sinful. *"Marriage is honourable in all, and the bed undefiled: but whoremongers and adulterers God will judge"* (Heb. 13:4). From the beginning, the Bible defines lawful marriage as a holy union between one man and one woman (Gen. 2:21-25), and Christ pointed back to the beginning as the divine standard (Mat. 19:4-6). The Law of Moses defined marriage as a covenant relationship between one man and one woman (Mal. 2:14-15). Since sexual relationships outside of marriage are sinful and since the Bible nowhere legitimizes marriage between a man and a man or a woman and a woman, it is obvious that homosexuality is forbidden. It is nowhere legitimized by Scripture. To say that homosexual unions are right is to reject the authority of the Bible.

In the Old Testament, homosexual practice is condemned severely. The homosexuals in Sodom and Gomorrah were destroyed by fire from heaven (Genesis 18:1-24). Homosexual activists claim that the cities were destroyed for their lack of hospitality or for some reason other than homosexuality, but the New Testament makes it clear that they were destroyed for their "filthy conversation" (2 Peter 2:6-8) and their "fornication" (Jude 7).

Under the Law of Moses homosexuality brought the death penalty:

> "Thou shalt not lie with mankind, as with womankind: it is abomination" (Leviticus 18:22).

> "If a man also lie with mankind, as he lieth with a woman, both of them have committed an abomination: they shall surely be put to death; their blood shall be upon them" (Leviticus 20:13).

This Law of Moses was given to Israel and it is not in force in Gentile nations today, but it does teach us what God thinks of homosexuality. "Now we know that what things soever the law saith, it saith to them who are under the law: that every mouth may be stopped, and all the world may become guilty before God" (Romans 3:19).

What about the biblical term "sodomite"? Some say that it referred only to prostitution associated with pagan temple worship and not to homosexuality in general. It is true that the term refers to male prostitution and homosexual moral perversion practiced in connection with idolatry (Deut. 23:17; 1 Ki. 14:24; 15:12; 22:46; 2 Ki. 23:7). But the term is also identified with homosexuality and moral perversion in general. The 1828 Webster dictionary defined sodomy as "a crime against nature." The *Webster's Deluxe Unabridged Dictionary* of 1983 defines sodomy as "any sexual intercourse regarded as abnormal, as between persons of the same sex, especially males, or between a person and an animal." The term is descriptive of the moral perversion of the city of Sodom (Genesis 19; Jude 1:7).

The New Testament also treats homosexuality as a moral abomination. In Romans 1 homosexuality is described in especially intense terms.

> "Professing themselves to be wise, they became fools, and changed the glory of the uncorruptible God into an image made like to corruptible man, and to birds, and fourfooted beasts, and creeping things. Wherefore God also gave them up to uncleanness through the lusts of their own hearts, to dishonour their own bodies between themselves: Who changed the truth of God into a lie, and worshipped and served the creature more than the Creator, who is blessed for ever. Amen. For this cause God gave them up unto vile affections: for even their women did change the natural use into that which is against nature: And likewise also the men, leaving the natural use of the woman, burned in their lust one toward another; men with men working that which is unseemly, and receiving in themselves that recompence of their error which was meet. And even as they did not like to retain God in their knowledge, God gave them over to a reprobate mind, to do those things which are not convenient" (Romans 1:22-28).

Paul identified homosexuality as the product of men's rejection of God and God giving them up to their own sinful ways. This passage calls homosexuality "vile affections" (v. 26), "against nature" (v. 26), "leaving the natural" (v. 27), "unseemly" (v. 27), "reprobate mind" (v. 28), and "not convenient" (v. 28).

The passage warns that homosexuality is the corruption of the imagination. It is the product of a reprobate mind. When the imagination is allowed to pursue wicked things it is dragged farther and farther into darkness and moral perversion, and this can begin at a very young age.

In 1 Corinthians 6:9, we learn that some of the members of the church at Corinth had been involved in homosexuality before they were saved.

> "Know ye not that the unrighteous shall not inherit the kingdom of God? Be not deceived: neither fornicators, nor idolaters, nor adulterers, nor effeminate, nor abusers of themselves with mankind."

The term "effeminate" is from the Greek word "malakos." It is used three times in the New Testament and twice it is translated "soft" (Mat. 11:8; Lk. 7:25). Webster defines it as "having the qualities of the female sex; soft or delicate to an unmanly degree; womanish." The woman is supposed to be effeminate, but 1 Corinthians 6:9 refers to moral perversion. It refers to the passive, feminine side of homosexuality.

The term "abusers of themselves with mankind" refers to the masculine side of homosexuality. It refers to that which is "against nature" (Rom. 1:26-27). The Greek word "arsenokoites" means "to lie with, or to cohabit with, a male." Matthew Henry (1662-1714), exemplifying the common interpretation of this term in earlier centuries, identified "abusers of themselves with mankind" with sodomy. *The Bible Exposition Commentary* says: "'Effeminate' and 'abusers' describe the passive and active partners in a homosexual relationship."

Some try to make the case that Jesus didn't mention homosexuality, pretending that this (if it were true) would prove that Christians should also be silent on the subject. The fact is that He did mention homosexuality. He mentioned the destruction of Sodom and Gomorrah twice in His teachings (Mark 6:10; Luke 17:29). Christ also upheld the Law of Moses (Mat. 5:18-19). Further, after His resurrection and ascension Christ sent the Holy Spirit to lead the disciples into all truth and to inspire the completion of the Scriptures (John 16:7-15). All of the words of the New Testament are given by divine inspiration and are inerrantly authoritative and come to us as revelation from Jesus Christ.

The New Testament commands us to abhor and reprove the evil works of darkness.

To say that it is wrong for Christians to reprove sin in society is to reject the Bible's own instruction.

> "But Herod the tetrarch, being reproved by him for Herodias his brother Philip's wife, and for all the evils which Herod had done" (Luke 3:19).
>
> "Abhor that which is evil; cleave to that which is good" (Romans 12:9)
>
> "And have no fellowship with the unfruitful works of darkness, but rather reprove them" (Ephesians 5:11).
>
> "Preach the word; be instant in season, out of season; reprove, rebuke, exhort with all longsuffering and doctrine" (2 Tim. 4:2).

The homosexual can be saved by repentance and faith in Jesus Christ.

Paul speaks of the homosexuality in the church at Corinth in the past tense -- *"and such WERE some of you"* (1 Cor. 6:11). The members of the church at Corinth had repented of their sin and had become new creatures in Christ. No sinner is so evil that God cannot save him, but he must repent of his sin rather than justify it, and when God saves He changes (2 Corinthians 5:17).

The modern movement to allow homosexuals into churches without repenting of homosexuality is unscriptural. Bible believers are not "homophobic" any more than they are "adulteryphobic" or "thiefphobic" or "lierphobic." They do not hate homosexuals. They want to see them come to Christ and be converted to holiness. They simply believe that the Bible teaches that men must repent of sin in order to be saved and join a church that teaches homosexuality is a sin.

They also know that homosexuality is a special kind of sin in the sense that it is a sin against nature itself and a sin that is a particular attack upon biblical marriage and therefore has the power to corrupt society in a unique way.

LIBERAL EMERGING CHURCH ERROR #15
WEAK ON THE SUBSTITUTIONARY ATONEMENT

The substitutionary atonement of Jesus Christ is the doctrine of salvation through the cross-work of Christ, salvation through the blood. God condemns and judges sin and only through the blood and death of His sinless Son, who suffered as man's substitute, is God propitiated and His Law satisfied. On the basis of Christ's atonement, the believing sinner is justified or declared righteous.

This is called substitutionary atonement, penal substitution, and other terms, and there is a great attack upon this doctrine today not only from theologically liberal circles but from evangelicals, as well, and many within the liberal emerging church reject it.

Doug Pagitt says:

> "I certainly believe in sin and forgiveness, but they are not built around a Greek judicial model of separation, rather around a relational call to return to a life in full agreement and rhythm with God. So God does not move away in the midst of our sin, but he moves closer" (*Listening*

to the Beliefs of the Emerging Churches, p. 134).

According to this emerging doctrine of the atonement, God does not separate from sin and does not, then, need to be propitiated by a blood offering. When Pagitt speaks of the "judicial model," he is referring to the doctrine that God is a holy Judge and His Law can only be satisfied by the payment of a proper price. This is not merely a "Greek" model, but a biblical one.

Karen Ward writes:

> "... We are looking for nonpropositional ways of coming to understand the atonement, ways that involve art, ritual, community, etc. ... Upon reflection, it seems to us that theories of atonement are just that, theories, which many faithful Christians will continue to posit and then disagree with. ... We have been drawn to lay down theories and enter atonement as the totality of what God did, does, and will do in Christ (life, death, resurrection, and return). ... WE ARE BEING MOVED, AS A COMMUNITY, BEYOND THEORIES ABOUT ATONEMENT, to enter into atonement itself, or at-one-ment--the new reality and new relationship of oneness with God which God incarnated (in life, cross, and resurrection) and into which we are all invited 'for all time'" (*Listening to the Beliefs of the Emerging Churches*, pp. 163, 164).

According to this emergent leader, the doctrine of Christ's substitutionary blood atonement is only one possible "theory" among many, and their preferred theory is that atonement refers not just to Christ's death, but to His life, death, resurrection, and return.

Brennan Manning says the God of the substitutionary atonement does not exist:

> "[T]he god whose moods alternate between graciousness and fierce anger ... the god who exacts the last drop of blood from his Son so that his just anger, evoked by sin, may be appeased, is not the God revealed by and in Jesus Christ. And if he is not the God of Jesus, HE DOES NOT EXIST" (Brennan Manning, *Above All*, p. 58-59; the foreword to this book is written by CCM artist Michael W. Smith).

Steve Chalke, in his book *The Lost Message of Christ*, denies the substitutionary atonement of Christ, calling it "cosmic child abuse."

Alan Jones says:

> "The Church's fixation on the death of Jesus as the universal saving act must end, and the place of the cross must be reimagined in Christian faith. Why? Because of the cult of suffering and the vindictive God behind it" (*Reimagining Christianity*, p. 132).

> "The other thread of just criticism addresses the suggestion implicit in the cross that Jesus' sacrifice was to appease an angry god. Penal substitution was the name of THIS VILE DOCTRINE" (p. 168).

In a podcast interview in January 2006 with Leif Hansen, Brian McLaren said that the traditional doctrine of the substitutionary atonement makes God into a strange monster that wants to kill his own son and needs to be restrained. He also says the substitutionary atonement detracts from social justice issues. He even mocks the atonement by saying that if it is true it would mean that God can't forgive one person unless he "kicks someone else." Consider this very foolish statement:

> What's so bad about sin? Now, I can just imagine some people quoting--See, McLaren doesn't think sin is a problem. I take sin really, seriously. But here's the problem, If I were to make this sort of analogy or parable. When I had little children, if one of my little children--Let's say my son Brett, was beating up on his little brother, Trevor. Now, Trevor is bigger. But back then--What was the problem? Was the problem that I don't want my younger son to get hurt and I don't want my older son to be a bully? I want my older son to be a good person. I want my younger son to be a good person. I want them to have a great relationship. Then the problem of sin is what it does to my family and what it does to my boys, you know. That's the problem with sin.

> But what we've created is, the problem of sin is that I am so angry at my son Brett for beating up his younger brother, I'm going to kill him. So now the problem we've got to solve is how to keep me from killing my son. Does that make sense?

> And so now it seems to me the entire Christian theology has shifted so now the problem is, how can we keep me from killing Brett? And I don't think that's the kind of God that we serve. I think the problem is God wants His children to get along with each other. He wants them to be good people. Because He's good. And His vision for creation is that they'll love each other and be good to each other and enjoy each other and have a lot of fun together. ...

> We have a vision that the real problem is God wants to kill us all. And we've got to somehow solve that problem. ...
>
> The traditional understanding says that God asks of us something that God is incapable of Himself. God asks us to forgive people. But God is incapable of forgiving. God can't forgive unless He punishes somebody in place of the person He was going to forgive. God doesn't say things to you--Forgive your wife, and then go kick the dog to vent your anger. God asks you to actually forgive. And there's a certain sense that, a common understanding of the atonement presents a God who is incapable of forgiving. Unless He kicks somebody else (McLaren, http://www.understandthetimes.org/mclarentrans.shtml and http://str.typepad.com/weblog/2006/01/brian_mclaren_p.html).

What McLaren ignores is God's holiness and justice. God is not just a father like a human father. He is a holy and just God who has given man His righteous Law. That Law, having been broken, must be satisfied. The wages of sin is death. Without the shedding of blood is no remission. And to provide the atonement, God hasn't "kicked" anyone but Himself!

WHAT DOES THE BIBLE SAY?

Atonement speaks of the price that was demanded by God's just and holy Law for man's sin.

The word is used 80 times in the Old Testament, and it refers to the payment of a price to propitiate God, either by money (Ex. 30:16) or by a blood sacrifice (e.g., Lev. 16:15-16). The Old Testament sacrifices pointed to Christ as *"the Lamb of God, which taketh away the sin of the world"* (John 1:29).

The word is used only once in the New Testament, referring to the blood and death of Christ, and it is used in association with the terms "justified" and "reconciled."

> "Much more then, being now justified by his blood, we shall be saved from wrath through him. For if, when we were enemies, we were reconciled to God by the death of his Son, much more, being reconciled, we shall be saved by his life. And not only so, but we also joy in God through our Lord Jesus Christ, by whom we have now received the atonement" (Romans 5:9-11).

In this passage we see that the atonement refers to a sinner being declared righteous (justified) and saved from wrath and reconciled to a holy God through Christ's sacrifice. Both blood (Rom. 5:9) and death (Rom. 5:10) were required to make the atonement. Death was required, because *"the wages of sin is death"* (Rom. 6:23), and blood was required, because *"without shedding of blood is no remission"* (Heb. 9:22).

We don't have to fully understand the Bible's doctrine of the atonement; we only have to believe it and rejoice in it!

A corresponding Bible term is "propitiation" (1 Jn. 2:2; 4:10; Rom. 3:25), which means satisfaction, as when a debt is satisfied and paid in full. The Greek word translated "propitiation" (*hilasmos*) is also translated "mercy seat" in Hebrews 9:5. The atonement was signified by the fact that the Old Testament mercy seat perfectly covered the tables of the Law in the Ark of the Covenant, and it was sprinkled with blood every year at the Day of Atonement (Lev. 16:15-16).

The cross-work of Christ was the SUFFICIENT payment that satisfied the demand of God's Law, so that the believing sinner is set at liberty.

> "Surely he hath borne our griefs, and carried our sorrows: yet we did esteem him stricken, smitten of God, and afflicted. But he was wounded for our transgressions, he was bruised for our iniquities: the chastisement of our peace was upon him; and with his stripes we are healed. All we like sheep have gone astray; we have turned every one to his own way; and the LORD hath laid on him the iniquity of us all" (Isaiah 53:4-6).

> "Even as the Son of man came not to be ministered unto, but to minister, and to give his life a ransom for many" (Matthew 20:28).

> "Being justified freely by his grace through the redemption that is in Christ Jesus: Whom God hath set forth to be a propitiation through faith in his blood, to declare his righteousness for the remission of sins that are past, through the forbearance of God" (Romans 3:24-25).

> "Purge out therefore the old leaven, that ye may be a new lump, as ye are unleavened. For even Christ our passover is sacrificed for us" (1 Corinthians 5:7).

"For ye are bought with a price: therefore glorify God in your body, and in your spirit, which are God's" (1 Corinthians 6:20).

"And all things are of God, who hath reconciled us to himself by Jesus Christ, and hath given to us the ministry of reconciliation; to wit, that God was in Christ, reconciling the world unto himself, not imputing their trespasses unto them; and hath committed unto us the word of reconciliation" (2 Corinthians 5:18-19).

"For he hath made him to be sin for us, who knew no sin; that we might be made the righteousness of God in him" (2 Corinthians 5:21).

"Who gave himself for our sins, that he might deliver us from this present evil world, according to the will of God and our Father" (Galatians 1:4).

"I am crucified with Christ: nevertheless I live; yet not I, but Christ liveth in me: and the life which I now live in the flesh I live by the faith of the Son of God, who loved me, and gave himself for me" (Galatians 2:20).

"And walk in love, as Christ also hath loved us, and hath given himself for us an offering and a sacrifice to God for a sweetsmelling savour" (Ephesians 5:2).

"For there is one God, and one mediator between God and men, the man Christ Jesus; Who gave himself a ransom for all, to be testified in due time" (1 Timothy 2:5-6).

"Who gave himself for us, that he might redeem us from all iniquity, and purify unto himself a peculiar people, zealous of good works" (Titus 2:14).

"For such an high priest became us, who is holy, harmless, undefiled, separate from sinners, and made higher than the heavens; Who needeth not daily, as those high priests, to offer up sacrifice, first for his own sins, and then for the people's: for this he did once, when he offered up himself" (Heb. 7:26, 27).

"Neither by the blood of goats and calves, but by his own blood he entered in once into the holy place, having obtained eternal redemption for us" (Heb. 9:12).

"So Christ was once offered to bear the sins of many; and unto them that look for him shall he appear the second time without sin unto salvation" (Heb. 9:28).

"By the which will we are sanctified through the offering of the body of Jesus Christ once for all. And every priest standeth daily ministering and offering oftentimes the same sacrifices, which can never take away sins: But this man, after he had offered one sacrifice for sins for ever, sat down on the right hand of God" (Heb. 10:10-12).

"Forasmuch as ye know that ye were not redeemed with corruptible things, as silver and gold, from your vain conversation received by tradition from your fathers; but with the precious blood of Christ, as of a lamb without blemish and without spot" (1 Peter 1:18-19).

"Who his own self bare our sins in his own body on the tree, that we, being dead to sins, should live unto righteousness: by whose stripes ye were healed" (1 Peter 2:24).

"Hereby perceive we the love of God, because he laid down his life for us: and we ought to lay down our lives for the brethren" (1 John 3:16).

"And from Jesus Christ, who is the faithful witness, and the first begotten of the dead, and the prince of the kings of the earth. Unto him that loved us, and washed us from our sins in his own blood" (Revelation 1:5).

"And they sung a new song, saying, Thou art worthy to take the book, and to open the seals thereof: for thou wast slain, and hast redeemed us to God by thy blood out of every kindred, and tongue, and people, and nation" (Revelation 5:9).

It is necessary to emphasize the fact that both BLOOD *and* DEATH were required by God's Law. Some modern teachers claim that the blood is merely symbolic of Christ's death, and some modern Bible translations exchange the word "blood" for "death." This is a great error. Christ's shed blood was required as surely as His death. We have seen how that in Romans 5:9-10 both aspects of the atonement are in view. Leviticus chapters 1-9 describe the Old Testament sacrifices, which depicted Christ's atoning sacrifice. In this passage the word "death" is mentioned 22 times, whereas the word "blood" is mentioned 44 times. Again, we see that BOTH blood and death were required for the atonement.

An example of the denial of the blood atonement is found in the writings of Bible Society leader Eugene Nida.

"Most scholars, both Protestant and Roman Catholic, interpret the references to the redemption of the believer by Jesus Christ, not as evidence of any commercial transaction by any *quid pro quo* between Christ and God or between the 'two natures of God' (his love and his justice), but as A FIGURE of the 'cost,' in terms of suffering" (Nida and Charles Taber, *Theory and Practice*, 1969, p. 53, n. 19).

Nida was co-author (with Barclay Newman) of the United Bible Societies' publication *A Translator's Handbook on Paul's Letter to the Romans*. Commenting on Romans 3:25, which says, "Whom God hath set forth to be a propitiation through faith in his blood," this commentary states:

> "... 'blood' is used in this passage in the same way that it is used in a number of other places in the New Testament, that is, to indicate a violent death. ... Although this noun [propitiation] (and its related forms) is sometimes used by pagan writers in the sense of propitiation (that is, an act to appease or placate a god), it is never used this way in the Old Testament."

In *Good News for Everyone*, Nida's defense of the *Today's English Version* (also known as the *Good News for Modern Man*), he says:

> "To translate *haima* as 'blood' in Acts 20:28 (as in traditional translations ...) could give the impression that Christ's blood became an object of barter, as though focus were on the substance of the blood rather than on the death of the person, for which the substance is a FIGURATIVE substitute" (p. 77).

Nida's view of the atonement is held by many theologians today, but the fact remains that it is heretical. The sacrifice of Christ was not just a figure; it WAS a placation of God--of His holiness and of the righteous demands in His Law. Christ's sacrifice WAS a commercial transaction between Christ and God, and was NOT merely *a figure* of the cost.

The sacrifice of Calvary was a true sacrifice, and that sacrifice required the offering of blood--not just a violent death. Blood is blood and death is death, and we believe that God knows the meaning of words. Had Christ died, for example, by hanging, it would not have atoned for sin because blood is also required.

Those who tamper with the blood atonement claim to believe in justification by grace, but they are rendering the Cross ineffective by reinterpreting its meaning. There is no grace without a true propitiation. Grace is a gift, and a gift is something that is purchased with a price.

Christ's atonement is FULL and is UNLIMITED. Paul Reiter notes that Christ died for all (1 Tim. 2:6; Isa. 53:6). He died for every man (Heb. 2:9). He died for the world (John 3:16). He died for the sins of the whole world (1 John 2:2). He died for the ungodly (Rom. 5:6). He died for false teachers (2 Pet. 2:1). He died for many (Mat. 20:28). He died for Israel (John 11:50-51). He died for the Church (Eph. 5:25). He died for "me" (Gal. 2:20).

LIBERAL EMERGING CHURCH ERROR #16 FEMALE CHURCH LEADERS

Eddie Gibbs and Ryan Bolger of Fuller Seminary, who authored a study of the emerging church, said, "Virtually all these communities support women at all levels of ministry…" (p. 11).

The contributors to *An Emergent Manifesto of Hope* include many female church leaders, including Heather Kirk-Davidoff, a minister of the Kittamaqundi Community; Nanette Sawyer and Karen Sloan, ordained ministers in the Presbyterian Church USA; and Deborah Loyd, a founding pastor of The Bridge Church in Portland, Oregon.

Loyd says that "one of our distinctives was the demand that women be afforded equality in every area of endeavor" (*An Emergent Manifesto of Hope*, p. 274).

Sally Morganthaler, a contributor to *An Emergent Manifesto*, seeks to broaden the role of women into "new forms of leadership" (p. 176). She complains that while females make up well over 60 percent of the average congregation's constituency their "representation as leaders outside of children's and women's programs is usually less than 1 percent" (p. 183). She condemns the "engineered neutralization of well over half of the human voices" and "the debilitating DNA of patriarchy" (pp. 183, 184). She claims that Jesus liberated women to positions of leadership (pp. 184, 185). She says, "Women with leadership abilities need to lead because, more often than not, they get this new world and they get it really well" (p. 187).

WHAT DOES THE BIBLE SAY?

The emerging church position on female church leaders is refuted by Jesus' example.

The Lord Jesus Christ honored women greatly and they had an important part in His earthly life and ministry. Many women assisted Him (Lk. 8:2-3). It was a woman that anointed Jesus for His burial prior to His death (Mat. 26:6-13). It was mostly women that stood at the cross (Mat. 27:55-56). It was women that observed Jesus' burial place and came to anoint His body (Lk. 23:55-56). It was women that first came to the empty tomb and first believed the resurrection (Mat. 28:1-6). And it was women that first reported the resurrection to the apostles (Mat. 28:7-8).

But the simple and telling fact remains that there were no female apostles. In Jesus' earthly life and ministry, women were helpers but they were not leaders.

The emerging church position on female church leaders is refuted by Paul's instruction in 1 Timothy 2:11-14.

> "Let the woman learn in silence with all subjection. But I suffer not a woman to teach, nor to usurp authority over the man, but to be in silence. For Adam was first formed, then Eve. And Adam was not deceived, but the woman being deceived was in the transgression."

We see that the woman is to have a humble, teachable spirit and is not to push herself into leadership positions. She is to learn in silence with all subjection. Compare 1 Peter 3:4, *"But let it be the hidden man of the heart, in that which is not corruptible, even the ornament of a meek and quiet spirit, which is in the sight of God of great price."*

The apostle gives two simple restrictions on the woman's ministry. First, she is not allowed to usurp authority over the man. Obviously, then, she can never hold a position such as pastor, since that is an authoritative position. Second, she is not allowed to teach men. This does not mean that a woman can never talk to a man about the Lord. Not long ago I received an e-mail from a woman who wanted to talk to her father-in-law about the Lord and asked if I thought that would be appropriate. I told her that she should definitely talk to her father-in-law about Christ. The women who arrived first at Christ's empty tomb were told to go and tell the disciples that Jesus had risen (Mat. 28:7-8). We cannot ignore plain restrictions in other passages, such as 1 Timothy 2:12, but the example in Matthew 28 does tell us that women can testify to men under certain conditions. What 1 Timothy 2:12 means that the woman cannot teach with authority. She is forbidden to teach or preach from the pulpit to a mixed congregation or to teach a mixed Sunday School class or to teach at a Bible conference to mixed crowds or to teach biblical subjects in a Bible college class. When a woman stands before a mixed crowd that includes men and opens the Bible and preaches or teaches, she is taking authority. There is no more authoritative thing in the world than to teach or preach the Bible. God's Word forbids a woman to do that.

God tells us the reason for these limitations. First, the order of creation requires them. The woman was created after the man to be his helpmeet and not his head (1 Tim. 2:13). Second, the woman's nature requires these limitations (1 Tim. 2:14). The woman was not created to lead but to serve and she was given the equipment to do the latter and not former. As a result of this, she is more easily deceived than the man. There are exceptions, of course, but this is the rule. In the Garden of Eden Satan targeted the woman with his deception.

The emerging church position on female church leaders is also refuted by Paul's teaching in 1 Corinthians 14:34-35.

"Let your women keep silence in the churches: for it is not permitted unto them to speak; but they are commanded to be under obedience, as also saith the law. And if they will learn any thing, let them ask their husbands at home: for it is a shame for women to speak in the church."

The context here is teaching and prophesying. The woman is not allowed to speak out in the church services in the sense of teaching or preaching. She is forbidden to teach men or to usurp authority over them (1 Tim. 2:12). I do not believe it is appropriate for a woman to lead in public prayer in a mixed congregation. 1 Timothy 2:8 says it is the men who should lead in prayer. I do not believe that it is appropriate for a woman to lead the singing in a mixed congregation or choir. She simply should not be put into any position whereby she is leading men in spiritual matters.

This does not mean, though, that a woman can never say anything in church. She can sing and testify in due order. A woman can testify about what God has done in her life without getting into a teaching/preaching mode, but she must be careful that she limits herself to a proper capacity. If there is an open question and answer time, women can participate, but she is not to blurt out questions in a disorderly fashion in other contexts. What Paul is warning about in the context of 1 Corinthians 14 is disorderliness and the exercise of ministry gifts.

The emerging church position on female church leaders is refuted by the biblical qualifications for church office.

God's standards for pastors and deacons do not fit a woman, in that one of the qualifications is that the officeholder be *"the husband of one wife"* (1 Tim. 3:2, 12; Titus 1:6). As for the women leaders in the Old Testament, such as Deborah, I have replied to that in the article "Women Leaders in the

Bible." See http://www.wayoflife.org/fbns/fbns/fbns150.html.

THE CONSERVATIVE EMERGING CHURCH

As we mentioned at the beginning of this book, there are two distinct streams that feed the broad river of the emerging church.

One is the more radical side that is represented by Brian McLaren and the Emergent Village. We will call it **THE LIBERAL EMERGING CHURCH**. *In doctrine*, it is flexible, tolerant, non-dogmatic, rethinking, evolving. It is dismissive of the Bible as verbal-plenarily inspired, infallible, and the sole authority for faith and practice. It is hesitant about holding a doctrinal statement of faith and if it does hold one it is usually very limited (such as the so-called Apostles' Creed). *In worship*, it is experimental and borrows heavily from "ancient spirituality," incorporating candles, incense, dim lighting, ambient music, labyrinths, icons, prayer stations, art, dance, meditation, silence. *In mission*, the emphasis of the liberal emerging church is on kingdom building in the world today and developing relationships with the unsaved, with no strict line between the church and the world. It is heavily involved with a social-justice-environmentalist gospel and often accepts people as part of God's family even when they do not have personal faith in Jesus Christ.

The other stream is less radical. For lack of a better term we will call it **THE CONSERVATIVE EMERGING CHURCH**. It is represented by men such as Mark Driscoll of Seattle and the Acts 29 church planting network. They have a higher view of the Bible and want to maintain a solid doctrinal foundation (particularly Calvinistic Reformed theology), but they are open to worldly, "cultural affirming" techniques of church growth because "the old methods aren't working." One report says that they are "not necessarily trying to rewrite theology, but offer innovative methods of ministry" ("Conference examines the emerging church," Baptist Press, Sept. 25, 2007). Driscoll claims to be "theologically conservative and culturally liberal."

Many men have made an effort to distinguish between various streams of the emergent church.

Mark Driscoll uses the terms "emergent liberals" and "emerging evangelicals," putting himself into the latter group (*Confessions of a Reformission Rev.*, pp. 21-23).

We believe, though, that an attempt to make a sharp distinction between the terms *emergent* and *emerging* is confusing to the average person and won't hold up in the long term. The two terms are often used today as synonyms. Further, even those of the liberal stream of the emerging church fall within the broad category of "evangelicals," so the distinction between "emerging liberals" and "emerging evangelicals" cannot be maintained. The emerging church in all of its facets fits under the broad umbrella of modern evangelicalism, so it is "evangelical" even when it is liberal. (If you find that confusing, I am not surprised, but it is only because of the confusion that reigns within contemporary evangelicalism.)

Ed Stetzer of the Southern Baptist Convention coined the term "relevant" to describe the more conservative stream, because they want to be "relevant" to modern culture. Yet the term "relevant" could as easily be applied to both streams of the emerging church, since the desire to be relevant to modern culture is a distinguishing feature of the entire field. They differ only in how far they will go in this venture.

Some use the term "missional" to describe the conservative side of the emerging church, but the liberal emerging churches also like that term, so it is of little help in distinguishing between various aspects of the movement.

I considered using the terms *doctrinal* and *non-doctrinal* to distinguish the two major streams of the emerging church, since one stream is much more oriented toward doctrinal truth and less relativistic than the other. But in the end I decided that those terms are too cumbersome.

We have decided to use the terms "liberal" and "conservative" to describe the two branches, though these are not ideal. While "liberal" is a perfectly good term for the most radical side of the emerging church, it is with great difficulty that we use the term "conservative" to describe the less liberal type of emerging churches. They are "conservative" only when compared to the liberal stream!

SOME INFLUENTIAL VOICES

JOHN BURKE is the founder of Gateway Community Church in Austin, Texas, and the Emerging Leadership Initiative (ELI), which is "devoted to partnerships that empower planters of emerging churches." Prior to this, he was on the management team of Willow Creek Community Church. He is the author of *No Perfect People Allowed*.

MARK DRISCOLL (b. 1970) is co-founder of Mars Hill Church in Seattle and president of the Acts 29 church planting network. Driscoll was once closely affiliated with the men who have gone on to form the liberal emerging church, but he has pulled away from them. He says:

> "In the mid-1990s I was part of what is now known as the emerging church and spent some time traveling the country to speak on the emerging church in the emerging culture on a team put together by Leadership Network called the Young Leader Network. But, I eventually had to distance myself from the Emergent stream of the network because friends like Brian McLaren and Doug Pagitt began pushing a theological agenda that greatly troubled me. Examples include referring to God as a chick, questioning God's sovereignty over and knowledge of the future, denial of the substitutionary atonement of the cross, a low view of Scripture, and denial of hell which is one hell of a mistake" (Mark Driscoll, http://theresurgence.com/?q=node/5).

DAN KIMBALL is pastor of Vintage Faith Church in Santa Cruz, California, and author of *They Like Jesus but Not the Church.*

ERWIN MCMANUS (b. 1958) is pastor of Mosaic in Los Angeles and author of *The Barbarian Way* (2005) and *Wide Awake* (2008). Mosaic is an old Southern Baptist Church that has been taken into the emerging direction by McManus.

TIM STEVENS is pastor of Granger Community church, Granger, Indiana, and author of *Simply Strategic Stuff, Simply Strategic Volunteers,* and *Simply Strategic Growth.*

RICK MCKINLEY is founding pastor of Imago Dei Community in Portland, Oregon. He is the author of *Jesus in the Margins: Finding God in the Places We Ignore* (Multnomah, 2005) and *This Beautiful Mess: Conversations on the Kingdom* (Multnomah, 2006).

RICK WARREN (b. 1954), pastor of Saddleback Church in southern California, is a mentor of the emerging church and is closely affiliated with all branches of it. Warren wrote the foreword to *The Emerging Church* edited by Dan Kimball.

The ACTS 29 church planting network follows this philosophy. It was co-founded by Mark Driscoll.

Many Southern Baptists are taking this path. Rick Warren is a Southern Baptist. McManus and other Mosaic leaders teach at the Southern Baptist Golden Gate Theological Seminary. Ed Stetzer, director of LifeWay Research, is on the Acts 29 board and some of their church plants are affiliated with the SBC.

Jason Jaggar of Mosaic spoke at Liberty University in Lynchburg, Virginia, in 2007.

NEW EVANGELICALISM SET THE STAGE FOR THE EMERGING CHURCH

The emerging church is simply the twenty-first century face of New Evangelicalism.

Andy Crouch calls the emerging church "post-evangelicalism." He says:

> "The emerging movement is a protest against much of evangelicalism as currently practiced. It is post-evangelical in the way that neo-evangelicalism (in the 1950s) was post-fundamentalist. It would not be unfair to call it postmodern evangelicalism" ("The Emergent Mystique," *Christianity Today*, Nov. 2004).

The late Robert Webber also observed the association between the emerging church and the neo-evangelicalism of the 1940s and 1950s. He taught that the emerging church is the latest of four movements that have occurred within evangelicalism since 1946, the first being neo-evangelicalism.

> "The new or neo-evangelicalism, as it was first called, broke away from its roots in the fundamentalism of the first half of the century. The new evangelicalism regarded fundamentalism as 'anti-intellectual, anti-social action, and anti-ecumenical.' Influential leaders called for engagement with philosophy and the intellectual ideas of the day, to the recovery of a robust involvement with social issues, and to a new form of ecumenical cooperation, especially in evangelism. ... The new evangelical theology distanced itself from fundamentalist biblicism ... They wanted to spar with the best, engage secularists and liberals on their own turf, and create institutions of higher learning that would command respect" (*Listening to the Beliefs of Emerging Churches*, p. 11).

The intimate association between New Evangelicalism and the emerging church is witnessed by *Christianity Today*. This magazine was founded by Billy Graham and his friends in 1956 as a mouthpiece for the New Evangelical movement. Today it is a mouthpiece for the emerging church. A section of their web site, called "The Emergence of Emergent," is dedicated to it, and they have published many positive articles dealing with it, including several by Brian McLaren.

Marshall Shelley, vice president of *Christianity Today*, said of Spencer Burke's *An Heretic's Guide to Eternity*, which is foreworded by McLaren: "Spencer is a winsome walking companion for those who find traditional dogma too narrow. It's a thoughtful conversation" (http://www.spencerburke.com/pdf/presskit.pdf).

The emerging church is the natural progression of New Evangelicalism. Let's go back a half century and consider some of its history.

The founders of New Evangelicalism grew up in fundamentalist homes as the fundamentalist-modernist controversy of the first half of the twentieth century was winding down. They were the proverbial new generation. *"And also all that generation were gathered unto their fathers: and there arose another generation after them, which knew not the LORD, nor yet the works which he had done for Israel"* (Judges 2:10).

In the first half of the 20th century, evangelicalism in America was largely synonymous with fundamentalism. George Marsden (*Reforming Fundamentalism*) says, "There was not a practical distinction between fundamentalist and evangelical: the words were interchangeable" (p. 48). When the National Association of Evangelicals (NAE) was formed in 1942, for example, participants included such fundamentalist leaders as Bob Jones, Sr., John R. Rice, Charles Woodbridge, Harry Ironside, and David Otis Fuller.

By the mid-1950s, though, a clear break between separatist fundamentalists and non-separatist evangelicals occurred. This was occasioned largely by the ecumenical evangelism of Billy Graham. The separatists dropped out of the NAE. The terms *evangelicalism* and *fundamentalism* began "to refer to two different movements" (William Martin, *A Prophet with Honor*, p. 224).

The sons and grandsons of the old-time evangelical-fundamentalist preachers determined to create a "New Evangelicalism." They would not be fighters; they would be diplomats, positive in their emphasis rather than militant. They would not be restricted by a separationist mentality.

The very influential Harold Ockenga claimed to have coined the term "new evangelical" in 1948. He was pastor of Park Street Church in Boston, founder of the National Association of Evangelicals, co-founder and first president of Fuller Seminary, first president of the World Evangelical Fellowship, president of Gordon College, on the board of directors for the Billy Graham Evangelistic Association, chairman of the Gordon-Conwell Theological Seminary, and one-time editor of *Christianity Today*.

Following is how Ockenga defined New Evangelicalism:

> "Neo-evangelicalism was born in 1948 in connection with a convocation address which I gave in the Civic Auditorium in Pasadena. While reaffirming the theological view of fundamentalism, this address REPUDIATED ITS ECCLESIOLOGY AND ITS SOCIAL THEORY. The ringing call for A REPUDIATION OF SEPARATISM AND THE SUMMONS TO SOCIAL INVOLVEMENT received a hearty response from many evangelicals. The name caught on and spokesmen such as Drs. Harold Lindsell, Carl F.H. Henry, Edward Carnell, and Gleason Archer supported this viewpoint. We had no intention of launching a movement, but found that the emphasis attracted widespread support and exercised great influence. Neo-evangelicalism... DIFFERENT FROM FUNDAMENTALISM IN ITS REPUDIATION OF SEPARATISM AND ITS DETERMINATION TO ENGAGE ITSELF IN THE THEOLOGICAL DIALOGUE OF THE DAY. IT HAD A NEW EMPHASIS UPON THE APPLICATION OF THE GOSPEL TO THE SOCIOLOGICAL, POLITICAL, AND ECONOMIC AREAS OF LIFE. Neo-evangelicals emphasized the restatement of Christian theology in accordance with the need of the times, the REENGAGEMENT IN THE THEOLOGICAL DEBATE, THE RECAPTURE OF DENOMINATIONAL LEADERSHIP, AND THE REEXAMINATION OF THEOLOGICAL PROBLEMS SUCH AS THE ANTIQUITY OF MAN, THE UNIVERSALITY OF THE FLOOD, GOD'S METHOD OF CREATION, AND OTHERS." (Harold J. Ockenga, foreword to *The Battle for the Bible* by Harold Lindsell).

Regardless of who coined the term "New Evangelical," it is certain that it described the mood of positivism and non-militancy that characterized that generation.

Ockenga and the new generation of evangelicals determined to abandon a militant Bible stance. Instead, they would pursue dialogue, intellectualism, non-judgmentalism, and appeasement. They refused to leave the denominations, even though they were permeated with theological modernism, determining to change things from within. The New Evangelical would dialogue with those who teach error. The New Evangelical would meet the proud humanist and the haughty liberal on their own turf with human scholarship rather than follow the humble path of being counted a fool for Christ's sake by standing simply upon the Bible. New Evangelical leaders also determined to start a "rethinking process" whereby the old paths were to be continually reassessed in light of new goals, methods, and ideology.

New Evangelicalism further called for a social aspect to the gospel -- "a new emphasis upon the application of the gospel to the sociological, political, and economic areas of life" (Ockenga, foreword to the *Battle for the Bible*).

New Evangelicalism rejected the old traditional standards of separation from the world, and the result has been the strange rock & roll Christian culture.

In 1978 Richard Quebedeux wrote *The Worldly Evangelicals*, documenting the dramatic changes that were already occurring within evangelicalism a mere thirty years after the onslaught of the spirit of "Newism." He said:

> "Evolutionary theory, in a theistic context, is now taken for granted by many evangelical scientists. ... Biblical criticism has now made inroads in almost all evangelical colleges and seminaries. In fact, a few evangelical biblical scholars actually stand to the left of their liberal counterparts on some points. ... it is becoming more and more difficult to recruit young pastors who have not been deeply influenced both by biblical criticism and by the behavioral sciences. ... Prior to the 60s, virtually all the seminaries and colleges associated with the neo-

evangelicals and their descendants adhered to the total inerrancy understanding of biblical authority (at least they did not vocally express opposition to it). But it is a well-known fact that a large number, if not most, of the colleges and seminaries in question now have faculty who no longer believe in total inerrancy. ... The position affirming that Scripture is inerrant or infallible in its teaching on matters of faith and conduct, but not necessarily in all its assertions concerning history and the cosmos, is gradually becoming ascendant among the most highly respected evangelical theologians. ... Indeed, the new theological heroes of the evangelical left are Karl Barth, Emil Brunner, and Dietrich Bonhoeffer... Clearly and undisputedly, the evangelical left is far closer to Bonhoeffer, Brunner, and Barth than to Hodges and Warfield on the inspiration and authority of Scripture" (*The Worldly Evangelicals*, pp. 15, 30, 88, 100).

Quebedeaux observed that "the wider culture has had a profound impact on the evangelical movement as a whole" (p. 115). Though Quebedeaux didn't make the connection, this is a direct result of the repudiation of separation. He said:

"In the course of establishing their respectability in the eyes of the wider society, the evangelicals have become harder and harder to distinguish from other people. Upward social mobility has made the old revivalistic taboos dysfunctional. ... the COCKTAILS became increasingly difficult to refuse. Evangelical young people LEARNED HOW TO DANCE AND OPENLY 'GROOVED' ON ROCK MUSIC. ... And evangelical magazines and newspapers began REVIEWING PLAYS AND MOVIES. ... The Gallup Poll is correct in asserting that born-again Christians 'believe in a strict moral code.' BUT THAT STRICTNESS HAS BEEN CONSIDERABLY MODIFIED DURING THE LAST FEW YEARS ... DIVORCE AND REMARRIAGE are becoming more frequent and acceptable among evangelicals of all ages, even in some of their more conservative churches. ... Some evangelical women are taking advantage of ABORTION on demand. Many younger evangelicals occasionally use PROFANITY in their speech and writing . . . Some of the recent evangelical sex-technique books assume that their readers peruse and view PORNOGRAPHY on occasion, and they do. Finally, in 1976 there emerged a fellowship and information organization for practicing evangelical LESBIANS AND GAY MEN and their sympathizers. There is probably just as high a percentage of gays in the evangelical movement as in the wider society. Some of them are now coming out of the closet, distributing well-articulated literature, and demanding to be recognized and affirmed by the evangelical community at large. ... It is profoundly significant that evangelicals, even the more conservative among them, have ACCEPTED THE ROCK MODE. This acceptance, obviously, indicates a further chapter in the death of self-denial and world rejection among them. ... When young people were converted in the

> Jesus movement, many of them simply did not give up their former habits, practices, and cultural attitudes--DRINKING, SMOKING, AND CHARACTERISTIC DRESS AND LANGUAGE. ... Young evangelicals drink, but so do conservative evangelicals like Hal Lindsey and John Warwick Montgomery (who is a member of the International Wine and Food Society). ... But EVEN MARIJUANA, now virtually legal in some areas of the United States, is not as forbidden among young evangelicals as it once was. A few of them, particularly the intellectuals, do smoke it on occasion..." (*The Worldly Evangelicals*, pp. 14, 16, 17, 118, 119).

When light associates with darkness, when truth associates with error, the result is always the corruption of light and truth. *"Be not deceived: evil communications corrupt good manners"* (1 Cor. 15:33), and, *"A little leaven leaveneth the whole lump"* (1 Cor. 5:6; Gal. 5:9).

Quebedeaux observed that evangelicals were fluid in their doctrinal convictions, moving toward "the left":

> "In the present 'identity confusion' among evangelicals, MANY ARE IN TRANSITION, moving from one stance to another (GENERALLY FROM RIGHT TO CENTER OR LEFT)" (*The Worldly Evangelicals*, p. 27).

Over the past 30 years since Quebedeaux published *The Worldly Evangelicals*, the apostasy within evangelicalism has continued to spread and exercise its corrupt leaven in countless ways.

It is obvious that the emerging church is not something new. It is just another wrinkle in New Evangelicalism's deeply compromised history and the latest wrinkle of end-time apostasy.

Those who reject "separatism" feel that they are only rejecting "extremism," but in reality they are rejecting the God-ordained means of protection from spiritual pollution.

(For more about this see our book *New Evangelicalism: Its History, Characteristics, and Fruit*, available from Way of Life Literature.)

ERRORS OF THE CONSERVATIVE EMERGING CHURCH

Following are some of the chief errors of the conservative emerging church. As we will see, it shares some errors with the liberal emerging church, but it draws back from major heresies such as universalism and the rejection of the substitutionary atonement.

CONSERVATIVE EMERGING CHURCH ERROR # 1
WORLDLINESS

They claim that they relate to the world without being conformed to it, but in reality they are deeply conformed to it. They don't think of themselves as worldly, but in reality they are very worldly!

Dan Kimball uses the term "missional," which is the same term used by the liberal emerging church, and defines this as being "very much in the world and engaged in culture but not conforming to the world" (*They Like Jesus*, p. 20).

In spite of such bold claims, the capitulation to the world among conservative emergents is obvious to those who have eyes to see. But the frog that jumps into a pot of water that is gradually warmed is unable to detect what is happening to him until it is too late.

Scott Thomas, director of Acts 29, says:

> "God is significantly using our network to influence and shape the church planting culture through BOTH rock-solid theology and contextualizing the gospel. We will not waver on either of these commitments. We won't water down our theology to reach more people AND WE WON'T ATTACK THE CULTURE IN THE NAME OF CHRISTIANITY" (http://www.acts29network.org/about/welcome/).

These are contradictory statements. You can't be faithful to the Bible (having rock-solid theology) if you "contextualize the gospel" and refuse to attack the sinful and satanic side of culture, which is a very large side of it in a world in which the devil is god (2 Cor. 4:4)!

God's Word commands, *"And have no fellowship with the unfruitful works of darkness, BUT RATHER REPROVE THEM"* (Eph. 5:11).

Imago Dei Community in Portland, Oregon, rejects the "isolationist" position of relating to mainstream culture, which "out of fear of being tainted by the degrading elements" removes itself and sets up rules such as "don't watch R-rated movies, listen to mainstream music, or read the wrong books" (http://www.imagodeicommunity.com/worship--beauty/cultural-engagement/cultural-engagement-vision).

Emergents mockingly call the separatist stance the "Christian ghetto" or "fortress mentality."

Mark Driscoll claims to be "THEOLOGICALLY CONSERVATIVE AND CULTURALLY LIBERAL" ("Pastor Provocateur," *Christianity Today*, Sept. 21, 2007). He criticizes "hardcore fundamentalism that throws rocks at culture" (ibid.). He defines himself as "relevant," "contextual," and "cool" ("Conference examines the emerging church," Baptist Press, Sept. 25, 2007).

Driscoll continually talks against "rules." He says, "But rules, regulations, and the pursuit of outward morality are ultimately incapable of preventing sin" (*The Radical Reformission*, p. 40). In a sermon that I heard him preach on January 27, 2008, he blasted rules and regulations as contrary to grace. While it is true that rules can be misused in the Christian life and obedience to rules as the means of holiness apart from regeneration and the power of the Holy Spirit is vain, it is foolish for a preacher to attack rules without making himself clear on this point. If "rules" were wrong and unnecessary, the New Testament would not be literally filled with rules for Christian living. In the epistle of Ephesians alone, which is the epistle that says we are saved by grace without works, I have counted 88 particular rules that the believer is exhorted to live by in chapters 4-6.

Driscoll describes Jesus as a party guy who hung out with "the kids in high school who always wear black concert T-shirts, sport greasy male ponytails, and smoke cigarettes just off school property during lunch" (*The Radical Reformission*, p. 30). He says Jesus started his ministry "as a bartender" and told "knock-knock jokes to miscreants who loved his sense of humor" (p. 30).

Driscoll's book *The Radical Reformission* contains testimonies of members of his church who proudly work in occupations that are drenched in sin, including a country music radio disc jockey who says, "I don't think you separate the sacred from the secular (p. 63); an owner of tattoo studios who claims that those who reject the tattoo culture are Pharisees (p. 114); a rock band manager who says that "it isn't the job of my band to preach the gospel" (p. 137); the owner of a brewery, who says, "I have been unable to find evidence in my own experience or from my friends' experience that drinking is habit-forming or addictive in and of itself" (p. 156); and a television broadcast analyst who says, "As believers, we need to be involved in Hollywood" (p. 179).

Driscoll says, "Restrictive Christians go too far and name everything a universal sin, forbidding some culture activities that the Bible does not, such as listening to certain musical styles, getting tattoos, watching movies, smoking cigarettes, consuming alcohol, and body piercing" (*The Radical Reformission*, p. 103).

Driscoll says that he learned to preach by "studying stand-up comedians." He said that seeing the filthy comedian Chris

Rock live was "a better study in homiletics than most classes on the subject" (*Confessions of a Reformission Rev.*, p. 70).

Mark Driscoll's church sets up a "champagne bar" at its New Year's Eve parties. The December 2007 party was called "Red Hot Bash2" and featured Bobby Medina and his Red Hot Band, "one of the top dance bands in the Northwest," which play everything "from Swing to Latin to Motown and beyond." Participants were invited to "come bust a move on the enormous dance floor" and were reminded to bring their IDs so they could enjoy the champagne. The church auditorium was "transformed into a post club" and there was a dance contest. Can a woman be biblically modest when she is "busting a move" in modern dance fashion?

Mars Hill has "beer-brewing lessons" for men and operates the Paradox Theater which has hosted hundreds of secular rock concerts for kids. At one concert, a Japanese punk band performed naked. The church didn't approve, but what should you expect from the filthy world of rock & roll? The church also hosts a secular jazz festival. Mars Hill has shown the really cool Seattlites that they can be cool, too.

Mars Hill shows R-rated movies. In fact, Driscoll says that some of his sermons on sex are R-rated and that visiting youth groups have been embarrassed and walked out halfway through the message (*Confessions of a Reformission Rev.*, p. 134).

Driscoll's messages on the Song of Solomon are an example. These were preached in conjunction with the 1978 Song of Solomon Bible Conference tour. He says that the Song of Solomon describes the practice of oral sex and striptease dancing!

Driscoll's blog for September 22, 2007, described his trip to Las Vegas to watch men beat one another to a bloody pulp in Extreme Fighting championships, to take in a raunchy, anti-God comedy routine by George Carlin, and to tour some of the clubs on Sunset Strip (http://www.theresurgence.com/md_blog_2007-09-21_vegas).

Darrin Patrick, founding pastor of the Journey in St. Louis, is the vice president of Acts 29. The Journey hosts a "Theology at the Bottleworks" which is advertised as "grab a brew and give your view" (*Christianity Today*, June 29, 2007).

The Journey also views and discusses R-rated movies at their "film night."

Another Acts 29 church, Damascus Road Church in Marysville, Washington, has a "Men's Poker Night" and invites men to play cards for money. They also have a "Men's Bible and Brew" and a "Men's Movie Night."

Rick Warren's Saddleback Church in California is not to be outdone. The following is from their website for 2005:

> "Our dances have become some of the most anticipated of our social events with hundreds of people attending. This Summer's Night dance in our Worship Center promises to be the same. It will begin with a light buffet style dinner followed by dancing to the sounds of our DJ on a huge 3,000 square foot ballroom competition floor. Professional lighting, effects and sound all blend together for a high-quality experience, all at an extremely reasonable price! Whether you bring a special friend, come alone or with a group, make sure you come ready to have fun! Music will consist of a wide variety providing for specific dances and freestyle. And what's a summer night without some beach music and reggae?"

Saddleback Church features nine different "worship venues." There is a worship style to suit every worldly taste. The Overdrive venue is "for those who like guitar-driven rock band worship in a concert-like setting that you can FEEL." The Ohana venue comes "complete with hula and island-style music," and on the first Saturday of every month you can take hula lessons during the potluck following the service. The Country venue features line dancing.

On April 17, 2005, when Rick Warren announced his P.E.A.C.E. program to Saddleback Church, he sang Jimi

Hendrix's drug-drenched song "Purple Haze" to the congregation, accompanied by his "praise and worship" band! He said he had wanted to do that for a long time.

A Saddleback Worship concert in December 2006 featured teenage girls doing immoral dance moves that included pelvic thrusts.

A video containing a slide show from an Argentina missionary trip by Saddleback Church members featured John Lennon's atheistic song "Imagine." The trip, made August 1-12, 2006, was part of Rick Warren's P.E.A.C.E. program, and the video was published on YouTube. The soundtrack uses several pieces of music, including John Lennon's original recording of *Imagine*. The lyrics say: "Imagine there's no heaven/ It's easy if you try/ No hell below us/ Above us only sky."

Dan Kimball is opposed to "people who are always saying negative things about the world" (*They Like Jesus but Not the Church*, p. 191). He says, "We should be telling people about Jesus and his saving grace rather than judging and condemning them" (p. 106). He sympathizes with unbelievers who "fear that organized religion will try to control how they think, dress, and act" (p. 75). He says we should listen to unbelievers when they criticize us and quotes one who says, "I don't see the point of having to add on all these organized rules like the church leaders think you should do" (p. 74).

The conservative emerging church's illegitimate fusion of the world and Christ is illustrated in the name of Dan Kimball's first worship service. He called it "Graceland," because "it took something familiar in pop culture (Elvis Presley's mansion) and fused it with spiritual meaning." Kimball adds, "Plus, I was a big pre-1960 Elvis fan!" (*The Emerging Church*, p. 37).

Kimball tells about an unbeliever he met at a gym who was surprised that he, a pastor, appreciated rebellious rock groups such as the Cure, the Smiths, Siouxsie, and the Banshees. "She said there was no way that a pastor would ever have liked the Smiths or the Cure, and she was shocked because I seemed normal and not at all what she thought a Christian and especially a pastor would be like" (p. 26).

By just "hanging out" with unbelievers and by loving secular rock & roll and by not condemning sin in a plain manner and by not warning of the dire consequences of unbelief, Kimball appears "normal" to unbelievers, meaning normal after a worldly definition. He is a cool Christian because he loves worldly things and isn't "judgmental" and "negative."

Kimball criticizes fundamentalists who have strong opinions on things such as "the role of women in the church, what type of music to listen to, and which Bible version to use" (p. 54). He agrees with unbelievers who condemn churches for being judgmental about things such as music, smoking, drinking, and dress (p. 98). He says it is wrong to tell homosexuals that unless they change they will go to Hell (p. 99).

Kimball tells of a heavy-metal rocker who was into heavy-metal music and had long hair and an earring and dressed in black leather jackets and "other clothing that fit with the genre of music he liked" (p. 108-109). After he professed Christ and had grown in the Lord he "adopted the dress code of the church," cutting his hair, removing his earring, and such. Kimball complains that this young man's old worldly friends were probably distressed that he had "lost his uniqueness" and had "adopted the dress code of the church" and "conformed to a church subculture." Kimball says, "They probably couldn't help but imagine that becoming a Christian means losing your uniqueness..." (p. 109).

Kimball is a rebel. It is the Bible that teaches that long hair on a man is shameful and that we should not conform to the world or follow the ways of the heathen. We are strangers and pilgrims in this world and we should be different. It is the Bible that dictates the "dress code of the church" and that creates the "church subculture" that the New Evangelical "Relevants" so despise.

Erwin McManus calls upon Christians to live "the barbarian way" in contrast to the traditional Bible path, which he describes as "civilized." He says those on the barbarian way "have little patience for institutions" and do not focus on "requirements" (*The Barbarian Way*, p. 6). He says: "It's hard to imagine that Jesus would endure the agony of the Cross just to keep us in line. Jesus began a revolution to secure our freedom" (p. 7). He says that "raw and untamed faith" should not be restrained and domesticated (p. 10). Just follow your dream without restraint. Those who follow the barbarian way "are not required or expected to keep in step" and "there is no forced conformity" (p. 71). He says that those who are on the barbarian way follow Christ's voice but this voice is not necessarily found in the Bible (p. 84). He says, "Not even God will hold us or control us by fear" (pp. 101, 102). (Contrast this doctrine with Romans 11:20; 2 Corinthians 7:1; Philippians 2:12; 1 Timothy 5:20; Hebrews 4:1; 12:28; 1 Peter 1:17; Jude 23.)

A video clip at McManus' Mosaic web site is a dance sequence set to funky music "where these cool dancers come out on stage and they are beset by these ominous people in suits. In the end the cool people overcome the suit people, who lose their suits and become like the cool people. Message: Don't be a suit--be cool." (This is Brian Snider's description, after watching the video on November 26, 2007.) The meaning of this video, of course, is that professing Christians should "loosen up" and not be so uptight and restrictive about how they dress and how they act. It is an attack against the position of separation from the world.

On March 2, 2008, Granger Community Church in Texas used a song by the rock group Van Halen to accompany a sermon entitled "Tight Like Spandex" (*Slice of Laodicea*, April 14, 2008).

The freedom that the New Evangelical Relevants envision is freedom to listen to raunchy music, watch raunchy movies, dress as I please, frequent bars and sensual rock concerts, pierce and tattoo my body, smoke, dance, drink, gamble, cuss, you name it.

Victory Church in Amarillo, Texas, hosted its third annual Fashionably Loud event on February 24, 2008, featuring fashion models, rock and hip hop music, light shows, break dancing, an electric guitar battle, and other things. The fashions included very low-cut necklines, short skirts, bare midriffs, punk hair styles, and tight pants. The church's senior pastor, David Brown, said, "It helps us to suggest to people that Christians are not living in another world, but the same one everyone else lives in and that Christians can be interested in fashion. Christians can be Christians and yet trendy too" ("Victory Church Is Letter It's Hair Down," Amarillo.com, Feb. 23, 2008). Mike Eminger, associate pastor of student ministries, said: "We will challenge the attendees with the fact that God has fashioned us and that he wants us to live loud, full lives."

The latest attraction among many "relevant" churches is "red hot" conversations on sex. CHARLOTTE SOUTH FELLOWSHIP IN MATHEWS, NORTH CAROLINA, featured a five week series in February 2007 called "Sex Crazy." Two of the messages were "Single and Sexually Satisfied" and "Raising Sexually Satisfied Kids." (Don't ask me what either of those concepts could possibly mean!) In February-March 2007 EASTLAKE COMMUNITY CHURCH IN KIRKLAND, WASHINGTON, had a "Thank God for Sex" campaign. Sermons titles included "Sex is Good" and "Learn Some New Moves." Eastlake advertises itself as a new kind of church and invites attendees to wear their shorts. ROCKY RIVER COMMUNITY CHURCH IN CONCORD, NORTH CAROLINA, had a "Desperate Sex Lives" campaign in February-March 2007. They fretted that "the only time most churches talk about sex is when they speak against it" and promised to "bring sex out of the dark and into the light." This hip church has "all the cool stuff like multimedia, a live band, and Krispy Kreme donuts" and deals with Bible issues "in a casual, no pressure environment." REVOLUTION CHURCH IN CANTON, GEORGIA, is also into the sex campaign business. The sermon series was accompanied by secular rock songs, including "Feel Like Making Love" by Bad Company and "Your Body is a Wonderland" by John Mayer. GRANGER COMMUNITY CHURCH IN GRANGER, INDIANA, had a "My Lame Sex Life" campaign featuring billboards with two pair of feet in a very suggestive configuration. One sermon title was "The Greatest Six You'll Ever Have." CORNERSTONE CHURCH IN CHANDLER, ARIZONA, had a "Bringing Sexy Back" campaign in August-September 2007. One of the sermon titles was "Greatest Sex Ever." THE GATHERING IN SEVIERVILLE, TENNESSEE, had a "Red Hot Sex" campaign in October 2007. It claimed that a "red hot sex life empowers every part of marriage." One sermon title by Pastor Gene Wolfenbarger was "God has designed you for sex and how to make it hot." REVOLUTION CHURCH IN LONGBEACH, CALIFORNIA, kicked off their "God Loves Sex" campaign in July 2007 with a "sex party." The web site explained, "Nothing dirty or weird--just an opportunity to celebrate God's gift of sex and intimacy," and the advertisement said, "God wants you to have great sex." OAKLEAF CHURCH IN CARTERSVILLE, GEORGIA, had a "Your Great Sex Life" campaign in March 2007. The advertisement complained that "the church either ignores sex or brings down a judgmental hammer."

Many other examples could be given.

My friends, this is carnal and foolish and wicked. Bible-believing churches have always taught God's people what the Bible says about sexual relations, but there is no place for this type of thing. What about the single people who attend these campaigns? What are they supposed to do when the church focuses on great sex! What about married couples when one or both partners have become physically disabled? In spite of these churches' claims to the contrary, such campaigns are *not* holy and are *not* faithful to God's Word. The Bible never deals with this issue in a shocking or lascivious manner. The fact is that western society is sex crazy, and these worldly churches are no different.

WHAT DOES THE BIBLE SAY?

We have refuted the error of worldliness in the section on the liberal emerging church. See "Liberal Emerging Church Error # 9: *Worldliness*."

We would add here that the emerging church position is hypocritical. Mark Driscoll mocks those who "separate from culture" and "hide out in a Christian culture" (*The Radical Reformission*, p. 140), but he does the same thing, if only to a different degree.

He teaches his people to give up fornication and to get married and have children and avoid pornography and tithe to God's work and many other things that are contrary to the prevailing culture of the Pacific Northwest where his church is located, so he is guilty of the very thing that he labels Pharisaical! He has created a distinct Christian culture that he believes is based on the Bible.

The world looks at him and his church as separatists! Secular newspaper articles have even called him "fundamentalist." A group calling itself People Against Fundamentalism threatened to picket his church because of his statements about wives submitting to their husbands.

He rejects the fundamentalist's dress standards as "legalistic," *yet he has dress standards*. He wouldn't allow a woman to participate in the worship band in a bathing suit. In fact, Driscoll has many rules for his members and leaders, even requiring that they give to the church and tracking their giving.

Yet he mocks the rules of the fundamentalist as Pharisaical and continually speaks about rules in a disparaging manner.

This is hypocrisy. I can't speak for all biblical fundamentalists, but I can speak for the thousands of them with whom I am associated throughout the world, and I can say that we don't set up rules out of fear or pride or in an effort to become holy through rules. We know that our salvation is through God's grace alone and our holiness is in Jesus Christ and by the indwelling Holy Spirit. We have rules because the New Testament has rules. Period.

We believe that we have to apply the principles of the Bible to our lives in every age. The Bible nowhere specifically forbids heroin use, but Driscoll would not allow his fellow elders to use it. Why? Because there are principles in the Bible that, when applied, forbid believers to get high on heroin. Likewise, the Bible teaches us to be modest in dress and to avoid nakedness and teaches us that men are lustfully attracted to women who are improperly clad, and our guidelines about fashion are simply an attempt to be obedient to this teaching.

The Bible instructs us not to be conformed to the world and to avoid the works of darkness but rather to reprove them, and by avoiding such things as rock music and bar hopping, we are simply trying to be obedient to the Bible's commands.

It is NOT legalistic or Pharisaical for a blood-washed believer to take the Bible seriously and to try to apply it to every area of life!

CONSERVATIVE EMERGING CHURCH ERROR # 2
CONTEMPLATIVE MYSTICISM

We have already documented this in the section on the liberal emerging church, and it is a serious matter. Contemplative mysticism is one of the glues that is bringing together all branches of the emerging church and evangelicalism at large with Roman Catholicism and paganism.

See "Liberal Emerging Church Error # 5: *Contemplative Mysticism*."

CONSERVATIVE EMERGING CHURCH ERROR # 3
THE "INCARNATIONAL DOCTRINE"

A foundational teaching of the conservative emerging church is the idea that Jesus was incarnated into the culture of this world and the Christian is commissioned to do the same thing. They call this "missional." Note the following statements by Mark Driscoll:

> "Jesus' incarnation is in itself missional. God the Father sent God the Son into culture on a mission to redeem the elect by the power of God the Holy Ghost. After his resurrection, Jesus also sent his disciples into culture, on a mission to proclaim the success of his mission, and commissioned all Christians to likewise be missionaries to the cultures of the world (e.g., Matt. 28:18-20; John 20:21; Acts 1:7-8). Emerging and missional Christians have wonderfully rediscovered the significance of Jesus' incarnational example of being a missionary immersed in a culture" (*Confessions of a Reformission Rev.*, p. 26).

> "Missions is every Christian being a missionary to their local culture" (*Confessions of a Reformission Rev.*, p. 19).

The liberal emerging church believes the same thing. Mars Hill Graduate School proclaims:

"We believe a person or community can never receive a hearing, nor offer the gospel, unless it incarnates the gospel through joyful participation in a culture's glory and honest engagement in its darkness. We wish to develop lovers of language, story, drama, film, music, dance, architecture, and art in order to deepen our love of life and the God of all creativity" (Mars Hill Graduate School, http://www.mhgs.edu/common/about.asp#scpriture).

WHAT DOES THE BIBLE SAY?

In answering this we must first emphasize that every Christian IS to be a missionary, and this is an important and biblical challenge.

Too many members of even staunch Bible-believing churches are half-hearted at best about evangelism and have little or no concern for the unsaved. Too often we don't even pass out gospel tracts; we don't spend time each week sharing the gospel with sinners; we don't befriend unbelievers with the goal of winning them to Christ; and we don't have any unbelievers on our daily prayer list.

The conservative emerging church challenges believers to take their responsibility as ambassadors for Christ seriously, and that is something that needs to be shouted from the rooftops. Consider the following challenge:

> "At a recent staff retreat we each wrote out 'missionary letters' like overseas missionaries do when they raise support. We wanted to ask how we are doing as 'missionaries' and what stories we would tell. How do we schedule our week as missionaries?" (*Listening to the Beliefs of Emerging Churches*, p. 103).

This is a good idea. Each member of a New Testament church should consider himself or herself a missionary and should be fully engaged in missionary work. Writing a missionary prayer letter would help the individual see how seriously he is taking this work.

Along this line, it is important for believers to be equipped to deal with the people they meet, whether they are Hindus or Buddhists or New Agers or agnostic evolutionists or whatever. Consider the following statement:

"Our culture is now flooded with pluralistic religions and mixed spiritual beliefs. Our culture is spinning out of control with sexual, religious, and moral confusion and choices. How do we respond to the somewhat parallel words of Jesus and Buddha? How do we answer the pro-gay theological arguments given today? What about euthanasia? What about women in ministry?" (*Listening to the Beliefs of Emerging Churches*, p. 87).

That is a good challenge. Believers should be trained to deal with people wherever they might be in their thinking. In particular, we need to learn how to use the Bible effectively. It is not enough to know a simple Romans Road plan of salvation.

In 1973 I was pursuing a self-centered life of pleasure and had cobbled together a religious philosophy from bits of the Bible, Hinduism (via Paramahansa Yogananda and the Self-Realization Fellowship Society), Christian Science, Buddhism (via Herman Hesse), New Age (via *The Aquarian Gospel of Jesus the Christ*), and other things. One day I was driving in my car near Miami, Florida, and passed by a man riding on a bicycle. For some reason, I turned the car around and pulled alongside of him and asked him where he was going. He said he was going to Mexico. I told him that I was going a couple hundred miles north to Lakeland and offered to give him a ride. He agreed, so we put the bicycle into the trunk of the car and drove down the road. I broached the subject of religion and asked him if he believed in God. He said, "Yes," and pulled a Bible out of his pocket and we began discussing the serious issues of life. As it turned out, I spent four or so days with the man, traveling from Florida to Mexico and back to Florida, and I was converted to Christ at the end of that journey.

The reason why I was willing to travel with him to Mexico in the first place was that I was impressed with his knowledge of the Bible. He was able to answer my questions and challenges with appropriate and powerful statements from Scripture, and he could take me right to the passages. I was amazed that the Bible was so practical. When I told him that

I believed in reincarnation, he showed me Hebrews 9:27, which says that men are appointed to die once and then the judgment. When I told him that I was following my heart, he showed me Jeremiah 17:9, which says the heart is deceitful above all things and desperately wicked. When I told him that I believed that God will accept any man as long as he is sincere in his faith, he showed me Proverbs 14:12, which says there is a way that seems right to a man but the end thereof are the ways of death. When I told him that I believed that there were many paths to God, he showed me John 14:6 and Acts 4:12. When I told him that I didn't believe it was possible to know the truth for certain, he showed me John 7:17 and 8:31-32.

I am thankful that this man was equipped to deal with me effectively.

The challenge that churches need to equip the saints to do the work of evangelism in this age is an important one that we need to take seriously. Churches should offer courses on how to understand and deal with Islam, Hinduism, Buddhism, New Age, and whatever other isms that we have to confront today. At the very least they should make good literature readily available for private study on these things.

But above all, they should train the people to be serious students of the Bible so they can answer people with God's infallible Word.

The emerging church also challenges Christians to be hospitable to unbelievers and not to keep them at arm's length, and that is a good challenge. Consider the following:

> "Very simply, we need to show grace-giving acceptance more than behavior-centered judgment to an unbelieving world. The problem with practicing this theology comes down to messiness. If we really live out grace, not just as words we say, but as a way we treat people, all kinds of messy people may just feel accepted enough to crash our church-party, and that would feel a lot different than the party of near-perfect people some of us have come to enjoy. But that's how grace works--by making beauty out of ugly things. If you owned a Rembrandt covered in mud, you wouldn't focus on the mud or treat it like mud.

> Your primary concern would not be the mud at all, though it would need to be removed. You'd be ecstatic to have something so valuable in your care. But if you tried to clean the painting by yourself, you might damage it. So you would carefully bring this work of art to a master who could guide you and help you restore it to the condition originally intended. When people begin treating one another as God's masterpiece waiting to be revealed, God's grace grows in their lives and cleanses them. We have watched gay people, radical feminists, atheistic Harvard grads, homeless crack addicts, couples living together, porn addicts, and greedy materialists come into our church, hang out around the body of Christ, find faith, change, and grow to wholeheartedly follow Christ (but for some it takes a long time, and some never change). Could those people, good and bad, come to your church? Can you picture it?" (*Listening to the Beliefs of Emerging Churches*, pp. 66, 67).

While we reject the New Evangelical non-judgmental philosophy in no uncertain terms (see Ephesians 5:11; 2 Timothy 4:2; Titus 2:15), it is true that believers should extend God's grace to other sinners in a compassionate and friendly and patient manner.

I am thankful that I know many Biblicist churches that do this.

I think of the man who led me to Jesus Christ. When I met him I was a hitchhiking, drug-abusing, jail-going, Hindu meditation practicing reprobate, but he loved me enough to spend a few days with me, putting up with my worldly behavior, my constant smoking, my foul mouth and pathetically proud attitude, patiently answering my brash challenges from Scripture. After a couple of days I told him it was ridiculous to base all of one's thinking on the Bible and that he should toss his Bible out the window so we could have a decent conversation. I reproved him for quoting Scripture and not having any thoughts of his own. In spite of this he stayed with me and even shared his hard-earned money with me, because I didn't have any, and he bought me a beautiful leather-bound Bible and a Strong's Concordance.

I think of the first church I joined after I was saved. The founding family of that church, the Hooveners, opened their home to young people who were in the world and loved many of them to Christ and discipled them, and as a result young people went out of there to Bible College and then on to serve the Lord in various ministries. I was already saved when I met them, but I was a new Christian and still had shoulder-length hair and smoked and loved rock music and trashy movies and had a lot of emotional problems that stemmed from heavy drug use. They loved me and instructed and discipled me, and as a result I gradually cut my hair and quit smoking and gave up rock music and gained some emotional stability and confidence and began to be grounded in a right understanding of the Scripture.

I think of one of my cousins in Florida. He opens his home one evening each month to people who are visiting America from other countries. He has traveled extensively to various parts of the world and thus understands foreigners better than the average American, but it is his Christian love and kindness that is the main attraction. He invites some of his Christian friends and relatives to join them, and they play games and talk and just get to know one another, and they also witness to the unbelievers and invite them to church.

I think of a church in Norfolk, Virginia, pastored by a friend named Jerry Matson. For decades, he has ministered to sailors who work on commercial ships that dock at the nearby shipyard. He goes on the ships and meets the men and invites them to visit his service center. There they are befriended and loved and fed and entertained and allowed to make phone calls home and are patiently taught the gospel of Jesus Christ. As a result, some have come to Christ and gone back to their homes in various parts of the world as missionaries.

In our missionary work in South Asia, we try to make Hindus feel welcome in our church services and encourage them to stay afterwards so that we can answer their questions about Christ and the Bible. We serve snacks and drinks. It usually takes several weeks and even months before they really understand the gospel and come to repentance and faith. Some Hindus have also lived at our house for various periods of time.

That being said, we do not agree with the idea that Jesus was a missionary to culture or that believers are missionaries to culture.

First, Jesus was not a missionary to culture but to people.

Christ came to seek and to save sinners (1 Timothy 1:15). It is the people in the world that God loves, not the culture of the world (John 3:16). Jesus did not adapt Himself to man's culture so much as He challenged it. He did not do what was expected, neither what was expected by the Jews nor what was expected by the Gentiles. He boldly disregarded the tradition of the Jews as well as that of the Samaritans (Matthew 15:1-2; Luke 6:1-9; John 4:9, 20-23). Christ did not give us an example of being a "missionary to culture" but of being a missionary to men while challenging culture.

Second, believers are not commanded to be missionaries to cultures but to preach the gospel to people.

Driscoll actually sites the Great Commission as support for his doctrine (Matthew 28:18-20; John 20:21; Acts 1:8-8), but these passages say nothing about being incarnated like Jesus or being a missionary to culture. The Great Commission says we are to preach and baptize and teach and disciple. We are to *"Go ye into all the world, and preach the gospel to every creature"* (Mark 16:15). Preaching the gospel to every nation and baptizing and making disciples does not add up to the emerging church's incarnational doctrine or to the idea of being a missionary to culture.

John 20:21 is perhaps vague enough to support such a doctrine, but only if it had support from elsewhere in the New Testament. In John 20:21 Jesus said, *"Peace be unto you: as my Father hath sent me, even so send I you.*" If this verse were isolated, it might be construed as saying that as Jesus was incarnated so must the believer be incarnated, but this interpretation is contradicted by the wider context. The Lord Jesus gave the Great Commission five times in the Gospels and Acts (Matthew 28:28-20; Mark 16:15-16; Luke 24:44-48; John 20:21; Acts 1:8). To interpret John 20:21 as saying something different than the other references is a presumptuous exegesis. What Jesus was saying in John 20:21 is that as the Father sent Him to save sinners (1 Timothy 1:15; 1 John 4:14), even so should His followers dedicate their lives to the same task.

Third, the book of Acts gives the divinely-inspired example of the fulfillment of the Great Commission, and there we do not see the Christians being incarnated like Jesus or being missionaries to culture.

In Acts we see the believers living holy, separated lives, preaching the gospel to unbelievers in the power of the Holy Spirit, and baptizing and discipling those that God saved.

What is needed to reach unbelievers is not incarnating into their culture but simply preaching the gospel with power. You don't have to understand or appreciate their music or know anything about their movie stars or think their fashion is cool. You just have to care about them and proclaim God's message of reconciliation in a biblical fashion. That is what we see in the book of Acts.

I think of my wife. She has worked with Hindus in South Asia since she first went there as a single missionary nurse in 1975. She doesn't dress like a Hindu or listen to their music or watch their movies. She isn't even an expert on Hinduism. She just loves them and patiently tells them about Jesus, and she has seen many of them come to Christ.

I think about my maternal grandmother. When I was out in the world far from Christ, she didn't know anything about my music and philosophies and ways, but she loved me and always reminded me of Jesus and the Bible and prayed for me with fasting and tears, and in this way she had a great part in my conversion.

It is true that people live in cultures and we must try to communicate the gospel in a way that they can understand, but this does not add up to being a missionary to a culture.

The missionary to culture idea smacks of an excuse to be worldly even while claiming to be holy, to love rock & roll, beer and gambling, R-rated movies, and champagne dance parties.

Fourth, culture is not innocent.

Culture is permeated with sin and idolatry, because it was fashioned by rebellious men and is part of the darkness of this world ruled by the devil (2 Cor. 4:4). Take the South Asian culture, for example. It is permeated with idolatrous Hinduism and Buddhism as well as evil western influences, and the missionary must teach the people to reject *everything* in the culture that is associated with idolatry and darkness. We do not build western style churches there, but we do teach the believers to reject everything within the culture that is wrong. In the churches we plant in South Asia the people speak their own languages and sit on the floor and shake their heads sideways to indicate yes and wear saris and kurta sudawals and eat daal baht with their fingers and never hand you something with the right hand and typically come to services late, all of which are cultural customs. But they do not wear "holy strings" or tikas or red saris or anything else associated with Hinduism, and they learn how to wear their saris and kurta sudawals in a modest manner and how to reject the immodest unisex fashions that are coming from the West and they learn that "spiritual songs" acceptable to a holy God are different in character than the world's party music. The music that our churches sing is largely indigenous, written by national Christians, but it sounds distinctly different from the music that is heard on the FM pop stations or in the pagan festivals.

Finally, the apostle Paul did not support the "be like them to win them" philosophy.

Paul's statements that "all things are lawful to me" and "I am made all things to all men" have been wrongly used to justify the "missionary to the culture" philosophy. We have considered these verses in their proper context in the chapter on the liberal emerging church. See "Liberal Emerging Church Error # 9: *Worldliness*."

CONSERVATIVE EMERGING CHURCH ERROR # 4
A POSITIVE, NON-JUDGMENTAL APPROACH

Dan Kimball warns of "judgmental finger-pointing Christians focusing on the negatives in the world" (*Listening to the Beliefs of Emerging Churches*, p. 85).

John Burke says it is wrong to use the Bible "in a defensive or aggressive way or brow-beating people into unquestioning belief" (*Listening to the Beliefs of Emerging Churches*, p. 36). He rejects "judgmentalism" (p. 37). He says, "As I understand Scripture, we're misrepresenting Jesus if the world hears our message as a message of judgment" (p. 65).

The conservative emerging church is practicing what Robert Schuller wrote about in his 1982 book: "Essentially, if Christianity is to succeed in the next millennium, it must cease to be a negative religion and must become positive" (*Self-Esteem the New Reformation*, p. 104).

The preaching at Willow Creek Community Church, founded by Bill Hybels, is described in this way: "There is no fire and brimstone here. No Bible-thumping. Just practical, witty messages."

As we have seen, this has been a principle of New Evangelicalism from its inception. Harold Ockenga said: "The strategy of the New Evangelicalism is the positive proclamation of the truth in distinction from all errors without delving in personalities which embrace the error. ... Instead of attack upon error, the New-Evangelicals proclaim the great historic doctrines of Christianity."

The conservative emerging church crowd will state in theory that preaching should be authoritative, but in practice their preaching is very weak, and they spend more time criticizing the "fundamentalist's" approach than the liberal emergent's.

WHAT DOES THE BIBLE SAY?

First, the prophets of old were not positive-focused emergents.

Consider Enoch's sermon:

> "And Enoch also, the seventh from Adam, prophesied of these, saying, Behold, the Lord cometh with ten thousands of his saints, to execute judgment upon all, and to convince all that are ungodly among them of all their ungodly deeds which they have ungodly committed, and of all their hard speeches which ungodly sinners have spoken against him" (Jude 14-15).

This Bible sermon is exceedingly negative! In fact, Enoch did not say one positive thing. You won't hear a message like this in any kind of emerging church. It would be considered disrespectable of the feelings of people, dehumanizing, lacking humility and the proper "tone."

Second, the Lord Jesus Christ was not a positive-focused emergent.

Christ preached more about Hell than Heaven, at least 14 times in the four Gospels, and He preached it red hot and terrible (e.g., Mark 9:42-48), warning people in the strongest terms not to go there. Christ rebuked error in the severest manner (Mat. 23:13-33). He scalded the Pharisees because they perverted the way of the truth and corrupted the gospel of grace, calling them hypocrites, blind guides, fools and blind, serpents, generation of vipers. Roman Catholic priests and theologically liberal Protestant ministers corrupt the truth at least as much as the Pharisees did, yet the emerging church does not speak out against them after the fashion of Christ. He told the Pharisees that they were of their father the devil (John 8:44), and a more "judgmental" statement has never been made! After forgiving and healing people Christ warned, *"... sin no more, lest a worse thing come unto thee"* (John 5:14). That is the type of thing that people in the "emerging culture" do not want to hear.

Christ's message cut against the grain of society in His day, and it still cuts against the grain of society. One thing is certain. His type of preaching would not be at home in any branch of the emerging church.

Third, it is also obvious that the apostles were not positive-focused emergents.

Paul was constantly involved in doctrinal controversies and was brutally plain about the danger of heresy. He called false teachers "dogs" and "evil workers" (Phil. 3:2). Of those who pervert the gospel he said, *"Let them be accursed"* (Gal. 1:8, 9). He called them *"evil men and seducers"* (2 Tim. 3:13), *"men of corrupt minds, reprobate concerning the faith"* (2 Tim. 3:8), *"false apostles, deceitful workers"* (2 Cor. 11:13). Paul named the names of false teachers and called their teaching *"vain babblings"* (2 Tim. 2:16, 17). He warned about *"philosophy and vain deceit"* (Col. 2:8). He described their *"cunning craftiness."* When Elymas tried to turn men away from the faith, Paul wasted no time with dialogue. He said, *"O full of all subtilty and all mischief, thou child of the devil, thou enemy of all righteousness, wilt thou not cease to pervert the right ways of the Lord?"* (Acts 13:10). He warned about false teachers who would come into the churches, calling them *"grievous wolves"* (Acts 20:29) and characterizing their teaching as *"perverse things"* (Acts 20:30). He called those who denied the bodily resurrection "fools" (1 Cor. 15:35-36). He warned about false christs, false spirits, false gospels (2 Cor. 11:1-4). He labeled false teaching *"doctrines of devils"* (1 Tim. 4:1). In the Pastoral Epistles Paul warned of false teachers and compromisers by name 10 times.

Peter was also plain-spoken about heresy. Almost two thirds of his second epistle is dedicated to warning about false teachers. He labeled their heresies "damnable" and warned of their "swift destruction" (2 Pet. 2:1). He called their ways "pernicious"; said their words were "feigned"; and boldly declared that *"their damnation slumbereth not"* (2 Pet. 2:3). He warned them of eternal Hell (2 Pet. 2:4-9) and called them "presumptuous" and "selfwilled" (2 Pet. 2:10). He likened them to *"natural brute beasts, made to be taken and destroyed"* (2 Pet. 2:12) and he exposed their deception (2 Pet. 2:13), which is a really fierce, severely uncomplimentary judgment.

John, "the apostle of love," was also busy warning about antichrists (1 John 2:18-19), calling them liars (1 John 2:22) and seducers (1 John 2:26) and deceivers (2 John 7); saying that they deny the Son (1 John 2:23) and that they don't have God (2 John 9). He put a great emphasis on testing the spirits (1 John 4:1-3). John even forbade the believers to allow the false teachers into their houses or to bid them God speed (2 John 10-11), which sounds very dehumanizing!

This strong biblical emphasis on reproving error does not characterize the emerging church in any of its aspects.

Fourth, biblical preaching is not just positive.

Biblical preaching always has a strong element of warning and plain correction. There is both "negative" and positive in the Bible, and the preacher's job is to preach it all. He is to *"reprove, rebuke, exhort"* (2 Timothy 4:2) and *"speak, and exhort, and rebuke with all authority"* (Titus 2:15). The preacher is to preach *all* things whatsoever Christ has taught us (Mat. 28:20). He is to speak the *whole* counsel of God (Acts 20:27).

A few years ago a "Positive Bible" was published by Kenneth Caine (Avon Books, 1998). Reflecting the philosophy that prevails in evangelicalism, the author determined to remove all of the "negative" statements from Scripture. The result was a very thin Bible!

Fifth, biblical Christianity is not just positive.

It is not only the preacher's job to reprove sin and warn of error. God commands *every* Christian to reprove sin (Eph. 5:11), to contend for the faith (Jude 3), and to separate from error (Rom. 16:17).

WHAT THE BIBLE SAYS ABOUT JUDGING

First, the Bible requires that we judge everything by the divine standard (1 Thess. 5:21).

We are to judge righteous judgment (Jn. 7:24).
We are to judge all things (1 Cor. 2:15-16).
We are to judge sin in the church (1 Cor. 5:3, 12).
We are to judge matters between the brethren (1 Cor. 6:5).
We are to judge preaching (1 Cor. 14:29).
We are to judge those who preach false gospels, false christs, and false spirits (2 Cor. 11:1-4).
We are to judge the works of darkness (Eph. 5:11).
We are to judge false prophets and false apostles (2 Pet. 2; 1 John 4:1; Jude; Rev. 2:2).

Second, we are not to judge hypocritically (Mat. 7:1-5).

In the Sermon on the Mount Jesus did not condemn all judging; He condemned hypocritical judging (*"Thou hypocrite, first cast out the beam out of thine own eye; and then shalt thou see clearly to cast out the mote out of thy brother's eye*," Mat. 7:5).

That Christ does not condemn all judging is evident from the immediate context. In the same sermon He warned about false teachers (Mat. 7:15-17) and false brethren (Mat. 7:21-23). It is impossible to beware of false prophets without judging doctrine and practice by God's Word.

That Christ did not condemn all judging is also evident by comparing Scripture with Scripture. We have seen that other Scriptures require judging.

Third, we are not to judge in matters of liberty (Romans 14).

Romans 14 is an exhortation not to judge things about which the Bible is silent, such as diet (Rom. 14:2-3) and holy days (Rom. 14:5-6). There are no laws in the New Testament about diet and holy days. In all such things there is personal liberty and the believer is not to judge others.

Romans 14 is *not* saying that some things in the Bible are of "secondary" importance and therefore should not be a matter of judgment. When he says we are not to judge one another, Paul is not speaking of things clearly taught in the Bible, but of things *not* taught in the Bible. If something *is* taught in the Bible, the believer is obligated to follow it and to judge on that basis.

Fourth, we are not to judge in an evil way (James 4:11-12).

This is defined in the context. It means to speak evil (Jam. 4:11). Proper judging, on the other hand, is to speak the truth in love. The truth is not evil and speaking the truth in love is not evil. The type of judging condemned by James is judging in the sense of tearing down, tale bearing, and slander. It is judging with an evil intent. When one judges sin and error scripturally, it is never with a desire to hurt anyone. The Pharisees judged Jesus in an evil manner (Jn.

7:52). The false teachers at Galatia and Corinth judged Paul in this manner, trying to tear him down in the eyes of the churches (2 Cor. 10:10).

To judge in an evil way is also to judge in a way that is contrary to the law of God (Jam. 4:12). This refers to judging others by human standards rather than divine, thus setting oneself up as the lawgiver. The Pharisees did this when they judged Jesus by their traditions (Mat. 15:1-3). On the other hand, when a believer judges things by God's Word in a godly and compassionate manner, he is not exercising his own judgment; he is exercising God's judgment. When, for example, I say that it is wrong for a woman to be a pastor, this is not my judgment; it is God's (1 Tim. 2:12). This is *not* evil judgment.

The judge-not philosophy has permeated evangelicalism today, but it is not Scriptural.

CONSERVATIVE EMERGING CHURCH ERROR # 5 *ECUMENICALISM*

Andy McQuitty, pastor of Irving Bible Church in Irving, Texas, was one of the speakers of the 2008 Song of Solomon Bible Conferences, which also featured Mark Driscoll and other "conservative emerging church" leaders. McQuitty has publicly stated that the late Pope John Paul II and Mother Teresa are in Heaven. The May 2007 issue of *Chatter,* the church's magazine, featured a picture of the two. McQuitty called the differences between Protestants and Catholics "theological pettiness" and said, "It is just plain silly to write each other off as far as true Christianity is concerned. We'll have plenty of time in Heaven to figure out who was right about Purgatory and Mary" (quoted from Shane Trammel, "The Death of Discernment In The Church," July 9, 2007, http://blog.shanetrammel.com/2007/07/09/the-death-of-discernment-in-the-church/).

McQuitty says that Protestants and Catholics should be able to cooperate in "building the kingdom of our common Lord Jesus Christ." He called John Paul II, who was utterly devoted to Mary, "a Man of God" and "a great man whom all Christians should admire, thank and emulate." McQuitty said that his personal spiritual life and faith had been enriched by this pope.

Erwin McManus, founder of Mosaic Church in Los Angeles, has the goal of breaking down the walls between Christian leaders of every kind, "whether they are modern, postmodern, emergent or megachurch" ("Interview: Cultural Architect on Rethinking Church Methods," *Christian Post*, Jan. 22, 2008). In January 2008 he was co-host of Robert Schuller's Rethink Conference, joining hands with a wide variety of heretics.

Dan Kimball says: "I ended up moving from a personal doctrinal statement with twenty things I would rigidly hold to--to about ten things. I became more of a Nicene Creed believer and then left more to mystery after that" (*Listening to the Beliefs of the Emerging Church*, p. 94).

The conservative emerging church favors friendship and dialogue with heretics rather than separation from them.

This is why the conservative emerging leaders contribute to books such as *Listening to the Beliefs of the Emerging Church*. In these endeavors, they join hands with liberals who hold to many heresies, such as denying the infallibility and sole authority of Scripture and the substitutionary atonement of Jesus Christ.

The book *Breaking the Missional Code* by Ed Stetzer and David Putman is interdenominational and ecumenical in outlook. They describe churches as diverse as Willow Creek, Anglican, and Charismatic and there is no significant warning about doctrinal error. They mention Mother Teresa and Billy Graham as positive examples (p. 67).

WHAT DOES THE BIBLE SAY?

We have refuted the ecumenical doctrine in the section on the liberal emerging church. See "Liberal Emerging Church Error # 11: *Ecumenism*."

CONSERVATIVE EMERGING CHURCH ERROR # 6
TRADITIONAL WAYS OF EVANGELISM AND CHURCH PLANTING NO LONGER WORK

In *Faith of My Fathers* Chris Seay, a third generation Baptist preacher, says that the "church in North America is in danger of self-destruction", claiming that the crisis has been growing over the past 50 years and has not reached its pinnacle. He describes how that his father and grandfather pastored traditional Southern Baptist churches. His grandfather pastored Magnum Oaks Baptist Church in Houston, Texas, for 28 years but it closed its doors in 2002, soon after he retired. Seay claims that a new way of doing church is necessary today. The answer, he believes, lies along the lines of Ecclesia, the church which he founded in Houston. It is a non-judgmental, inclusive, hip, artsy, liturgical, "missional" type of church.

Dan Kimball begins his book *They Like Jesus but Not the Church* by showing how that American society has changed. He says:

> "In our increasingly post-Christian culture, the influences and values shaping emerging generations are no longer aligned with Christianity. Emerging generations don't have a basic understanding of the story of the Bible, and they don't have one God as the predominant God to worship. Rather, they are open to all types of faiths, including new mixtures of religions. ... I once heard someone explain that the church in America is not above what happened in Europe. European nations have truly become post-Christian nations" (pp. 15, 16).

Kimball describes theologically orthodox churches that are populated by a few old people who have lost their children to the world and have no spiritual power. We are told that the problem with these churches is that they have not adapted to the times and what they need is a good dose of emerging churchism.

WHAT DOES THE BIBLE SAY?

In fact, the problem with dead but theologically sound churches is that they are not taking the Bible seriously. It has never been enough just to be sound in doctrine.

Victorious Christian living begins with the new birth. It requires genuine spiritual conversion, followed by surrender to Christ and dedicated pursuit of His will.

> "I beseech you therefore, brethren, by the mercies of God, that ye present your bodies a living sacrifice, holy, acceptable unto God, which is your reasonable service. And be not conformed to this world: but be ye transformed by the renewing of your mind, that ye may prove what is that good, and acceptable, and perfect, will of God" (Romans 12:1-2).

The Bible teaches that born again Christians need to be sound in doctrine *and* zealous in Christian living. Titus was instructed to *"speak thou the things which become sound doctrine"* (Titus 2:1), and the things that become sound doctrine in that same chapter are the aged men being *"sober, grave, temperate"* (v. 2) and the aged women being *"in behaviour as becometh holiness"* (v. 3) and young women being sober and chaste and loving their husbands and children (vv. 4-5) and young men being sober minded (v. 6) and preachers showing a pattern of good works and sound speech (vv. 7-8) and servants being obedient and honest (vv. 9-10) and every believer *"denying ungodliness and worldly lusts, we should live soberly, righteously, and godly, in this present world"* (v. 12).

This combination of sound Bible doctrine and holy Christian living works! It backs up the profession that we make and the gospel that we preach, and gives us power with God. Children see it and want to follow in the same footsteps as their parents and grandparents. It works today just as well as it did 50 years ago or 200 years ago or 2,000 years ago. My wife and I have spent 35 years in the ministry, both in North America and in Asia, and this old-fashioned, fundamentalist way works today as well as it did decades ago. I have the privilege of preaching each year in churches in various parts of the world, and the majority of those churches are not dead by a long shot. They are seeing Christians mature in the faith. They are seeing souls saved. They are seeing children grow up and serve Christ.

It is common that young people who grow up in Christian homes and churches will struggle some as they reach maturity. There are no true second generation Christians. Jesus said that true Christianity requires being born again. It is not merely learning what to believe and how to act. True Christianity does not come by baptism and confirmation. Each individual must acknowledge his fallen condition and receive Christ for himself, and each individual must make the decision of whether to serve Christ or self.

We live in a vile society that is aggressively opposed to the Bible way, but I personally know of thousands of fundamentalist Christians who are experiencing victory in the midst of these times and whose children and grandchildren are following in their footsteps. There are hundreds of fundamentalist Bible Colleges and Institutes in North America and abroad that are populated by thousands of young people who are zealous for Christ.

On a recent preaching trip to Canada, for example (which is not the "Bible belt" by any stretch of the imagination), what I witnessed was a great encouragement, and I experience this each year in various places. The first church I preached in was Victory Baptist Church in Sherwood Park, Alberta, near Edmonton. The church was founded about 30 years ago by Pastor Dave Harness. Today they have a beautiful building and lovely property. The pastor has 12 happy, well-adjusted children who are serving the Lord in the same faith as their parents. Next I preached in Pembina Valley Baptist Church in Winkler, Manitoba. This church of several hundred people recently built a beautiful large new auditorium because they outgrew the old one. I preached a three-day meeting, and each night people were still there fellowshipping at 11 pm. The church operates a Bible College for young people who want to be trained for the ministry. Another meeting on that trip was Bethel Baptist Church in London, Ontario. This church is 25 years old and it is moving forward spiritually in the face of the devil's attacks. The church built a printing operation by faith 15 years ago and has sent Christian literature to many parts of the world. The founding pastor's children are serving the Lord and some of his grandchildren are preparing for the ministry. The final meeting on that trip was New Hope Baptist Church in Tillsonburg, Ontario. It is a growing church that has its own school for educating children. The five-day mission conference was well attended each night, and a good percentage of the young people who grow up in the church go on to serve the Lord. All of the pastor's grown children are involved in the ministry.

I could write an entire book along this same strain. The "old fashioned" Bible church movement is far from dead. In fact, it is very lively. There are thousands of fundamentalist missionaries planting churches throughout the world.

Further, if some fundamentalist or evangelical churches are "dead," that is no reflection on the truth and effectiveness of the "traditional" Bible way. Dedicated, holy, separated Christian living and preaching the simple gospel of Jesus' cross and the new birth "works" today just as well as it ever has. This doesn't mean that multitudes will be saved in any given locale. The response to the gospel is different in different places and circumstances. Only God knows why that is true, but it is. And the Bible instructs us that the last days will witness a great turning away from the faith, which we are clearly observing.

The bottom line is that we are called to be faithful to God's Word regardless of the response. The true Christian faith and ministry is not "pragmatic." Its objective is not "success" as measured by any worldly standard or church growth pattern. Its objective is obedience to God.

> "Let us hear the conclusion of the whole matter: Fear God, and keep his commandments: for this is the whole duty of man. For God shall bring every work into judgment, with every secret thing, whether it be good, or whether it be evil" (Ecclesiastes 12:13-14).

CONSERVATIVE EMERGING CHURCH ERROR # 7
ANTI-FUNDAMENTALIST

Mark Driscoll hits out at "hardcore fundamentalism" frequently. He claims that fundamentalists rarely take the gospel out of their churches and that they replace the gospel with "rules, legalism, and morality supported with mere prooftexts from the Bible" (*The Radical Reformission*, p. 22). He claims that letting go of culture is "fundamentalist sectarianism" and states that "sectarianism is the huddling up of God's people to enjoy each other and Jesus without caring about anyone who is lost and dying outside of Christ" (p. 143). He likens fundamentalists to Pharisees and describes them as "avoiding sinners and hiding out in a Christian culture" (p. 140). He calls them "arrogant, self-righteous, and judgmental" who "do little more than yell at [the unsaved] to be moral when they should be explaining how to be redeemed" (p. 140). He mocks a church that advertised itself as "Separated" and "Reaching out to Seattle" (p. 141), claiming that these are contradictory ideas. He calls fundamentalists "mixed nuts" and "old legalists who want to argue about the King James Bible" ("The Last of the Hepcat Churches," *The Relevant Church*, p. 25).

Driscoll even blames fundamentalism for liberal emerging church heresy.

"Fundamentalism is really losing the war, and I think it is in part responsible for the rise of what we know as the more liberal end of the emerging church. Because a lot of what is fueling the left end of the emerging church is fatigue with hardcore fundamentalism that throws rocks at culture. But culture is the house that people live in, and it just seems really mean to keep throwing rocks at somebody's house" ("Pastor Provocateur," *Christianity Today*, Sept. 21, 2007).

In this interview, Driscoll mocks fundamentalists who warn about rock music and says that this is a "stupid" thing to do.

Driscoll often makes fundamentalists the brunt of his jokes. He says, for example, that his old church building was "as hard to find as a fundamentalist having fun" (*Confessions of a Reformission Rev.*, p. 126).

Dan Kimball speaks in deeply sympathetic and understanding terms about atheists and homosexuals and every sort of worldly rebel, but he refers to biblical fundamentalists only in the most severe terms, repeatedly describing them as ignorant, hatemongering people who give Jesus a bad name. Kimball is opposed to Christians who hand out tracts and tell people they are going to Hell or who warn rock & rollers about sin and who are judgmental (*They Like Jesus but Not the Church*, p. 32).

Rick Warren blasts fundamentalism at every opportunity. He called it "one of the big enemies of the 21st century" ("The Purpose-Driven Pastor," *The Philadelphia Inquirer*, Jan. 8, 2006). In his interview on *Larry King Live* on December 2, 2006, Warren said: "There are all kinds of fundamentalists, Larry, and they're all based on fear. There are Christian fundamentalists. There are Muslim fundamentalists. I've met some Jewish fundamentalists. You know that there are secular fundamentalists. They're all based on fear. Secular fundamentalists are afraid of God."

Speaking before the Pew Forum in May 2005 Warren made the following comments:

"Today there really aren't that many Fundamentalists left; I don't know if you know that or not, but they are such a minority; there aren't that many Fundamentalists left in America. ... Bob Jones is not a mega-church. That's right exactly, it's not, and that group is shrinking more and more and more. ... when I say there are very few fundamentalists, I mean in the sense that they are all actually called fundamentalist churches, and those would be quite small. There are no large ones. ... that group is shrinking more and more and more" ("Myths of the Modern Mega-Church," May 23, 2005, transcript of the Pew Forum's biannual Faith Angle conference on religion, politics and public life).

He also said,

"Now the word 'fundamentalist' actually comes from a document in the 1920s called the *Five Fundamentals of the Faith*. And it is a very legalistic, narrow view of Christianity..."

We could give many more examples of this, because rarely does a conservative emergent preach or write unless he takes a potshot at the fundamentalist.

WHAT DOES THE BIBLE SAY?

Fundamentalism is a broad term, but the fundamentalists that I know are simply trying to take the Bible seriously. Some fundamentalists hold to the King James Bible and some use the modern versions; some are dispensational and some aren't; some are Calvinists and some are anti-Calvinist; some are Baptist and some are Protestant; some believe in formal theological education and some don't, and there are plenty of other differences. But at the heart of fundamentalism is the attitude that everything in the Bible is true and we should not only believe it but be willing to fight for it. It is summarized in Psalm 119:128: "Therefore I esteem all thy precepts concerning all things to be right; and I hate every false way."

George Dollar, in his history of fundamentalism, defined it this way: "Historic fundamentalism is the literal interpretation of all the affirmations and attitudes of the Bible and the militant exposure of all non-biblical affirmations and attitudes" (*A History of Fundamentalism in America*, 1973).

Looking back over the fundamentalist movement since the 1930s, John Ashbrook defined it as follows: "Fundamentalism is the militant belief and proclamation of the basic doctrines of Christianity leading to a Scriptural separation from those who reject them" (*Axioms of Separation*, p. 10).

That is the type of fundamentalism that tens of thousands of churches throughout the world seek to emulate and that Mark Driscoll and his crowd are taking every opportunity to ridicule.

When I read what the emergents say about fundamentalists, it makes me wonder if they actually know any of them or have actually visited their churches and read their books, because their statements about fundamentalists are filled with errors, slanders, and straw men.

What about the claim that fundamentalists replace the gospel with "rules, legalism, and morality supported with mere prooftexts from the Bible"? I personally have preached in at least 500 fundamentalist churches in 16 countries and I don't know any who are guilty of this. We preach the gospel of the grace of Jesus Christ, the gospel that is a free gift that was purchased by Christ on the cross. We don't intermingle works of any kind with the gospel of salvation. Further, the morality we preach is not based on "mere prooftexts" but upon the whole thrust of the Bible and upon Scripture rightly interpreted in context and by comparing Scripture with Scripture.

What about the claim that fundamentalists huddle up to "enjoy each other and Jesus without caring about anyone who is lost"? Again, I don't know who this is referring to, because most of the fundamentalist churches I know tend to be very evangelistic. My wife and I have spent nearly two decades preaching the gospel to Hindus in South Asia and another decade in jail ministries and other types of evangelism, and there are tens of thousands of fundamental

Baptists who have done the same. In what way can this be characterized as not caring about the lost? It is true that there are fundamentalist churches that are not evangelistic, but in my experience that is the exception more than the rule.

What about the claim that fundamentalists are "arrogant, self-righteous, and judgmental"? How can the emergent make such a claim without knowing the motives of another man's heart? Arrogance is a personal problem. I suspect that there are at least as many arrogant emergents as there are arrogant fundamentalists. As for self-righteousness, the fundamentalists that I know are not self-righteous; they know that their righteousness is a gift of God's grace in Jesus Christ. It is a vicious slander to label a Christ-trusting, Christ-loving fundamentalist a self-righteous Pharisee.

What about the claim that fundamentalists "do little more than yell at them [the unsaved] to be moral when they should be explaining how to be redeemed"? Again, I don't know any fundamentalists who do this, and if there are some I would suspect that the number is very small. The fundamentalists that I know around the world preach the gospel to the unsaved. Yes, we mention sin because sin must be acknowledged and repented of before God. We mention sin in the same manner that Jesus mentioned to the woman at the well that she was living with a man who was not her husband and to the rich young ruler that he was covetous. The unbeliever must acknowledge that he is a sinner, and it is the job of God's Law to reveal his sinful condition (Romans 3:19-20). A change of mind about sin is the essence of repentance, but we don't confuse works with the free gift of salvation.

What about the claim that fundamentalism is based on fear? I would reply that if fear is a central aspect of biblical fundamentalism it is the fear of God that leads to strict obedience to His Word, and that is scriptural and right and godly. This was exactly how Paul instructed the believers at

Corinth to live: *"Having therefore these promises, dearly beloved, let us cleanse ourselves from all filthiness of the flesh and spirit, perfecting holiness in the fear of God"* (2 Cor. 7:1). Paul instructed the church at Philippi to *"work out your own salvation with fear and trembling"* (Phil. 2:12). Hebrews 12:28 says we are to *"serve God acceptably with reverence and godly fear."*

What about the claim that fundamentalism is very small and shrinking? To set the record straight, fundamentalist churches are growing both in size and in number and many of them run in the thousands. Consider Lancaster Baptist Church north of Los Angeles, in Warren's own state of California, with a membership of 4,000. The fundamental Baptist movement has tens of thousands of churches in America alone, many of them with a membership of 500 and more, and it has a large and aggressive missionary arm that probably exceeds that of the Southern Baptist Convention. And fundamental Baptists form only one segment of fundamentalism. Even one small, insignificant fundamentalist ministry like mine touches tens of thousands of people. My sermons have been downloaded 120,000 times from just one web site.

What about the claim that the name "fundamentalist" came from a document in the 1920s called the *Five Fundamentals of the Faith*? In fact, there was no document by this name. I have practically every book that has been written about the history of fundamentalism, and the fact is that the name "fundamentalist" derived from a series of books called "The Fundamentals" that was published from 1910-1915. With the financial backing of two wealthy Christian businessmen, some three million copies of the 12 volumes of *The Fundamentals* were distributed to Christian workers in the United States and 21 foreign countries. The series, composed of 90 articles written by 64 authors, did not promote "five fundamentals" but rather dozens of fundamentals. (For more about the history of fundamentalism see http://www.wayoflife.org/fbns/fundamen1.htm)

What about the idea that fundamentalism is a "narrow view of Christianity"? This is correct. It seeks to be as narrow as the Bible, and if that is a sin, the apostles and early churches didn't know about it. They left us with a once-delivered faith and solemnly exhorted us to keep it (Jude 3).

As for the idea that fundamentalism is a form of "legalism," what kind of "legalism" is it for a blood-washed, saved-by-grace saint to aim to preach all of the truths of God's Word and to be faithful to God's Word in all matters? Though we are saved by grace without works, we are saved *unto* good works (Ephesians 2:8-10). If that is legalism, Paul was a great legalist, for he testified, "For I have not shunned to declare unto you all the counsel of God" (Acts 20:27). By my count, there are 88 specific duties that Christians are instructed to follow in the book of Ephesians alone, the very book that emphasizes salvation without works!

As for the idea that letting go of culture is "fundamentalist sectarianism," Driscoll's problem is with the Bible and not with the fundamentalist, because it is the Bible that forbids God's people to be conformed to the world (Romans 12:2) or to love the world (1 John 2:15) or to make friendship with the world (James 4:4) or to yoke together with unbelievers (2 Corinthians 6:14).

Driscoll might not like our way of obeying these Scriptures, but then again, we don't like his way of not obeying them.

I am sure that I speak for many fundamentalists when I say that my passion is to be faithful to my God and Saviour Jesus Christ and to obey His eternal Word as recorded in the Scripture. I did not grow up a fundamentalist. I am a fundamentalist by Bible-based conviction. I became a fundamentalist when I was saved at age 23 and began to study the Bible and saw there that it is God's will for me to hate every false way (Psalm 119:128) and to preach with reproof and rebuke (2 Timothy 4:2) and to love not the world (1 John 2:15) and to have no fellowship with the unfruitful works of darkness but rather to reprove them (Ephesians 5:11) and to earnestly contend for the faith that was once delivered to the saints (Jude 3) and to mark and avoid those who teach false things (Romans 16:17).

It was this type of teaching from the Bible itself that convinced me to be a fundamentalist separatist as opposed to a wishy washy evangelical tolerationist, and it is this type of teaching that has convinced me to remain a fundamentalist in the face of the severe opposition that we face today from literally every direction.

Should this sincere Bible conviction be held up as the object of ridicule by fellow Christians who profess to believe the Bible?

Further, the emerging church's attack upon fundamentalism is highly hypocritical. They say that we shouldn't use labels, but they are quick to label the fundamentalist. They say we shouldn't be judgmental, but they are viciously judgmental of the fundamentalist. They claim to hold the high ground on Christian compassion, but they are anything but compassionate toward fundamentalists. They mock the fundamentalist's standards and rules, but they have plenty of standards and rules of their own.

CONSERVATIVE EMERGING CHURCH ERROR # 8
A SOCIAL JUSTICE, KINGDOM-BUILDING EMPHASIS

Rick McKinley of Imago Dei of Portland says:

> "I hope that we can leave the next generation great theology on the Kingdom of God that seems to have gotten confused in the enlightenment. I hope that we can expand our theology of the Trinity from a static doctrine to a dynamic and living theology of community and transformation" ("My Thoughts on the Emerging Church," blog dated October 18, 2007).

Erwin McManus says the church is the place where dreams should be nurtured and unleashed. He describes the "wild and God-sized dreams and visions" that people have caught from his congregation and have gone forth to be social workers and artists and chefs and dancers and fashion designers and psychologists and environmental engineers (*The Barbarian Way*, p. 103). The glaring omission from this strange list is evangelists and soul winners and pastors and Bible teachers and defenders of the faith!

In 2005, Rick Warren announced his P.E.A.C.E. plan. The objective is to erase poverty and illiteracy and fight world disease, among other things. P.E.A.C.E. stands for

P - plant a church or partner with an existing one in every village
E - equip local leaders
A - assist the poor
C - care for the sick
E - educate the next generation.

Warren says, "We'll work with everyone who wants to help. I'll work with an atheist who wants to stop AIDS" ("Pastor Warren Lays out a Global Vision," *Orange County Register*, April 17, 2005).

Relevants use the term "missional" to describe this program, as opposed to the old terms "mission" or "missions."

WHAT DOES THE BIBLE SAY?

See "Liberal Emerging Church Error # 6: *A Social-Justice, Kingdom Building Gospel*."

CONSERVATIVE EMERGING CHURCH ERROR # 9
REJECTING "AGENDA" OF WINNING THE LOST TO CHRIST

The emerging church calls upon Christians to build intimate relationships with the unsaved but not necessarily with the objective of leading them to Christ.

Mars Hill Church in Seattle operates a secular rock club called Paradox which has hosted hundreds of rock concerts. Senior pastor Mark Driscoll says the focus of this operation is simply to show hospitality. "So we welcomed kids into a safe place where we could build relationships of grace on Jesus' behalf RATHER THAN PREACHING AT THE KIDS or doing goofy things like handing out tracts" (*Confessions of a Reformission Rev.*, pp. 126, 127).

In *They Like Jesus but Not the Church*, Dan Kimball begins by relating a talk he gave to a group of pastors. He told them that he spends a considerable part of his time as a pastor developing relationships with unbelievers. He said that he gets invited to [rock & roll drinking] clubs to hang out and see bands, and "how this also is a way to hang out with and build trust and credibility with those I'm befriending" (p. 12). He said, "I shared how incredibly refreshing it is to be friends with people outside of church circles" (p. 13).

When one of the pastors asked him if he had won them to Christ, he replied, "No, I'M JUST TRYING TO BE THEIR FRIENDS [sic] and get to know them" (p. 14).

Another pastor commented that the emerging generation of people are "pagans" and "they just need to hear solid preaching, which will cause them to repent of their ways," but Kimball strongly disagrees.

Kimball says the term "missional" means that "we don't 'bring Jesus' to people but that we realize Jesus is active in culture and we join him in what he is doing," and, "we serve our communities, and that we build relationships with people in them, rather than seeing them as evangelistic targets" (*They Like Jesus*, p. 20).

Kimball quotes from many unsaved people that he has befriended, giving their opinions about Christ and the church, and he says: "I DIDN'T SET OUT TO PROSELYTIZE THEM; I SIMPLY MET THEM TO BEFRIEND THEM, enjoy their company, and ask their opinions. ... I see them as friends, not as evangelistic targets" (p. 61).

Kimball says he thinks Christians have done more harm than good by witnessing to unbelievers using "traditional" methods of confronting them with their sin and need for Christ (p. 38). He says that instead of street witnessing we should develop "relationships in which we dialogue and build trust with people" (p. 43).

We agree that believers should be friendly to the unsaved and should be ready to befriend them, but this friendship must be done very carefully in the context of holiness.

It is far better to invite the sinner to spend time with us than for us to spend time with them on their own turf (bars, rock concerts, and such).

And there should always be the objective of reaching the unsaved for Christ. Yes, we have an agenda, because we are commanded by our Master to preach the gospel to every person (Mark 16:15). That is the agenda Jesus has given us. For a believer, the most important way to be a friend to the unsaved is to confront him with the gospel. Assuming that Hell is real and that salvation is only through faith in Christ, *nothing* is friendlier or more compassionate than this!

In his book *Peril of Islam*, Gene Gurganus, who was a missionary to Muslims for 17 years, gives a proper biblical philosophy of befriending unbelievers in the context of evangelism. The first of his nine suggestions for winning Muslims to Christ is the following:

> "If we are going to evangelize Muslims, the first thing we have to do is to cultivate a friendship. Saying, 'Hello. How are you?' is not enough. We need to come along side and get to know him, know his problems, his frustrations, his ambitions, and his fears" (p. 61).

Gurganus is saying we should befriend the unsaved, but he is not saying what the emerging church is saying. Gurganus is saying that the objective is not merely to befriend the unsaved but to win them to Christ!

That is what we see in the life and ministry of Jesus Christ. He was a friend of sinners above all friends and He spent time with them, but He never sinned in any way with them; He was not a "party animal"; and He definitely had the objective of saving those He befriended. He said, *"For the Son of man is come to seek and to save that which was lost"* (Luke 19:10). Jesus did not come to earth just to make friends and help people in some vague sense!

Further, Christ preached very plainly to people; He was not afraid of offending them with direct truth. He demanded repentance (Luke 13:3-5) and warned often of Hell, at least 14 times in the Gospels (i.e., Mark 9:43-48). Christ's preaching was so plain and uncompromising that most of his own followers eventually turned away from Him because they were offended at His words (John 6:60-66).

God has made us ambassadors for Christ and has given us the ministry of reconciliation (2 Cor. 5:17-21). The believer's chief job in this present world is to urge sinners to be reconciled to Christ. This is not a peripheral part of our purpose in this present world; it is the very heart of it!

Further, our ministry to the unsaved must have a great sense of urgency to it. The Bible says that today is the day of salvation (2 Cor. 6:2). It warns against banking on tomorrow (James 4:13-14). *"The night is far spent, the day is at hand"* (Romans 13:12). See Matthew 24:42, 44; 25:13; 1 Thess. 5:1-6.

Evangelist D. L. Moody had it right when he said, "I look upon this world as a wrecked vessel. God has given me a lifeboat and said to me, 'Moody, save all you can.'"

CONSERVATIVE EMERGING CHURCH ERROR # 10
ONLY "MAJOR" DOCTRINES SHOULD BE POINTS OF DIVISION AMONG CHRISTIANS

The conservative emerging church, following the standard evangelical philosophy today, divides doctrine into major and minor. The major doctrines are called "cardinal," "essential," and "fundamental," and anything beyond the major doctrines is not supposed to be important enough to cause divisions among Christians. A popular quotation is "In essentials unity, in non-essentials liberty, in all things charity."

Mark Driscoll says that "skirmishes over secondary issues will overtake primary issues like evangelism and church planting" ("Conference examines the emerging church," Baptist Press, Sept. 25, 2007).

Driscoll divides doctrine into four categories that he calls Christianity 1.0, 2.0, 3.0, and 4.0. Christianity 1.0 refers to that "handful of essential beliefs" the "different Christian faith communities" must hold in common in order to have unity. These are things such as the deity of Christ and salvation by grace alone. Thus, unity is based only on the "essential" doctrines. Christianity 2.0 refers to the doctrinal standards of an individual church (Baptist, Methodist, Calvinist, etc.). Christianity 3.0 refers to the beliefs that parents impart to their children. Christianity 4.0 refers to "personal beliefs and preferences by which someone lives their life of faith that includes far more precise convictions on a wide number of matters."

Dan Kimball says that "following Jesus means we can say with confidence that we believe in certain fundamental things," such as the deity, virgin birth, substitutionary atonement, and resurrection of Christ, the divine inspiration of Scripture, and salvation by grace through faith; but we shouldn't add anything to the "core fundamental beliefs" (*They Like Jesus but Not the Church*, p. 190). He is opposed to those who go beyond "the five fundamentals" to make an issue of such things as the woman's role in ministry, the doctrine of end times, creationism, the mode of baptism, dress codes, worship styles, evangelistic methods, and divine election (pp. 190, 205). He says, "When we take subtle or not so subtle jabs at those who have different opinions on non-core issues, that is un-Christlike and only shows how Christians fight and bicker at each other, why would someone want to become like us?"

WHAT DOES THE BIBLE SAY?

First, this principle is refuted by the Bible's silence.

This popular philosophy simply has no biblical basis. The Bible nowhere says that some doctrine is of such a non-issue that it should not cause divisions.

Second, this principle is refuted by Christ's teaching.

Consider Matthew 23:23, where Christ taught that while not everything in the Bible is of equal importance everything has some importance and nothing is to be despised or neglected.

> "Woe unto you, scribes and Pharisees, hypocrites! for ye pay tithe of mint and anise and cummin, and have omitted the weightier matters of the law, judgment, mercy, and faith: these ought ye to have done, and not to leave the other undone."

It is also refuted in Matthew 28:20, where Christ taught that the churches are to teach the believers to observe ALL THINGS whatsoever He has commanded. He did not say or even hint at the idea that some things are not worth making an issue over in certain Christian contexts.

Third, this principle is refuted by Paul's example and teaching.

He taught the whole counsel of God (Acts 20:27).

He taught Timothy to value all doctrine and not to allow ANY false doctrine (1 Tim. 1:3).

He further taught Timothy to keep all doctrine "without spot" (1 Tim. 6:13-14). Spots refer to the small things, the seemingly insignificant things. The context of Paul's instruction in 1 Timothy 6:14 is an epistle that has as its theme church truth (1 Tim. 3:15). In this epistle, we find instruction about such things as pastoral standards (1 Tim. 3), deacons (1 Tim. 3), the restriction upon the woman's work in the church (1 Tim. 2), and the ordination and discipline of elders (1 Tim. 5). These are the very kinds of things that are typically considered of very secondary importance by evangelicals.

If we obey Paul and have the mindset that we must keep all of the things taught in the New Testament without spot, it is impossible to hold to the lackadaisical principle that we should not cause divisions based on "secondary truth."

Fourth, not all heresies are of equal weight as far as destructiveness, but all heresies are to be opposed.

A heresy is a doctrinal error. The word describes the self-will that characterizes such sin. A "heretic" is one who exercises his own will over the Word of God and chooses an error over the truth. The error can be as serious as denying the deity of Christ or as seemingly slight as allowing a woman to usurp authority over men.

Some heresies are *"damnable heresies"* (2 Peter 2:1), which are heresies that affect eternal salvation. To accept a damnable heresy is to bring upon oneself eternal damnation. The damnable heresy described by Peter was that of denying the Lord Jesus Christ. The apostle John also described the doctrine of Christ as a crucial doctrine (2 John 9). The doctrine of Christ pertains to teachings about His person, such as His Deity, humanity, virgin birth, sinlessness, atonement, and bodily resurrection. In 2 Corinthians 11:4 Paul mentioned three areas of damnable heresies. These are those pertaining to the person of Christ, the gospel, and the Holy Spirit. This would include the doctrine of salvation by grace alone and the Trinity.

There are also less serious heresies.

> "For there must be also heresies among you, that they which are approved may be made manifest among you. When ye come together therefore into one place, this is not to eat the Lord's supper. For in eating every one taketh before other his own supper: and one is hungry, and another is drunken" (1 Corinthians 11:19-21).

In this passage Paul was referring to errors in the church at Corinth, and in the immediate context he is describing errors relating to the Lord's Supper. He called these "heresies," but they are not damnable heresies. A born again child of God can hold to such errors.

That not all heresies have the same consequence does not mean that some heresies are to be ignored. Every wind of false doctrine is to be resisted. See Ephesians 4:14.

David Nettleton refuted the emergent philosophy in "A Limited Message or a Limited Fellowship," which describes his experiences in an interdenominational youth ministry in the 1950s. Consider an excerpt from this:

> This message, like many, is born out of an experience. It may be some others are going through similar experiences. Therefore, let me recount the one which brought this message to light. I was brought up as a Presbyterian. I was saved at a college which was interdenominational in student body, but was managed by the Church of the Brethren. From there I went to a seminary which was not a denominational school, and from there to another seminary which was United Presbyterian. I entered the Baptist pastorate with no Baptist training except that which came from reading of the Scriptures.
>
> A few years later I was drawn into an interdenominational youth movement and was given the leadership of a local Saturday night rally. I cooperated with any who were evangelical, regardless of their associations. I was advised by top leaders in the movement to seek the names of outstanding modernists for my advisory committee. I didn't do that. But I did follow advice which led me to send all converts back to the churches of their choice, churches I knew to be liberal in some cases. This greatly troubled my conscience and I prayed and thought about it.
>
> Another problem connected with this work was the failure on my part to instruct any converts on the matter of Christian baptism, which in the Scriptures is the first test of obedience. I felt that I should do this inasmuch as Peter and Paul did it. But how could it be done when on the committee of the work there were close friends who did not believe it? By such an association I had definitely stripped my message and my ministry of important Bible truths which many called 'nonessentials.'
>
> In the follow-up work it was not convenient to speak of eternal security in the presence of Christian workers who hated the name of the doctrine. Thus the ministry was pared down to the gospel, just as if there was nothing in the Great Commission about baptizing converts and indoctrinating them. I had found the least common denominator and I was staying by it. But my conscience had no rest.
>
> Then it was that Acts 20:27 came to mean something to me. The great apostle had never allowed himself to be drawn into anything which would limit his message. He could say with a clean conscience, 'I am

pure from the blood of all men. For I have not shunned to declare unto you all the counsel of God.' Why cannot many say that today? In my case, and in many other cases, it was due to a desire to teach a larger audience and to work with a larger group of Christians.

Many have been carried away from full obedience by a noble-sounding motto which has been applied to Christian work. 'In essentials unity, in nonessentials liberty, and in all things charity.' Some things are not essential to salvation but they are essential to full obedience, and the Christian has no liberty under God to sort out the Scriptures into essentials and nonessentials! It is our duty to declare the whole counsel of God, and to do it wherever we are.

Today we are choosing between two alternatives. A LIMITED MESSAGE OR A LIMITED FELLOWSHIP. If we preach all of the Bible truths, there are many places where we will never be invited. If we join hands with the crowds, there will be limiting of the message of the Bible. Bear this in mind--it is the Baptist who lays aside the most! It is the fundamental Baptist who makes the concessions! Think this through and you will find it to be true. We believe in believer's baptism. We believe in separation. We preach eternal security. We believe in the imminent coming of Christ. We consider it an act of obedience to reprove unbelief in religious circles. The Sadducee and the Pharisee are to be labeled. But according to a present philosophy we must lay these things aside for the sake of a larger sphere of service.

Which is more important, full obedience or a larger sphere of service? And yet I do not fully believe these are the only two alternatives. It is our first duty to be fully obedient to God in all things, and then to wait upon Him for the places of service. It may be that we will be limited, and it may be that we will not. Charles Haddon Spurgeon did not travel as widely as some men of his day, but his sermons have traveled as far as the sermons of most men (David Nettleton, "A Limited Message or a Limited Fellowship," GARBC).

CONSERVATIVE EMERGING CHURCH ERROR # 11 MUSIC IS A MATTER OF PREFERENCE

All emerging church leaders hold the principle that music is a matter of preference, that music itself is neutral and that only the words have consequence. They even go beyond this and say that those who make an issue of music are sinning.

In *Breaking the Missional Code,* Ed Stetzer lists music under the category of "the sin of preferences" (p. 50).

In chapter 8 of *The Purpose Driven Life,* Rick Warren says:

> "God loves all kinds of music because he invented it all--fast and slow, loud and soft, old and new. You probably don't like it all, but God does! ... Christians often disagree over the style of music used in worship, passionately defending their preferred style as the most biblical or God-honoring. But there is no biblical style! ... God likes variety and enjoys it all. There is no such thing as 'Christian' music; there are only Christian lyrics. It is the words that make a song sacred, not the tune. There are no spiritual tunes" (pp. 65, 66).

WHAT DOES THE BIBLE SAY?

The Bible nowhere says nor even hints that God loves all kinds of music. Rick Warren's only evidence for this outrageous statement is his reasoning that since God "invented it all" he must like it all. Yet, where is the evidence that God invented all music? Are you telling me that the devil and sinful men are not involved in the field of music? That is a ridiculous thought, seeing that the devil is called "the god of this world" and music is one of the most powerful influences in this world. Sinful men have used music since Cain's children built the first society apart from God and made musical instruments to satisfy their carnal pleasures (Genesis 4:16-21).

As for the idea that music is neutral, it is patently ridiculous, and the only people who make such a claim are Christians who are trying to defend the use of rock music in the ministry.

Those who hold this principle need to answer the following questions:

If all musical styles are neutral, WHY IS IT THAT THE MOVIE "TEXT PAINTER" CAN USE DIFFERENT STYLES OF MUSIC TO CREATE DIFFERENT EMOTIONS? This can be illustrated by the old silent movies. There were no words to the movies except the text shown on the screen, but the musicians (sometimes a lone pianist or organist; sometimes an orchestra) could create feelings of fear, happiness, sorrow, romance, anger, indignation, tension, uncertainty, merely by changing the style of music. If there was a scene with the bad guy slowly sneaking up on the unsuspecting, sleeping heroine, the music would be tense and gloomy. If upbeat classical or peppy march music were scored for that type of scene, the movie would be like a comedy, because the acting would be saying one thing and the music would be saying something different. The movie text painter can create different emotions with different styles of music for the simple reason that music is NOT neutral. Music is a language. John Debney, one of the top composers of movie films, says:

> "The best directors I've worked with--like Mel [Gibson], Steven Spielberg, Tom Shadyac--have told me that music is fifty percent of the experience of the film. I think music is the voice of the soul of the emotional fabric of the film. I talk to many college classes, and I love to show them a couple of scenes first without music and then with music. When there's no music, people are always struck by how incredibly two-dimensional it is. And when you add music, it invariably evokes an emotional response" ("The Passion of the Musicians," *Christianity Today* web site, Aug. 31, 2004).

Debney is talking about the power of music as a language. Each style of music played by an orchestra creates different feelings and thoughts in the listeners. Put in a different way, if all musical styles are neutral, why does a military march never sound like a romance ballad or a baby lullaby sound like a punk rock concert? The reason is that music is not neutral; music is a language.

If all musical styles are neutral, WHY DO TAVERNS AND NIGHT CLUBS ALWAYS PLAY A CERTAIN KIND OF MUSIC? They never play sacred Christian music. The reason is because music is not neutral, and taverns and bars play a kind of music that fits the lifestyle of that setting. Music is a language.

If all musical styles are neutral, WHY DID THE OLD BLUESMEN BELIEVE THAT CERTAIN KINDS OF RHYTHMS CAUSED WOMEN TO BE MORALLY LOOSE? For example, Professor Longhair's boogie-woogie piano music is said to have caused women to "jump and wriggle." Robert Johnson, one of the pioneering bluesmen who died young because of his womanizing, said of his blues rhythms: "This sound affected most women in a way that I could never understand" (Robert Johnson, quoted from *The Bluesmen*). B.B. King, one of the biggest names in the blues, said in his autobiography, "The women reacted with their bodies flowing to a rhythm coming out of my guitar..." (B.B. King, *Blues All Around Me*). Those are powerful statements about the effect of a specific kind of music and rhythm. Were the bluesmen confused about their music? No, they are testifying to the fact that music is not neutral; it is a language, and since they wanted to create a lascivious atmosphere, they used suitable rhythms.

If all musical styles are neutral, WHY DO ROCK MUSICIANS CLAIM THAT THEIR HEAVILY SYNCOPATED RHYTHM IS SEXY?

Following are just a few of the many quotes we could give along this line.

> "Rock music is *sex*. THE BIG BEAT matches the body's rhythms" (Frank Zappa of the Mothers of Invention, *Life*, June 28, 1968).

> "That's what rock is all about--*sex with a 100 megaton bomb, THE BEAT!*" (Gene Simmons of the rock group Kiss, interview, *Entertainment Tonight*, ABC, Dec. 10, 1987).

> "Rock 'n' roll is 99% *sex*" (John Oates of the rock duo Hall & Oates, *Circus*, Jan. 31, 1976).

> "Rock 'n' roll is *pagan and primitive, and very jungle*, and that's how it should be!" (Malcolm McLaren, punk rock manager, *Rock*, August 1983).

"The THROBBING BEAT of rock provides a vital sexual release for adolescent audiences" (Jan Berry of Jan and Dean, cited by Ken Blanchard, *Pop Goes the Gospel*).

"The great strength of rock 'n' roll lies in ITS BEAT ... it is a music which is basically *sexual, un-Puritan* ... and a threat to established patterns and values" (Irwin Silber, Marxist, *Sing Out*, May 1965).

"Rock and roll aims for liberation and transcendence, eroticizing the spiritual and spiritualizing the erotic, because that is its ecumenical birthright" (Robert Palmer, *Rock & Roll an Unruly History*).

"Rock and roll is fun, it's full of energy ... It's *naughty*" (Tina Turner, cited in *Rock Facts*, Rock & Roll Hall of Fame and Museum).

"Rock and roll was something that's *hardcore, rough and wild and sweaty and wet and just loose*" (Patti Labelle, cited in *Rock Facts*, Rock & Roll Hall of Fame and Museum).

"The sex is definitely in the music, and sex is in ALL ASPECTS in the music" (Luke Campbell of 2 Live Crew).

Rapper Missy Elliot's third album, "Miss E ... So Addictive," is described as "a seductive cocktail of quirky rhythms and hypnotic beats."

The blues music (predecessor to rock and roll) that was played in Gayoso brothels in Memphis in the early part of the 20th century is described as "SEXUALLY SYNCOPATED SOUNDS" (Larry Nager, *Memphis Beat: The lives and Times of America's Musical Crossroads*).

Why do these secular rock lovers describe the heavily syncopated rock rhythms as sexy, primitive, seductive, rough, hardcore, naughty, loose, wild, and hypnotic? What do they know, or what are they admitting, that the Contemporary Christian Music crowd denies? They are admitting that music is not neutral and that the heavy backbeat of rock & roll is sensual.

If all musical styles are neutral, WHY DOES ONE OF THE FOREMOST EXPERTS IN DRUMMING CLAIM THAT CERTAIN RHYTHMS CAN ALTER THE STATE OF ONE'S CONSCIOUSNESS? Mickey Hart, drummer for the Grateful

Dead, has traveled the world researching the power of drums. In his book *Drumming at the Edge of Magic* he observes: "Everywhere you look on the planet people are USING DRUMS TO ALTER CONSCIOUSNESS. ... I've discovered, along with many others, the extraordinary power of music, particularly percussion, to influence the human mind and body. . . . There have been many times when I've felt as if the drum has carried me to an open door into another world." Hart says this because he knows that music is not neutral and that certain music produces certain results. Those who want to use music to enter a trance and to alter their state of consciousness *never* use traditional sacred Christian music, because it simply isn't suitable.

If all musical styles are neutral, WHY WOULD A VOODOO PRIESTESS SAY THAT HER GODS RESPOND TO CERTAIN RHYTHMS? *Consider this quote carefully:* "The rhythm is more important than the meaning of the words. Our gods respond to rhythm above all else" (a Macumba priestess in Brazil, quoted from *African Rhythm & Sensibility*). The voodoo priestess says this because she knows that music is not neutral and that certain rhythms interact with the spirit world. What a loud warning to those who have ears to hear!

If all musical styles are neutral, WHY DID THE 1960s LSD NEW AGE GURU TIMOTHY LEARY SAY, "DON'T LISTEN TO THE WORDS, IT'S THE MUSIC THAT HAS ITS OWN MESSAGE" *(Leary, Politics of Ecstasy). Leary said this because he knew that music is a language.*

If all musical styles are neutral, WHY DID JIMI HENDRIX, ONE OF THE FOREMOST EXPERTS IN ROCK RHYTHMS, CLAIM THAT CERTAIN TYPES OF MUSIC CREATE A CERTAIN ATMOSPHERE? "Atmospheres are going to come through music, because the music is a spiritual thing of its own" (Jimi Hendrix, *Life* magazine, Oct. 3, 1969).

If all musical styles are neutral, WHY DID ROCK AND ROLL HISTORIAN ROBERT PALMER SAY THAT THE SENSUAL INFLUENCE OF ROCK AND ROLL INHERES IN THE RHYTHM? "I believe in the transformative power of rock and roll ... this transformative power inheres not so much in the words of songs or the stances of the stars, but in the music itself--in the SOUND, and above all, in the BEAT" (Robert Palmer, *Rock & Roll an Unruly History*).

If all musical styles are neutral, WHY DID HOWARD HANSON, WHO DIRECTED THE PRESTIGIOUS EASTMAN SCHOOL OF MUSIC FOR 40 YEARS, SAY: "MUSIC CAN BE PHILOSOPHICAL OR ORGIASTIC. IT HAS POWERS FOR EVIL AS WELL AS FOR GOOD"? (cited from Frank Garlock's *The Language of Music*; Dr. Garlock is a graduate of Eastman and sat under Hanson).

If all musical styles are neutral, WHY DID THE WORLD FAMOUS CONDUCTOR LEONARD BERNSTEIN SAY THAT MUSIC IS A LANGUAGE THAT REACHES THE HEART? "Music doesn't have to pass through the censor of the brain before it can reach the heart. An f sharp doesn't have to be considered in the mind; it is a direct hit, and therefore all the more powerful" (Bernstein, *The Joy of Music*).

If all musical styles are neutral, WHY DOES THE BIBLE SPECIFY THAT BELIEVERS SHOULD SING A CERTAIN KIND OF MUSIC? "*Speaking to yourselves in psalms and hymns and spiritual songs, singing and making melody in your heart to the Lord*" (Ephesians 5:19). The word "spiritual" means *set apart* for God, *different* in character from the things of the world. A tavern or nightclub owner would never play sacred psalms, hymns, and spiritual songs over the music system, even if the words were not included. It would create the wrong atmosphere. Why, then, should believers borrow the music that tavern owners use to entertain and lull or stir the drinking crowd to their lascivious pleasures?

If all musical styles are neutral, THAT MEANS THAT THE DEVIL HASN'T CORRUPTED MUSIC, but such an idea is nonsensical. The devil hates God and has attempted to corrupt everything that God has created. He is called "the god of this world" (2 Cor. 4:4) and "the spirit that now worketh in the children of disobedience" (Eph. 2:2), and he has corrupted religion, literature, art, fashion--you name it. Music is one of the most powerful influences in society. To think that the Devil has not corrupted music for his own wicked purposes and for the enticement of fallen man is contrary to everything the Bible teaches.

If all musical styles are neutral, WHY DID JOSHUA DISCERN THAT THE MUSIC COMING UP FROM THE CAMP OF ISRAEL WAS "A NOISE OF WAR"? (Exodus 32:17). If music is neutral, how could he make any judgment at all about the nature of what he was hearing?

If all musical styles are neutral, WHY DO CHILDREN REACT DIFFERENTLY TO VARIOUS KINDS OF MUSIC? After visiting a church while on vacation, one of my readers submitted the following, "Why did my children behave properly during the traditional morning service, but jump around like they had 'ants in their pants' for 45 minutes during the loud rockish night service at a church we were visiting?"

We conclude that music is not "neutral" or "amoral." Music is a language, and in the Christian realm the message of the music must match the message of the lyrics and both must be spiritual. There are many styles of worldly music that preach a message that is contrary to the Bible and therefore cannot be used in the service of a holy God.

CONSERVATIVE EMERGING CHURCH ERROR # 12
REJECTION OF DISPENSATIONAL THEOLOGY AND THE IMMINENCY OF CHRIST'S RETURN

One of the characteristics of the emerging church in all of its aspects is the rejection of dispensational theology and the acceptance of an amillennial approach to Bible prophecy.

Mark Driscoll brazenly rejects dispensational theology. He refers to it as "pessimistic dispensationalism" (*Listening to the Beliefs of Emerging Churches*, p. 146). The Lighthouse Trails gives the following information: "On a YouTube session Driscoll says those eschatology-minded Christians who come to his church are not welcomed there. In Driscoll's book *Confessions of a Reformissional*, he mocks the idea of a rapture for believers and a one-world government with an Anti-christ who makes people wear a mark to buy, sell or trade (pp. 49-50). He added that this kind of end-time 'mission' was not a message from Jesus but rather one 'concocted from a cunning Serpent'" ("Mark Driscoll Rejects McLaren but Embraces Contemplative," Jan. 11, 2008, http://www.lighthousetrailsresearch.com/blog/index.php?p=931&more=1&c=1).

Driscoll also mocks the imminent Rapture doctrine in *The Radical Reformission*. He claims that the Rapture doctrine is evidence of the sickness of American Christians and mocks those who have the goal of leaving "this trailer park of a planet before God's tornado touches down on all the sinners" (p. 78). He calls dispensationalists "nutty, Christian, end-times-prophecy Kaczynskis" (p. 165). [Ted Kaczynski was the "Unabomber" terrorist who murdered three people and maimed 23 others in his 18-year-long campaign against modern technology.]

In his contribution to *Listening to the Beliefs of Emerging Churches*, Dan Kimball describes how that he rejected dispensational theology and the doctrine of an imminent Rapture (pp. 87-90) to his current position, that "the kingdom of God is here, now" (p. 102).

In *Breaking the Missional Code*, Ed Stetzer, who is on the Acts 29 board, says it is wrong to worry about whether the Rapture is coming. "When the disciples had an inordinate interest in the end times, much like we do today in North America among evangelicals, Jesus said, 'Do not get focused on that'" (p. 40).

He is referring to Acts 1:6-8, but Jesus was not talking there about the timing of the Rapture but about the coming of the kingdom of God. The disciples were expecting the kingdom to be set up immediately, but Jesus told them to focus rather on preaching the gospel and leave the timing of the kingdom to Him. This passage corrects the emerging church doctrine that we are building the kingdom of God in the world today, but it does not support the idea that we shouldn't be concerned about the imminent return of Christ.

Rick Warren also downplays dispensational theology and the imminent return of Christ. In *The Purpose Driven Life* he says:

> "When the disciples wanted to talk about prophecy, Jesus quickly switched the conversation to evangelism. He wanted them to concentrate on their mission in the world. He said in essence, 'The details of my return are none of your business. What is your business is the mission I have given you. Focus on that'" (p. 285).

This is NOT what Jesus said, not even *in essence*!

> "When they therefore were come together, they asked of him, saying, Lord, wilt thou at this time restore again the kingdom to Israel? And he said unto them, It is not for you to know the times or the seasons, which the Father hath put in his own power. But ye shall receive power, after that the Holy Ghost is come upon you: and ye shall be witnesses unto me both in Jerusalem, and in all Judaea, and in Samaria, and unto the uttermost part of the earth" (Acts 1:6-8).

Christ said to the disciples that He was not going to give them any more information about His return and the establishment of the kingdom beyond what He had already told them and what is already written in Scripture, and that they needed to concern themselves with preaching the Gospel. Christ was NOT saying that the study of Bible prophecy is unimportant. In fact, He said in Revelation 1:3 that those who study prophecy are blessed. Christ did NOT say that His disciples should not be constantly looking for His return, for He had already taught them: *"Therefore be ye also ready: for in such an hour as ye think not the Son of man cometh"* (Mat. 24:44). I am constantly amazed at how emergents of all brands misuse Scripture.

Roger Oakland comments:

> "Jesus was telling the disciples they could not know the day or the hour, but nowhere does Jesus ever indicate that 'the details of my return are none of your business.' Rather than quickly changing the subject, we find in Matthew 24 and Luke 21 two of the longest passages in Scripture quoting Jesus' own words, and what's more, where He details the signs of His coming. ... Later on, one of those disciples, John, was given an entire book to write on the details of Jesus' coming. Jesus continually said to be alert and ready for when He returns. ... Christians are called to witness and be watchmen. No Scripture exists that tells us to ignore the events that have been pointed out as signposts indicating the return of Jesus. If we do, we might be like the foolish virgins who fell asleep waiting for the bridegroom (Matthew 25:1-13)" (*Faith Undone*, pp. 155, 156).

WHAT DOES THE BIBLE SAY?

We have defended dispensationalism and the biblical doctrine of the kingdom of God in the section on the liberal emerging church. See "Liberal Emerging Church Error # 6: *A Social-Justice, Kingdom Building Gospel*" and "Liberal Emerging Church Error # 7: *Rejection of Dispensationalism and the Imminency of Christ's Return.*"

BRIAN MCLAREN: THE EMERGING CHURCH'S BIGGEST MOUTH

As the most prominent voice in the emerging church, Brian McLaren represents the philosophy of the movement. He claims that truth is a shifting thing, exalts doubt as highly as faith, and rejects the infallible inspiration of Scripture, the substitutionary atonement of Christ, and the eternal punishment of Hell fire.

A REVIEW OF "A NEW KIND OF CHRISTIAN"

McLaren's book "A New Kind of Christian: a Tale of Two Friends on a Spiritual Journey" won a *Christianity Today* Award of Merit in 2002 and has found a wide and approving audience in "evangelical" circles.

"A New Kind of Christian" presents theological liberalism in the guise of a wiser, kinder, gentler type of Christianity called "Postmodern." The semi-fictional account is about an evangelical pastor who has a crisis of faith and submits himself to the guidance of a liberal Episcopalian who is a graduate of Princeton Divinity School and a former Presbyterian pastor. This Postmodern guide, who is named "Dr. Neil Oliver," is called "Neo" by his friends. Neo resigned the pastorate because he was too liberal for his denomination and is teaching high school when we meet him in McLaren's book.

The book recounts the evangelical pastor's journey from a position of faith in the Bible as the absolute standard for truth, a position in which doctrine is either right or wrong, scriptural or unscriptural, to a pliable position in which "faith is more about a way of life than a system of belief, where being authentically good is more important than being doctrinally right" (from the back cover of "A New Kind of Christian").

Gary E. Gilly hit the nail on the head in his review of "A New Kind of Christian" by observing: "More specifically, McLaren rejects absolute truth, authority, theology, objectivity, certainty and clarity. He embraces relativism, inclusivism, deconstructionism, stories (to replace truth), creative interpretation of Scripture, neo-orthodoxy, and tolerance."

As the evangelical pastor in "A New Kind of Christian" begins his sad journey into theological liberalism (which he wants to call "postmodern") he describes himself in these words:

> "I feel like a fundamentalist who's losing his grip--whose fundamentals are cracking and fraying and falling apart and slipping through my fingers. It's like I thought I was building my house on rock, but it turned out to be ice, and now global warming has hit, and the ice is melting and everything is crumbling" (p. 22).

When he first begins talking with "Neo," the evangelical pastor admits that he is afraid that Neo's ideas are corrupting him and turning him into a heretic (p. 26), but he quenches the fear and proceeds down the path of error.

Instead of opening his Bible and seeking the face of God alone and finding out what God has to say in His Word and re-orienting himself to the eternal Word of God, instead of confiding in a man of God who believes the Bible, this evangelical pastor turns, in his hour of doubt, to a clever unbeliever and is led into the deepest error. This is exactly what is happening to men and women throughout the evangelical world, because they have been brainwashed to think that separation from false doctrine is mean-spirited and that a "positive, non-judgmental" approach to Christianity is preferable. As a consequence, evangelicalism, over the past 50 years, has been infiltrated with every sort of heresy.

A visit to a typical evangelical bookstore is evidence of this. On the shelves of such a bookstore you will find Chuck Colson's radical ecumenism, Robert Schuller's Self-esteemism, C.S. Lewis's Anglo-Catholicism, and all sorts of Psycho-heresy. You will find Mother Teresa exalted as a model Christian, even though she was committed to a false gospel and thought Jesus was a Catholic wafer and believed that Hindus go to Heaven if they believe sincerely in their gods. You will find books by Bruce Metzger, who believes that Jonah is "popular legend" and Job is an "ancient folktale," and books by Kurt Aland, who rejected the infallibility of Scripture and claimed that even the canon of Scripture is yet unsettled. You will find Greek New Testaments edited by the Roman Catholic Cardinal Carlo Martini. You will find books by men who claim that Matthew and Mark and Luke didn't write their Gospels directly by divine inspiration but that they used various mythical sources such as a "Q" document. You will find histories that present the Roman Catholic Church as an authentic form of Christianity. You will find heretical "church fathers" such as Augustine and Origen exalted as men of God. You will find books by charismatics who believe that the Holy Spirit knocks believers onto the floor and glues them there and that the supernatural gift of tongues is a talent that can be learned. And we have only begun to describe the dangers that are found in a typical evangelical Christian bookstore today.

It is New Evangelicalism that has created the climate whereby the average Christian does not have a mindset of being on the constant lookout for heresy and of carefully testing everything by Scripture. It has created a gullible generation.

Brian McLaren's "A New Kind of Christian" is a dangerous book that ridicules a staunchly biblical, fundamentalist position on every hand. It slanderously describes such a position as Phariseeism and likens it to medieval Roman Catholicism. In the very beginning of the book, the

Postmodern guide Neo says: "I don't dislike fundamentalists, taken individually--they tend to be pretty nice folks. Get them together in a group though, and I get nervous. I start to twitch and break out in a rash" (p. 9).

That is the best thing the book has to say about those who hold a strict Biblicist stance, whereas theological liberals and Romanists are depicted in a much more sympathetic light.

Though purporting to represent a more intellectual approach to Christianity, the book is filled with strawman arguments, shallow reasoning, and Scripture taken wildly out of context.

It teaches that the Bible is not the infallible Word of God and that all doctrines and theologies are non-absolute, that we need to approach the Bible "on less defined terms" (p. 56). It teaches that the Bible alone should not be our authority, but that the Bible should be one of many authorities, such as tradition, reason, exemplary people and institutions one has come to trust, and spiritual experience (pp. 54, 55). It teaches that it is wrong and Pharisaical to look upon the Bible as "God's encyclopedia, God's rule book, God's answer book" (p. 52). It teaches that the authority of the Bible is not in the text itself but in a mystical level above and beyond the text (p. 51).

It teaches that Christians should not try to judge right from wrong in an absolute sense because all of our understanding of the Bible is colored and conditioned by extra-biblical things such as one's time and culture. It teaches that the postmodern Christian is one who "relativizes your own modern viewpoint," thus understanding that everything he believes about the Bible and Christianity is only relative and uncertain (p. 35). It teaches that there is no such thing as "the Christian worldview," that every doctrinal position, "no matter how resplendent with biblical quotations--can claim to be the ultimate Christian worldview, because every model is at the least limited by the limitations of the contemporary human mind, not to mention the 'taste in universes' of that particular age" (pp. 36, 37).

It teaches that ecumenism is good and that all "denominations," including Roman Catholicism, can contribute to a proper form of Christianity. We are informed that "there are good Catholics, good Greek Orthodox, good Pentecostals, and good Episcopalians" (p. 73). It teaches that labels such as Catholic, Protestant, liberal, and evangelical "are about to become inconsequential" in a postmodern Christianity (p. 41). It teaches that mystical Catholic practices are authentic and desirable (p. 58).

It teaches that people should not ask pastors questions such as, "Do you believe in inerrancy?" or "What's your position on homosexuality?" because to make them answer such questions is to "cheapen" them and to make them sell themselves (p. 61).

It teaches that the real issue for Jesus is "goodness, not just rightness" (p. 61), as if goodness and righteousness and truth are in some sort of conflict.

"A New Kind of Christian" teaches that Jesus' objective was "holistic reconciliation."

> "I think what Jesus was about ... was a global, public movement or revolution to bring holistic reconciliation, a reconnection with God, with others, with ourselves, with our environment" (p. 73).

Here the author is not referring to what Jesus will do when He returns to establish His kingdom but what he is allegedly doing today. He claims the proper objective of churches is not merely the salvation of souls but the renewal of the world and saving the planet from destruction (p. 83).

It teaches that it is right for Christians to use pagan practices such as the Native American sweat lodge, peace pipe, dance, dream catcher, and smoke (pp. 26, 74-78). Apparently McLaren thinks that God's warning, *Learn not the way of the heathen*," (Jer. 10:2), is no longer in effect.

It teaches that unbelievers and pagans can possibly be saved without personal faith in Christ (p. 92).

QUOTES FROM OTHER BOOKS AND ARTICLES BY MCLAREN

In *A Generous Orthodoxy*, McLaren says the Bible is "not a look-it-up encyclopedia of timeless moral truths, but the unfolding narrative of God at work..." (p. 190). He compliments the Anglicans because to them the Bible is *a factor* in their thinking "but it is never *sola*--never the only factor. Rather Scripture is always in dialogue with tradition, reason, and experience" (p. 235).

McLaren's doctrine of salvation is as murky as any I have ever read. He says:

> "I DON'T THINK WE'VE GOT THE GOSPEL RIGHT YET. What does it mean to be 'saved'? When I read the Bible, I don't see it meaning, 'I'm going to heaven after I die.' Before modern evangelicalism nobody accepted Jesus Christ as their personal Savior, or walked down an aisle, or said the sinner's prayer. I don't think the liberals have it right. But I don't think we have it right either. None of us has arrived at orthodoxy" ("The Emergent Mystique," *Christianity Today*, Nov. 2004, p. 40).

McLaren doesn't think we have the gospel right yet, but two thousand years ago the Lord Jesus commanded, *"Go ye into all the world, and preach the gospel to every creature"* (Mark 16:15). It is a little late to be trying to get the gospel right, isn't it!

In *A New Kind of Christian*, McLaren has his postmodern hero say that he rejects the idea that the gospel is about getting individual souls into Heaven because this "smacked of selfishness" and was unacceptable to postmodern thinking (pp. 82, 83).

McLaren identifies with Anabaptists because they (allegedly) teach that "one becomes a Christian through an event, process, or both, in which one identifies with Jesus, his mission, and his followers" (*A Generous Orthodoxy*, p. 229). Though Christ described salvation as a birth (John 3), McLaren thinks it might be more a process than an event.

McLaren has "a strong conviction that THE EXCLUSIVE, HELL-ORIENTED GOSPEL IS NOT THE WAY FORWARD" (*A Generous Orthodoxy*, p. 120, f. 48).

McLaren says the emerging approach is "less rigid, more generous" (*A Generous Orthodoxy*, p. 190), and it is "conversational, never attempting to be the last word, and thus silence other voices" (p. 169). He says it "doesn't claim too much; it admits it walks with a limp" (p. 171). He says, "To be a Christian in a generously orthodox way is not to claim to have the truth captured, stuffed, and mounted on the wall" (p. 293). He likens doctrinal dogmatism to smoking cigarettes, saying that "it is a hard-to-break Protestant habit that is hazardous to spiritual health" (p. 217).

In his books *The Secret Message of Jesus* and *Everything Must Change*, McLaren says that "the essential message of Jesus" is the kingdom of God, and this is "not just a message *about* Jesus that focused on the afterlife, but rather the core message *of* Jesus that focused on personal, SOCIAL, AND GLOBAL TRANSFORMATION IN THIS LIFE" (*Everything Must Change*, p. 22). He says that THE KINGDOM OF GOD IS "ABOUT CHANGING THIS WORLD" (p. 23).

McLaren mocks the "fundamentalist expectations" of a literal second coming of Christ with its attendant judgments on the world and assumes that the world will go on like it is for hundreds of thousands of years (*A Generous Orthodoxy*, p. 305). He calls the literal, imminent return of Christ "pop-Evangelical eschatology" (*Generous Orthodoxy*, p. 267) and the "eschatology of abandonment" (interview with Planet Preterist, Jan. 30, 2005, http://planetpreterist.com/news-2774.html).

McLaren says that the book of Revelation is not a "book about the distant future" but is "a way of talking about the challenges of the immediate present" (*The Secret Message of Jesus*, 2007, p. 176). He says that phrases such as "the moon will turn to blood" "are no more to be taken literally than phrases we might read in the paper today" (*The Secret Message*, p. 178).

McLaren epitomizes the emerging church's radical ecumenism by calling himself "evangelical, post-protestant, liberal/conservative, mystical/poetic, biblical, charismatic/contemplative, fundamentalist/Calvinist, anabaptist/anglican, Methodist, catholic, green, incarnational, emergent" (*A Generous Orthodoxy*, subtitle to the book).

The fact that these various doctrinal positions are contradictory and non-reconcilable does not bother the man one iota. He is fully committed to "orthoparadoxy," being convinced that he can hold contradictions in harmony.

In June 2006 McLaren joined the blasphemous Marcus Borg of the Jesus Seminar, who boldly denies the Jesus of the Bible, at the Center for Spiritual Development in Portland, Oregon. The center promotes New Age and occultic practices such as Yoga, Sufism, Tai Chi, Enneagram, and Reiki. The Episcopalian heretic John Shelby Spong has also spoken at this Center.

McLaren wrote a glowing recommendation of Alan Jones' book *Reimagining Christianity*. Jones calls the gospel of the cross a vile doctrine, claims that there is no objective authority, and says that Hindus and Buddhists are God's people:

> "But another ancient strand of Christianity teaches that we are all caught up in the Divine Mystery we call God, that the Spirit is in everyone, and that there are depths of interpretation yet to be plumbed. ... At the cathedral [Grace Episcopal Cathedral in San Francisco] we 'break the bread' for those who follow the path of the Buddha and walk the way of the Hindus" (*Reimagining Christianity*, 2005, p. 89).

Of this book McLaren says:

> "It used to be that Christian institutions and systems of dogma sustained the spiritual life of Christians. Increasingly, spirituality itself is what sustains everything else. Alan Jones is a pioneer in reimagining a Christian faith that emerges from authentic spirituality. His work stimulates and encourages me deeply" (endorsement on back cover).

McLaren says, "I DON'T THINK IT'S OUR BUSINESS TO PROGNOSTICATE THE ETERNAL DESTINIES OF ANYONE ELSE" (p. 92) and offers a quote from a C.S. Lewis novel as his authority. In this novel Lewis's character was a soldier who served a false god named Tash all his life, but he was accepted nonetheless by Aslan, who represents Christ.

> "Alas, Lord, I am no son of Thine but the servant of Tash. He answered, Child, all the service thou has done to Tash, I account as service done to me. ... Therefore if any man swear by Tash and keep his oath for the oath's sake, it is by me that he has truly sworn, though he know it not, and it is I who reward him."

According to C.S. Lewis, who is deeply loved by all branches of the emerging church, an individual might be saved even if he follows a false religion in this life and makes no personal profession of faith in Jesus Christ.

McLaren said that the Indian Hindu leader Gandhi "sought to follow the way of Christ without identifying himself as a Christian" (*A Generous Orthodoxy*, p. 189).

McLaren teaches that there is much good in pagan religions, that they have been a good thing for the world.

> "My knowledge of Buddhism is rudimentary, but I have to tell you that much of what I understand strikes me as wonderful and insightful, and the same can be said of the teachings of Muhammad, though of course I have my disagreements. ... I'd have to say that the world is better off for having these religions than having no religions at all, or just one, even if it were ours. ... They aren't the enemy of the gospel, in my mind..." (pp. 62, 63).

The man needs to spend a few years living in India or Nepal to see how the Hindu religion has corrupted and debased the people, how it has turned women into chattel, cows and snakes into gods, certain classes of people into untouchables, and human life in general into something of little value, how it has encouraged pride and self-centeredness and corruption at every level of society and has discouraged humility and compassion. Or maybe he should spend a few years in an Islamic country such as Saudi Arabia or Pakistan to see what the Muslim religion has done to people. Are they better off because they can change their religion only on the pain of death and because a woman has no real rights and because she can be killed just because she does something that the male members of the family consider unacceptable?

McLaren says that Buddhism is not the enemy of the gospel, but how can a religion that teaches that Jesus Christ is not God and not the only Saviour of the world NOT be an enemy of the gospel? He says the Muslim religion is not the enemy of the gospel, but how can a religion that teaches that Jesus was not God and did not die for our sins and that forbids its members to convert to the Christ of the Bible NOT be an enemy of the gospel?

In a podcast interview in January 2006 with Leif Hansen, McLaren said that if the doctrine of Hell is true then the Christ's message and cross is "false advertising." He said that since Christ taught that God's kingdom doesn't come through violence and coercion, this would be contrary to the judgment of Hell. He also said if Hell is true then people can legitimately question God's goodness.

This interview is truly amazing in a fearful way. Hansen says that he doubts God's very existence and even casts a profanity at Jesus. And yet the two of them ramble on in a very knowing sort of way, mocking fundamentalists and Calvinists and anyone else who won't accept the emerging church's unbelief. It is a great warning that if you reject the truth you are walking in utter darkness.

McLaren says:

> "Does it make sense for a good being to create creatures who will experience infinite torture, infinite time, infinite--you know, never be

numbed in their consciousness? I mean, how would you even create a universe where that sort of thing could happen? It just sounds--It really raises some questions about the goodness of God. ...

"The traditional understanding says that God asks of us something that God is incapable of Himself. God asks us to forgive people. But God is incapable of forgiving. God can't forgive unless He punishes somebody in place of the person He was going to forgive. God doesn't say things to you--Forgive your wife, and then go kick the dog to vent your anger. God asks you to actually forgive. And there's a certain sense that, A COMMON UNDERSTANDING OF THE ATONEMENT PRESENTS A GOD WHO IS INCAPABLE OF FORGIVING. UNLESS HE KICKS SOMEBODY ELSE. ...

"... one of the huge problems is the traditional understanding of hell. Because if the cross is in line with Jesus' teaching then--I won't say, the only, and I certainly won't say even the primary--but a primary meaning of the cross is that the kingdom of God doesn't come like the kingdoms of this world, by inflicting violence and coercing people. But that the kingdom of God comes through suffering and willing, voluntary sacrifice. But in an ironic way, THE DOCTRINE OF HELL BASICALLY SAYS, NO, THAT THAT'S NOT REALLY TRUE. THAT IN THE END, GOD GETS HIS WAY THROUGH COERCION AND VIOLENCE AND INTIMIDATION AND DOMINATION, just like every other kingdom does. The cross isn't the center then. The cross is almost a distraction and false advertising for God" (McLaren, http://www.understandthetimes.org/mclarentrans.shtml and http://str.typepad.com/weblog/2006/01/brian_mclaren_p.html).

Hansen replies as follows:

"Oh, Brian, that was just so beautifully said. I was tempted to get on my soap box there and you know--Because as you and I know there are so many illustrations and examples that you could give that show why THE TRADITIONAL VIEW OF HELL COMPLETELY FALLS IN THE FACE OF--IT'S JUST ANTITHETICAL TO THE CROSS. But the way you put it there, I love that. It's false advertising. And here, Jesus is saying, turn the other cheek. Love your enemy. Forgive seven times seventy. Return violence with self-sacrificial love. But if we believe the traditional view of hell, it's like, well, do that for a short amount of time. Because eventually, God's going to get them."

McLaren also said:

"The church has been preoccupied with the question, 'What happens to your soul after you die?' AS IF THE REASON FOR JESUS COMING CAN BE SUMMED UP IN, 'JESUS IS TRYING TO HELP GET MORE SOULS INTO HEAVEN, AS OPPOSED TO HELL, AFTER THEY DIE.' I JUST THINK A FAIR READING OF THE GOSPELS BLOWS THAT OUT OF THE WATER. I don't think that the entire message and life of Jesus can be boiled down to that bottom line" ("The Emerging Church," Part Two, *Religion & Ethics*, July 15, 2005, http://www.pbs.org/wnet/religionandethics/week846/cover.html).

In the same interview McLaren said that the traditional doctrine of substitutionary atonement makes God into a strange monster that wants to kill his own son and needs to be restrained. He also says the substitutionary atonement detracts from social justice issues. He even blasphemously mocks the atonement by saying that if it is true it would mean that God can't forgive one person unless he "kicks someone else." Consider this very foolish statement.

"What's so bad about sin? Now, I can just imagine some people quoting--See, McLaren doesn't think sin is a problem. I take sin really, seriously. But here's the problem, If I were to make this sort of analogy or parable. When I had little children, if one of my little children--Let's say my son Brett, was beating up on his little brother, Trevor. Now, Trevor is bigger. But back then--What was the problem? Was the problem that I don't want my younger son to get hurt and I don't want my older son to be a bully. I want my older son to be a good person. I want my younger son to be a good person. I want them to have a great relationship. Then the problem of sin is what it does to my family and what it does to my boys, you know. That's the problem with sin.

"But what we've created is, the problem of sin is that I am so angry at my son Brett for beating up his younger brother, I'm going to kill him. So now the problem we've got to solve is how to keep me from killing my son. Does that make sense?

"And so now it seems to me the entire Christian theology has shifted so now the problem is, how can we keep me from killing Brett? And I don't think that's the kind of God that we serve. I think the problem is God wants His children to get along with each other. He wants them to be good people. Because He's good. And His vision for creation is that they'll love each other and be good to each other and enjoy each other and have a lot of fun together. ...

"We have a vision that the real problem is God wants to kill us all. And we've got to somehow solve that problem. And what that does to me, Leif, that is so significant, is that it then minimizes the concern about injustice between human beings. That becomes a peripheral concern. But what if that's God's real concern, from beginning to end, see? ...

"The traditional understanding says that God asks of us something that God is incapable of Himself. God asks us to forgive people. But God is incapable of forgiving. God can't forgive unless He punishes somebody in place of the person He was going to forgive. God doesn't say things to you--Forgive your wife, and then go kick the dog to vent your anger. God asks you to actually forgive. And there's a certain sense that, a common understanding of the atonement presents a God who is incapable of forgiving. Unless He kicks somebody else" (McLaren, http://www.understandthetimes.org/mclarentrans.shtml and http://str.typepad.com/weblog/2006/01/brian_mclaren_p.html).

What McLaren ignores is God's holiness and justice. God is not just a father like a human father. He is a holy and just God who has given man His righteous Law. That Law, having been broken, must be satisfied. The wages of sin is death. Without the shedding of blood is no remission. And to provide the atonement, God hasn't "kicked" anyone but Himself!

On the issue of homosexuality, McLaren says:

> "Frankly, many of us don't know what we should think about homosexuality. ... We aren't sure if or where lines are to be drawn, nor do we know how to enforce with fairness whatever lines are drawn. ... Perhaps we need a five-year moratorium on making pronouncements" ("Brian McLaren on the Homosexual Question," Jan. 23, 2006, http://blog.christianitytoday.com/outofur/archives/2006/01/brian_mclaren_o.html).

In December 2006, McLaren spoke at the Open Door Community Church in Sherwood, Arkansas. The church's web site says:

> "The leadership at Open Door Community Churches are excited to see gay and non-gay Christians worshiping together as one. We believe that gay and non-gay Christians can and should come to the table of the Lord together, side by side, without labels. We believe that as these two historically separate communities join together at the cross of Jesus Christ a healing and a new understanding of oneness in Christ occurs in both groups. We are part of a growing revival of grace-filled Christians transcending either the terms 'conservative' or 'liberal.' Above all things, we are a GRACE CHURCH! We are a family embracing the full spectrum of race, age, gender, family status, sexual orientation, economic status and denominational background."

On his own web site McLaren even recommends the writings of New Ager Ken Wilber.

Roger Oakland remarks:

> "Ken Wilber was raised in a conservative Christian church, but at some point he left that faith and is now a major proponent of Buddhist mysticism. His book that Bell recommends, *A Brief History of Everything*, is published by Shambhala Publications, named after the term, which in Buddhism means the mystical abode of spirit beings. ... Wilber is perhaps best known for what he calls integral theory. On his website, he has a chart called the Integral Life Practice Matrix, which lists several activities one can practice 'to authentically exercise all aspects or dimensions of your own being-in-the-world' Here are a few of these spiritual activities that Wilber promotes: yoga, Zen, centering prayer, kabbalah (Jewish mysticism), TM, tantra (Hindu-based sexuality), and kundalini yoga. ... *A Brief History of Everything* discusses these practices (in a favorable light) as well. For Rob Bell to say that Wilber's book is 'mind-blowing' and readers should spend three months in it leaves no room for doubt regarding Rob Bell's spiritual sympathies. What is alarming is that so many Christian venues, such as Christian junior high and high schools, are using *Velvet Elvis* and the *Noomas*" (*Faith Undone*, p. 110).

In *Up from Eden: A Transpersonal View of Human Evolution* (1981, 2004), Ken Wilber calls the Garden of Eden a "fable" and the biblical view of history "amusing" (pp. xix, 3). He describes his "perennial philosophy" as follows:

> "... it is true that there is some sort of Infinite, some type of Absolute Godhead, but it cannot properly be conceived as a colossal Being, a great Daddy, or a big Creator set apart from its creations, from things and events and human beings themselves. Rather, it is best conceived (metaphorically) as the ground or suchness or condition of all things and events. It is not a Big Thing set apart from finite things, but rather the reality or suchness or ground of all things. ... the perennial philosophy declares that the absolute is One, Whole, and Undivided" (p. 6).

CONCLUSION

Beware of Brian McLaren and the emerging church!

A good test is to ask Christian leaders what they think of this man. Assuming they are familiar with his writings, if they fudge and hedge, refusing to come right out and mark him as a dangerous heretic, they are heretics themselves or at least well down the road of serious compromise!

CAIN THE FIRST EMERGENT WORSHIPER

The emerging church says Christians should worship God in their own individual ways, through art, dance, whatever.

Rick Warren says, "There is no one-size-fits-all approach to worship and friendship with God" (*The Purpose Driven Life*, p. 103).

On pages 22-28 of his book *Sacred Pathways: Discover Your Soul's Path to God*, Gary Thomas says that there are nine ways that people draw near to God: *Naturalists* are inspired to love God out-of-doors; *sensates* love God with their senses; *traditionalists* love God through rituals, liturgies, unchanging structures; *ascetics* love God in solitude and simplicity; *activists* love God through battling injustice; *caregivers* love God by meeting people's needs; *enthusiasts* love God through celebrations; *contemplatives* love God through adoration; and *intellectuals* love God by studying.

This sounds like Cain, who was the first emerging worshipper. He wanted to approach God and delve into spiritual things, but he wanted to do it on his own terms rather than follow the precise instructions of God's Word. He didn't want to be "boxed in."

Cain was the firstborn son of Adam and Eve and his younger brother Abel was a prophet (Luke 11:50-51). God spoke through Abel and instructed the family that He was to be approached through the sacrifice of a lamb, which pointed to the coming of the Lamb of God, Jesus Christ (Hebrews 12:24). Abel obeyed and brought the prescribed offering, shedding its blood and killing it as God had instructed. Cain decided to come on his own terms, instead, and brought an offering of the vegetables that he had grown with his own hands. It was an emerging, cool, artsy type of worship!

Abel offered by faith in God's Word, whereas Cain offered in the presumption of his own thinking (Heb. 11:4). God rejected Cain's offering and accepted Abel's (Genesis 4:1-11), and as a result the cool Cain killed his own brother.

As David Moss says in *God's Song*, (Fundamental Evangelistic Association, Fresno, CA):

> "Cain thought that the most important thing in life was for him to express himself. He thought God would be pleased if he used his own imagination in offering a creative form of sacrifice. Why was God not pleased? Because God did not want human imagination or 'creativity' as a gift. Rather, He wanted conformity to His precise plan. Humans reject this dogmatic rigidity and substitute for it their theory of existential relativism. As each one tills and cultivates his own life, he will inevitably express reality differently from others. There must be, therefore--according to man's imagination--many legitimate roads to follow in order to accommodate the many different orientations of people and the many different ways in which they express themselves.
> ...
>
> It is when we allow the agents of sensuality to enter our worship that the order and peacefulness of worship is destroyed, not enhanced. The expressiveness of the individual becomes more important than what pleases God. God is expected to be happy because men and women are giving Him something they 'grew with their own hands,' but in the process, the sacrifice of Cain is repeated over and over again to the music of the modern church (David Moss, *God's Song*, pp. 46, 49).

CHARLES SPURGEON EXPOSED THE EMERGING CHURCH

The emerging church represented by Brian McLaren and the Emergent village is not as new as it appears to be. It was already raising its head in the late 19th century, because Charles Spurgeon described it perfectly in his comments on James 5:19-20.

He called it "modern thought" and "deceitful infidelity."

Spurgeon also described the tolerant attitude of modern evangelicalism that puts up with emerging heresies. He called this "latitudinarianism."

"Brethren, if any of you do err from the truth, and one convert him; Let him know, that he which converteth the sinner from the error of his way shall save a soul from death, and shall hide a multitude of sins" (James 5:19-20).

It was not merely that he fell into a mistake upon some lesser matter which might be compared to the fringe of the gospel, but he erred in some vital doctrine--he departed from the faith in its fundamentals. There are some truths which must be believed, they are essential to salvation, and if not heartily accepted the soul will be ruined. This man had been professedly orthodox, but he turned aside from the truth on an essential point.

Now, in those days the saints did not say: 'We must be largely charitable, and leave this brother to his own opinion; he sees truth from a different standpoint, and has a rather different way of putting it, but his opinions are as good as our own, and we must not say that he is in error.'

That is at present the fashionable way of trifling with divine truth, and making things pleasant all round. Thus the gospel is debased and another gospel propagated.

I should like to ask modern broad churchmen whether there is any doctrine of any sort for which it would be worth a man's while to burn or to lie in prison. I do not believe they could give me an answer, for if their latitudinarianism be correct, the martyrs were fools of the first magnitude.

From what I see of their writings and their teachings, it appears to me that the modern thinkers treat the whole compass of revealed truth with entire indifference; and, though perhaps they may feel sorry that wilder spirits should go too far in free-thinking, and though they had rather they would be more moderate, yet, upon the whole, so large is their liberality, that they are not sure enough of anything to be able to condemn the reverse of it as a deadly error.

To them black and white are terms which may be applied to the same colour, as you view it from different standpoints. Yea and nay are equally true in their esteem. Their theology shifts like the Goodwin Sands, and they regard all firmness as so much bigotry. Errors and truths are equally comprehensible within the circle of their charity.

It was not in this way that the apostles regarded error. They did not prescribe large-hearted charity towards falsehood, or hold up the errorist as a man of deep thought, whose views were 'refreshingly original'; far less did they utter some wicked nonsense about the probability of their having more faith in honest doubt than in half the creeds.

They did not believe in justification by doubting, as our Neologians do; they set about the conversion of the erring brother; they treated him as a person who needed conversion: and viewed him as a man who, if he were not converted, would suffer the death of his soul, and be covered with a multitude of sins.

They were not such easy-going people as our cultured friends of the school of 'modern thought,' who have learned at last that the deity of Christ may be denied, the work of the Holy Spirit ignored, the inspiration of scripture rejected, the atonement disbelieved, and regeneration dispensed with, and yet the man who does all this may be as good a Christian as the most devout believer!

O God, deliver us from this deceitful infidelity, which while it does damage to the erring man, and often prevents his being reclaimed, does yet more mischief to our own hearts by teaching us that truth is unimportant, and falsehood a trifle, and so destroys our allegiance to the God of truth, and makes us traitors instead of loyal subjects to the King of kings (C.H. Spurgeon, "Restoring Those Who Have Erred," *Words of Counsel for Christian Workers*, pp. 139-142).

BIBLIOGRAPHY

EMERGING CHURCH

Ashley, Jennifer, ed. *The Relevant Church: A New Vision for Communities of Faith*. Chapters by Brian Kay, Alex McManus, Mark Driscoll, Sandra Barrett, Ian Nicholson, Tommy Kyllonen, Mike Bickle, Timothy Keel, Karen Ward, Todd Spitzer, Dustin Dagby, Jason Zahariades, Holly Rankin Zaher, Mark Seandrette, and Mark Howerton. Lake Mary, FL: Relevant Books, 2004. 171 pp.

Batterson, Mark. *In a Pit with a Lion on a Snowy Day*. Recommendations on the inside of the book by Frank Wright, Brian McLaren, Ed Young, Lindy Lowry, Craig Groeschel, and Margaret Feinberg. Colorado Springs: Multnomah Books, 2006. 182 pp.

Bell, Rob (1970-). *Velvet Elvis: Repainting the Christian Faith*. Grand Rapids: Zondervan, 2005. 194 pp.

Campolo, Anthony (1935-). *Carpe Diem: Seize the Day*. Dallas: Word Publishing, 1994. 234 pp.

———. *The God of Intimacy and Action: Reconnecting Ancient Spiritual Practice*.

———. *How to Be Pentecostal Without Speaking in Tongues*. Dallas: Word Publishing, 1991. 176 pp.

———. *How to Rescue the Earth Without Worshiping Nature*. Nashville: Thomas Nelson, 1992. 211 pp.

———. *The Kingdom of God Is a Party*. Dallas: Word Publishing, 1990. 150 pp.

———. *Partly Right: Christianity Responds to Its Critics*. Waco, TX: Word Books, 1985. 222 pp.

———. *A Reasonable Faith: Responding to Secularism*. Waco, TX: Word Books, 1993. 199 pp.

———. *Red Letter Christians: A Citizen's Guide to Faith and Politics*. Foreword by Jim Wallis. Ventura, CA: Regal, 2008. 240 pp.

———. *Speaking My Mind: The Radical Evangelical Prophet Tackles the Tough Issues Christians Are Afraid to Face*. Nashville: W Publishing Group, 2004. 240 pp.

———, and Gordon Aeschliman. *50 Ways You Can Reach the World.* Downers Grove, IL: InterVarsity Press, 1993. 148 pp.

Chesterton, Gilbert Keith (1874-1936). *Orthodoxy.* Introduction by Philip Yancy. New York: Image Books, 2001 reprint of the 1908 original. 170 pp.

Claiborne, Shane (1975-). *Irresistible Revolution: Living as an Ordinary Radical.* Foreword by Jim Wallis. Grand Rapids: Zondervan, 2006. 367 pp.

Driscoll, Mark (1970-). *Confessions of a Reformission Rev. Hard Lessons from an Emerging Missional Church.* Grand Rapids: Zondervan, 2006. 207 pp.

———. *The Radical Reformission: Reaching out without Selling out.* Grand Rapids: Zondervan, 2004. 204 pp.

Foster, David (c. 1969-). *A Renegade's Guide to God: Finding Life Outside Conventional Christianity.* Recommendations on back cover by Brian McLaren, Stephen Baldwin, Mike Huckabee, Pat Williams, and Ken Abraham. New York: Faith Words, 2006. 295 pp.

Gibbs, Eddie, and Ryan Bolger. *Emerging Churches: Creating Christian Community in Postmodern Cultures.* Recommendations in the front of the book by Robert Webber, Karen Ward, John Franke, Doug Pagitt, Alan Roxburgh, and Jonny Baker. Grand Rapids: Baker, 2005. 345 pp.

Grenz, Stanley James (1950-2005), and John Franke. *Beyond Foundationalism: Shaping Theology in a Postmodern Context.* 2000.

Jones, Alan. *Reimagining Christianity.*

Jones, Tony. *Postmodern Youth Ministry: Exploring Cultural Shift, Creating Holistic Connections, Cultivating Authentic Community.* 2001

———. *The Sacred Way: Spiritual Practices for Everyday Life.* Grand Rapids: Zondervan, 2005. 222 pp.

———. *Soul Shaper: Exploring Spirituality and Contemplative Practices in Youth Ministry.* 2003.

Kimball, Dan. *The Emerging Church: Vintage Christianity for New Generations.* Forewords by Rick Warren and Brian McLaren. Articles by Rick Warren, Howard Hendricks, Brian McLaren, Sally Morgenthaler, Chip Ingram, Mark Oestreicher. Recommendations by John Ortberg, Luis Palau, Bob Buford, Erwin McManus, Nancy Beach, Brian McLaren, Marshall Shelley, Tic Long, Chris Seay, David Crowder, Sally Morgenthaler, Rick Warren, Howard Hendricks, Spencer Burke, Carol Childress, Daniel Hill, Tony Jones, Dieter Zander, Paul Allen, Gary Tuck, Les Christie, Josh Fox. Grand Rapids: Zondervan, 2003. 266 pp.

———. *The Emerging Worship: Creating Worship Gatherings for New Generations.* Forewords by David Crowder and Sally Morgenthaler. Grand Rapids: Zondervan, 2004. 238 pp.

———. *They Like Jesus, but Not the Church: Insights from Emerging Generations.* Grand Rapids: Zondervan, 2007. 271 pp.

McCullough, Donald. *If Grace Is So Amazing Why Don't We Like It? How God's Radical Love Turns the World Upside Down.* Recommendations on back cover: M. Craig Barnes of Pittsburgh Theological Seminary, Nancy Ortber formerly teaching pastor of Willow Creek Community Church, and Alan Jones, dean of Grace Cathedral, San Francisco. San Francisco: Jossey-Bass, 2005. 245 pp.

McLaren, Brian D. (1956-). *The Church on the Other Side.*

———. *Everything Must Change: Jesus, Global Crises, and a Revolution of Hope.* Nashville: Thomas Nelson, 2007. 327 pp.

———. *A Generous Orthodoxy.* Grand Rapids: Zondervan, 2004. 348 pp.

———. *A New Kind of Christian: A Tale of Two Friends on a Spiritual Journey.* San Francisco: Jossey-Bass, A Wiley Imprint, 2001. 195 pp.

McManus, Erwin Raphael (1958-). *The Barbarian Way: Unleash the Untamed Faith Within.* Nashville: Nelson Books, 2005.148 pp.

Miller, Donald (1971-). *Blue Like Jazz: Nonreligious Thoughts on Christian Spirituality.* Recommendations on back cover: *Christianity Today*, Dan Kimball, *Revelant* magazine. Nashville: Thomas Nelson, 2003. 243 pp.

———. *Searching for God Knows What.* Nashville: Thomas Nelson, 2004. 246 pp.

Murphy, Nancy. *Beyond Liberalism and Fundamentalism.*

Nouwen, Henri Jozef Machiel (1932-1996). *In the Name of Jesus: Reflections on Christian Leadership.* New York: Crossroad, 1989. 107 pp.

———. *Sabbatical Journey: The Diary of His final Year.* New York: Crossroad Publishing Company, 1998.

Oakland, Roger (1947-). *Faith Undone: The Emerging Church...A New Reformation or an End-time Deception.* Silverton, OR: Lighthouse Trails Publishing, 2002, 2007. 261 pp.

Pagitt, Doug (1966-). *Church Reimagined.* Grand Rapids: Zondervan, 2003. 233 pp.

———. *Preaching Reimagined.*

————, and Tony Jones, ed. *An Emergent Manifesto of Hope*. Chapters by Brian McLaren, Dan Kimball, Sally Morgenthaler, Will Samson, Tim Keel, Barry Taylor, Samir Selmanovic, Karen Sloan, Ryan Bolger. Grand Rapids: Baker Books, 2007. 318 pp.

Pope, Randy. *The Intentional Church: Moving from Church Success to Community Transformation*. Foreword by John Maxwell. Recommendations by John Haggai, Carl George of Cunsulting for Growth; Crawford Loritts, associate director of Campus Crusade for Christ; Steve Brown, professor at Reformed Theological Seminary; Bob Reccord, president of the Southern Baptist North American Mission Board; Scotty Smith, pastor of Christ Community Church; Rick Warren; Andy Stanley; Bill Hybels; Bob Buford, founder of Leadership Network; R.C. Sproul. Chicago: Moody Press, 2002, 2006. 222 pp.

Richardson, Rick (1955-). *Reimagining Evangelism: Inviting Friends on a Spiritual Journey*. Forewords by Brian McLaren and Luis Palau. Downers Grove, IL: InterVarsity Press, 2006. 167 pp.

Seay, Chris (1972-). *Faith of My Fathers: Conversations with Three Generations of Pastors about Church, Ministry, and Culture*. Foreword by Donald Miller. Grand Rapids: Zondervan, 2005. 179 pp.

————. *The Gospel according to Tony Soprano: An Unauthorized Look into the Soul of TV's Top Mob Boss and His Family*. New York: Jeremy P. Tarcher/Putnam, 2002. 159 pp.

Sjogren, Steve (1955-), and David Ping, Doug Pollock. *Irresistible Evangelism: Natural Ways to Open Others to Jesus*. Loveland, CO: Group, 2004. 190 pp.

Sloan, Karen. *Flirting with Monasticism*.

Sweet, Leonard (1961-). *The Gospel according to Starbucks: Living with a Grande Passion*. Waterbrook, 2007.

————. *Jesus Drives Me Crazy*. Grand Rapids: Zondervan, 2003.

————. *Postmodern Pilgrims: 1st Century Passion for the 21st Century World*. Broadman and Holman Publishers, 2000. 194 pp.

————. *Quantum Spirituality: A Postmodern Apologetic*. Dayton, OH: Whaleprints, 1991.

————, ed. *The Church in Emerging Culture: Five Perspectives*. Contributions by Andy Crouch, Michael Horton, Frederica Mathewes-Green, Brian McLaren, Erwin McManus. Grand Rapids: Zondervan, 2003. 263 pp..

Stetzer, Ed, and David Putman. *Breaking the Missional Code: Your Church Can Become a Missionary in Your Community.* Recommendations on the inside of the book by Dan Kimball, George Hunter III, Mark Driscoll, Alan Hirsch, Bob Roberts, Reggie McNeal, Dave Travis, Eddie Gibbs, Elmer Towns, and Bob Reccord. Nashville: Broadman & Holman Publishers, 2006. 244 pp.

Webber, Robert (1933-2007), ed. *Ancient-Future Faith: Rethinking Evangelicalism for a Postmodern World.* Grand Rapids: Baker Books, 1999. 240 pp.

———. *The Divine Embrace: Recovering the Passionate Spiritual Life.* Grand Rapids: Baker Books, 2006. 282 pp.

———. *Evangelicals on the Canterbury Trail: Why Evangelicals Are Attracted to the Liturgical Church.* Harrisburg, NY: Morehouse Publishing, 1985. 174 pp.

———. *Listening to the Beliefs of Emerging Churches: Five Perspectives.* Chapters by Mark Driscoll, John Burke, Dan Kimball, Doug Pagitt, and Karen Ward. Grand Rapids: Zondervan, 2007. 240 pp.

———. *The Younger Evangelicals: Facing the Challenges of the New World.* Grand Rapids: Baker Books, 2002. 283 pp.

Yungen, Ray. *A Time of Departing: How Ancient Mystical Practices Are Uniting Christians with the World's Religions.* Silverton, OR: Lighthouse Trails Publishing, 2002. 245 pp.

CONTEMPLATIVE SPIRITUALITY

Brother Lawrence (c. 1611-91). *The Practice of the Presence of God.* New Kensington, PA: Whitaker House, 1982. 95 pp.

De Mello, Anthony (1931-87). *Awakening: Conversations with the Masters.* New York: Random House, 1998. 202 pp.

———. *Sadhana: A Way to God: Christian Exercises in Eastern Form.* Garden City, NY: Image Books, 1984. 140 pp.

Foster, Richard. J. (c. 1945-). *Celebration of Discipline: The Path to Spiritual Growth.* New York: Harper & Row, 1978. 184 pp.

———. *Celebration of Discipline: The Path to Spiritual Growth.* New York: HarperSanFrancisco, 1988. 228 pp.

———. *Celebration of Discipline: The Path to Spiritual Growth.* New York: HarperSanFrancisco, 1998. 228 pp.

Flynn, Brian (1958-). *Running against the Wind: The Transformation of a New Age Medium and His Warning to the Church.* Silverton, OR: Lighthouse Trails Publishing, 2005. 238 pp.

Fry, Timothy, ed. (1915-). *The Rule of Saint Benedict.* New York: Vintage Spiritual Classics, 1981. 73 pp.

Griffiths, Alan (1906-93). *The New Creation in Christ: Christian Meditation and Community.* Springfield, IL: Templegate, 1994.

Ignatius of Loyola (1491-15456). *The Spiritual Experiences.* New York: Vintage Books, 2000. 177 pp.

Johnston, William (1925-), ed. *The Cloud of Unknowing,* and *The Book of Privy Counseling.* Foreword by Huston Smith. New York: Image Books, 1996. 195 pp.

Jones, Tony. *The Sacred Way: Spiritual Practices for Everyday Life.* Grand Rapids: Zondervan, 2005. 222 pp.

Kempis, Thomas à (1380-1471). *The Imitation of Christ.* Trans. by Joseph Tylenda. New York: Vintage Books, 1998. 242 pp.

Kidd, Sue Monk (1948-). *The Dance of the Dissident Daughter: A Woman's Journey from Christian Tradition to the Sacred Feminine.* New York: HarperOne, 1996. 253 pp.

King, Ursula. *Christian Mystics: Their Lives and Legacies throughout the Ages.* Mahwah, NJ: HiddenSpring, 2001. 270 pp.

Merton, Thomas (1915-69). *The Ascent to Truth.* New York: Harvest Book, 1979. 342 pp.

———. *The Asian Journal of Thomas Merton.* New York: New Direction, 1975. 445 pp.

———. *Contemplative Prayer.* Introduction by Thich Nhat Hanh. New York: Image Books, 1996. 116 pp.

———. *Mystics and Zen Masters.* New York: Farrar, Straus and Giroux, 1967. 303 pp.

———. *New Seeds of Contemplation.* Foreword by Sue Monk Kidd. New York: New Directions, 2007. 297 pp.

———. *The Seven Storey Mountain.* New York: Harvest Book, 1998. 467 pp.

———. *Soul Searching: The Journey of Thomas Merton.* Duckworks, 2007. DVD

———. *Zen and the Birds of Appetite.* New York: New Directions, 1968. 141 pp.

Myss, Caroline. *Entering the Castle: Finding the Inner Path to God and Your Soul's Purpose.* Foreword by Ken Wilber. New York: Free Press, 2007. 391 pp.

Nouwen, Henri J.M. (1932-1996). *The Way of the Heart: Desert Spirituality and Contemporary Ministry.* New York: HarperSanFrancisco, 1991. 96 pp.

———. *With Open Hands.* Foreword by Sue Monk Kidd. Notre Dame, IN: Ave Maria Press, 2006. 125 pp.

Pennington, M. Basil (1931-2005), and Thomas Keating (1923-), Thomas Clarke. *Finding Grace at the Center: The Beginning of Centering Prayer.* Woodstock, VT: Skylight Paths Publishing, 2002. 105 pp.

Schuller, Robert Harold (1926-). *Prayer: My Soul's Adventure with God.* New York: Image Books, 1996. 295 pp.

Talbot, John Michael (1954-). *Come to the Quiet: The Principles of Christian Meditation.* New York: Jeremy P. Tarcher/Putnam, 2002. 287 pp.

———. *Hermitage: A Place of Prayer and Spiritual Renewal: Its Heritage and Challenge for the Future.* New York: Crossroad, 1989. 194 pp.

———. *The Lover and the Beloved: A Way of Franciscan Prayer.* New York: Crossroad, 1987. 123 pp.

———. *Meditations from Solitude: A Monastic Mystical Theology from the Christian East.* Eureka Springs, AR: Troubadour for the Lord, 1994. 338 pp.

———, with Dan O'Neill. *Regathering Power.* Ann Arbor, MI: Servant Books, 1988. 113 pp.

———, with Steve Rabey. *Ancient Wisdom for Experiencing God Today: Lessons from Thirteen Holy Men and Women.* San Francisco: Jossey-Bass, 2005. 234 pp.

———, with Steve Rabey. *The Lessons of St. Francis: How to Bring Simplicity and Spirituality into Your Daily Life.* New York: Plume, 1998. 255 pp.

Teasdale, Wayne (1945-2004). *A Monk in the World.*

———. *Mystic Heart: Discovering a Universal Spirituality in the World's Religions.*

Teresa of Avila (1515-82). *The Life of Saint Teresa of Avila by Herself.* Trans. by J.M. Cohen. New York: Penguin Books, 1957. 316 pp.

———. *The Way of Perfection.* Trans. by E. Allison Peers (1891-1952). New York: Image Books, 1964. 280 pp.

Yungen, Ray. *A Time of Departing: How Ancient Mystical Practices Are Uniting Christians with the World's Religions.* Silverton, OR: Lighthouse Trails Publishing, 2002. 245 pp.

INDEX

Acts 29, 18, 127, 396, 455
Allegoricalism, 147, 281
Allender, Dan, 24, 122
Anderson, Leith, 12
Anglican, 37
Anthony, 162
Anti-Fundamentalism, 50, 429
Artress, Lauren, 155
Ascetism, 182
Atonement, 373
Augustine, 159
Baker Books, 8
Baker, Jonny, 44, 278
Batterson, Mark, 28, 332
Baylor University, 31
Beatles, 194
Bell, Rob, 28, 52, 57, 61, 89, 108, 123, 209, 246, 299, 334, 347, 362
Benedict, 168
Bible Translation, 172
Bible translations
Latin, old, 174
Biola University, 24
Black Madonna, 232, 234
Blue Like Jazz. *See* Miller, Donald
Blue, Debbie, 90, 292
Bolger, Ryan, 28, 39, 46, 122, 188, 246, 286, 290, 333, 347, 381
Bonaventure, 169
Bonhoeffer, Dietrich, 24
Born Again, 84
Breath Prayer, 143, 194
Brennan, Manning, 374
Bronsink, Troy, 93

Buber, Martin, 12
Buddhism, 201, 208, 210
Buford, Bob, 11
Burke, John, 388, 417
Burke, Spencer, 28, 91, 211, 247, 296, 345, 367
Campbell, Jonathan, 88
Campolo, Peggy, 368
Campolo, Tony, 29, 76, 94, 124, 188, 213, 238, 241, 247, 279, 287, 346, 357, 368
Cecil, Brad, 292
Celibacy, 181
Centering Prayer, 129, 215
Chalke, Steve, 374
Chesterton, G.K., 29
Chopra, Deepak, 133
Christ and the Scripture, 73
Christianity Today, 30, 128, 390
Christ's Return, 259, 278, 454
Claiborne, Shane, 331
Cleaveland, Adam, 93, 108, 299
Clement of Alexandria, 157
Club Culture, 299
Condor, Tim, 30, 62, 93, 108, 331
Contemporary Christian Music, 446
Crouch, Andy, 88, 90, 390
Dalai Lama, 204, 209
Dallas Theological Seminary, 22
Darkness, 221
Darling, Mary, 188
De Mello, Anthony, 204
Desert Fathers, 157

Dialogue, 238, *See* Interfaith Dialogue
Dionysius the Areopagite, 160
Discursive Meditation, 216
Dispensationalism, 281
Divinity of Man, 231
Doctrine, 98, 441
Doctrine, Major and Minor, 441
Dodridge, Anna, 43
Doubt, 108
Drew University, 40
Drinking, 324
Driscoll, Mark, 22, 127, 312, 388, 397, 406, 423, 429, 441, 454
Drucker, Peter, 12
Drum Circle, 125
Eastern University, 29
Ecclesia. *See* Seay, Chris
Ecumenism, 30, 120, 124, 197, 236, 270, 391, 423
Edson, Ben, 79, 293, 313, 344
Emergent Village, 7, 30, 32, 330
Emmaus Way. *See* Condor, Tim
England, 37, 44, 79, 80, 278, 299, 313, 343, 344
Environmentalism, 272
Epicentre Network. *See* Mobsby, Ian
Erdman, Chris, 31
Eucharist. *See* Mass
Evangelism, 290, 425, 438
Faith, 114
Fasting, 183
Female Pastors, 381
Flash Prayer, 137
Foolish Questions. *See* Questions, Foolish
Foster, David, 31, 51, 92, 296, 331
Foster, Richard, 134, 136, 204, 217
Francis of Assisi, 172
Franke, John, 32
Friesen, Dwight, 31, 56, 93, 293
Fuller Theological Seminary, 28, 31, 39, 46, 55, 122, 286, 347
Fundamentalism, 431
Gibbs, Eddie, 28, 122, 188, 246, 290, 333, 381
Global Warming, 274
Goddess, 155, 231, 234
Golden Legend, 173
Gospel, 84, 254
Gospel of the Kingdom, 358
Grace Cathedral, 155
Granger Community Church. *See* Stevens, Tim
Great White Throne, 353
Grenz, Stanley, 31
Griffiths, Alan, 205, **233**
Hairshirt, 184
Hall, Simon, 292, 343
Hansen, Leif, 363
Harrison, George, 194
Headspace, 344
Hell, 362, 364
Heresy, 444
Heretic, 112
Hinduism, 82, 95, 133, 194, 197, 205, 208, 210, 220, 233, 239
Hirsh, Alan, 32
Hochschild, Joshua, 332
Homosexuality, 30, 366
Houston, Jean, 155

Hybels, Bill, 11, 240
Idolatry, 195, 310
Ignatius of Loyola, 135, 178
Ikon. *See* Rollins, Peter
Imagination Prayer. *See* Visualization Prayer
Imago Dei, 127, 389, 397, 436, *See* McKinley, Rick
Imminency. *See* Christ's Return
Incarnational Doctrine, 408
Inquisition, 159, 174
Interfaith Dialogue, 12, 203
InterVarsity, 8
Ireland, 38, 88, 293
Jacob's Well. *See* Keel, Tim
Jacobs, Alan, 332
Jager, Willigis, 196, 206
Jaggard, Jason, 389
Jerome, 158
Jesus Prayer, 142, 194
John 17, 67, 336
Johnston, Si, 344
Jones, Alan, 349, 375
Jones, Andrew, 12
Jones, Tony, 12, 32, 61, 122, 127, 139, 225, 279
Jossey-Bass, 13
Judge Not. *See* Non-Judgmentalism
Keating, Thomas, 129, **203**, 216
Keel, Tim, 26, 32
Kidd, Sue Monk, 208, **226**
Kierkegaard, Soren, 12, 24
Kimball, Dan, 12, 19, 126, 389, 401, 417, 424, 425, 430, 438, 455
Kingdom of God, 264, 436
Kundalini, 223
Labyrinth, 154

Latin, 174
Le Saux, Henri, 205
Leader to Leader Institute, 12
Leadership Network, 11
Lectio Divina, 143
Legalism, 316
Lewis, C.S., 24, 33
Liberty University, 389
Loeser, Alois, 120
Loyd, Ken, 33
Maddock, Geoff, 55
Main, John, 202
Manning, Brennan, 211, 221, 242
Mantra, 131, 194
Mars Hill Bible Church, 28, *See* Bell, Rob
Mars Hill Church, 24, 325, 388, 438
Mars Hill Graduate School, 24, 30, 32, 35, 122, 295
Mary, 167, 177
Mass, 150, 167, 175, 317
McCullough, Donald, 33, 44, 62, 96, 250, 298, 342, 367
McKinley, Rick, 20, 389, 436
McKnight, Scot, 33, 76, 332
McLaren, Brian, 5, 12, 29, **34**, 60, 75, 89, 122, 209, 273, 278, 330, 340, 363, 366, 375
McManus, Erwin, 57, 389, 403, 424, 437
McQuitty, Andy, 423
Merton, Thomas, 136, 176, 179, 196, **200**
Miller, Calvin, 141
Miller, Donald, 21, 36, 41, 50, 55, 62, 96, 247, 298, 344, 362, 367

Mirror of the Blessed Life, 173
Mobsby, Ian, 37, 80, 299
Monastic Interreligious Dialogue, 203
Monasticism, 124, 145, 156, 163, 238
Moreland, J.P., 24
Morganthaler, Sally, 36, 381
Mosaic. *See* McManus, Erwin
Mother Teresa, 153, 225, 241
Murdoch, Rupert, 13
Music, 446
Myss, Caroline, 208
Mystery, 100
National Council of Churches, 31
New Age, 133, 155, 207, 208, 209, 232
New Birth. *See* Born Again
Newbigin, Lesslie, 23, 24, 37
Nida, Eugene, 379
Non-judgmentalism, 212, 216, 300, 311, 412, 420, 421, 422
Non-Judgmentalism, 417
North Park University, 33
Nouwen, Henri, 37, 344
Ockenga, Harold, 392
Origen, 158
Orthoparadoxy, 93
Pagitt, Doug, 12, 38, 92, 123, 209, 249, 367, 373
Patrick, Darrin, 18, 400
Peace, 285
Pennington, M. Basil, 204, 216
Pseudo-Dionysius. *See* Dionysius the Areopagite
Purgatory, 180
Putman, David, 424
Quest, 123
Questions, 108
Rahner, Karl, 116
Rapture. *See* Christ's Return
Ratzinger, Joseph, 206
Rauschenbusch, Walter, 250
Regent College, 31
Repentance, 83
Repetition, 194
Revive, 44, 343
Riverview Community Church, 325
Rollins, Peter, 38, 88, 293
Roman Catholic Church, 29, 37, 120, 129, 135, 156, 166, 197, 233, 317, 331, 332
Rome, 174
Ryan, Thomas, 204
Saddleback Church. *See* Warren, Rick
Samson, Will, 61
Sanctus 1, 344
Sawyer, Nanette, 43, 82, 220, 293, 345
Scandrette, Mark, 38
Schuller, Robert, 38, 271
Schutz, Roger, 120
Seay, Chris, 12, 39, 61, 297, 333, 367, 425
Second Vatican Council, 150, 166, 177
Selmanovic, Samir, 346
Separation, 197, 271, 391
Sermon on the Mount, 285
Shambhala Publications, 208
Shannon, William, 242
Shapevine, 18, 39
Shenk, Wilbert, 39
Silence, 185
Sloan, Karen, 39, 124

Smith, Brad, 12
Social Gospel, 250
Sojourners, 34, 40, 249, 252, 368
Solomon's Porch. *See* Pagitt, Doug
Soularize. *See* Burke, Spencer
Southeastern Baptist Theological Seminary, 18
Southern Baptist, 8, 15, 17, 18, 224, 226, 389, 425
SpiritVenture Ministries, 40
St. Romain, Philip, 223
Stations of the Cross, 149
Stetzer, Ed, 17, 424, 447, 455
Stevens, Tim, 389
Storytelling, 97
Substitutionary Atonement. *See* Atonement
Sutton, Dave, 343
Sweet, Leonard, 40, 116, 249, 272, 343
Swish Prayer, 137
Taize, 120
Talbot, John Michael, 171, 179, 218, 223, 237
Taylor, Barry, 55, 97, 108, 286
Teasdale, Wayne, 206, 209
Teresa of Avila, 178, 180
Terra Nova, 13
The Cloud of Unknowing, 130, 168, 170, 178, 180
The Journey, 325, *See* Darrin, Patrick
TheOOze. *See* Burke, Spencer
They Like Jesus But Not the Church. *See* Kimball, Dan
Thomas, Scott, 396
Three Nails, 270

Tickle, Phyllis, 17
Toulouse, Council of, 172
Trinity Evangelical Divinity School, 33, 40
Unity, 336, 441
Universalism, 241, 340
Vain Repetition. *See* Repetition
Vatican II Coucil. *See* Second Vatican Council
Velvet Elvis, 57, 61, 90, 108, 209, 246, 299, 347, 362
Veriditas, 155
Visualization Prayer, 135, 219
Wallis, Jim, 270, 288, 368
Ward, Karen, 19, 41, 60, 90, 291, 343, 374
Warren, Rick, 8, 11, 389, 400, 430, 437, 447, 455
Webber, Robert, 76, 124, 332, 390
Wheaton College, 332
Wilber, Ken, 209
Willard, Dallas, 344
Willow Creek Community Church, 240, 417
Women Pastors. *See* Female Pastors
World Council of Churches, 37
Worldliness, 295, 394, 396
Wright, N.T., 246, 279
Young Leaders Network, 12
Youth Specialities, 140
Zondervan, 8, 13